Do-It-Yourself
PROJECTS
F R O M
ATTIC TO BASEMENT

Bernard Price

Published by Popular Science Books

Distributed to the trade by Rodale Press

Copyright 1976, 1977, 1978, 1979, 1980
  1981, 1982, 1983, 1986 by Bernard Price

Published by
  Popular Science Books
  Times Mirror Magazines, Inc.
  380 Madison Avenue
  New York, NY 10017

Distributed to the trade by
  Rodale Press
  32 East Minor Street
  Emmaus, PA 18049

Library of Congress Cataloging-in-Publication Data

Price, Bernard (Bernard L.)
  Do-it-yourself projects from attic to basement.
  Includes index.
  1. Dwellings — Remodeling — Amateurs' manuals.
2. Do-it-yourself work. I. Title.
TH4816.P75   1986   643'.7   85-29023
ISBN 0-943822-65-3

Manufactured in the United States of America

Contents

Preface

The National Hardware Show is held in Chicago during the second week of August. It was there that John Sill, the publisher of Popular Science Books, came up with the idea for this book. He suggested that I assemble a group of my home projects, which had been published over the years in *Homeowner's How To* (now *The Homeowner*), *The Family Handyman* and *Mechanix Illustrated* (now *Home Mechanix*) into a book. This volume is the result. It contains a broad spectrum of projects that will enhance every area of the home and garden. These projects may be used directly by the do-it-yourselfer, or as a back-up when dealing with contractors. For those who contemplate taking on major projects, a technical section includes instructions for masonry, carpentry, tiling, wallpapering and other skills.

I wish to thank the following companies and organizations for their valued cooperation and assistance in the preparation of both the book itself as well as the projects which made this work possible.

The concrete block sequence in Chapter 37 is through the courtesy of the Portland Cement Association and some of the major drawings in Chapter 38 were supplied by the American Plywood Association, Southern Forest Products Association and Teco. Some of the drawings in Chapter 39 are from the American Gypsum Association. The molding shapes and combination drawings in Chapter 40 are from the Wood Moulding and Millwork Producers, while Georgia-Pacific supplied the modular panel photographic sequence and Townsend provided the planked wall photograph. In Chapter 41, Hartco supplied some drawings and the parquet floor sequence, while photographs from Armstrong World Industries were used in some of the vinyl floor sequences. Some drawings and the mosaic tile countertop photographic sequence were supplied by American Olean Tile in Chapter 43.

I would also like to thank:

American Gypsum Association
American Olean Tile Company
American Plywood Association
American Standard
Amerec Corporation
Amerock Corporation
Armstrong World Industries
Arrow Fastener Company
Benchmark Tool Company
Bruce Hardwood Floors
Black and Decker
California Redwood Association
Caradco Windows
Congoleum Corporation
Delta
E.I. DuPont de Nemours and Co.
Emperor Clock
Alliance Manufacturing Company
General Electric
General Hardware Manufacturing
  Company
Georgia-Pacific
Goldblatt
Grant Hardware
Halo Lighting Division of
  McGraw-Edison
Harris Flooring
Hartco, Tibbals Flooring
Heatilator
Hirsh Company
Jacuzzi Whirlpool Bath
Koppers Company
L. & M. Surco
Mannington
Masonite Corporation
NuTone
Oak Flooring Institute
Paeco

Porter Cable Corporation
Portland Cement Association
Potlatch Corporation, Townsend Unit
Reed Wallcoverings
Rubbermaid
Sears
Skil Corporation
Southern Forest Product Association
Stanley Door Systems
Stanley Hardware, a Division of the Stanley Works
State Industries
StuccoStone of California
Thermosol
Thomas Industries
Vermont-American
Wallcovering Information Bureau
Weyerhaeuser Company
Wiremold Company

Wood Moulding and Millwork Producers

Part I

Attic

1

Disappearing Attic Stairs

There are dozens of good reasons to have convenient access to your attic. But the fact is that many homes either have minimal or no access. Others have an attic access stuck away in a closet, requiring the removal of stored articles before the homeowner does a circus act to "get up there."

The solution is simple, inexpensive and one you can handle yourself: a set of disappearing stairs designed to accommodate normal-sized adults.

Once installed, you'll appreciate it every time you need to install or perform maintenance on a TV antenna, air-conditioning unit, attic vent fan or central vacuum system. You'll find it easier to use your attic's unfinished area for storage, or you might decide to finish a room for either guests or storage.

Even occasional jobs like installing insulation or additional circuits will be easier.

In the parts area, you'll need a stairs kit, some 2×6s, a little molding to trim the opening and some paint. (The latter two items should match the existing room or hall decor.) Any home shop will have the required tools, which include hammer, saw, rafter and miter squares, chalk line and drill.

Half the battle is choosing the right place in the room or hall. Compare the installation sketch with the physical layout of the room, the location of the walls and doors, and especially the attic ceiling clearance with the specs provided for the particular model stair kit you're using. Then you'll be able to lay out the opening in no time.

Installation

Mark the rough opening on the ceiling with the chalk line and rafter square to assure 90° corners. To be on the safe side, cut out a small opening in the center of the outline with a drywall saw and check the area to eliminate any possibility of conflict with electrical lines, vacuum tubes or other obstructions. (It's best to cut off all electri-

cal power to avoid the possibilities of dangerous electrical shocks.)

If all's in order, proceed to remove the drywall ceiling cutout. For safety, and to avoid the possibility of ceiling cracks as well as nonalignment of the headers with the trimmed-off joists, jam studs between the floor and a plank laid up flush with the ceiling along the long edges of the opening. The opening size is determined by the stair kit model specs, but the joist headers and blocking between must fit into this dimension, so here's what you do.

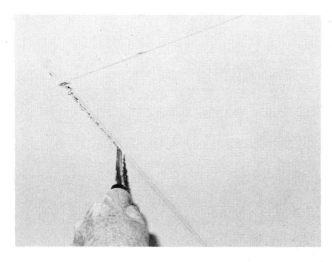

Select the stair location. Check the installation sketch to insure attic ceiling clearance. Mark the opening and cut ceiling out.

Stretch chalk lines between the new marks and snap the string. Do this on both sides of the opening.

Place a 2×4 flat against the ceiling and support it with studs from the floor to prevent sagging joists and ceiling cracks.

Nail in bolts supplied for corner support plates. Nail flat end of bolt to header, adjust plate and nut until plate is flush with ceiling.

Use a square to mark joists for cutting. Cut the joists 1½" back from edge of opening so header will be flush to finish ceiling.

Set the stair frame into the opening with the corners resting on support plates. Shim the frame shingles and nail.

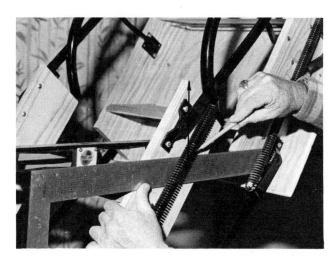

Extend stairs to floor. Place a square across stringers so blade just touches upper stringer's high corner. Draw line, measure to the lower stringer's top corner (arrow).

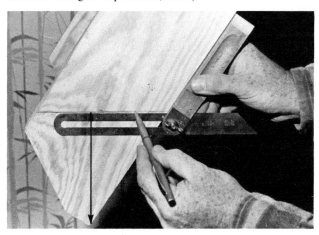

Use the distance determined in the step above and measure up from the floor. Draw a line parallel to the floor. Repeat the process on opposite side and cut both ends.

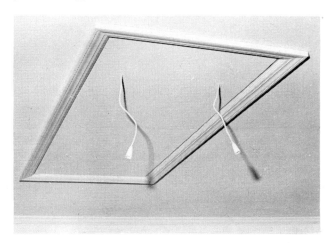

Trim the opening with molding set back ¼″ from stair frame edge and corners mitered to 45°. Drill ¼″ holes for cord. Install the cord through holes and attach tips.

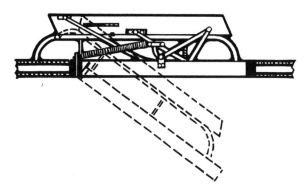

The stairs fold into the attic area, flush with the ceiling. Keep in mind the arc described as the stair swings down: distance A must be great enough to provide clearance. If you know your ceiling height, the dealer can provide the other minimum dimensions.

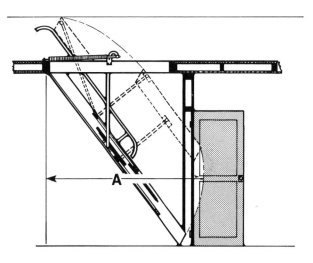

Mark the joists at the ends of the opening right at the drywall ceiling edge. Carry these marks up the joist using a miter square. Then place marks on these joists 1½″ farther out from the marks you made first. This will allow the joist headers and blocking that box in the opening to fit flush with the ceiling opening. Stretch chalk lines between the new marks and snap the string. Do this on both sides of the opening. Carry the new marks down to the upper surface of the ceiling with the miter square.

It's best to saw out the joists near the middle of the opening first to get yourself some stroking room for the saw. Then cut out the remaining pieces. Trim the 2×6 joist headers so they span between the existing uncut joists, and then nail them in place. The face of the headers, as well as the face of the blocking between them, should be flush with the ceiling opening when you are through. Remove the temporary bracing.

The kit we used provided special plates and bolts with nuts. One end of these bolts was flattened and had a nailing hole in the flat. Nail one bolt in at each corner and assemble the plate and nut on it. Run up the nut far enough to make the plate flush with the bottom surface of the ceiling. The plates support the stair assembly in the correct position in the opening. When that is done, they can be pushed up (just the bolts) into the gap that will exist between the stair frame and the headers and blocking.

Before lifting the stairs up into the opening, some preparation is necessary. Fasten the handrail and strut brackets to the carriage bolts provided in the stair assembly stringers. Also connect the power spring to its anchor on both sides with the bolts and nuts. This requires a little muscle, so stretch the spring either with a small length of chain or a multiple loop of mason's cord.

Get some help and lift the entire assembly up into the opening so that it rests on the metal corner plates. Then shim the gap between the stairs frame and the blocking and headers of the rough opening. Do this on all four sides, using pairs of undercourse siding shakes. The tapers, installed this way, provide a means of reducing gaps and keeping things parallel.

Close up the stairs from time to time as you're shimming to make sure the gaps are kept constant at $\frac{1}{8}''$. Complete this work by nailing through the stair frame and shims into the rough opening.

Next, lubricate all strut joints and axles. Then pull the stairs down. Adjust the power spring nuts until you reach the desired tension. You can drill a pair of holes in the stair panel row and install the pulls.

With the stairs in the down position, mark off the lines and measurements on the stair stringers necessary for the cutoff required at the lower end of the lower stair section. This cutoff will allow the lower section to rest on the floor with the stairs completely open and the two sections locked at their junction.

Add molding to trim the opening, mitering it at the corners with a miter box. Sand everything, plug all nail holes and paint.

2

Attic Theater

An odd-shape attic space that doesn't seem suitable for anything other than musty storage can, with a little imagination and craziness, be turned into a gem of a living addition. Our problem, for example, couldn't have been more difficult—nor the solution more spectacular.

There we were with a distorted space in the attic—very little headroom, due to the $^4/_{12}$ roof slope, and a large 4'-deep drop on the end that is the living room of our split-level home. Given the angulations and the drop, both similar to a movie theatre, we had the answer: Build a Little Theater for the kids. By the time we were done, it had turned into an entertainment center complete with Super 8 movie and slide projection, a TV with a VCR deck and electronic games for the tube.

Of course, there were structural problems. The existing 2×6 ceiling joists (in the drop) were not strong enough to support the weight of people. The answer: Beef them up by spiking 2×8 sister joists along the full length of the existing joists.

Next problem: How do you get 4×8 plywood sheets up through a small attic access? Solution: We partially disassembled the struts on the disappearing stairway.

The last problem of how to muscle all that heavy stuff to the attic yielded quickly when we bribed a few strong friends with steak and brews at a moving party.

Following is a guide to developing a similar split-level attic. It begins with a temporary plywood platform that spans the joists and allows you a secure perch while working.

Preparation and Re-creation

First remove all insulation from the joist bays and reposition any electrical cable that may prove to be a problem later. To eliminate the possibility of an uneven floor, crown all joists before nailing them to the existing ones. Be sure to nail them from both sides.

Sister joists (2×8s) are nailed to existing 2×6 ceiling joists in preparation for use as the load-bearing floor.

Framing (openings) for the TV and VCR deck are built into the knee wall at the lower or sloping end of the room.

The upper ends of studs are cut at a bevel or angle equal to the roof slope. Ends are toenailed to the top plate.

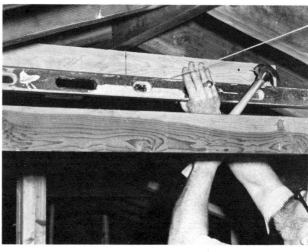

Rafter collars are raised as high as possible—one on each rafter pair—and become ceiling supports for furring strips.

The top plate may not be located directly under a rafter. If so, you have to nail in a series of joist blocks for support.

R-11 Insulation goes into stud bays and R-19 in rafter bays, both foil-side inward. Patch any tears with duct tape.

Add the bridging between joists. Also reinforce the first 4' of the deck above the drop and raise the collars that tie the rafters together. Add extra collars so each rafter pair has one.

Replace the insulation and nail in the subfloor on both deck and pit areas using rosin-coated box nails. Run the first layer of subfloor (particleboard underlayment) with the long edges at right angles to the joist run, butting the shorter edges over the joists. Run the second layer at right angles to the first, lapping the joists. You end up with a heavy, strong and inexpensive subfloor.

Now, square off the room by snapping chalk lines. Set the sole (bottom) plates for the stud walls, which run parallel to the rafters. If luck is with you, the top plates will line up with the rafters and may be nailed directly to them. If not, nail some blocking between the adjacent rafters and nail the top plates to these.

Set the top plate plumb (relative to the bottom plate) using a long level and straight stud. Mark off your 16" intervals on the bottom plate and, again using a level and stud, transfer these marks to the top plate. Set your portable saw at the roof slope angle and trim the studs to length. Nail them in place. Where they are higher than 8', slip in some blocking to prevent vibration.

Build up the knee-wall end of the room with framed openings for the TV and VCR deck. Then construct the wall at the rear of the deck (platform), including the framing for the door.

Drill holes through the studs for the electrical cable (as far back as practical to keep cable away from nails). Then install outlet boxes for duplex receptacles and switches. A strut-mounted box between the rafters takes care of ceiling fixtures. While you're at it, wire in either a TV cable or antenna, as you won't be able to get into that area later.

After insulation and power lines are in, drywall is installed on all vertical surfaces, including built-ins.

Panel interiors of built-ins, cutting with a saber saw, then block-plane all the edges for a good, snug fit.

The lower level of finished panels is installed. Carefully measure, cut and install top pieces with slanted ends.

Ceiling tiles are stapled through flanges (use 9/16"-long staples) to the lines of uniformly spaced furring strips.

Allow all electrical boxes to protrude from studs and rafters in order to accommodate sheathing and panels.

Now, staple up your R-11 insulation in the stud bays and R-19 in the rafter bays, foil face to the living space.

Cut, fit and nail all the wallboard in place on the vertical surfaces. Don't bother to tape and joint. As the panels are the next order of business, figure where your vertical joints fall and spray brown paint in vertical lines at these locations—just in case there's a panel-edge discrepancy.

Accuracy isn't required when cutting the tops of the panels to the roof slope, as the thickness of the furring, tiles and molding eat up quite a bit of space beneath the rafters, thus hiding any discrepancies. Just measure the right and left sides with a tape at the centers of the appropriate studs, mark the panels and cut them.

It's okay to cut on the finish side if you use a jigsaw with a metal-cutting blade. The fine-tooth blade prevents splintering. Fit the back panels in the built-in boxes so the grooves are aligned with those on the walls. At the corners, panels should first be sawn to rough fit, scribed with a compass and blockplaned for a neat fit. This eliminates the need for inside corner molding.

The ceiling tiles are stapled to a network of 1×2 or 1×3 furring strips. These strips must be installed perpendicularly to the rafter run and shimmed for levelness.

When you've checked your furring job carefully, square the room and balance the tiles according to the instructions in the packaging. For the installation, work several rows at a clip from the right to the left side. The end pieces must be individually cut with a utility knife, leaving about a ¼" space between the end tile and the wall. Use ⁹⁄₁₆" staples and be careful not to crunch the beveled face of the tiles with the stapler. If you get a couple of joints that don't quite close up, take a scrap tile, match its edge with the one you're installing and tap the scrap a bit. Make the cutout for the strut-mounted electrical box in the tiles.

We used track lighting. Just hacksaw it carefully to the required length and install the dead end. Extra holes may be drilled in the track for mounting, if needed.

Attach the live end to the outlet-box cover (supplied with the track parts), remove the access cover from the live end and pull the load (black), neutral (white) and bare ground through the live end. Screw the cover (live end) assembly to the outlet box and connect the three wires to the indicated terminal screws. Then close the access cover.

Align the track and push it onto the live end. Then, using the toggle bolts supplied (or panhead screws), mount the track to the wide furring strip—right through the tiles. Snap the fixtures in place, aim them and load them with R-16 40-watters.

If you plan on using a Masonite base for the floor covering, make sure that you get the underlayment type available in either 3'×4' or 4'×4' sizes. Do not use the wall type. Keep the joints tight but not forced, nail from the center of each panel outward and allow a ¼" gap at the wall. Nailing should be on a 6" pattern.

The flooring can be loosely laid, with no adhesive or tape. Roll out the material and align it squarely with two adjacent walls, trim all inside and outside corners with a utility knife, then trim the long runs. Do this by forcing the material into the wall/floor joint with a piece of 2×4 or a rafter square, cutting it along the steel edge of the square.

Allow the material to settle for a day or so, then recheck and, if necessary, trim it back ¼" from the wall. Avoid sharp kinking. Prepaint the base molding and install it over the perimeter of the flooring material.

Make up the steps, cabinet face-frame, doors, rail posts, rail, handrail and deck edge-molding from oak except the door panels, which are pieces of wall panel.

When all your woodwork is ready to go, cleat-mount the face-frame on the deck along with a plywood return and its panel cover. Next, mount a cleat on the wall behind the face-frame and on the back edge of the face-frame. Drill these cleats so you'll be able to attach the top with screws from beneath. Make the top from particle-board (or plywood with laminate) and cover the exposed edges with a routed, stained oak molding. Hang cabinet doors, install a sliding platform inside the centrally located openings.

Cabinetry for the raised-deck end of the theater is framed of oak and fitted to walls and floor by scribing and planing.

The outside corners of floor covering must be relieved before trimming long-wall runs. Do not cut over, onto the field.

Hang the door, shimming the side and head jambs to suit, nail in the stop and set and putty the holes. Then prepaint all pine moldings, including the door casing. Install all moldings.

If it takes two pieces for a run, make scarf joints. Install the rail posts and rail, then the handrail for the steps. Note that all fastening screws on the exposed surfaces of the stained parts are plugged, sanded and restained. Notch into the deck edge-molding for the tops of step stringers and mount steps.

After touch-up and installing screen and equipment, you're ready to roll'em.

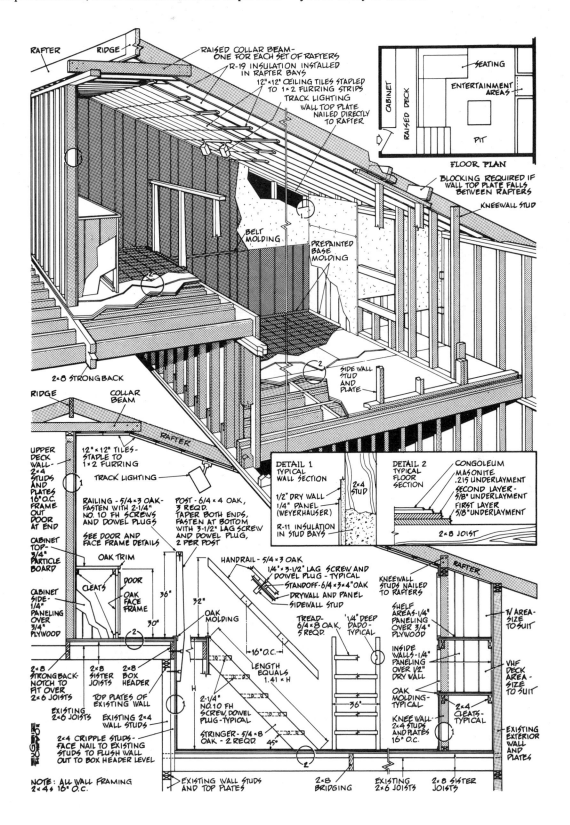

3

Attic Vent Fan

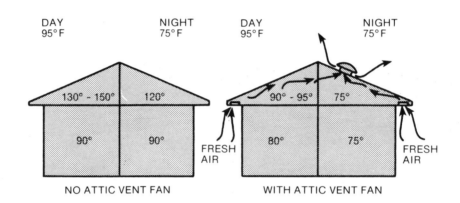

DAY 95° F   NIGHT 75° F   DAY 95° F   NIGHT 75° F

130° - 150°   120°   90° - 95°   75°

90°   90°   80°   75°

FRESH AIR   FRESH AIR

NO ATTIC VENT FAN   WITH ATTIC VENT FAN

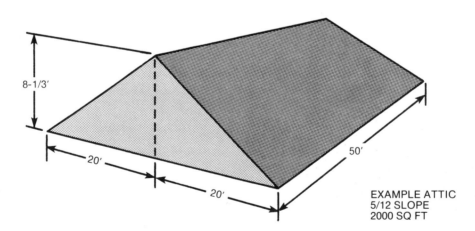

8-1/3'

20'

20'

50'

EXAMPLE ATTIC
5/12 SLOPE
2000 SQ FT

A   { VOLUME OF ATTIC = (2) × (1/2) × (8-1/3) × (20) × (50) = 8330 CU FT

FOR 10 CHANGES OF ATTIC AIR PER HOUR, 10 TIMES 8330 = 83,300 CU FT/HR

B   { IF FAN CAPACITY IS 1400 CU FT PER MINUTE

$$\frac{1400 \text{ CU FT}}{\text{MIN}} \times \frac{60 \text{ MIN}}{\text{HR}} = \frac{84,000 \text{ CU FT}}{\text{HR}}$$

A IS EQUAL TO B;
THERE OUR RULE OF THUMB USING 0.7 IS JUSTIFIED.

You can maintain a comfortable atmosphere in your home—and reduce utility bills—by installing an automatic vent fan in your attic. It's a quick, inexpensive project.

On hot summer days, an attic acts like a solar collector. Temperatures in it may go as high as 150° F, and part of the heat is transferred to the main living areas of the home. This forces air conditioners to work longer, raising electrical energy costs. An automatic vent fan draws in fresh supplies of cooler air from the outside, preventing heat buildup in the attic, and it costs a lot less to run than an air conditioner.

Automatic attic vent fans have a thermostatic switch that you can set to a desired cut-in temperature. The fan then operates until the attic temperature is reduced slightly below the preset point. If, for example, you set the switch to cut in the fan motor at 100° F, the motor will run until the attic temperature goes down to 85° F, and it will not cut in again until the temperature hits 100° F. This 15° differential prevents unnecessary cycling of the fan. There is also an upper temperature cutoff point to prevent dangerous drafting in the event of a house fire.

The fan you select will depend on your attic area. It should move enough cubic feet of air per minute (CFM @ 0.03″ pressure is the industry standard) to perform ten changes of attic air per hour. Because air will be moved out of the attic, a fresh supply of air from the outside must be drawn in through a properly sized venting area, or areas, to keep the attic pressure at the rated figure of 0.03″. These vents are typically a combination of gable, ridge and under-the-eave installations.

CFM Requirements

1. Multiply the length by the width of your attic floor to get its area.
2. Multiply the area by 0.7 to get fan CFM requirements.
3. If you have a dark roof—dark colors absorb more heat than light ones—multiply the fan CFM (from item 2 above) by 1.15

For example, if your attic is 40′ × 50′, you would first multiply those dimensions (40×50) to get 2000. To get the fan CFM requirements, you would then multiply the area (2000) by 0.7. That would give you a CFM of 1400. In the event the roof is a dark one, you would then multiply the 1400 by 1.15 and come up with a 1610 CFM.

This rule-of-thumb computation is easily verified by the accompanying diagram, which computes the volume of air enclosed in an attic. Multiply this volume by ten to get the total volume of air that must be moved to provide ten changes per hour. Now, compare this number with the result of multiplying our example CFM rating of 1400 CFM by 60 minutes per hour.

Venting Area

If your attic insulation has a vapor barrier on the side facing the living space of your house, compute the total vent area by dividing the attic floor area by 300. If you don't have this vapor barrier, you may still use the 1/300 ratio (divide attic floor area by 300) if at least 50% of the total venting area is located 3′ or more above the under-the-eave vents. When conditions are such that neither vapor barriers nor 50% upper attic venting is present, you must use the 1/150 ratio (divide attic floor area by 150).

You can get back to the 1/300 ratio by:

1. Installing a vapor barrier, which would be to your advantage in preventing winter heat loss through the attic as well, or...
2. Increasing upper attic venting area in the gable ends to meet your 50% requirement. If you do this, it's best to increase the size of existing gable vents, because installing additional ones may detract from the appearance of your home.

Whichever ratio you use, you'll probably install some under-the-eave vents, but these vents are inexpensive, easy to mount and unobtrusive.

Vent example 1. The attic floor is 2000 square feet and there is a vapor barrier. Divide 2000 square feet by 300 and get 7 square feet of total vent area.

Vent example 2. The attic floor is again 2000 square feet, but there is no vapor barrier. The gable vents are 4 square feet in area. Divide 2000 square feet by 300 and you get 7 square feet of total vent area. Since 4 out of the 7 square feet of required vent area (more than 50% are 3′ or more above the eave vents), simply make sure to provide the remaining 3 square feet in under-the-eave vents.

Vent example 3. Same conditions as in Example 2, but this time only 3 square feet of gable vent exist. Again, divide 2000 square feet by 300 and get 7 square feet of total venting. The gable vents this time provide 3 out of 7 square feet (less than 50% of the total venting is 3′ or more above the eave vents). This means that you must either:

1. Add a vapor barrier and provide 7 square feet of total venting, or...
2. Use the 1/150 ratio and divide 2000 square feet by 150 to get 14 square feet of total venting, or...
3. Increase the gable vent area to more than 3.5 square feet (50% of the total venting is 3′ or more above the eave vents) and provide a total of 7 square feet of venting.

Fan Installation

Once you've calculated the CFM requirement and purchased the appropriate unit, proper installation is next. First, choose the location. Generally, the best spot for the fan is at the center of the rear slope of the roof, far enough down from the ridge so that the dome of the fan is below the ridge line.

Drill through the roof at the midpoint of the central rafter bay as shown. Also drill holes through the roof right next to each rafter. This provides markings to indicate the limits of the opening.

Assemble all the tools and equipment you will need on the roof before beginning the outside work.

Mark a starting location from the inside of the attic in the centermost rafter bay and drill a hole through the roof at the midpoint between the two rafters. Next, drill a hole through the roof right next to each of these rafters to mark the limits of the opening which you'll be sawing. If the fan you are installing requires a circular opening, push a dowel through the center hole, so it protrudes through the roof.

Assemble all the equipment you'll need on the roof. This includes drill motor, saw, rafter square, hammer, chalk, string, broad-edged or electrician's chisel, Sheetrock knife, caulking gun and compound, torch and igniter and roofing nails.

If your fan requires a circular cutout, simply attach a string and chalk to the dowel you pushed through the center hole and mark a circle using the dowel as the compass center. If, as in the case of the installation illustrated, your fan requires a rectangular opening, mark it out with the aid of a rafter square. Then drill a hole at each corner and saw along the outline between the holes.

Center the fan over the hole and, with the fan lying flat on the roof, mark the outline of the large metal flange with chalk.

The top section of the flange must be tucked underneath the roof shingles in that area, so you'll have to lift these shingles. Asphalt shingles are self-sealing—the tab sections of the shingles above adhere to the solid section of those below. They also tend to become brittle, especially as they age. To lift them safely, heat your Sheetrock knife with the torch, and work the hot knife blade underneath the tabs. As the heat penetrates the asphalt seal, you'll be able to slide the knife blade in farther. Don't force the knife when it cools—just reheat it. This whole operation won't take more than two or three minutes, so be patient and do it right.

Next, load up your caulking gun and apply compound generously all around the opening within the area outlined in chalk, except at the top where the flange fits under

To mark out circular opening, use dowel you pushed through as compass center; swing circle with chalk and string.

Mark out rectangular opening with the aid of a rafter square. Drill a hole in each corner and saw between the holes.

the shingle tabs. In this upper area, caulk under the lifted shingle as far up as you can go.

Place the fan in position according to the chalked outline and caulk the top of the metal flange where it goes underneath the shingles. Make sure to get the flange all the way under the exposed shingles at the top, so that the top edge of the metal flange is above the tab slots of the shingle covering it. Otherwise, you'll have to caulk the slot areas very heavily to prevent leaks. Finish the roof work by driving caulked roofing nails right through the flange.

If your calculations indicated the need for additional air vents, install them now in the eaves.

Caulking within the chalked outline on the roof is best done with a wavy pattern, plus a straight line. It is also necessary to caulk both under the top shingles and over the flange upper section, which will go underneath the top shingles.

The fan is centered over the hole and upper shingle tabs as shown, prior to marking the flange outline with chalk.

Use roofing nails to fasten fan flange to the roof. Drive the nails right through flange and caulk them at the same time.

A rough chalk outline is marked on the roof. Heat Sheetrock knife blade with a torch. That will facilitate lifting the shingle tabs at the top of the opening.

These vents are ideal for under-the-eave installation and each supplies about 85 square inches of vent air.

Looking at the installation from inside the attic, notice the armored cable and box containing the thermostatic switch. When mounting this box to the rafter edge, first remove the switch from the box and hold it aside while nailing through the box support to avoid damage to the switch. For the safety of anyone who may have to work on the fan at a later date, it's best to install a positive disconnect. Wire up the fan according to local electrical codes and make sure of proper grounding throughout.

Under-the-eave installation of vent is shown here. Just mark the outline in pencil around the vent, remove the vent and remark the hole outline about ¾″ in from the pencil line. Drill a hole in each corner and saw in between the holes.

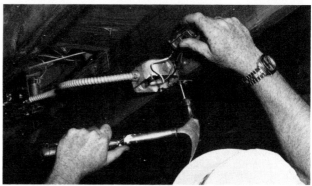

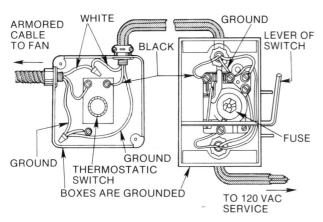

Electrical schematic of the power source, positive disconnect and thermostatic switch. Remember to check your local electrical code, and to ground all boxes and devices properly. Only after all else is done should you hook up to the power. That's a good habit to get into.

Attic view of fan installation (top) shows armored cable and switch box, ready for electrical work to be done. To avoid damage, remove the thermostatic switch from box before mounting box support to rafter edge (center). Typical positive disconnect box for use between power source and thermostatic switch (bottom) may be switched off if later work on fan is required—a worthwhile safety precaution.

4

Solar Hot Water

The ever-increasing energy costs hit the homeowner in home heating, electricity and domestic hot water heating dollars. Barring conservation and insulation attempts, it's tough to make serious inroads in the first two problems. But you *can* do something about the energy costs of heating your hot water, which accounts for 20% to 30% of your heating bills.

If you put in a solar hot water heating system, you'll probably eliminate upwards of 50% of the energy costs of heating hot water and be able to pay back the cost of the installation in a reasonable period, say 6 to 8 years. By installing the system yourself, you'll pocket another $500 to $1,000. This is not a difficult job, as it requires only modest carpentry, plumbing and minor electrical skills.

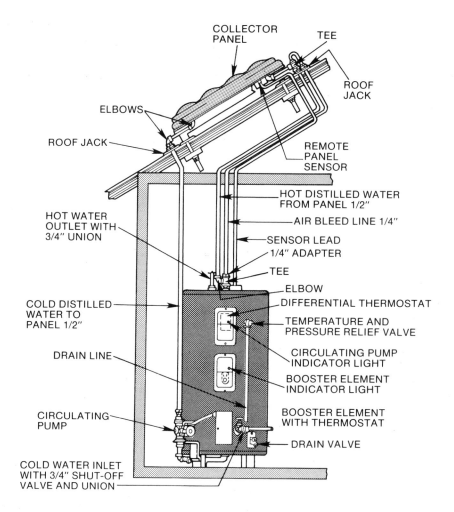

The Solarcraft II water heater system that was installed. This shows circulating pump, hooked up independently with a flat panel mounting upon the roof. This diagram is designed only to show the location of the components in an overall view.

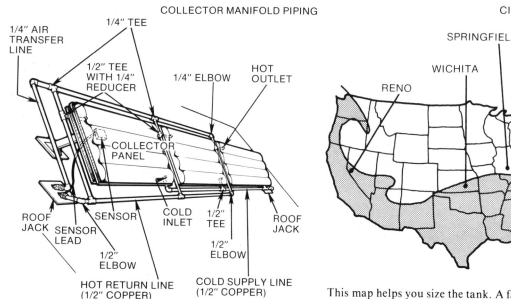

This illustration shows the collector manifold piping for a typical 40″ tilted collector panel set up on a sloped roof.

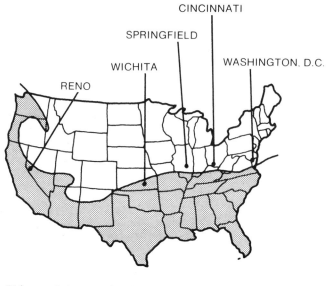

This map helps you size the tank. A family of four living in the shaded area needs an 82-gallon tank. A family of four in the unshaded area needs a 120-gallon tank, while a family of six in either area needs a 120-gallon tank.

How Does This System Work?

We installed a well-made solar heating system that is quite simple to operate despite the fact that it's completely automatic. The two main components of the system are roof collector panels and a combination tank/heat exchanger, which are connected by piping. The medium, distilled water, flows in the system, gaining heat from the sun when it's in the collectors and releasing heat to the domestic hot water when it's in the exchanger. The two waters never touch or mix. The system is technically an active one with a pump to move the medium up when activated by command signals from a differential thermostat and its sensors.

The medium can't freeze because it drains back to the heat exchanger/tank at night or when dense cloud formations combine with frigid temperatures. If this cloud cover persists, the exchanger has a backup electrical heater that goes on by thermostatic signal. We valved in an additional gas backup, which we'll show later.

Planning Your System

As your collectors are really the direct access to solar energy, you want them to be as efficient as possible. The main factors here are tilt, orientation, number of collectors (area) an an open "window" to the sun's rays.

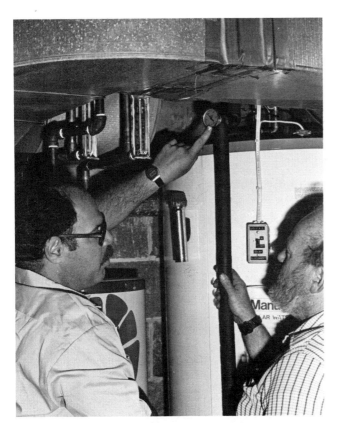

Having just harnessed the sun, we made a quick check on the system's thermometers to make sure all was in order. The only work left on the roof was trimming the support pipes.

The optimum orientation would be on a roof facing directly south, but according to HUD, slight deviations, certainly up to 15° either side of direct south won't have any appreciable loss of efficiency. In fact, experience shows that a major deviation such as 90° (that is facing east or west) can be accommodated by flattening out the tilt angle, with an efficiency loss of only about 17% from optimum. The tilt or raising of the panels from horizontal depends on the latitude of the site. As the north latitude or distance from the equator increases, the tilt also increases in order to get the maximum effective radiation. The same idea holds for trees or large buildings that might shade the collectors.

The collector area or number of panels basically determines your savings. If you have insufficient area, most of the heating will not be handled by the solar unit, and the small savings per year will make the payback time excessive. On the other hand, if you overkill with too many collectors, you'll have more than you need and also have an excessive payback time, due to the extra cost. Somewhere in the middle is the optimum number of panels.

There are two tank sizes available, 82 or 120 gallons, and the choice of which one is simple. It depends on your homesite and family size, according to the sizing information chart.

Another consideration is the vertical distance from the tank to the collectors. If it's greater than 21', you'll need an additional pump to carry the elevation head. But this is no problem—you simply install it in series, or you can order it that way from the factory.

The basic system is typically sold as a group including the heat exchanger/tank, pump, collectors (3) and collector mounting kits (3). Extra pumps and collectors plus kits can be purchased to suit the conditions.

Installation

The solar heating installation is basically a three part job: (1) installation of the collector panels on the roof; (2) installation of the heat exchanger/tank; (3) collector manifold and lines.

Before starting the actual roof work, get the tools ready for the mounting of the panels and fabrication of the collector manifolds. These include drill, wrenches, chalk line, large square, flexible tape, hammer, marking keel, caulking gun with silicone sealer and all soldering necessities. Also get the panel hardware mounting kits along with the copper pipe roof jacks and foam rubber insulation.

The panels should be handled carefully to avoid damaging the plastic faces. When unpacking them, be sure to save the package mounting nuts, as these will be used to start the hardware onto the panels.

We found that the best method of getting the panels from the ground to the roof was by two men pushing from below and two men pulling from the roof while the collector panel slides up a ladder on its back side with its long side more or less vertical.

Next, lay out the mounting hardware pattern with chalk line, tape and a large square according to the panel arrangement you have selected. Make sure that the holes for the threaded rods will fall *between* the rafters and that your layout is squared and aligned with the roof (not skewed). Drill the holes.

Assemble the hardware to the panels with your helper (only two people are needed on top once the panels are on the roof). Place the panels, one at a time, over the mounting holes; guide the rods into the holes; and apply silicone sealer under the large washers, which will rest on the roof shingles. Do this for all panels, while another helper works inside the attic fastening up the 2×6 struts, compression washers and nuts.

Make up the water and air manifolds from ½″ copper tubing and brass fittings. When soldering, be sure to clean

Before locking down the threaded rod mounts, we applied a generous amount of silicone sealer between the shingle and the metal washer.

Holes are drilled through the roof with an auger bit at the layout locations to accept the threaded rod mountings for collector panel hardware.

To set the solar angle for the collector panels, we used an angle gauge placed up under the channel flange. Then we locked them in place.

Here's a view of the roof jack at the hot water line, air line and sensor cable end. Insulation is taped and jack is cut in before silicone sealer.

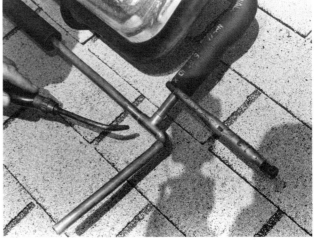

Foam insulation is placed over tubing and held back out of the way with small Visegrip pliers during soldering. When cool, foam snaps back.

Here's how the pipes and valves appear in a complete installation: It'll look like a rat's nest of copper tube, valves and fittings, but it works.

The heat exchanger here acts as a preheater for the existing gas heater. Note the two circulation pumps in series.

When distilled water is raised over 21', two pumps in series are required. Throttling valve adjustment is above pump(s).

and flux all tube ends and fitting hubs properly to avoid any leaks. Fit foam rubber pipe insulation over the entire network (install it as you go along) and tape up all insulation splice areas. All water tubing must slope *downward* so the water will drain back to the heater when the pump stops. You can use leftover brackets to help this or purchase separate pieces. We used ½″ for the air line as well as on top of the roof because insulation for that size is easy to obtain. Once inside the house, we switched over to ¼″.

It's best to rent an appliance hand truck to move the heat exchanger where you want it, as this will enable you to negotiate stairs as well.

There are two ways to use this heat exchanger: (1) as an independent water heater or (2) as a preheater for an existing heater, such as the gas heater in this case. If you use it independently, supply the backup heat with 220 volts and simply hook the tank between the cold water supply and the house hot water. If you use it as a preheater, skip the electric backup and set up the plumbing as shown. This will give you the options of solar only, gas only or a combination.

From the roof, the hot line, cold line, air line and sensor cable must be routed through jacks (plastic flanges) on their way through the attic, closets and whatever convenient areas you can find in route to the exchanger.

The upper end of the sensor cable is connected to a screw-in sensor at the end of the panel nearest the hot outlet where the lines pierce the roof. Signals from this sensor and the sensor on the tank are used by the differential thermostat to control pump operation.

When all connections are made, the system must be filled with distilled water medium. *Never* turn on the power *before* this is done. Note that when used as a preheater, no initial drain down is necessary, but when used independently, a specific quantity drain down is required depending upon the tank size and tube lengths. This job will most probably take you several days, but it's worth the effort when you consider the savings you'll be making from that time forward.

ROOF PITCH CONVERSION	
Inches of Vertical Rise Per Foot at Horizontal Run	Approximate Tilt Angle in Degrees
2	10
4	18
6	27
8	34
10	40
12	45

Valve #	Solar	Gas	Both	Function
1	O	S	O	Solar In
2	O	S	O	Solar Out
3	S	O	O	Gas In
4	S	O	O	Gas Out
5	S	O	S	Cold Diverter
6	O	S	S	Solar Out To House Hot H$_2$O

S = SHUT   O = OPEN

Solar collector angle depends on location. The collectors should be mounted facing south at an angle from the horizon equal to the geographical latitude if possible. Installation with the collector panel facing southeast or southwest by up to 15° will work almost as well as due south. Local weather conditions should guide panel orientation. Example: If you have morning fog that lasts until noon, face the panel southwest because you get very little morning sun. Conversely, if you have daily afternoon showers, face panels to the southeast.

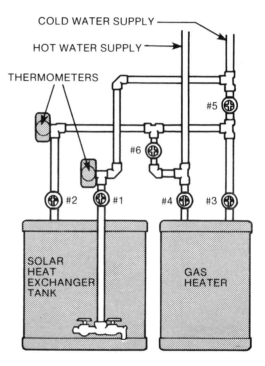

If you're using the heat exchanger as a preheater, this schematic shows a good way to get the maximum flexibility with a valving scheme.

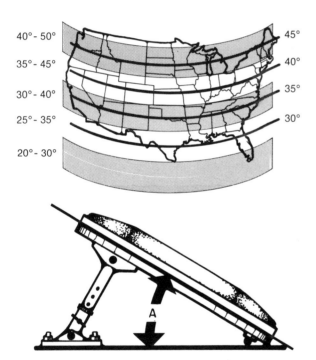

Angle "A" of the solar collector panel equals the geographical latitude.

Part II

Family Living Areas

5

Custom Bedroom Storage

Bedrooms in most homes lack built-in storage facilities. You must still invest in "bedroom furniture" to get sufficient space and convenience.

To demonstrate practical solutions for the do-it-yourselfer, we designed and built the wall storage modules shown here. Two modules are for a man's clothing, three for a woman's. You may want to build one, or, as your budget permits, all of them and the soffit that houses dimmer-controlled, recessed lighting, unifying the wall. Construction details include a vanity with lights and mirror and mirror-backed niches with glass shelves.

Despite their contemporary look, these modules demand only average carpentry skills. The cabinets and doors require only butt joints, cleats, glue, nails or screws for assembly, and a perfect finish is assured with prefinished panels.

The modules are sized to hold storage units and racks, while the doors' depth is designed to take inexpensive storage bins.

Soffit

Begin by building the soffit framing, using a stretched string and line level to get a straight, horizontal line (ignore all floor and ceiling discrepancies). Cover the framing with plasterboard and plywood, but leave the face open. This will allow you to cut the light holes, install the fixtures and do the wiring. Close the soffit face, install all molding, paint the soffit, then install the light bezels.

Cabinets, Box Doors

The cabinets and doors are laminated with ¼" pecan panel over the "D" side of the A-D plywood, so it's necessary to prepare only the "A" sides and those "D"

Smart, contemporary styling of storage modules is boldly accented by ebony soffit and trim, mirrored niches and a simply elegant vanity. Dimmer-controlled recessed lighting lets you adjust light level.

The complete system includes five modules separated by mirror-backed glass-shelved niches.

Beautiful carpeting complements the rich tones of this real hardwood-faced veneer, planked-effect paneling.

sides that will be exposed (some shelf bottoms). With this in mind, cut out all the main surfaces from the A-D plywood and fill the voids only on those "D" shelves that require it. Next, cut out all pine pieces, sand them; then all "A" surfaces and the filled "D" surfaces.

Prime the pine parts with a brush. Prime the plywood surfaces (all "A" and the filled "D") with a roller using thinned enamel underbody. Leave the glue assembly areas bare. When they're dry, sand and dust all primed parts. Then apply latex paint, again leaving the glue surface areas bare.

Lay out and mark the cleat and shelf locations on the cabinet sides, then begin the assembly of both cabinets and box doors, using white glue and nails. Or better yet, use 1¾" No. 8 flathead, Phillips drive hardened screws. These may be driven quickly and easily with a ⅜" drill motor and No. 2 Phillips bit. Both the screws and bit are available at industrial hardware stores.

After removing all existing base molding from the area, lay out and mark the cabinet positions along the wall, leaving stud location marks on the wall between the cabinets so you'll be able to fasten the cabinet backs to the studs. Slide the cabinets into place, then level and set them in with nails or screws driven into the floor, soffit and studs.

Remove the door casing and trim the ¼" A-D plywood to fit the niche, door and vanity areas. Prepaint the plywood for the door and vanity areas and install it with panel adhesive and colored nails. Trim and sand the door area plywood flush with the door jamb, then replace the door casing. Next, install the niche plywood with panel adhesive and nails.

Cut and scribe all cabinet side panels to the soffit and back wall as shown. Then laminate them to the plywood cabinet sides using panel adhesive cartridges in a caulking gun. Use matched color panel nails 1" long, driven in at a slight angle to avoid piercing the inner walls of the cabinets. Make sure that the combined ¾" ply and ¼" panel form a flush front edge to receive the feature strips by checking with a combination square.

Next, laminate the doors, using the *exact* panel overlap scheme shown in the drawing. Note that this overlap permits slight chamfering of the face panel edge on the door hidden by the batten of the mating door. This edge will be painted black like the feature strips and faces.

Trim, fit and install all feature strips, faces and shelf face strips with glue and nails, making sure to remove the excess glue while it's wet. Set all nails, fill the holes, sand and touch up all paint required on the cabinets and the doors as well.

Open, the modules are (left to right above) storage for woman's skirts, jackets, shoes; corner module; woman's full-length unit; man's suits, shoes; man's clothing and built-in TV. Shirts and underwear are visible in nylon-covered wire baskets. Two space-saving drawers, under TV, (left, center) hold accessories. Woman's short-length module (right, center) has slide-out racks for shoes and removable wall bins ideal for small items. Corner module (right) has clever door arrangement to open wide. Amerock's "Revolving Shelves" bring purses to fore, while baskets hold lingerie, sweaters, linens; belts are conveniently on doors.

To hang the doors, lay one leaf of continuous hinge down on the face of the outer feature strip 4½″ from the top and let the other leaf overhang the edge. Then, press the hinge knuckle in until it contacts the feature strip edge. Punch-mark the hinge hole centers and drive in the screws. Although No. 4 screws are conventionally used, we did the job with ⅝″ No. 6 screws, using the drill motor and Phillips No. 2 bit. **Caution:** This is pine, so take it a little easy until you get the "feel" of it.

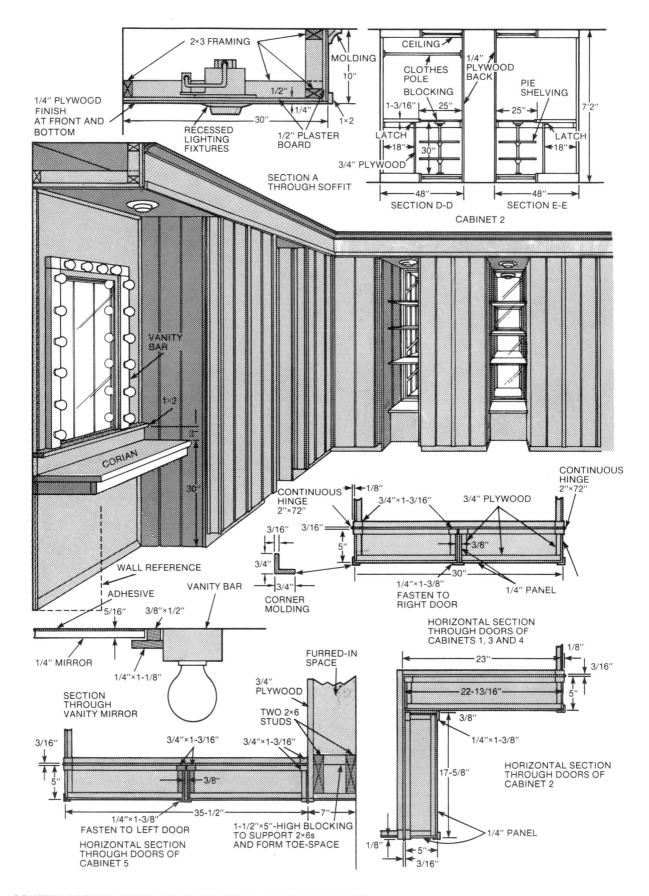

2×3 FRAMING

MOLDING

10"

1/4" PLYWOOD FINISH AT FRONT AND BOTTOM

1/2"

1/4"

1×2

30"

RECESSED LIGHTING FIXTURES

1/2" PLASTER BOARD

SECTION A THROUGH SOFFIT

CEILING

1/4" PLYWOOD BACK

CLOTHES POLE BLOCKING

PIE SHELVING

1-3/16"

25"

25"

7'2"

LATCH

18"

30"

LATCH

18"

3/4" PLYWOOD

48"

48"

SECTION D-D

SECTION E-E

CABINET 2

VANITY BAR

1×2

3"

CORIAN

30"

WALL REFERENCE

ADHESIVE

5/16"

3/8"×1/2"

VANITY BAR

1/4" MIRROR

1/4"×1-1/8"

SECTION THROUGH VANITY MIRROR

CONTINUOUS HINGE 2"×72"

1/8"

3/4"×1-3/16"

3/4" PLYWOOD

CONTINUOUS HINGE 2"×72"

3/16"

3/16"

5"

3/8"

3/16"

3/4"

3/4"

CORNER MOLDING

1/4"×1-3/8"

30"

1/4" PANEL

FASTEN TO RIGHT DOOR

HORIZONTAL SECTION THROUGH DOORS OF CABINETS 1, 3 AND 4

23"

1/8"

3/16"

22-13/16"

5"

3/8"

1/4"×1-3/16"

HORIZONTAL SECTION THROUGH DOORS OF CABINET 2

FURRED-IN SPACE

3/4" PLYWOOD

TWO 2×6 STUDS

3/16"

5"

3/4"×1-3/16"

3/4"×1-3/16"

3/8"

1/4"×1-3/8"

35-1/2"

7"

17-5/8"

FASTEN TO LEFT DOOR

1-1/2"×5"-HIGH BLOCKING TO SUPPORT 2×6s AND FORM TOE-SPACE

1/8"

5"

3/16"

1/4" PANEL

HORIZONTAL SECTION THROUGH DOORS OF CABINET 5

CONSTRUCTION PLAN FOR COMPLETE MODULAR STORAGE SYSTEM.

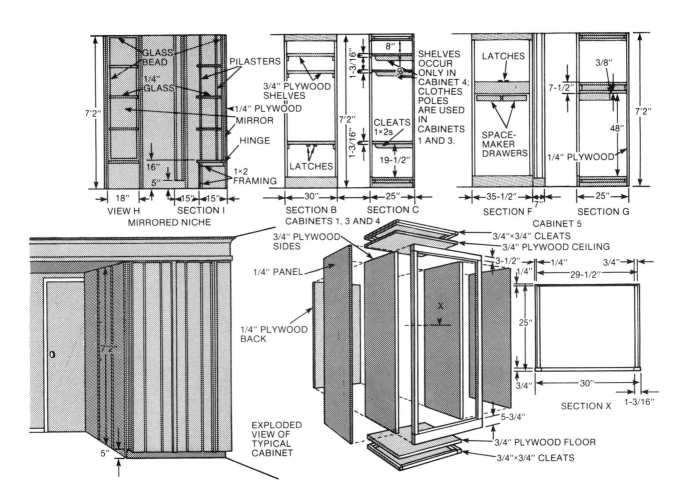

GLASS BEAD
PILASTERS
1/4"
GLASS
1/4" PLYWOOD
MIRROR
HINGE
1×2 FRAMING
7'2"
16"
5"
18"
15" 15"
VIEW H
SECTION I
MIRRORED NICHE

3/4" PLYWOOD SHELVES
LATCHES
1-3/16"
1-3/16"
7'2"
30"
SECTION B
CABINETS 1, 3 AND 4

8"
SHELVES OCCUR ONLY IN CABINET 4; CLOTHES POLES ARE USED IN CABINETS 1 AND 3.
CLEATS 1×2s
19-1/2"
25"
SECTION C

LATCHES
SPACE-MAKER DRAWERS
35-1/2"
SECTION F
7"
CABINET 5

3/8"
7-1/2"
48"
1/4" PLYWOOD
7'2"
25"
SECTION G

3/4" PLYWOOD SIDES
1/4" PANEL
1/4" PLYWOOD BACK
EXPLODED VIEW OF TYPICAL CABINET
7'2"
5"

3/4"×3/4" CLEATS
3/4" PLYWOOD CEILING
3-1/2"
1/4"
1/4"
X
25"
3/4"
5-3/4"
3/4" PLYWOOD FLOOR
3/4"×3/4" CLEATS

1/4" 3/4"
29-1/2"
30"
1-3/16"
SECTION X

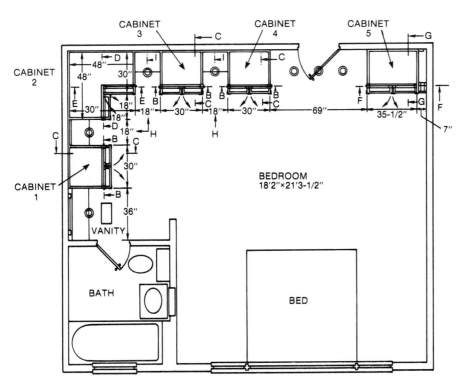

CABINET 3
CABINET 4
CABINET 5
C
C
I
I
G
CABINET 2
48"
48"
30"
D
E
30"
18"
18"
18"
18"
E B
18"
30"
B
C
B C
B
30"
B
C
69"
35-1/2"
F
F
G
7"
C
D
18"
H
H
C
CABINET 1
B
C
30"
B
36"
VANITY
BEDROOM
18'2"×21'3-1/2"
BATH
BED

CONSTRUCTION PLAN FOR COMPLETE MODULAR STORAGE SYSTEM.

Place the door and attached hinge against the cabinet and raise it until there is a ¼″ gap between the top of the door and the bottom of the soffit. Make a small mark on the cabinet feature strip to indicate the top of the hinge. You may want to get the hinge leaf onto the cabinet strip and the door strip in equal parts, so proceed as shown in the drawing. When all is in order, punch-mark the holes and drive the screws. Mount the battens, outside moldings and latches.

Then nail a piece of prepainted blocking to cover the wall-soffit joint. Now, cut, fit and install the niche storage boxes, using prepainted lids, lid supports and front faces.

Cut all mirrors—except the vanity—¼″ smaller than the actual dimensions for ease of fit. Spot small amounts of mirror adhesive through the niche plywood area, then place the mirror in position between the adjacent cabinets on the sides and the blocking piece and lid support on the top and bottom respectively. Press the mirror against the wall, compressing the adhesive; then fit and install the prepainted glass bead molding over the glass edges, nailing into the cabinets, top blocking and niche box lid support. (Note that second surface mirrors require the inside surface of the molding to be painted to avoid the reflection of raw wood.)

Install top blocking—in each of the cabinet doors that get mirrors—72¼″ up from the inside of the bottom door piece. Then mount the mirrors and install the glass bead as before. Install the pilasters and clips, but leave the glass shelves out until the job is finished to avoid breakage. Locate and mark the position of the vanity bar electrical strip hole and pull an electrical lead out there.

Vanity

Start work on the vanity by nailing in the substructure, which supports it with its top edges 29¼″ from the floor, and paint the front face. If you've never handled Corian® before, here are a couple of tips:

1. Circular saws, portable or bench type, that are used to cut this material must be carbide-tipped. If you're forced to use a jigsaw, fit it with a 14-tooth-per-inch metal cutting blade.
2. Edges may be routed using carbide bits with roller bearing guides.

After cutting the countertop and backsplash for the vanity bar, rout the front edge of the top with a rounding-over bit, but don't cut into the Corian with the square bit corner. Coat the top surface of the substructure with panel adhesive (cartridge and caulking gun). Place the countertop on this adhesive bed, then press it down. Next apply some beads of adhesive to the sanded wall behind the backsplash area. Then apply some sealer (cartridge and gun) to the Corian-to-Corian joint. Now place the backsplash in position and press it home to the wall and downward to the countertop. You should either clean away the excess sealer immediately with a putty knife and

treat the adjacent areas with alcohol or allow it to dry and trim it out at that time with a razor blade.

Cut the vanity mirror to 23¾″ × 36⅞″, which will provide a ⅝″ space on three sides between the mirror and the vanity bars. Glue and nail the prepainted molding on top of the Corian backsplash, then mount the mirror to the wall as before, butting the bottom edge on the molding.

Install the electrical strips and vanity bars according to the maker's instructions, but don't install the lamps until the mirror molding has been completed to avoid damage. Make up this molding for all three sides from parting strip and lattice, forming an "L"-shaped section.

Miter the two top corners and then install the molding, prepainted, with panel adhesive. Your vanity is complete.

Finish Work

Starting with the pie-shelf assembly in cabinet 2, begin by adding a block of ¾″ plywood to the underside of the middle "L"-shaped shelf, using the supplied template as a location aid. This is necessary because the maximum post height is 29⁷⁄₁₆″, but the framework in the lower section requires a 30″ shelf separation. Now, install the pie shelves according to the manufacturer's instructions. If you make any assembly errors and have to dismantle these units, merely place a wood block between the hammer face and the metal parts.

In a given framework, only one width basket may be used, but you may choose a variety of depths to suit your requirements.

The space-saving drawers mounted under the TV shelf of cabinet 5 require spacing away from the shelf to clear the face edge. The easiest way to handle this is to use either nuts or washers as spacers and wood screws as fasteners. Also in cabinet 5, we filled a shallow shelf with small organizers to hold small items and jewelry.

Many of the box doors are equipped with tie and belt racks type or ladder-type trouser hangers suspended on hooks. Still others are loaded with wall bins. These are excellent for storing hosiery, small items, cosmetics and sprays.

After installing lamps, put the glass shelving in place and display your favorite art objects. Install the carpet and get ready for lots of compliments on your craftsmanship.

Cabinet Side Panels

- With plywood cabinets set in place and plumb, measure the maximum horizontal distance from the front cabinet edge to the wall. At this level, there will be a maximum gap between the back of the cabinet and the wall.
- Start by cutting the panel width to maximum horizontal distance. (Keep a standard distance between the front edge of the panel and the nearest

groove on all cabinets.) That means adding the extra panel width for scribing purposes onto the back edge of the panel.

- Rough trim the panel height so that you can place the panel next to the cabinet side, with the panel grooves plumb. The panel will extend past the front edge of the cabinet until the scribing corrections are made. Use a compass or dividers set to the maximum gap, with one leg riding the wall and the other leg scribing (marking) the rear of the panel. Remove the panel, plane or saw away the error, then replace the panel for a final fit. You may have to do this more than once, but the first correction is the major one.

Hinge Leaves

Here's the procedure for getting the hinge leaves equally located on both door and cabinet feature strips:

- Place door with the hinge installed in position against the cabinet feature strip at the height already determined.
- Then, place 90° edge of a combination square against the inner edge of the cabinet feature strip.
- Extend the blade of the square until it touches the edge of the cabinet hinge leaf. This dimension should be the same as a similar measurement taken between the inner edge of the door feature strip and its hinge leaf edge.

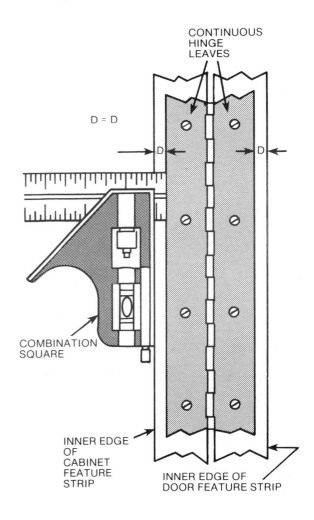

6

Dining Room Redo

The before photo, above, was the inspiration for the total make-over, left. Note the terrific impact of the panelled door window treatment, wallcovering and new chandelier.

The party got out of hand. It all began with plans for a dinner party, and the casual observance that the paint in the dining room was looking a little dingy. Maybe we could postpone the dinner party until we had time to give the walls and ceilings a fresh coat of paint. But the farther we looked, the worse it got: Walls, floors, ceiling, lighting—even the furniture—needed attention.

The chandelier was a "builders' special" of uncertain vintage; the carpet looked as though it had served as Astro Turf for the Super Bowl; the paint on the ceiling had turned from white to gray and the walls were 50′ of blandness, an ideal subject for wallcovering. The window

was an early aluminum model combination that needed replacement or concealing.

Preparation

Our first step was to wade through acres of brochures, wallcovering books and magazines showing window treatments to get a handle on the direction we might take.

Short of ripping the old window out, our best bet seemed to be to conceal it behind some fancy sliding doors. I designed 16′ of new doors I could assemble in the shop. New wallcovering would liven up the walls. Could we get material for the door curtains color-coded to the wallcovering? We could and did. By this time we were pasting color samples on our rough sketch of the room. The project looked great except for one thing. The chairs, though upholstered in quality fabric, had become worn and soiled. We could buy extra curtain fabric and upholster the chairs to match.

A careful time study for the project showed that the upholstery and doors would take the most time. By removing the old upholstery carefully, we were able to use the old material for patterns. Armed with these "patterns" and our measurements, we cut out the curtains, chair seats, valance and chair piping in that order. While my wife got the sewing machine going, I went down to the shop and started on the doors.

The result of the shop work was four large, raised panel sliders, ready to be painted. I decided on a spray finish for the doors, which called for several coats of paint.

Between paint coats I took advantage of the drying time to rip up the old carpeting, the tackless perimeter and padding. I found you can make the sanitation department's hit list if you put out a mess of this stuff several days running.

To replace the old carpet we chose parquet flooring, with an Oriental area rug. I removed the shoe molding for repainting and laying of the parquet floor.

Paint and Wallcovering

The first step in painting was to repaint the ceiling and install a new chandelier. Then I painted all room moldings that were still in place—stool, apron, base and case— to get ready for wallcovering application. Registers and outlet covers came off at this point.

Pretrimmed wallcovering is a boon for non-pros, and eliminates the need for a long steel trimming edge. Must tools are a long table, roller and handle, drywall knife, utility knife, smoothing brush, a bucket and mixing stick and a long level. Most of these can be borrowed from your wallcovering supplier.

The first step of wallcovering should be hung next to a plumb line penciled in an obscure area on the wall. Measure the wall height, check out the repeat in the pattern, leave some overage (about 6″ on each end) at the top and bottom, and cut enough pieces to do the entire room. To paste the pieces, stack them all face down on the table and roll the adhesive on them, one at a time. Fold the ends of the wallcovering in toward the middle, and carry the wallcovering to the wall. Unfold the top section and align it, allowing at least 2″ overlap at the ceiling line or molding. Match the long edge either to the plumb line or the adjacent strip of wallcovering. Smooth the covering with the brush, checking the job by taking an oblique sighting over the covering. When the piece is smoothed and matched, trim the top and bottom by placing the drywall knife against the juncture of the wall and ceiling or the

The base molding was removed for installation of parquet floor tile. Pails served as a workbench for painting the base.

All room moldings that remained in place were painted before starting the wallcovering.

base molding. Then cut across the covering with the utility knife, guided by the edge of the drywall blade. Sponge away all adhesive from ceilings, moldings and the face of the wallcovering.

To conceal electric outlet covers, cut a section of wallcovering large enough so that you can match the pattern on the wall, usually about one square foot. Turn off the power to the outlet, then match the piece to the wall pattern. Stick an awl in the center (screw) hole, and with this hole punched in the covering, install the cover plate. The outlet cover will squeeze down on the wallcovering, imprinting its outline. Then remove the cover plate and trim the edges and holes in the wallcovering. Apply adhesive to the outlet cover and attach the wallcovering, folding the edges around to the back of the outlet cover.

A long table is needed for pasting the wallcovering. Using a roller and roller tray speed application of the paste.

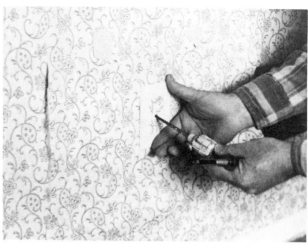

A scrap of wallcovering is placed so the pattern will match, and a hole is punched through the screw hole of cover.

The wallcovering is smoothed in place with the brush. Inspect the wallcovering in oblique light for bubbles.

The cover is aligned with the center hole punched in photo right, above. Wallcovering is then cut to fit the cover.

A wallboard finishing knife is used as a straightedge for trimming the wallcovering; notch is cut for door rail.

Flooring

When painting and wallcovering are done, it's time to install the parquet floor. Snap a pair of lines at right angles to each other, with the lines intersecting at the center of the room. The chalk lines will provide a straight starting line in both directions, and you'll have tiles of equal width at the perimeter, for a professional-looking border.

The tiles are as easy to install as advertised. To be on the safe side of the manufacturer's guarantee, use the adhesive recommended in the instructions. The adhesive is applied with a notched spreader trowel. Spread only as much adhesive as you can cover within the curing time noted on the adhesive label, and remember that a high room temperature will shorten the cure time of the adhesive. Be sure to provide adequate ventilation, and to leave a ¼″ gap at all edges of the room to allow for expansion of the wood. The ¼″ gap will be covered by the base shoe.

Tile mastic is spread using the notched spreader trowel. Apply only a small area at each stage and ventilate the room.

Apply parquet tile, starting in the center of the room. Allow at least ¼″ on all sides of room for tile expansion.

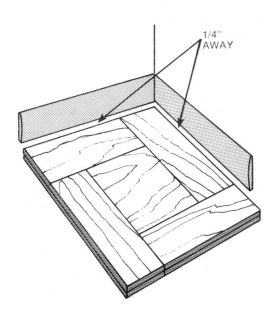

Upholstery

Sewing new upholstery and curtains was a straightforward job. If piping is involved in the upholstery, you have to make the piping from bias-cut material, sewn around commercially available cording. There is a special foot for your sewing machine for sewing piping.

Once the pieces and sewn assemblies are done, reupholstery is a matter of stapling on a muslin undercover and then the material itself. Most often, you stretch and fasten the material to the corners of the chair frame, then pull and staple the areas between corners. Pull the fabric tight enough so the surface is smooth over the padding, but not tight enough to cause puckers or wrinkles.

New material is stapled on the chair back. Material used for upholstery matches the door insets and wallcovering.

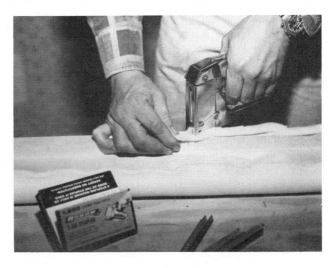

Valance is covered with foam rubber padding, attached with a heavy-duty stapler capable of penetrating the 1×6 pine.

The fabric is applied. The staple gun must have capacity for staples long enough to penetrate through padding.

The valance is attached to the ceiling joists using screws. The valance will conceal the aluminum door track.

Window and Door Treatment

The sliding doors for the dining room are large double units with two raised panels and two insert openings each. The basic door structure is of 5/4 (1⅛″ thick) pine stock for the side stiles, center stiles and rails. The panels are made of ½″ thick plywood, the raised panels of ¼″ thick plywood. All the tenons are ½″ thick and ¾″ long and the dadoes are the same thickness. This allows a continuous dado to hold both the ½″ plywood panels and the tenons.

In our project, the two inner doors slide and the two outer doors are stationary on the tracks, although this is optional. The completed doors are equipped with trolleys that ride on a bypassing sliding track fastened to the ceiling. At the floor, the doors are held by adjustable guides.

When sizing the doors, the height should be checked at several places along the wall, and the thickness of the existing rug and/or proposed flooring should be considered in your calculations. The combination of the track and trolley plus the new flooring should be subtracted from the total height from ceiling to original floor. This number is the height of the doors to be constructed. Allow ¼″ to prevent future binding.

Next, divide the length of the wall by four (or the number of doors you require). This dimension plus ½″ for overlap is the width of each door.

Start construction by cutting out the component blanks. Remember to include the length of the tenons on the pieces that require tenons.

All tenons and dadoes can easily be made on a table saw. The dadoes are ½″-wide grooves that run the full length of all pieces. The tenons are made in a two-step operation. First make the stop cuts, with the rip fence set to control the length of the tenon and the miter head set to keep everything square. The next step is to remove the waste. Remove the miter head, leaving the fence, and rapidly pass the stock over the blade transversely with an oscillating motion, while advancing forward from infeed to the output side of the blade. If you haven't made tenons before, practice on some scrap lumber first.

Dry-fit all pieces to be sure they are the correct size. Then glue and clamp everything into assemblies, including the ½″-thick plywood lower section panels. When the glue is dry, sand all surfaces and rout out the rear shoulders of all the dadoes in the top sections. Use a self-guiding roller bearing bit, and let the roller ride in the bottom of the dado. Do this routing step slowly to avoid splintering the wood. This routing operation will convert the dadoes into rabbets, where the inserts—curtains, grilles or plastic—will be housed.

After sanding the rabbets, glue and nail the raised ¼″-thick plywood panels and add ¼″ quarter-round molding around the edges of the bottom section, where the molding will appear as beading. Cut the miter corners of the molding with a modeler's saw. Use tiny brads or "beauty brads," available at cabinetmakers' supply shops, to fasten the molding.

You must bore ⅜″-diameter holes with the aid of a drill guide to fit the gang trolley for the track to the top of the doors. Place scrap stock between the drill guide clamps and the doors to protect the doors from damage.

Screw the track to the ceiling joists. Note there are notches in the ends of the track to get the trolleys started. Do not cut these notches off if the track must be cut to fit.

Finally, hang the doors and adjust them. Be sure to use floor guides that are wide enough to accommodate the 5/4 wood stock. You can adjust the doors so they travel easily in the tracks and hang plumb, as shown in the illustration. Two wrenches for adjustment are usually supplied with the track kit.

All tenons and dadoes can be made on the table saw. The dadoes are ½″ wide and run the full length of all pieces.

Use a router with a self-guiding roller bearing bit to cut the rear shoulders of the dadoes, making rabbets for the panels.

To make tenons, first make the stop cuts, then remove the waste.

Use modelers' saw to miter the ¼″ moldings.

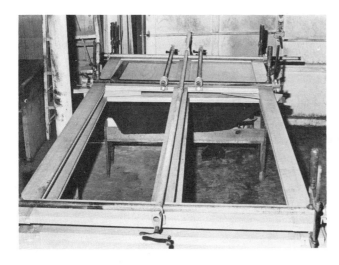

Dry-fit all the door pieces to be sure they fit. Then use pipe clamps and glue for the final assembly. Allow time to dry.

Add the ¼″ quarter-round molding as beading around the bottom section edges.

We built a valance to hide the top of our new doors, and the track they ride on. If you don't use doors for your project, you may still be interested in a valance to hide your drapery rods. The valance was cut from 1×6 pine, then 1″ was ripped from the width so the board could be screwed to the upper rear of the main piece. (See sidebar illustration). The valance was covered with foam padding, and the material was stapled on. Then the valance was screwed to the ceiling joists.

The face-lift is now complete. Our only remaining expense will be the menu for the dinner party we'll have to christen our "new" dining room.

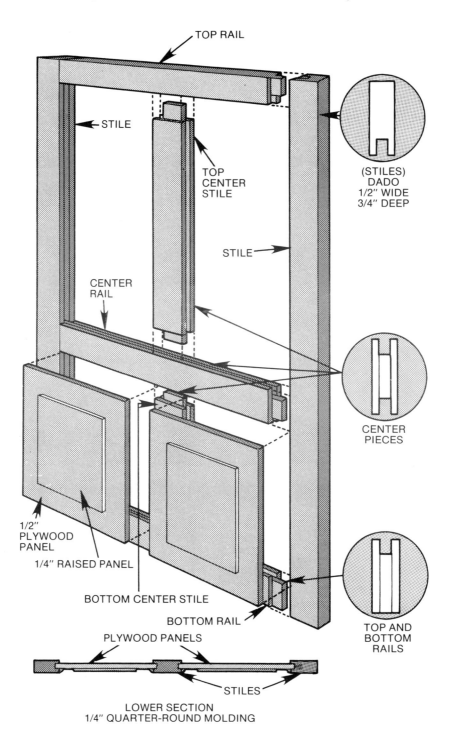

TOP RAIL

STILE

TOP CENTER STILE

(STILES) DADO 1/2″ WIDE 3/4″ DEEP

STILE

CENTER RAIL

CENTER PIECES

1/2″ PLYWOOD PANEL

1/4″ RAISED PANEL

BOTTOM CENTER STILE

BOTTOM RAIL

TOP AND BOTTOM RAILS

PLYWOOD PANELS

STILES

LOWER SECTION
1/4″ QUARTER-ROUND MOLDING

7

Beamed Ceiling

Wooden ceiling beams can add colonial charm to a family room and relieve the monotony of the totally unadorned ceilings found in so many of today's homes. Here's how to install them.

Beamed Layout

The beams should span the shorter wall-to-wall dimension of the room, and there should be an odd number of beams to get an even number of equally wide inter-beam spaces—the design that is most pleasing to the eye. All beams should be full width, except those on end walls, which should be half the width to give the appearance of continuing past the wall line.

Beams are constructed of readily available dimensioned lumber and are fastened to plates supported by the ceiling joists in one of three ways:

1. If ceiling plates run perpendicular to joists, it's a simple matter to nail or screw a plate to each joist in line.
2. If plates run parallel to, and line up with joists, just nail or screw plate along an entire joist.
3. If plates run parallel to, but do not line up with joists, it's best to install inter-joist blocking to serve as a nailer for plates that run between joists. This support method allows you to place beams wherever your design requires, regardless of joist spacing.

Divide the ceiling into an even number of spaces to provide for an odd number of beams. Try for an inter-beam spacing of 3' to 4'. Then mark the ceiling and snap chalk lines across it at each of the beam centerlines. Snap an additional chalk line 1¾" on either side of each centerline for the plates, which should be 5/4 or 2×4 (3½" wide) and run the complete width of the room.

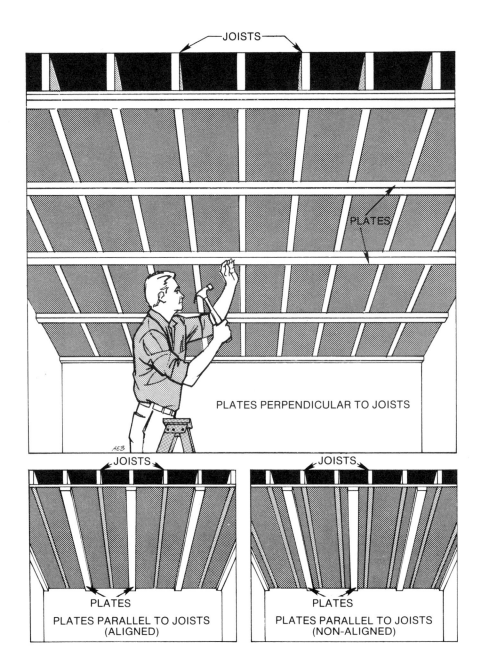

Three situations you may come upon in beam installation: Top, plates perpendicular to joists; bottom left, plates parallel to and lined up with joists; bottom right, plates parallel to, but not aligned with joists, which here need blocking.

Mounting Plates

If you are installing plates perpendicular to the joists, drive in No. 10 screws or 16d nails through the plates and gypsum board into the joists. You can find the joists by looking for nailhead marks or by tapping the gypsum. A hollow, drumlike sound indicates no structure above the gypsum, whereas a hard, nonresonant knock indicates a joist directly above. You can also probe for the joist with a small nail by tapping it through the gypsum. This plate-mounting procedure also works if plates are parallel to and line up with joists.

If the plates are parallel to but do not line up with joists, mark out an opening to be cut in the gypsum board between the two outer chalk marks (3½″ apart), about 1′ long, every 4′. Cut out the openings with a plasterboard saw, keyhole saw or jigsaw and set the cutout piece aside so it can be refitted later.

Insert a zig-zag rule with the extension slide for inside measurements into the opening and measure the horizontal distance from joist face to joist face. It should be about 14½″ for joists 16″ on center and 22½″ for joists 24″ on center. Repeat these measurements in all cutouts and record them in sequence.

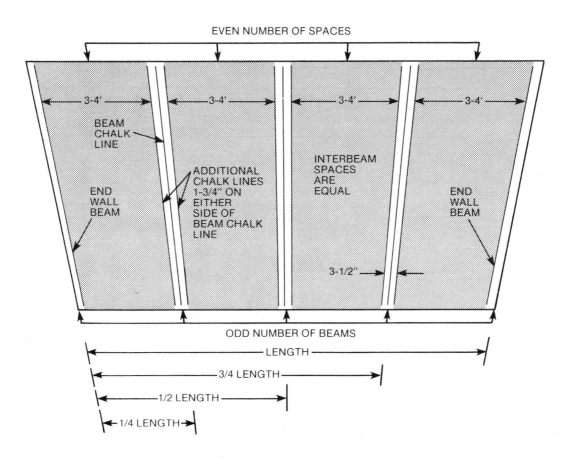

EVEN NUMBER OF SPACES

3-4'   3-4'   3-4'   3-4'

BEAM
CHALK
LINE

ADDITIONAL
CHALK LINES
1-3/4" ON
EITHER
SIDE OF
BEAM CHALK
LINE

INTERBEAM
SPACES
ARE
EQUAL

END
WALL
BEAM

END
WALL
BEAM

3-1/2"

ODD NUMBER OF BEAMS

LENGTH

3/4 LENGTH

1/2 LENGTH

1/4 LENGTH

A basic scheme for dividing ceiling into even number of spaces and odd number of beams. Broken lines indicate beam centerlines and plate outlines.

Nail one end of chalked mason's cord at the mark on one side of the room; then stretch the cord to the mark on the opposite side and snap the cord.

If joists and plates are either perpendicular or parallel and aligned, prop up one end of the plate and drive nails or screws into joists.

Cut a piece 5/4 or 2×4 blocking to each of the dimensions just made. You'll be driving four screws in on both ends of all these blocking pieces to lock them to the joists, so first prepare the pieces by drilling eight 11/64"-diameter holes (body clearance for No. 8 screws) obliquely in the ends of each one. If you have a No. 2 Phillips screwdriver bit with your reversible, variable-speed drill, you can save time by installing the blocking pieces with the drill motor, using No. 8 hardened Phillips "twin-fast" screws 3" long, which are made for power driving.

Begin by inserting the blocking piece through the cutout, placing it between the joists, flush with the backside of the gypsum. Next, get your drill motor in position, usually with the body and handle up in the joist bay, and drive in the eight screws. If properly installed, the blocking will support upward of 150 pounds.

Indicate the centerlines of the blocking on the adjacent gypboard with a pencil (don't use a pen: ink will tend to bleed through any paint you apply later) and replace the cutouts. Now, line the plates up with the chalk marks, and

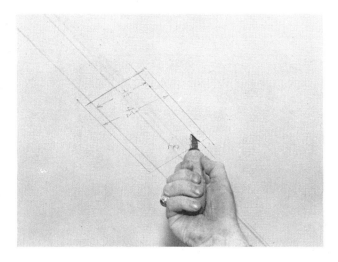

Saw out 3½"×12" plasterboard piece on beam centerline for insertion and installation of blocking; if necessary, enlarge cutout to 4½" maximum.

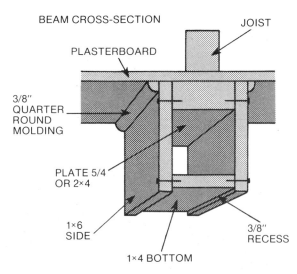

Beams have 1×6 sides and 1×4 bottoms, all common pine. Keep a ⅜" recess at bottom-side joint and hide the side-ceiling joint with molding.

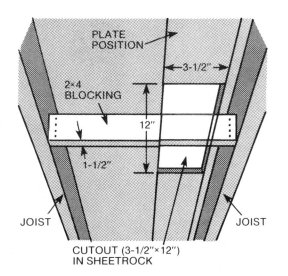

Measure joist face-to-joist face distances and record in sequence. Blocking is indicated in opening.

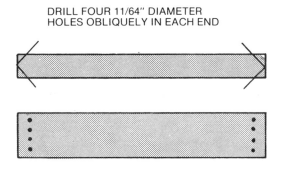

Trim 2×4 blocking to lengths measured; then drill four oblique clearance holes for No. 8 screws in each.

nail or screw the plates to the blocking, using the blocking centerline marks as guides.

Beams Construction

Construct the beams right on the spot from No. 2 common pine (clear pine is about 2½ times as expensive and, because a relatively coarse look is quite acceptable, common pine is actually the better choice). The sides of the beam are 1×6 and the bottoms are 1×4.

Measure the width of the room at each centerline using the method shown here, but add 1/16" to this when transferring the measurement to the boards. The slightly overlength boards tend to stay in place after you flex them into position against the plates. Prop 2×4s under the bottom edge of the sides to straighten them as much as possible. Now, check for a gap between the top edge of the side and the ceiling. Ceilings are not generally true and, quite often, you'll find that a gap exists. Gaps up to ⅛" will never be noticed because the side-ceiling joint will be covered by a molding; if gaps are larger than that, plane high points carefully, until you get an adequate closure.

When the side fits properly against the ceiling, nail or screw it to the plate (No. 8 flathead screws, 2" long, or 8d nails).

Measure and cut to size a 1×4 bottom and set it in place, butting against the inner surface of the side already mounted. Adjust the recess at the bottom using a ⅜"-thick spacer as a guide and clamp the side and bottom piece together. Nail or screw the side to the bottom and remove the clamps.

Measure and cut the second side and place it up against the ceiling, propping with 2×4s if necessary. Now, clamp it to the bottom piece, spacing the recess as you go along,

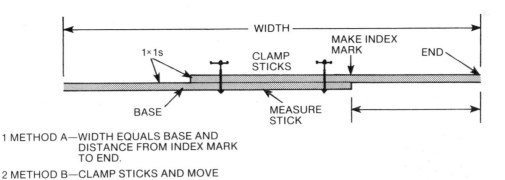

1 METHOD A—WIDTH EQUALS BASE AND
DISTANCE FROM INDEX MARK
TO END.
2 METHOD B—CLAMP STICKS AND MOVE
AS A UNIT.

It's a long way from wall to wall, so use 1×1 sticks to measure width accurately. Measurements may be transferred with sticks clamped or apart.

With the side fastened to the plate, clamp the bottom to the inside surface of the side, adjusting the recess as you go, before fastening with nails or screws.

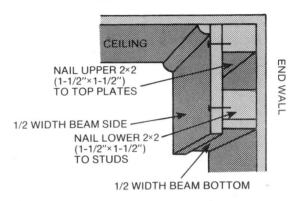

CROSS SECTION OF END WALL

For the half-width beams at the end wall, first nail or screw 2×2s in position as shown. The upper nailer is the plate and the lower nailer plumbs the side.

and then nail or screw it to both the plate and bottom piece. This method will handle all beams except those at the end walls.

For the half-width beams at the end walls, fasten two nailers. The top nailer serves as a plate and the lower one will keep the side plumb. Scribe both bottom and side pieces, then assemble with nails or screws.

Finish Work

This is an excellent time to paint the ceiling between the beams. A textured finish will enhance the effect—the beamed ceiling pictured has the interbeam spaces painted with sand added and applied with a stipple-finish roller. (Adding sand greatly reduces the paint coverage.) The ceiling was primed first.

Now you have only to conceal the slight gaps between the sides and ceiling. Prime enough ⅜" quarter-round molding to handle the job. Choose a contrasting low-gloss enamel or semigloss paint. Prepaint the moldings and install them with small finishing nails, fill all nail or screwhead holes, then paint the beams themselves.

After the paint is dry, step back, admire the job and consider some colonial furniture as your next project.

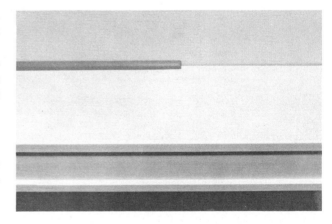

Attach ⅜" quarter-round prepainted molding to cover side-ceiling joints, which are either a maximum ⅛" gap or scribed or planed to that dimension.

8

Hardwood Plank Floor

You can now lay a handsome, random-width oak floor with a trowel.

Would you like an elegant, pegged, plank oak floor? You may think it's too tricky a job to handle, but it's not. There are now easy-to-apply plank floors that go over a variety of subfloors and require only a special adhesive and trowel. It only takes a couple of days to floor an average-size room.

The hardwood planks are made by several manufacturers, and installation techniques are similar. The better planks are actually a bonded laminate, composed of three 1/8" layers: a bottom layer of rough oak with relief grooves to facilitate bonding; an oak center; and an oak top surface that is prefinished and designed to give years of troublefree service, with virtually no maintenance. Each plank is alternately tongued and grooved on all four edges. The planks come in both 3.5" and 7" widths, enabling you to lay a random pattern.

If you would like to put one of these floors in your home, some advance planning and subfloor preparation are necessary. The rest is easy.

Subfloor Preparation

The flooring comes in bundles of 25 square feet. To determine how much you need, measure the room area and then allow an additional 5% planking for waste.

When you order, also get any special trowel suggested by the manufacturer and enough hardwood flooring adhesive to do the job properly. The average rate is 50 square feet per gallon for normal floors, 35 to 40 square feet per gallon for marginal concrete floors. Remember, not enough adhesive makes for difficult bonding, while too much may seep up through the joints.

All materials should be left in the house at 70°F, or slightly higher, for a couple of days before starting the floor. That temperature also should be maintained until the job has been completed.

The preparatory work will depend on the existing subflooring:

- If the existing subfloor is wood (plywood, tongue and groove, hardwood), sand all rough edges and check the area for loose boards.

Lock down any loose or squeaky boards with 10d, rosin-coated box nails, driven in angled pairs for extra holding power. If squeaking is caused by a gap between the subfloor and the joists, which cannot be nailed closed, drive wedges in from the basement side. Other squeaks may be removed by driving screws up through the subfloor into the existing hardwood flooring above it. Before proceeding, fill any cracks with water, wood putty, and sand.

- If the subfloor is new, ⅜″ plywood, start by performing the work described above. Next, nail down the plywood, using as many full sheets as possible arranged in a brick-lap pattern. The best fastener for this job is the annular-grooved underlayment nail, available at any lumber yard. Drive the nails into the main areas of the plywood, spacing them 6″ to 8″ apart, but "sewing" the edges together with a really tight nailing pattern. Again, sand all high spots, fill cracks and make sure all nailheads are flush.

- If the existing floor is resilient (vinyl, but not rubber, tile), you can lay the wood planks directly over the existing tiles, after they have been sanded or chemically stripped of wax with ammonia solution. Check for loose tiles and for squeaks and high spots, as described above. Never remove tiles with the intention of laying the plank down on the tile mastic, since this mastic is not compatible with the latex patch adhesive.

  If the floor tiles are loose or broken, repair the damage with new tiles and sand them smooth. Or, if you want to level the new plank floor with a slightly higher floor in an adjacent room, apply a ⅜″ plywood subfloor over the tiles, which is what was done in the case of the floor pictured.

- If the subfloor is concrete, the concrete should be level, dry, sound and clean. It must not vary more than 3/16″ for every 10′. If this is not the case, gradually fill in with latex patch in layers not exceeding ⅛″ at a time. No dampproofing membrane should be used in concrete, as the planks should be bonded directly to the concrete with LP adhesive. Concrete with known moisture problems should not be used as a subfloor for wood plank. Remove all grease, oil and stains; then take down any high spots with a carborundum stone or a terrazzo grinder (which can be rented). Finally, vacuum.

Starting the Floor

Once the subfloor is ready, remove the base molding, collect the tools you'll need and you're ready to start on the floor. First, snap a chalk line down the length of the room for a plank-starting guide. This mark should be about 2′ from the wall, allowing a work access area.

Now apply a 2′-wide band of adhesive, using the recommended special trowel. Start at the chalk line and extend

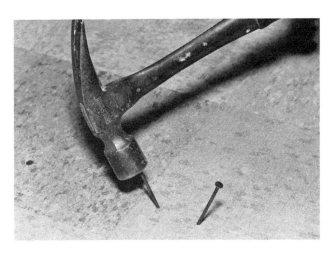

Use 10d, rosin-coated box nails to lock down any loose or squeaky boards in a wood subfloor. To really get a bite in the joist below, angle the nails.

If squeaking is caused by a stubborn gap between the subfloor and the joist and it cannot be nailed closed, drive in a wedge from the basement side.

For a new plywood subfloor, use full sheets in a lapped pattern. Drive annular-grooved underlayment nails, 6″ apart, except at the edges.

the adhesive the length of the room. To make sure there is enough tack or bonding strength to hold down any bowed planks, allow the adhesive to set for 40 minutes to two hours, depending on temperature, humidity and circulation, before laying any planks. A good way to learn when the adhesive is ready is to form a small ridge with the notched trowel; the apex of the ridge should be dry and semi-hard, but the rest of ridge should yield to finger pressure and be relatively soft.

When you're satisfied the adhesive is properly set, start laying in the planks, with their tongued edges facing the chalk line. Get a good, straight start and make sure the tongued and grooved ends lock together. Start alternate rows with a cut plank and you'll avoid a line of pegs near the wall. Continue planking by engaging the tongues and grooves on the long edge first, then those on the ends.

To get a good, tight joint, engage a scrap of plank into the grooved edge of the plank you're laying, and strike the scrap with a hammer, forcing the joint closed. Initially, before you have a large field of planks to work against when striking the scrap, previously-laid planks may tend to slide away, instead of closing the joint. To avoid this, temporarily drive a couple of nails into the subfloor next to the chalk-indicated starting-plank row edge. Complete the flooring in this first 2' wide area, then lock it down with a 150-pound floor roller. The roller shown, borrowed from a local flooring store, weighed only 100 pounds, so an additional weight of 50 pounds was added from a weight-lifting set. Record the time it takes to complete this area.

Finishing the Job

When you trowel out the adhesive, cover as much space as you'll be able to plank in two or three hours (the setup time). Never let adhesive set for more than four hours before laying planks. If it has, trowel on additional adhesive, so that the solvent in the new layer will soften the adhesive beneath and make it reusable.

When fitting planks against walls, into doorways or around built-in cabinets, cut them to shape with a jigsaw equipped with a metal-cutting blade for the smoothest edge. Continue to trowel adhesive and lay plank across the room, applying rows of 3"-, 5"- and 7"-wide planks in sequence. Stagger the end edge joints by choosing adjacent planks of appropriate length.

When you approach a wall, there won't be enough space to engage the scrap and strike it with a hammer to close the joints. In this case, lay some scrap against the wall and hold another piece of scrap vertically against the plank you're setting. Then, insert a small pry bar into the space between and use a wedging motion. For very narrow spaces between the plank and the wall, insert a piece or two of scrap plank and wedge against the new plank to close the joint.

Materials and tools needed for flooring: solvent, latex patch adhesive, wax, jigsaw, scraps, chalk cord, trowel, square and hammer.

Using a special trowel, apply the latex patch adhesive in a sweeping motion. Extend a band of adhesive the full length of the room.

The adhesive should set for 40 minutes to two hours before planks are positioned on it. Here, first area is ready for planking. Note access area to the right.

To lay plank, engage the long edge tongue and groove, then slide plank until end tongue and groove mate and close joint. Make sure you get a straight start.

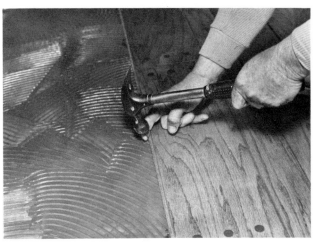

If the previously set planks tend to slide out as you strike the scraps, drive in back-up nails to hold the planks in place.

To avoid a continuous alignment of pegs along the wall, cut the starting plank of every other row. Engage tongues and grooves on long edge first.

Once you have placed planking in an area, lock it down with a 150-pound roller. To make this borrowed roller heavy enough, weight was added.

To get a good, tight joint, engage a scrap piece of plank into the grooved edge of the plank you're working on and strike the scrap with a hammer.

A jigsaw that is equipped with a metal cutting blade will give your planking the neatest cuts. Mark all cuts with the aid of a try square.

Roll each floor section as you finish it and remove any adhesive smears with mineral spirits, xylene or toluene. When you've completed the floor to the far wall, go back to the chalk line and lay in the planks from that point to the near wall. Replace the base molding. If your planked room is slightly elevated from an adjacent room, install a ⅜″ × 1½″ oak nosing at the threshold. In the room shown, such a piece was installed before starting the planking in order to get a neat-looking edge.

Never use water-emulsion self-polishing waxes on your hardwood floor. The better flooring planks are factory finished, waxed and polished, and most manufacturers recommend only occasional use of dark tone wax to keep the dark shade of the wood.

When you are approaching a wall and do not have room enough to swing a hammer, use this simple wedging technique.

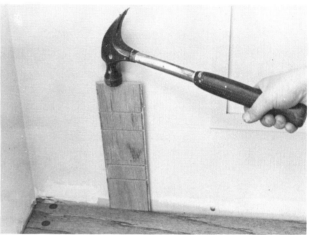

When you are really up tight against a wall, you can wedge with scrap, or use scrap and a small pry bar.

9

Media Cabinet

Look around your house. More than likely you have a television, a stereo system (including turntable, tuner and cassette deck, among other items) and if you're really into electronics, a videocassette recorder or videodisc player.

Possibly you have a TV game or computer with accessories. How about a movie or slide projector? Then there are the records, tapes, videocassettes, film, slide carousels, extra wires, headphones, game joysticks and all else that is part and parcel of modern-day gadgetry.

Chances are you have these items strewn all over the house, with no central storage or even a central place to enjoy them all.

Here's your answer: your own entertainment cabinet... designed to house all the equipment you have, or ever hope to have, plus storage space to accommodate the paraphernalia that accompanies it. The cabinet provides a central spot for making use of all those goodies.

The entertainment cabinet is, of necessity, a large piece of furniture. But it'll provide a welcome addition to a family room, den or redone basement.

Cabinet Construction

To construct it, cut out all major pieces from ¾" birch-veneer plywood stock. This includes sides, tops, bottoms, all shelves and the divider. Don't cut the inset doors now as they must be carefully trimmed and fitted. Notice that the cabinet is built in two sections to facilitate handling should you move or redecorate.

Cut the front edge strips from 4/4 (13/16") birch veneer stock. This is to trim the front edges of the sides, shelves, divider, plus tops and bottoms. Also cut the reinforcing cleats, for interior-corner side/bottom joints, from the same stock.

Electronic components housed all in one cabinet you can build yourself. The bottom left compartment stores records or videodiscs. On top of that is a space for a videocassette or videodisc player. The small bay at desk height is ideal for a computer or video game. The TV goes just above that. There is storage area at left of TV. Behind the upper sliding doors go tapes and slide carousels. At the top of the assembly is a pullout mount for a movie screen. Down the right side of the cabinet are spaces for stereo components. A projector cart stows at bottom right.

Next, cut all dadoes and the top, bottom and rear rabbets of the sides. Glue the front edge strips to the sides. These should protrude about 1/32″ over the inner and outer surfaces of the sides. *Carefully* sand these edges flush with the surfaces of the sides using a belt sander with a 120-grit belt. Try to avoid cross-grain sanding since the marks of cross sanding would have to be eliminated, and you don't want to sand right through the thin birch veneer. Pad-sand to a final 220-grit finish.

Dry-fit the joints to check for square and snugness and to mark all shelves and the divider for size trimming. You want to make sure all rear edges do not extend beyond the depth of the rabbets at the rear of the sides, and that the front edges all come even. This ensures that the edging is

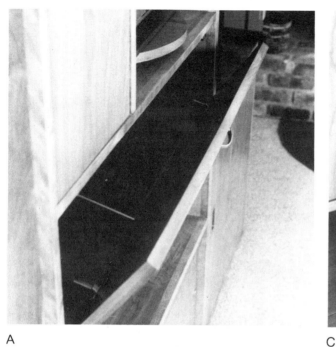

A

C

B

D

(A) The hinged front of the computer bay folds down to make a desk. (B) The TV mounts on a swivel that pulls out for viewing from any angle. (C) Doing the family budget at home is easy—when finished, fold up the front; the computer is out of sight. (D) The cart holds both slide and movie projectors. The canted top puts the projector at optimum angle.

flush when the assembly is done. The exception is with the two short shelves in the large cabinet that are covered by the smaller inset door. These shelves, *including birch front edges*, must come even with side and divider edges before trim is added, so the door can be properly closed. Glue the edges to the front of these small shelves and sand them.

Now, glue and clamp the cabinet assemblies. Make use of a carpenter's or rafter square for right-angle alignment. When the glue is dry, fit, glue and clamp all the remaining front edges in place.

Cut, trim and install the backs with glue and 4d box nails—after marking the rear edges of the sides to indicate the centers of the dadoes. Carry the center marks across the back after putting it in place, then nail the back into the shelves along these lines.

Fit the sliding doors and tracks, matching the grains as closely as possible and allowing ¾″ overlap where the doors meet. To get the best fit, trim the height of the doors so that when the top of each door is held up into the top (deeper) track, the bottom just clears the bottom-track flange as it's installed.

Measure, cut and fit the hinged doors. Set up the hardware. Chisel out the recesses for the door pulls.

Tape all door edges (using contact cement), then sand off the edges. Mount the doors and handles.

European hinges allow the doors to be adjusted forward and back and the hinge line gap to be increased or decreased. They also control the door swing limit.

Install the reinforcement cleats with glue and cabinet screws.

Cut, sand and edge the TV disc. Lay out its mounting holes on the slide/rotator, then mount the slide/rotator and completed TV disc.

Build the projector cart, using birch tape to trim exposed edges front and back. Install casters.

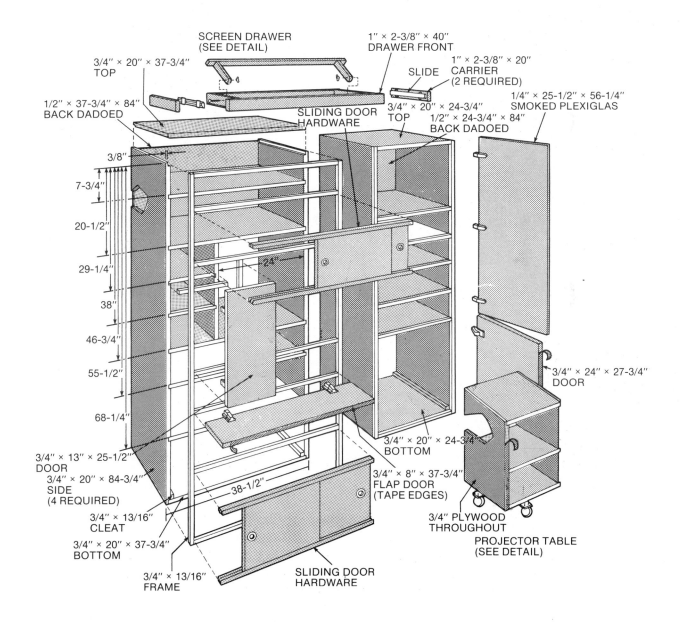

Rip the four main sides using a table saw with a guide. You might consider cutting oversize, with final trim later.

After final trim, dado the inner sides of cabinet wall and clamp 13/16″ trim to front using pipe clamps.

Glue shelves and sides of each cabinet section and clamp. Be sure to use scrap buffers to avoid marring wood.

Install the shelf trim of 13/16″ birch to only the front sides of the shelves. Sand overhang to match.

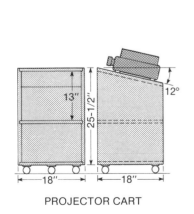

PROJECTOR CART

13″
25-1/2″
12°
18″ 18″

1/4″ × 19-1/4″ × 36-1/2″
DRAWER BOTTOM

3/4″ × 2-1/8″ × 35″
DRAWER BACK

3/4″ × 2″ × 40″
SCREEN HOLDER

3/4″ × 2″ × 8″
ARM

3/4″ × 2-1/8″ × 19-1/4″
SIDE

1″ × 2-3/8″ × 19″
CARRIER

1″ × 2-3/8″ × 40″
DRAWER FRONT

CLEAT

DRAWER

SCREEN

BORE

DRAWER SLIDE

CABINET

SLIDE

SCREEN HOLDER DETAIL

Clamp the trim securely and let dry. Then sand the surface of the trim to match the shelf surfaces.

Cut the dadoes and assemble the sliding screen mount. Cut the articulating arms, drill and mount them (using flathead bolts) to the sliding section. Tape whatever raw plywood edge shows. Mount the slider on the outer slide section, which is supported by a pair of carriers screwed to the cabinet tops.

Drill and mount the Plexiglas door using hinges that allow a 90° swing; add the door pull.

Drill holes to accommodate wires to the various components. Sand the cabinets. An application of Watco Danish Oil finishes them beautifully. Place the cabinets where you want and secure them together.

When you've installed the cabinets, mount your screen to the carrier and provide a hook down on the front of the cabinet to hold the screen open. Also provide a method of locking the drawer in position to hold screen angle for viewing.

With the right side of the cabinet closed, the stereo components are neatly hidden.

10

Room Divider

A room divider is a practical aid in defining areas and arranging furniture. It can be moved whenever your living habits change the uses of a room. Since this divider consists of 24″-wide modules, you can easily add to its length. The open, illuminated shelves (of glass so light penetrates them) brighten and lend spaciousness to adjacent areas. The base cabinets provide convenient storage.

Actual Assembly

Begin by cutting out all cabinet sides, tops, bottoms, dividers and shelves from ¾″ birch-faced plywood. Machine the dadoes in the sides, shelves and bottoms. Assemble both cabinet bodies with white glue and clamps.

Cut out all four face frame members (machine mortises and tenons, or drill for dowels if you prefer) and assemble with glue and clamps.

Cut out the eight doors from ⅝″ birch-faced plywood and the eight "raised" panels from ¼″ plywood. Edge the doors with backband (or corner guard) molding, trimmed down so it's flush with the rear surface of the doors. Complete the doors by installing raised panels.

When the face frames are dry, glue and nail them to the bodies, set nails, fill the nail holes, and sand. Cut the backband as shown and install it on the inner edges of all face frame top sections.

Final-sand the cabinets and doors with No. 220 grit paper, and prime with two coats of enamel undercoat, sanding after each coat. Then, apply two coats of low-gloss enamel.

Set up the lights as shown in the electrical drawing on next page, but mount the fixtures mechanically to the undersides of the shelves with round-head wood screws in addition to the nipples.

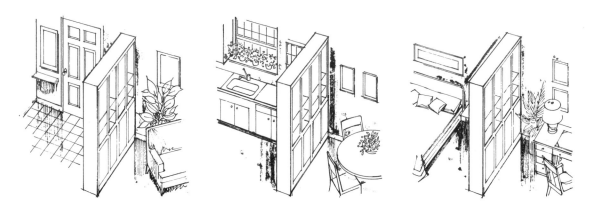

Room dividers are used to define an entrance hall (left), divide a kitchen work space from eating area (middle) and create a study area in a bedroom (right).

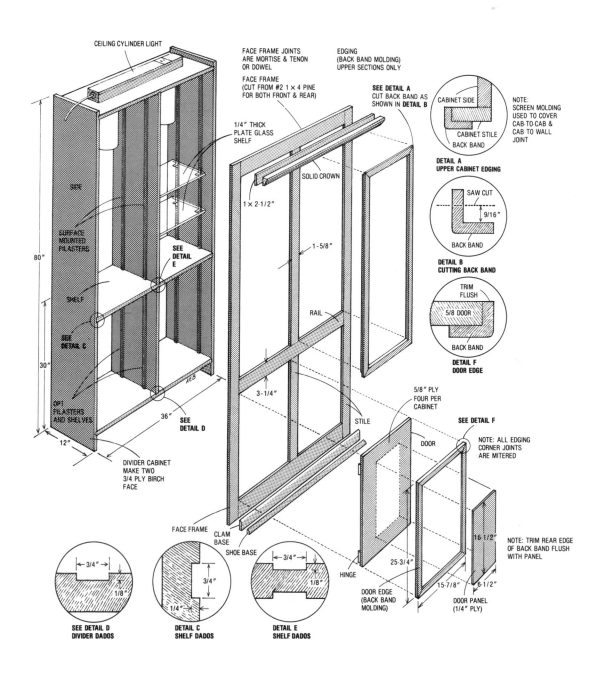

Provide a switch controlled outlet on the wall where the innermost cabinet will be attached, and cut a hole in the cabinet side facing the wall to provide room for the plug.

Predetermine a wall-stud location and fasten the innermost cabinet to the wall in a plumb position with wood screws driven in from below the shelf and above the top. Do the same when attaching the second cabinet to the first. Drive screws down into the floor from the lower face frame rail so they'll be covered by molding.

Add the 16 pilasters, clam base and shoe, upper fascia, and solid crown. Apply screen molding at cabinet and wall joints. Set all nails and fill holes, sand, and paint. Add glass shelves and lamps.

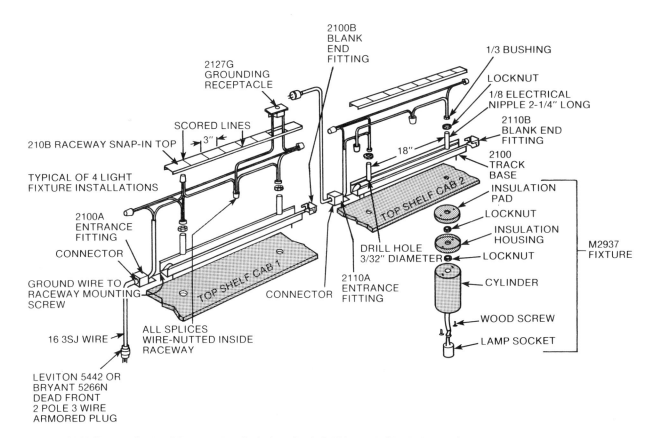

Replace M2937 fixture nipple with an ⅛ electrical pipe nipple 2¼″ long. Drill ¹³⁄₃₂″ holes in raceway bases on C's of fixtures (18″ apart). Drill ¾″ holes in top plywood shelves on same C's. Insert fixture nipples with wires through shelf, raceway base and secure with a locknut. Wire as shown. Insert receptacle in 3″ space in top where scored section was removed. All raceway parts are Wiremold®.

11

Fireplace

Many of today's homes include both a family room and a living room. Often, the living room is formally furnished and unused, while the family room bears the brunt of daily living and entertaining. Warm up a formal living room with a fireplace and you make it a true *living* room—a place where family and friends love to linger.

Today's manufactured fireplaces make do-it-yourself installation manageable. And there's a bonus for you in the work—the equity in your home is sure to go up two or three thousand dollars.

The fireplace shown here is a Heatilator Mark 123C Model 3138. Because of its zero-clearance construction it can be placed on or against combustible materials. Here is how it is installed.

After you decide where you want to locate your fireplace, you'll need to take a few measurements (see illustration) to ensure that you purchase the correct parts. These measurements are: (1) the height of the room in which the fireplace will be installed, plus the height of any room above it through which the chimney must pass (but minus height of the platform if you choose a raised hearth); (2) the height from the attic floor to the point through which the chimney will exit the roof; (3) the distance between the attic floor and the roof peak; (4) the horizontal distance between items 2 and 3 as indicated in the inset illustration; (5) the number and thicknesses of all ceilings through which the chimney will pass.

Platform Construction

Build the deck structure from 2×10 lumber. Drop the center area down 1" to recess the fireplace, thus hiding some sheet metal. Make sure the recess is level in both directions.

Install the decking in two layers: (1) ⅝" CDX plywood, butted tightly together; (2) ½"-A-C plywood, leaving ⅛" expansion joints between pieces.

Note the noncombustible cement board (concrete with fiberglass skin) in the hearth extension area. Cut this material to size with a masonry blade (wear eye protection) in your portable saw, or score it and crack it over a sharp edge. Install with roofing nails.

Now, get some help and position the fireplace; install the 2' starter chimney section.

Framing the Fireplace

Use a string and fishing weight as a plumb bob to align the top of the starter section with the ceiling above it and mark out an 18″×18″ opening. Saw out the drywall, box in the opening and then install the firestop and the first 3′ chimney section from above, twisting and locking it to the starter section.

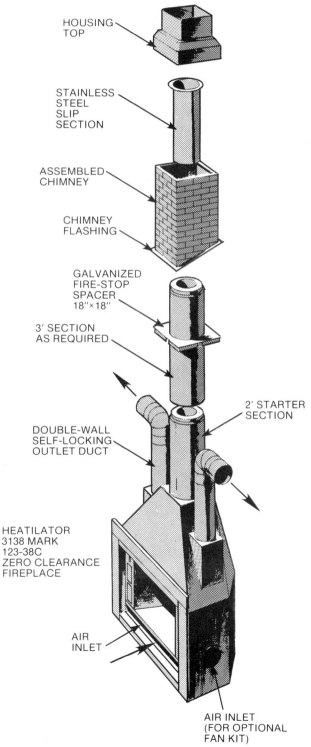

HOUSING TOP

STAINLESS STEEL SLIP SECTION

ASSEMBLED CHIMNEY

CHIMNEY FLASHING

GALVANIZED FIRE-STOP SPACER 18″×18″

3′ SECTION AS REQUIRED

DOUBLE-WALL SELF-LOCKING OUTLET DUCT

2′ STARTER SECTION

HEATILATOR 3138 MARK 123-38C ZERO CLEARANCE FIREPLACE

AIR INLET

AIR INLET (FOR OPTIONAL FAN KIT)

A

B

C

(A) The Heatilator rests on the platform with a noncombustible cement board hearth extension. (B) The first chimney section, which is twist-locked into the starter, emerges from the fire-stop between all floors. (C) The double-wall ducting that connects the unit to the warm-air outlet requires a 1″ ceiling.

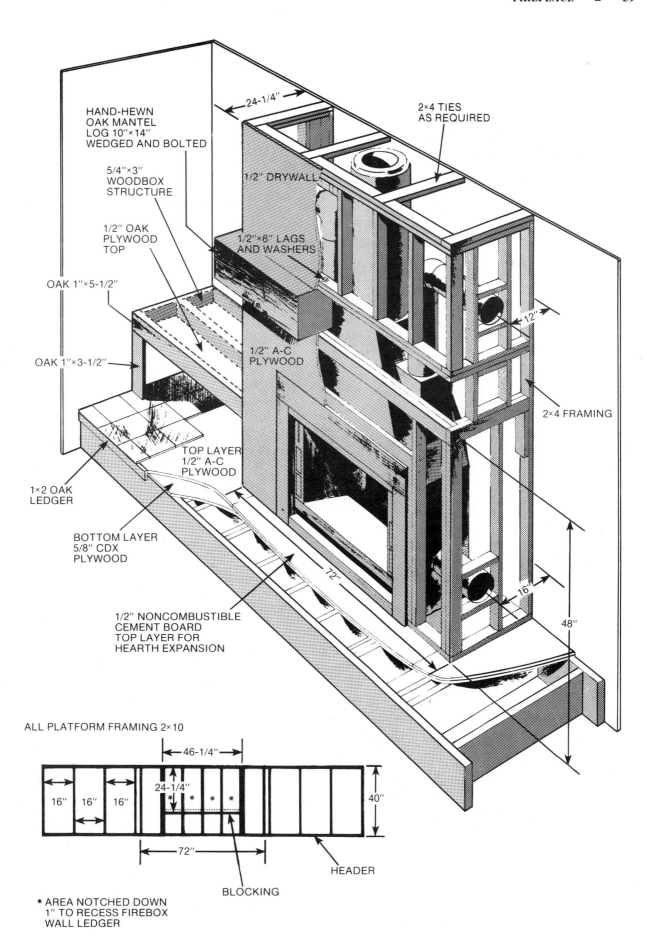

HAND-HEWN
OAK MANTEL
LOG 10″×14″
WEDGED AND BOLTED

5/4″×3″
WOODBOX
STRUCTURE

1/2″ OAK
PLYWOOD
TOP

OAK 1″×5-1/2″

OAK 1″×3-1/2″

1×2 OAK
LEDGER

BOTTOM LAYER
5/8″ CDX
PLYWOOD

1/2″ NONCOMBUSTIBLE
CEMENT BOARD
TOP LAYER FOR
HEARTH EXPANSION

TOP LAYER
1/2″ A-C
PLYWOOD

1/2″ A-C
PLYWOOD

1/2″ DRYWALL

1/2″×6″ LAGS
AND WASHERS

2×4 TIES
AS REQUIRED

24-1/4″

12″

2×4 FRAMING

16″

48″

72″

ALL PLATFORM FRAMING 2×10

46-1/4″

24-1/4″

16″ 16″ 16″

72″

40″

HEADER

BLOCKING

* AREA NOTCHED DOWN
1″ TO RECESS FIREBOX
WALL LEDGER

Frame around the fireplace with 2×4s. I chose to use a massive, 10″×14″ oak beam as a mantel.

Box in for the air inlets (optional fan kit) and the heat outlets. Install the housings, leaving enough protruding out so they will be flush with the surface when installed later. The outlets require the manufacturer's double-walled twist-lock ducting, but the inlets need only standard 6″ diameter, galvanized ducting.

Blank off the vertical inlets on the front face with pieces provided, and wire in a switch for the air-inlet blower motors.

Chimney

Add on enough sections of chimney to mark out the roof opening. Pierce the roof and construct the box-in. Then, with a helper, assemble the chimney on the roof and cut the bottom of chimney panels to match the roof pitch, leaving a minimum 4″ flap on the higher side panel to be tucked under the shingles.

Attach the chimney flashing and install the chimney assembly, less the housing top, caulking as needed. Do not caulk the lower side.

Remove the housing-top rain deflector, insert the slip section in the housing top and place the housing on the chimney brackets as you insert the slip section into the topmost chimney section. The slip section must extend at least 2″ into the chimney section.

Lock everything down, test for water leaks with a hose and start a fire with the damper open. Check the entire installation for smoke leakage.

Fireplace Finish Work

Nail ½″ plywood on the front face below the mantel opening. Prop the prestained mantel beam in place, wedge it with underscore shakes and lock it to the structure with ½″×6″ lag bolts. Then, cut the shakes flush.

Apply drywall surface to the remaining framing, metal corner bead to the two external corners and drywall tape

A

A

B

B

(A) Two optional air-inlet assemblies with standard 6″ galvanized ducting feed the fire and help push out warm air. (B) At roof level, caulk is applied to the side where the flashing fits. The chimney section is barely visible inside an 18″-square box.

(A) After the chimney assembly and flashing are installed, the housing and stainless steel slip section are fitted to the last section. (B) Heavy textured-base paint was applied with a trowel and brushed with a whisk broom for a serrated effect—just one of the texture possibilities.

A

B

(A) The chimney was completed with simulated brick applied to the proper adhesive base; the housing top was stuccoed with the same material applied with texture. (B) To do the job, use a trowel, level, nippers, tile cutter and chemicals (three-part epoxy mortar, brown floor grout and flexible additive).

to all internal corners. Tape the joint between the metal fireplace and the wood structure using heavy textured-base paint instead of joint compound. When dry, paint the plywood and platform with oil-based primer.

Fill in the cracks between the beam and the drywall with the heavy textured-base paint. Stain or paint the simulated bricks to match the mantel and install them around the fireplace margin with the white adhesive recommended by the manufacturer. Then seal with the recommended sealer when set.

The fireplace installed in this cold, hard-to-arrange room created an intimate, inviting conversation corner.

Use the drying times to construct the firewood boxes. Stain, finish and install them and their structural supports. After masking off all dark or stained edges, apply heavy textured-base paint to the main chimney surfaces, first with a trowel, then with a whisk broom to texture the surface.

While the paint is drying, go back on the roof and apply simulated brick to the chimney with the proper adhesive.

Platform Finish Work

Nail the prestained 1×2 oak ledger to the front face of the platform. Then, using nippers and tile cutter, cut, fit and dry lay the tile allowing a ⅜″ grout joint.

Remove the tiles from the platform and keep them in order, then dust off the platform surface. Mix the three-part epoxy mortar according to the manufacturer's instructions. Apply the mortar with a ¼×¼″ square-notched trowel, set the tiles in place and rack them down using a 2×4 on edge struck with a hammer. Check for level and alignment.

When the tile mortar has set (about 24 hours), apply sealer to the top surfaces of the tiles *only*. Mix the floor grout with flexible additive and apply it according to the instructions, as a very dry mix. Keep sweeping the grout dust off the tiles throughout the operation. If necessary, grout can be removed from the surface of this nonglazed tile using a suitable type of acid, but *carefully*, as sloppy or excessive acid cleaning can bleach the grout in the joints. **Caution:** Wear proper eye protection when working with acid.

Apply heavy textured-base paint to the front face of the platform beneath ledger.

12

Ceramic Tile Floor

The reward of careful work—years of virtually maintenance-free beauty.

You can enjoy the beauty and ease of maintenance of an Italian tile floor for a lot less effort than you'd expect, thanks to the development of epoxy mortars. They permit a practical way for you to lay a tile floor at a reasonable price without the complexity of traditional methods.

The epoxy mortar method employs a three-part epoxy mortar (two liquid epoxy components plus a premixed powder consisting of portland cement, sand and additives) that is easily prepared and spread with a serrated trowel. The mortar provides an instant bed that holds the tiles firmly upon full curing. Its initial curing time (working time) is about two hours, depending on ambient temperature and humidity. It is applicable to both plywood and concrete floors.

Compare this with the traditional method, which uses a bed of mud, made of portland cement, and sand with metal lath support. This bed must be skillfully and carefully prepared by means of large-area screeding and smoothing. In addition, the tiles must be soaked prior to setting. In this method, the work preceding the tile setting is critical, whereas the epoxy mortar method permits you to set and level the tile directly, which is relatively easy.

Both methods require that the existing floor be properly prepared, but for a durable result, the mud method requires you have a heavier floor than is found in most residential homes.

Other Methods

Thinset: In the thinset method, a mortar mix is applied to a depth of ¼″ with a ¼″ or 3/16″ serrated trowel. The tiles require no soaking, but this method may be used only over concrete floors such as in homes with radiant heating. Although easier than the mud method to install and level tile, it is not as simple as the epoxy mortar method.

Adhesive method: Here you must screed the adhesive on both the subfloor and tile, clearly more difficult than just one surface coating with the epoxy mortar. This method might prove satisfactory if you were installing a Japanese mosaic tile, but in the case of the Italian tile, whose working characteristics are somewhat different, cracks might develop.

Therefore, the epoxy mortar method proves to be the most practical for the homeowner inasmuch as it can be applied to both plywood and concrete floors, requires no mud-lath work, it is easily mixed, and the tiles can be leveled after setting, with excellent void coverage (these voids are areas beneath the tile that must be filled with mortar to prevent cracking).

Tile Selection

Japanese tiles are generally vitreous (glassy) because the clay is fully fired simultaneously with the pattern colors. Most Italian decorative ceramic floor tiles are made in a two-step process. The molded clay is partially fired and then sold to other manufacturers who silk screen and refire them. The Japanese tile is therefore slightly harder. But, due to the large number of designs, the Italian tile offers a wide range of patterns. Typically, Japanese tiles are smaller (usually up to 6″ size) due to technical limitations.

Job Approach

The general approach consists of preparation of the rough and subfloor, planning and aligning the pattern, cutting and dry layout, mixing and spreading the mortar, and setting and leveling the tile. This is followed by grouting, grout sealing, replacement of molding, and installation of threshholds. By removing molding before you begin the job, you can save a lot of critical fitting, cutting and cleaning up grout stain. See the chart for tools and material.

Except for cleaning, floor preparation is eliminated if you are working on a concrete floor. On all others begin by locking the existing floor down to the joints below. These loose areas can best be found by walking on the area and feeling the floor give beneath you. Another telltale sign is squeaking.

Drive 10d rosin-coated nails through the floor into the joints. If any troublesome area of your floor sinks into a hollow in the joist, go downstairs and drive wooden wedges between the floor and the joist, then come upstairs and drive more 10d nails into that same joist. This is very important since movement of a nonrigid floor can cause cracking tiles later. Any loose strip or parquet flooring should be locked down in the same manner.

Next, lay out your ¼″ or ⅜″ plywood subfloor that will cover linoleum, vinyl, vinyl asbestos, sheet goods, painted surfaces, strip or parquet flooring. Lap the main sheets

Nail down the plywood subfloor with annular ring underlayment nails. Keep 6″ spacing in the field and 1½″ along the edge.

Use a reciprocating or coping saw to work plywood in the corners of the floor.

Fitting around curves is no problem with the coping or reciprocating saw.

(like brickwork), and don't allow gaps to accumulate between edges (plane where necessary). Fit around any curved areas and into those nasty little nooks and crannys by cutting the plywood with a reciprocating or coping saw.

Now, drive in annular ring underlayment nails (specially designed for extra grip) spaced 6″ apart in the field and 1½″ apart along the edges.

Dry Laying, Aligning, Cutting

Divide the room in two using a nail at each end spanned by mason's cord at least 1½″ above the sub-floor so as not to conflict with the work. Start laying out the tiles, using a mason's cord as a guide for pattern alignment. Leave at least a ⅛″ gap between tiles (never butt tile as the rubbing may cause crazing, or stress cracks).

Make all straight cuts using the tile cutting machine by scoring first, then cracking the tile over the small ridge with the aid of the cutter handle. Irregular cuts must be done with nippers. It takes a little practice, but if you nip off small amounts at a time, you won't have any problems. Remove roughness from tile edges by rubbing them with the edge of a scrap piece of tile.

When you have done about 35 square feet, stop. It's time for the next operation. Move the field of tile you have just dry-laid to an adjacent area, but keep every piece in its proper order. Do this because you have only limited time to work once the epoxy has been mixed.

The three-part epoxy mortar comes with its own mixing bucket. Don't mix it until you have the serrated trowel, level, hammer, 2×4 and spatula on the site. There is only a two-hour initial curing time within which you can work. It's best to plan on 90 minutes to be safe. Mix the two cans of liquid together with a scrap piece of 1×2 and then add in the dry ingredients and stir until the mix is complete.

Spreading, Setting and Leveling

Using a deep serrated trowel, spread out approximately a ¼″ layer of epoxy mortar with a sweeping circular motion. Don't overextend because you have to work on the tiles within a reasonable arm's reach. Also, remember not to "paint yourself into a corner" because you can't walk on fresh set tile. Place a number of tiles from the dry-laid group prepared earlier. Keep the pattern square with the mason's cord and maintain the ⅛″ gap between tiles.

Now, lay the 2×4 down on edge on top of several adjacent tiles and hammer down moderately on the 2×4 all along its length, which will seat and level the tiles properly along this line. Next, rotate the 2×4 90° and repeat the operation. Check both these directions with your level and repeat if necessary to remove any discrepancies.

Scoring and cracking tile with the tile cutting machine is demonstrated here.

Take out small bites with the nippers to accommodate irregular shapes required.

Three-part epoxy mortar comes in its own mixing bucket. This unit is good for about 35 square feet.

Use a long circular sweeping motion when spreading the epoxy mortar with the deep serrated trowel.

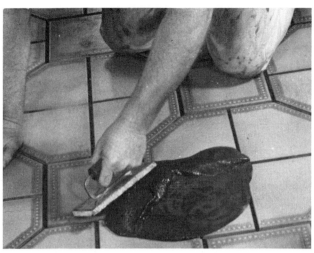

Spread the grout with the rubber float and work it thoroughly into the joints.

Place the tile down on the mortar, keeping the pattern aligned and maintaining a ⅛″ gap.

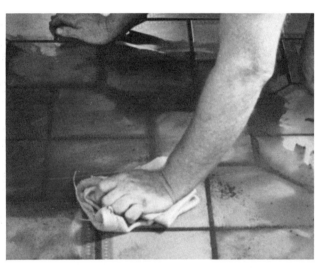

Wipe the tiles clean and dry with a burlap or other rough rap. The grout will remain in the joints.

Check the level of several tiles after working them with a scrap piece of 2×4.

Apply grout sealer to the joints after grout has dried for three days. This will retain the grout color.

If you're going to take a break or are interrupted, clean the excess mortar from the exposed edges of the last tiles with the spatula; it can harden and be difficult to clean out. Clean off the tops of the tile you have just set with a damp rag (uncured epoxy mortar is water soluble). Repeat the above steps across the whole room until the tile setting, aligning and leveling is complete. Do not walk on any part for 24 hours so that the epoxy can cure.

Grouting and Sealing

When the complete floor has set, you're ready to grout. Grout comes in a number of colors to match or contrast with the tile. If you're going to use more than one bag of grout, dry-mix all the bags together first to retain color consistency. Then mix small batches of the powder with water in a bucket, keeping track of the proportions or you may get color density variations (the grout should have the consistency of a thick, soupy mix).

Pour it on the floor on an area that you can reach with a spread of your arms. Apply it with a rubber float, being careful to leave no joint gaps. Next, wipe off the tile surface until it is clean and dry using a burlap or similar rough cloth that will not disturb the grout in the joints. Continue this procedure until the floor is complete.

After three days, apply grout sealer fluid to the joints with a brush in order to retain the grout color. Replace the moldings and casings (prepainted), install commercial threshholds and admire the results.

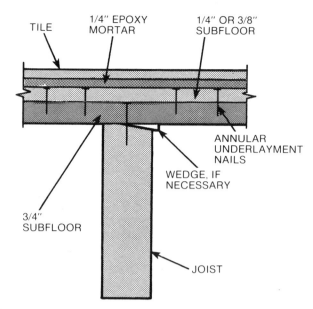

Cross-sectional view of floor, showing rough floor, subfloor, epoxy mortar and tile.

Maintenance

Sweep or vacuum the floor. Then damp mop. To replace a broken tile, strike it in the center with a hammer. Then remove the broken pieces and mortar with a brick chisel. Replace with a new tile as described in installation section.

13

Clock Kit

F ew colonial furniture pieces can give your home as much charm as an Early American tall-case clock, particularly the grandfather style. The clock shown started out as a kit—cartons of strange-looking walnut pieces and subassemblies, bags of hardware, weights, the movement itself, the face, pendulum and chimes.

When you first look at this rather formidable array, you may wonder if it can all go together and resemble the photo in the instruction manual. The answer is yes—it takes only about 30 hours of work for a first-class job—and you don't have to be a direct descendant of Seth Thomas to build a family heirloom that will give you years of pleasure.

You supply the glass, glue, nails, sandpaper and finishing materials—the kit has everything else. You also can order the moldings premitered with the kit. Take this option—it's a good deal. If you feel a little shaky about what finishing materials to apply and how to use them properly, the manufacturer can supply a finishing kit with instructions at a slight extra cost.

These clock kits use hardwood, and if you've never worked hardwood before, a couple of tips may help: (1) Chisels and saws must be very sharp to get clean, crisp cuts. (2) Both nails and screws require predrilled holes. Forcing a screw home without predrilling will either snap the screw or mangle the head. Driving a nail into hardwood, especially near an end or through thin stock, will almost certainly split the wood. Avoid these problems by using a combination bit for screw holes and a drill with a diameter slightly smaller than the nail diameter, for nail holes. Combination bits incorporate a pilot hole, shank clearance hole, countersink and stop. They're sold according to screw size (No. 8 is the most popular) at lumberyards and hardware stores. When driving a screw, always use soap as a lubricant. (3) Due to its density, hardwood takes a little more time to glue than a softwood

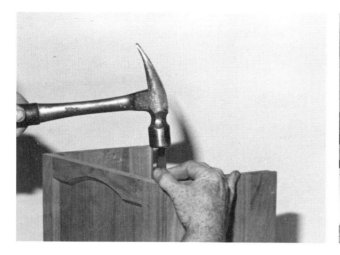

Drive clamp nails into the machined slots of mating pieces to align and draw them together. Use clamps to ensure a good, tight joint along glue line.

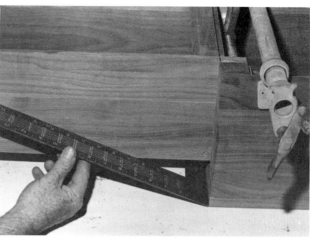

A square and blocks may be needed for lining up the waist and base subassemblies. The screw showing on the waist side will be covered by molding.

Insert a square into the corners of pieces being assembled to make sure that these are 90° joints, needed for easy mating of next assembly pieces.

This view of the base shows the four small predrilled leveler blocks that will receive plastic-threaded inserts and adjustable, threaded shank feet.

Remove the waste material by gently tapping a firmer type chisel along the grain of the wood. Take more than one cut to trim this without mishap.

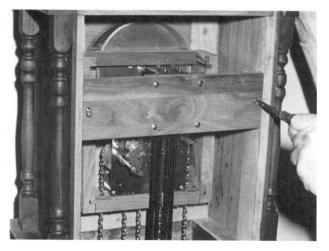

When the woodwork is finished and the clock works are installed, it's time to screw the chime board in place, then adjust the chime hammers.

such as pine. Although the kit supplies clamp nails (these fit in machined slots in mating wood pieces and are designed to align and pull these pieces together while the glue sets), it's best to use them mainly for alignment and rely on some auxiliary clamps to get a good, tight joint along the entire glue line.

Shaping and routing are eliminated because the manufacturer supplies the base front, waist door, hood door, dial frame, crown front and numerous other pieces in completely machined and/or subassembly form.

The manual suggests that you presand all wood pieces before assembly. This is a good idea, especially in and around awkward areas and inner surfaces. Do not, however, sand the outside corners of the premitered moldings where they'll join because you'll produce a slight radius that will appear more modern than colonial.

Assembly

As you begin to assemble and glue, dry-fit (no glue) some extra pieces to aid in getting the subassembly squared up. This will ensure that these pieces, to be installed later, will fit perfectly without any doctoring. As an example, dry-fit the base back when gluing the base front to the sides.

When the three major subassemblies (base, waist and hood) have been completed, the waist must be assembled to the base in true vertical alignment. This alignment will avoid an unsightly appearance and prevent any problems with the swing of the pendulum bob. After all the woodwork is done, fit the hardware, and then remove it for finishing. Leave the installation of the door glasses and clock movement for later—after the wood has been finished.

Finishing

The finishing process is begun by setting all nails and filling the holes with a mixture of hide glue and sanding dust. As you sand this mixture in, the holes will completely disappear. Now, go over the entire clock with sandpaper, working down to a No. 220 grit paper.

A number of finishing options are available: (1) Purchase the manufacturer's finishing kit and use it according to instructions. This entails a standard stain and varnish approach. (2) Use a wipe-on penetrating oil. This is a very easy material to handle, providing you follow the instructions on the can. (3) Apply the authentic colonial shellac finish used in the Cabinetmaker's Shop in Colonial Williamsburg. This is how the master of the shop goes about it:

Dampen the wood to raise the grain, and when dry, sand off the fuzz with worn-out No. 220 grit paper. (Create your own worn-out paper by rubbing two sheets of No. 220 together.) Remove all dust. Then, brush on water stain with one hand and wipe immediately with the other (using a soft, lint-free cloth).

Water stain will bring out the wood grain, but it's tricky to use. You've got to watch out for overlapping. Therefore, plan out the order of staining the surfaces so that a newly stained surface meets a previously stained surface at either a corner or edge, if possible.

When dry, sand again with wornout paper and remove all dust. Then apply linseed oil with a brush and wipe off excess with a cloth. Allow this to dry for three or four days. This oiling emphasizes the wood color and, at the same time, tends to start filling the pores. If you want to close the wood pores quickly, add natural paste filler at this point.

Now, apply six to 12 coats of shellac, sanding between each coat. (The wood pores will fill at least partially from the repeated shellac coats.) Fresh shellac may be mixed by adding shellac flakes to alcohol—two pounds per gallon for a two-pound cut. Allow a couple of hours drying time for each coat. If desired, buff and wax the finish because a shellac finish is not water-stain resistant.

When you're done with the finish, balance the clock where it will sit on the floor with the screw foot adjusters and mark this spot on the floor. Install the glass in the doors and replace the doors into the waist and hood. Mount the clockworks, chimes and pendulum. All that's left to do is adjust the pendulum bob to the correct length and adjust the chime hammers (both of these operations are amply covered in the manuals).

14

Fold-up Sewing Center

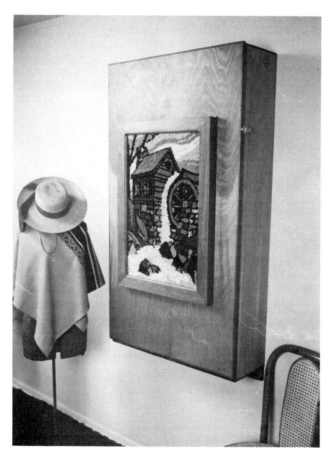

Your wife wants a sewing center, but you don't have a spare room. Solve the problem with a wall-mounted unit that takes as little as 30″ of wall space and can be made to look like a framed piece of art on a rich wood background.

Here are two wall-unit sewing centers that are inexpensive and easy to build. Each can be made in a weekend,

and, when you're done, you'll have a sewing center that folds back to the wall and returns the room to other uses. Your wife doesn't sew? Simple modifications turn these designs into home offices or hobbycraft centers.

The wall units are built of birch lumber core plywood, edged with mahogany and finished with a lustrous, penetrating oil.

Cutting the Pieces

The basic cutting schedules and construction for both types of center are shown in the drawings on the following pages. Because the techniques employed in the building are quite similar, only Type I is detailed here. With the guidelines provided, you can build the design that best fits your available wall space.

Type I, with the picture-frame support leg, requires only a single sheet of plywood. Make the sequenced cuts first, then trim down the individual pieces to the sizes indicated in the drawing. While you're at it, cut the edging, nailers and framing from mahogany.

Preparation of Joints

The corner joints, where top and bottom meet the sides, are rabbeted and edged with hardwood. These joints are strong, decorative and eliminate unsightly plywood edges.

The top and bottom butt ends nest in rabbets machined into the ends of the sides, so get out your router and a self-guided ⅜″ rabbeting bit (or a straight-sided bit plus your router edge guide). Set up the sides, inside faces up, on a flat surface and place a piece of scrap plywood of the same thickness on either side of the workpieces. Clamp all four pieces (two workpieces and two scrap pieces) together, so the edge formed by the four where you'll be routing is straight across (square). Now when you machine the

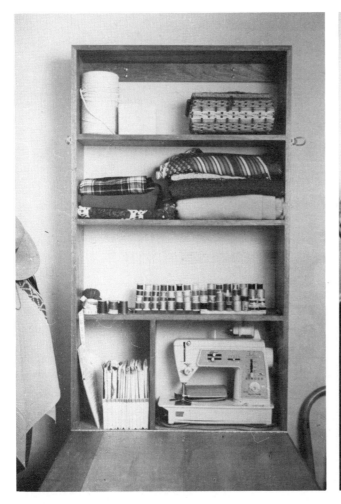

Close-up of open Type I center shows how much can be fit into storage area.

In the open position, the picture-frame leg sewing center (Type I) reveals generous work space and a handy storage area that includes a cubby hole into which the sewing machine fits. In closed position (opposite page), the work and storage areas disappear. All that is visible is a handsome wall unit—in this case, framing a tapestry-like work of art. Since the closed unit takes almost no space, it frees the room for other purposes.

rabbet (and the scrap as well), there won't be any runout at the ends of the workpieces because of the placement of the scrap pieces.

Check the fit of the rabbets with the tops, bottoms and the ⅜″ square corner edge pieces. If the dry fit looks good, you're ready to assemble the basic box.

Box and Flap Front

Use white glue and 6d finishing nails to assemble the major pieces. Keep the assembly square and add in the ⅜″ square corner edges, locking them with glue and No. 18 brads driven in diagonally. Don't worry if the hardwood corner edges stick out at the front or rear, as you'll sand them down later.

Close-up of the top-side joint shows the butt end of the top nested in the side piece rabbet, with the hardwood edge taking up the remaining space. Strength and beauty are combined in this joint.

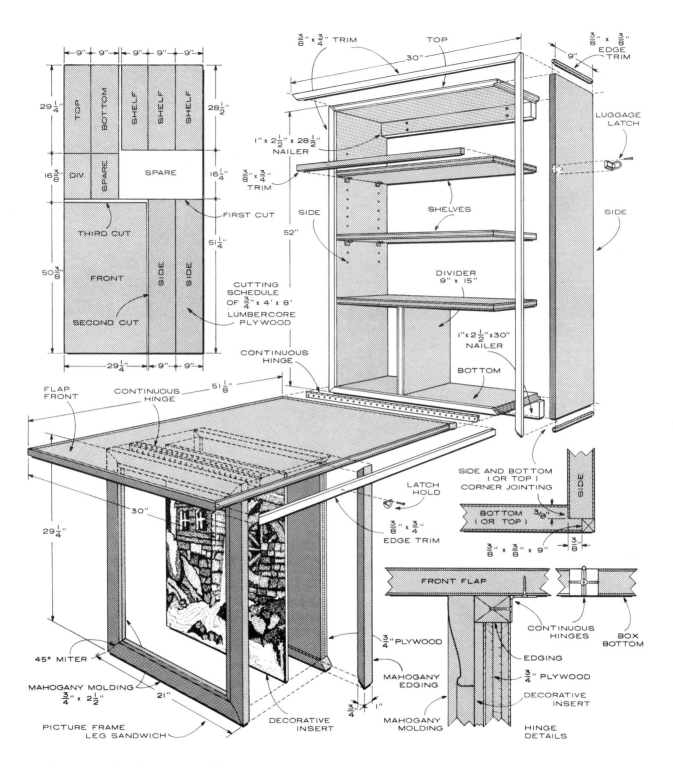

While the glue is drying on the basic box, edge the front flap with 3/8″×3/4″ hardwood mitered at the corners. In cutting the miters, use a scrap wood back-up behind the workpiece to avoid splintering and hand-fit pieces to get good, tight corners. Install the edges with glue and brads.

When the basic box has dried, sand the corner edges flush with the front and rear edges of the top, bottom, and sides. Now fit, glue, and nail in the lower shelf and divider, keeping the dimensions of the sewing machine space 15″ high × 17½″ wide. (If your machine is not standard size,

adjust the cubby hole accordingly.) Arrange the remaining shelves to suit your needs. While the flap edging is drying, start the picture-frame leg.

Leg Construction

The leg is basically a sandwich composed of a hardwood-edged scrap plywood panel, a picture insert and a picture-frame front. It is hinged at its top to the outer side of the front flap. In the open position, the front flap

Scrap plywood, clamped next to the workpieces, forms a square edge that prevents runout of the rabbet cut.

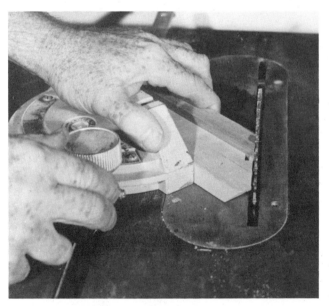

Cut all miters on the saw as shown, using a scrap back-up between the workpiece and miter head to control splintering. (Blade guard was removed for photo.)

becomes a 30″ high working surface, supported at the outer end by the picture-frame leg. In the closed position, the leg becomes a framed picture on a wood background. If the sewer prefers a lower working height, determine the length of the leg before building the frame.

To start the leg construction, cut the scrap plywood panel to size, then cut and miter the ¾″×1″ hardwood edging, using the same technique as shown in the illustration. Hand-fit the edging and attach it to the panel with glue and nails. Cut out and miter the picture frame members from hardwood to fit whatever picture you have

chosen—retaining the picture-frame leg height you need—and assemble them into a frame unit with glue and nails, using corner clamps.

When both subassemblies are dry, rout a decorative bead or groove on the frame. Insert a tasteful piece of art into the recess that is formed by the scrap panel and its edging. Then glue the picture frame to the panel edging. When dry, sand the frame and panel assembly and mount one side of a continuous hinge to the rear of the upper panel edge.

Edges, Nailers, Finish

Miter and hand-fit the ⅜″×¾″ hardwood front edge and attach it to the front box edges with glue and brads. In a similar manner, install the shelf and divider front edges. Cut the nailers to size and attach them to the top, bottom and sides with glue and 6d finishing nails.

Set all nails, fill holes, sand all surfaces and edges, working down to No. 220 grit paper. Dust off all work with a tack cloth and apply an oil finish according to

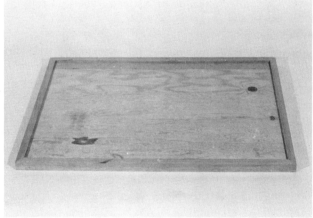

Edge scrap panel of picture-frame leg with ¾″×1″ hardwood, mitered at corners. The recess formed by the panel and its edging accommodates the work of art you choose to frame.

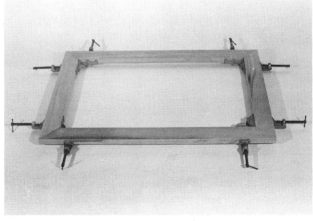

Using corner clamps of the kind shown in assembling the picture frame insures tight joints and squareness.

instructions on the container. Go for the extra step of rubbing the surfaces with 4/0 steel wool and penetrating oil as a lubricant. It's worth the extra trouble for the lustre that you'll get.

Final Assembly

Mount one side of a continuous hinge to the edge of the front flap nearest the box; then the other side of the hinge to the front edge of the box bottom. Install a pair of brass luggage latches (available at luggage repair shops).

Mount the box onto the wall as follows:

- Find two conveniently located stud centers and mark them with tape where the top and bottom nailers meet the wall.
- Mark nailers on the approximately 16″ centers (if such is the case in your home) and predrill clearance holes in the nailers for No. 10 × 3″ mounting screws.
- Get a helper to prop the sewing center (front flap closed and latched) at the correct height so that the predrilled holes in the nailers are in vertical alignment with the stud center marks. The correct height is 29¼″ from the floor to the lower surface of the box bottom at all points.
- The sides should check out plumb (dead vertical, as measured by a long level), so that the flap edges will line up with the sides in the closed position.

If all is in order, drive the mounting screws (well soaped) through the bottom nailer into the studs. Now open the latches and allow the flap to come down to a level position, supported by a suitable prop. Drive screws through the top nailer into the studs and remove all visible tape.

Finally, install the picture-frame leg. Close and latch the flap and center the picture-frame leg, marking the leg top with a horizontal strip of tape. Next, mark the locations of the left and right sides of the picture-frame leg on the tape. Align the hinge on these marks and punch-mark screw pilot holes to mount the continuous hinge to the flap front. Remove all tape, drive in the hinge corner screws and recheck the leg alignment before proceeding further. If the leg fits squarely, drive in the remaining hinge screws and your sewing center is finished.

Notes on Type II

Type II centers will require about 1⅓ sheets of birch plywood. The shelves and divider must be set back to provide clearance for the chains in the closed position, so pre-edge and sand these pieces prior to assembly into the box. Use brass chains and screweyes to support the front flap, instead of the picture-frame leg in the Type I design, and install three magnetic catches to hold the flap in the closed position (instead of the luggage latches). Edging, joinery and finish are the same as used in the Type I center.

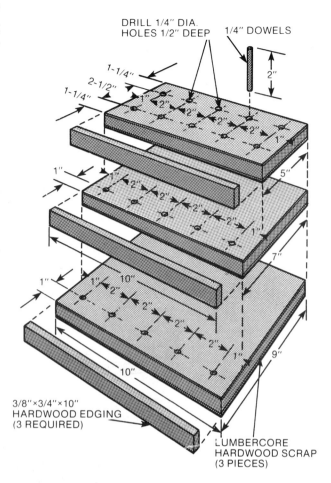

To make the large spool caddy above, cut the three main pieces from birch veneer plywood scrap and edge them with hardwood. Glue the three levels together and sand when dry. Drill dowel holes ½″ deep. Insert ¼″ diameter, 2″ long dowels and finish with penetrating oil.

Four-tier plastic caddy holds 32 small-size spools of thread.

Accessorizing Your New Fold-up Sewing Center

Once you have completed your sewing center, you're ready to consider how it should be accessorized. Storage devices such as those pictured here will make it an efficient "workshop" for the home sewer. Units to hold thread, tapes, bobbins, scissors, needles and patterns can be stored in the main shelf area, where the sewer can get at them, almost without getting up from the chair.

You can make the large spool caddy yourself in minutes, using some of the birch veneer plywood and hardwood left over from the sewing center construction project. The other items shown here are inexpensive and readily available in stores everywhere.

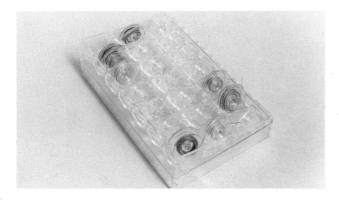

Container with a clear plastic cover holds 32 bobbins.

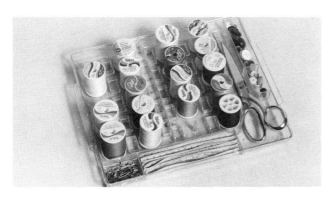

If the sewer in your house is the kind who likes to have a little bit of a lot of things at hand, the clear plastic organizer is just the ticket. Partitions accommodate a variety of sewing staples.

The home sewer can keep patterns handy and in perfect order in the sturdy plastic, hinge-top box. A carrying handle makes it portable.

Part III

Bathroom

15

Whirlpool Bath

After settling into the completely refreshing luxury of your own whirlpool bath, you will not remember any of the heavy construction work that it took to get it installed. As soothing jets of water massage your body, you'll feel *born again*—even before you leave the bath. After all, the entire NFL can't be wrong!

Whirlpool baths come in a variety of shapes, sizes and materials. The one shown is a 34″×60″ reinforced fiberglass tub and pan with a motor-driven pump and three adjustable jets. The plumbing, integral with the tub, in-

cludes trip-lever waste and overflow, an antisyphon vacuum breaker, a showertub fill diverter valve, hot and cold water valves, air induction controls, plus the connections between the system components. It does not include the rough waste, vent and water supplies. The pump motor is controlled by a timer, adjustable up to 60 minutes.

Although some of these baths are available with a removable front skirt for easy access to the working parts, it's not that much more work to build in a fully sunken installation. The only real difference is the construction of a platform with a rectangular opening for the tub and an access panel at the bottom of the back wall. This access panel allows you to put all the controls against the wall for a definite design plus. The reason for choosing a fiberglass tub over a cast iron one is a weight differential of about 400 pounds...an important consideration in a retrofit.

For those who wish to tackle the project, here's a blow-by-blow account of the planning and the work itself.

Planning

Planning is most important, so first check the available bathroom space and the floor's ability to sustain a load of 50 pounds per square foot. You'll need a 20-amp cable with a GFI (Ground Fault Interrupter) breaker on the panel end. The power for the pump motor will be switched by a timer that should be placed at least 5' away from the nearest tub edge. Check the current National Electrical Code's coverage of spas and tubs. You can also check your local building code for the load-carrying limit of the bathroom joists.

Next, get the complete information on the bath itself. This includes weight, physical dimensions, power requirement, rough plumbing setup, base support (mortar or plaster for those tubs that require it), sealing where the tub's flange meets the platform, and the size and location of required access panels. Actually, it's better to have the tub on the site for direct physical measurement.

Framework

The platform size should be keyed to the room size, whirlpool bath size and the size of the tiles you'll be using. For example, the bath shown here requires an opening of 8 tiles×14 tiles (34″×60″). Note that a line of tiles takes slightly more space than you'd figure due to the small projections on their edges, which provide the grout spacing. The best way to lay out a row of tiles is on a stick (like a story pole used in house construction) with the tile numbers corresponding to the *actual* space required for them. By working out the platform like this, you'll save yourself a mess of nipping and cutting.

The platform should be constructed with a 2×4 framework, a ¾″-thick skin of A-C plywood and a ½″-thick skin of cement board over this to serve as a substrate for the tile. In our case, we removed the existing steel bathtub

and then, to open up the bathroom, we removed a non-supporting wall separating the lavatory from the tub/toilet area. To provide enough room in the alcove, we moved a short end wall (from a closet in an adjacent room) back about 1½'. The bathroom had some tile in it at the time of this retrofit, so we stripped off both the tile and the drywall holding it. This provided a unique opportunity to add the proper amount of stud-bay insulation prior to nailing up the *green* water-resistant drywall.

Bathroom before the whirlpool installation.

Wall and tub removed, wall stripped, short wall at left cut back and rough plumbing exposed.

As long as the wall is open, add insulation, then put up water-resistant drywall.

Control panel of whirlpool bath.

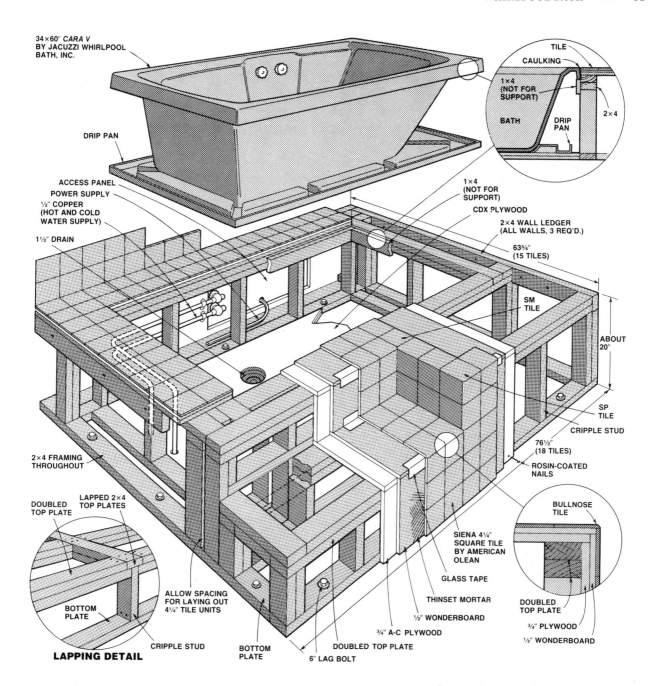

34×60″ *CARA V*
BY JACUZZI WHIRLPOOL
BATH, INC.

TILE
CAULKING
1×4
(NOT FOR
SUPPORT)
BATH
2×4
DRIP
PAN

DRIP PAN

ACCESS PANEL
POWER SUPPLY
½″ COPPER
(HOT AND COLD
WATER SUPPLY)

1½″ DRAIN

1×4
(NOT FOR
SUPPORT)
CDX PLYWOOD
2×4 WALL LEDGER
(ALL WALLS, 3 REQ'D.)
63¾″
(15 TILES)
SM
TILE
ABOUT
20″
SP
TILE
CRIPPLE STUD
76½″
(18 TILES)
ROSIN-COATED
NAILS

2×4 FRAMING
THROUGHOUT

DOUBLED
TOP PLATE
LAPPED 2×4
TOP PLATES

BOTTOM
PLATE
CRIPPLE STUD
ALLOW SPACING
FOR LAYING OUT
4¼″ TILE UNITS
BOTTOM
PLATE
DOUBLED TOP PLATE
6″ LAG BOLT

SIENA 4¼″
SQUARE TILE
BY AMERICAN
OLEAN
GLASS TAPE
THINSET MORTAR
½″ WONDERBOARD
¾″ A-C PLYWOOD

BULLNOSE
TILE
DOUBLED
TOP PLATE
¾″ PLYWOOD
½″ WONDERBOARD

LAPPING DETAIL

In the areas where the wall was removed, there were breaks in the existing mosaic floor. There we nailed some expanded metal to the subfloor and brought the depression up to floor level with concrete. The finish tile floor may be applied directly over the existing one and the concrete patch at the appropriate time. Run the power cable, switch cable and any other ancillary cables you require before installing the drywall. Also, work out the rough plumbing early on. This includes the 1½″ drain and the ½″ copper water supplies and their shutoff valves. Keep the platform plan handy to avoid any conflicts with electrical and plumbing routing.

If necessary, beef up any joists that have been notched where the old tub was, then bring this area up to floor level with CDX plywood, making sure to include the

5″×10″ cutout for the drain and overflow. Finish the drywall work, taping and jointing as you go.

When you lay the bottom plates for the platform, remember that the whole structure will have a combined skin thickness of 1¼″ (¾″plywood plus ½″ cement board), not including the tile that goes over this. You can figure the tile thickness at ⅜″, since the tiles are 5/16″ thick and the thinset mortar to adhere them will surely take up 1/16″. Inasmuch as the height of this whirlpool is close to 20″, you must build the structure five tiles high, not including the tiles set flat on the deck of the platform. Set the bottom plates in place over some adhesive or mastic to account for local discrepancies, and then drill through the plates and the floor to the joists below. Anchor these plates to the joists with lag bolts.

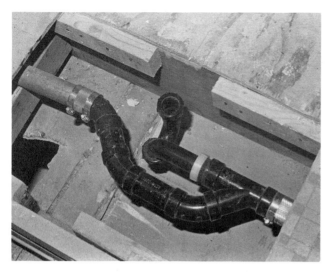

Work out the rough plumbing early in the project.

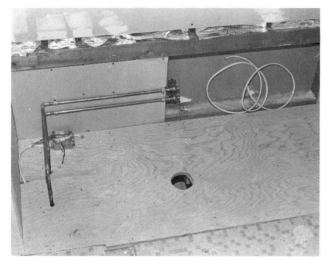

Rough plumbing should include the 1½" drain plus the ½" copper water supplies and their shutoff valves.

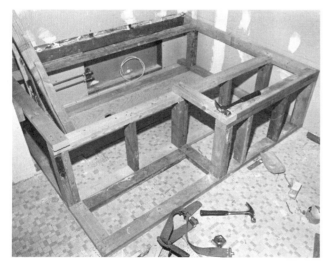

Frame whirlpool and platform area with 2×4s. Note ledgers in place and lapped top plates.

Next, nail up the wall ledgers at the designed structure height, less the skin thickness. Make sure that these ledgers are dead level since the platform top will be your gauge when you set the tub. Then work up a system of doubled top plates and cripple studs so you can lap-join the top plates between the short walls for extra strength. Build up the opening for the tub and the inset step. The tub opening must be 34"×60" and *square*.

Fasten the ¾" A-C plywood to the framework with rosin-coated box nails and a layer of cement board with roofing nails. Cement board, an excellent substrate for tile, is concrete with integrated fiberglass skin. Although it may be sawn with a masonry blade, you'll find it easier to score and crack it, just like gypsum board. Sawing creates a dense, gray cloud that is both messy and unhealthy. A special carbide-tip scoring knife is available at tile-supply stores at nominal cost.

Where pieces of cement board butt together, tape and joint them just like gypsum board, but use fiberglass tape and thinset mortar mixed with water. With the platform and walls done, you're ready for tiling.

Tiling

For external edges, we used a combination of bullnose tile butted against the edge of an adjacent flat tile for the external edges, and for the internal edges we used simple butting of flat tiles. On the deck of the platform, external and internal corners were treated with SCR-L and SM tiles respectively (roundout-and-square-in-angle tiles).

Basic tile operations are cutting, setting, grouting and cleaning. Three methods of tile setting were used in this project: (1) setting with latex-base mastic over drywall using a triangular-notched trowel; (2) setting over cement board using water-mixed thinset mortar with a ¼" square-notched trowel; (3) setting tile-over-tile with thinset mortar mixed with a latex mortar additive applied

Apply ¾" A-C plywood to frame, then a second skin of cement board, nailed in place with roofing nails, then taped and jointed with fiberglass tape and thinset mortar.

with a ¼″ square-notched trowel. If you're setting tile over a wooden subfloor, use an epoxy mortar and a square-notched trowel. Note that all mortars and mastics have well-defined curing times, so apply them only to an area you can tile within the given time period.

For straight line cutting, you can rent a hand-operated scorer/cracker and you can buy a carbide-tip nipper to handle the irregular shapes. Cut tile edges can be smoothed by rubbing a scrap piece of tile against them, edge-to-edge, or by holding the cut edge against a stationary belt sander (using goggles for eye protection, of course). If you lack tile-setting experience, your best bet is to lay the tile out dry, make any cuts needed, pick up the tiles in order before applying the mortar, and then do the actual setting.

When setting tile on drywall, place them in position over the mastic and press with a twisting motion for a good grab. Tiles set in thinset or epoxy mortar must be

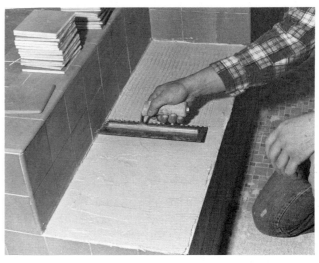

Begin tiling by troweling on thinset mortar on cement board with ¼″-notched trowel.

Rent a tile cutter for straight cuts. Score surface first with the diamond wheel, then press handle to crack.

Lay tiles in mortar in a planned order.

Use a carbide-tip nipper to handle irregular shapes.

Tiles set in thinset or epoxy mortar must be beaten in with a hammer and board after they are positioned.

beaten in after they're placed in position. When you have placed enough tiles to create a small field, lay a board down over them and smack it with a hammer—but not hard enough to crack a tile. Beat all over the field to get good adherence and ensure a flat surface. Make sure that all grout spaces provided by the tiles' small edge projections are clear of mastic or mortar so there will be room for grout later.

Clean the tile surfaces in small field groups by damp-sponging and dry-mopping with a burlap rag or similar material after a haze forms. The mortar or mastic must be set up before applying grout. The most common grout is the dry-cure type, which is mixed with water. But for extra dampproofing, use an acid-type grout mixed with a latex additive. In either case, use a rubber-bottom float to get it onto the surface and into the grooves. Then damp-sponge the surface, and dry-mop when the haze appears.

Plumbing and Setting the Tub

You might wish to finish all the tile work before fitting the tub to avoid damaging the fiberglass. The alternative is to install the tub first and then add the tile right up to the edge, but it's a bit tricky. Before setting the tub in place, fit the plumbing that can be done outside of the platform. This includes the trip lever waste and overflow unit and the diverter valve/ check valve/ hot and cold water valve connections. Some local codes allow you to eliminate the extra check valve included in the kit.

Set the tub on a bed of plaster or mortar (we used mortar) for a nonflexible support, while supporting the edges with 1×4s nailed to the inner faces of the platform structure. Note that these 1×4s do not support the tub itself. We made slings from fiberglass tape to lift the tub in and out for the trial fitting. The reason for this is that you must determine how much mortar is needed to keep the

Apply grout with a rubber float after mortar is dry. Work grout in with circular strokes.

Before setting in the tub you might want to finish all of the tile work.

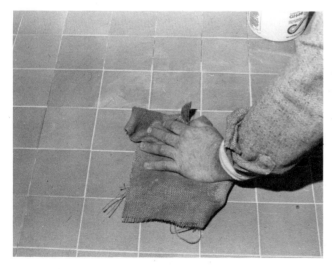

While damp remove excess and clean tile with damp sponges, changing sponges frequently.

When setting tub on mortar or plaster, check edges with level placed at various angles.

tub at the desired level and to position the 1×4s to accommodate this height.

It's best to have the access panel open during this work so that someone can see the work from that area. Now, mix the mortar, a little on the thin side, shovel it in place, and sling the tub into position. Check to see that the height is right and the tub is level. You can lower the tub by having someone walk in it. Make sure the tub and pan contact fully with mortar.

When the mortar has cured, hook up the final plumbing and electrical connections. Then seal around the flange of the tub where it meets the tile with a resilient-type sealer. This can be applied from a cartridge gun, smeared into place and cleaned, while wet, with sponges and water. Hooking up the waste tailpiece to the trap may require opening a ceiling below. But this gives you the best view to check for any possible leaks. When everything's set, haul your tired, aching body into your new whirlpool bath and have a blast.

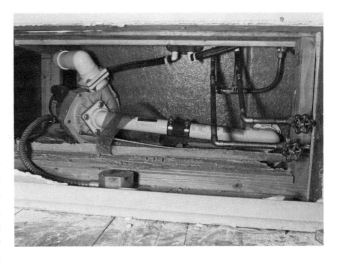

Not the most elegant view! It's looking in from the access panel at the rear showing pump, motor, electrical junction box, water supplies and valves.

16

Sauna/Bath

I f you have 100 square feet of floor space to spare and would like to treat yourself and the family to some permanent luxury, install a sauna. A session in a sauna is a great way to renew life after a hard day. The therapeutic benefits are legendary.

Better still, install a combination sauna and bathroom, as we did. We wanted the one, then opted for both, given the added convenience of an extra bathroom.

Planning

Our site is the basement, which meant we dealt with a concrete floor for the drain plumbing. It wasn't difficult. But if you'd like your setup on the first or second floor, the difference, actually, is to your advantage. Simply tie in to existing wall plumbing for the bathroom section.

Our site is the basement, which meant we dealt with a concrete floor for the drain plumbing. It wasn't difficult. But if you'd like your setup on the first or second floor, the difference, actually, is to your advantage. Simply tie in to existing wall plumbing for the bathroom section.

You'll want to start with a plan for your project, showing accurately the location of the toilet and shower waste lines, as well as the venting scheme for each of these units. Venting for different sizes of plumbing pipes requires different distances between the fixture and the vent stack. This is easily checked at your local building authority.

With your plans drawn and the waste line approximately located beneath the concrete floor, mark the wall positions and the main plumbing fixtures (shower and toilet)

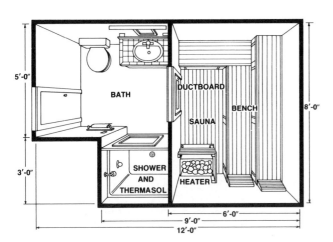

Combination sauna and bathroom is packed into about 100 square feet of floor space (above), allowing ample walk-around area in both rooms. Appointments for both (opposite page) add a nice touch of luxury. Sauna (top) is lined throughout with redwood, including slat benches, floor rack and headrests. Entry to sauna is through bathroom (top right); note sauna controls on wall. Sink area is well lighted with string of globelike bulbs in hooded housing. Stall shower (bottom right) is conveniently located to right of the sauna entry; general sauna-bath routine is to alternate sessions of dry heat with cold showers in the Finnish tradition.

with yellow crayon (it's easier to see that color on dull concrete).

Be sure to allow air-space between the sauna's free-standing walls and the basement walls for proper circulation. The upper portions of the first-floor joist bays accomplish this for the ceiling. Pay particular attention to the layout of the walls surrounding the shower alcove and use the product literature as a guide. This extra care is necessary because the framing serves as a fastening surface for the back and sides of the shower stall.

Be sure to provide a 12½″ clearance between the center of the closet flange and the proposed wall behind it (the ½″ is for the wallboard that is applied over the studs). Follow the manufacturer's drawing for the waste location in the shower area, as well.

It's best to make a plan of the new waste and vent plumbing, showing the connections to the existing waste-line and vent the proper diameter.

The concrete basement floor, in our example, had to be broken up to expose existing drain lines and to install new lines.

Plumbing

Our preliminary plumbing installation necessitated tearing up a little of the concrete floor. This is easier than it appears; it's just a matter of renting a hammer (either electric or pneumatic) and chopping away enough concrete to expose the existing lines and provide enough room for the new work. You will most probably find cast-iron pipes; simply remove the section of waste pipe required and insert a cast-iron, no-hub fitting. A rented soil-pipe cracker quickly gets the unwanted cast-iron section out for you. All that remains is the installation of the new ABS or PVC pipes and fittings.

During this part of the job, *do not* flush any toilets, showers, sinks or washers—a word to the wise is sufficient! Note also that the waste installation means maintaining a ¼″ pitch-per-foot down-grade.

Be sure to place a 5″- or 6″-diameter smoke pipe (sleeve) around the shower-waste stub before the concrete is poured. This allows the receptor hub (shower base) to fit in below the floor grade. This sleeve is collapsed and removed later. The shower waste sticks up out of the floor after the concrete is poured and is cut to proper length later.

The closet flange should be set up to a point ¼″ above the proposed finished floor. In our case, this meant ¼″ above the floor tiles; the tiles would be set near the end of the job, but they had to be figured in ahead of time. The lavatory waste should be laid out so it fits within the wall just behind the vanity cabinet.

Standard wall framing was used for enclosures. Powder-actuated spikes or pins were driven through plates, into deck.

Framework

After the concrete has set, re-mark the floor if the original marks have been obliterated by the breakout. Set down the sole plates for the walls, locking them in with concrete nails—or, better, with powder-actuated spikes.

Wallboard in sauna is covered with 6-mil polyethylene stapled in place. This prevents moisture from getting into walls.

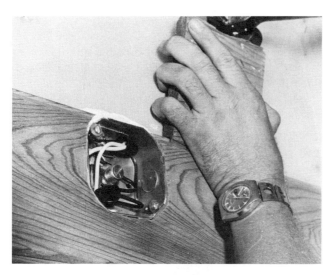

Installing redwood. Obstacles like electrical boxes are cut to fit with jigsaw. Boards are tapped together with scrap.

All nails used on faces (boards and benches) are set below surfaces; exposed nailheads get hot and can burn you.

Steam generator, water supply, steam-discharge pipe and electrical feed all sit out of the way on their own shelf.

Next install joist blocking where the wall top plates run parallel to the joists for the additional necessary support at the top.

Plumb down from the top with a bob, or up from the bottom with a level and a 2×4, to locate the top plates directly over the sole plates. Nail them into the joists or blocking, lapping at the corners for extra strength. Then mark your 16″ centers on all plates except for those in the shower alcove. *Note:* Stud placement and framing is critical; be sure to follow manufacturer's instructions. Now toenail your studs.

If there are any small pipes running under the first-floor joists that don't lend themselves to easy removal, install furring that clears them. The furring serves as nailers for the ceiling material. Make sure that all electrical cables and plumbing pipes routed through the wall or ceiling areas are protected by steel plates where they pass through wood. This avoids the possibility of nailing into them. *Note:* Nail in blocking to support the sauna heat and bathroom accessories.

Fit the hot- and cold-water supplies, clamping where necessary to eliminate vibrations that could cause wall noise after the job is completed. Work in the electrical cables and boxes, allowing them to protrude ½″ in the bathroom for the combined thickness of the wallboard plus redwood planks in the sauna. The sauna heater is chosen according to the amount of space to be heated; it requires a heavier amperage cable as the size of the room increases. Check your local building code for the required breaker style.

Insulation

With all rough plumbing and electricals in the walls, install unfaced insulation in both walls and ceiling bays. Batts are the easiest. Now go ahead with the wallboard in the sauna—but hold up on it in the bathroom until the shower is in place. Observing this order gives you a very neat jointing of the wallboard with the shower components. When you put up the wallboard in the bathroom, use the green, water-resistant type over the shower.

Sauna Finish Work

Now back to the sauna. Staple up some 6-mil plastic over the wallboard to retain any moisture that may occur during the time the sauna operates. Then fit the sauna jamb and door. Most likely, you'll have to do some chopping on the door's bottom rail, but there's plenty of meat there...not to worry. Remember to allow for the tile floor and the marble sill that fits directly under the door. Remove the door while you're working on the redwood ceiling and walls.

Redwood for sauna use comes in assorted lengths from 3′ to 20′. The redwood we used is from the California Redwood Association and is 1″×6″ Clear All Heart, kiln-dried, tongue-and-groove, V-groove. This is the material to use, both from a practical and an aesthetic standpoint. When you order redwood, be sure to allow 15% extra to make up for the wood lost or hidden in the joints and an additional 3% to 5% for the wood lost in trimming to exact length.

All fastening should be done with either aluminum, stainless-steel or hot-dipped galvanized finishing nails. See to it that all nails, whether blind-nailed (at the tongues) or face-nailed, are set flush at the tongues but under any surface. The first set produces a proper fit at the tongue-and-groove joints and the second set prevents sauna users from getting burned by a hot nail. The special material or finish on the nails prevents any staining of the walls.

First, plank the ceiling. Then, starting at the lowest point along the walls (no basement, for example, is truly level), scribe the bottom plank so that its top edge (the groove) is dead level. Face-nail this piece on the bottom and at the ends, and blind-nail it at the tongue. You may find it necessary to predrill the redwood, especially near the ends, to prevent splitting. The final result justifies the extra effort.

At the tongue, the nails driven in blindly at a 45° angle are hidden by the groove of the plank above it. When the planking is complete, all internal corners are fitted with ¾″-square molding; do only the ceiling at this time. Install all benches and duckboards, then do the rest of the moldings.

The 2×4 redwood frames for the benches are all half-lapped to the uprights that support them; the ledgers are nailed or lagged to the studs in the walls behind the benches. The bench heights are appropriate for sitting or lying down (headrests are provided for this purpose). When you have made up the slatted benches, headrests, duckboards and heater fence, the sauna is complete except for the final electrical work.

Bathroom Finish Work

Now go back to the bathroom. The hot- and cold-water supplies should have been installed by this time, as well as the stubs for the shower, toilet, lavatory and steambath discharge. The steam generator sits on a shelf behind the shower. Cave in the temporary sleeve around the shower's wasteline and you're ready to set the receptor (base). We used a 36″ stall shower (they are available in 48″ size, as well). The stall consists of the receptor, two sides and a back, plus sealing and face stripping that hide the hardware.

Start the receptor installation by leveling it with shims, where necessary, and nailing it in place to the framing. This is the critical part of the job. If the receptor is out of level, the back and sides will be out of plumb. Also make sure that the waste stub is centered in the receptor hub hole.

Temporarily position the back and the side that accommodates the shower valve and spray heads. Check the joint where the back meets the rear edge of the side wall. Any slight gap is easily corrected by inserting a shim on the structure behind the back wall. Mark the places where the valves and heads go through the side wall and remove

With back of shower in place, fit the sides, then fasten. When fastening, make sure any shims are under screw holes.

Edge of hole in lavatory top is prepared with sealant before the sink is set.

it for cutting with a jigsaw or hole saw (depending upon the hole size). Now place the opposite side in position against the back wall and repeat the fitting procedure at the joint.

Complete the cutting or drilling. If everything's ship-shape, apply sealant to the channels before installing the sides to the back with screws. Incidentally, shimming should be done only at screw locations. Any excess sealer can be quickly sponged away after closure.

Owens-Corning provides an elastomeric drain seal, which sets in place between the waste pipe and the hub.

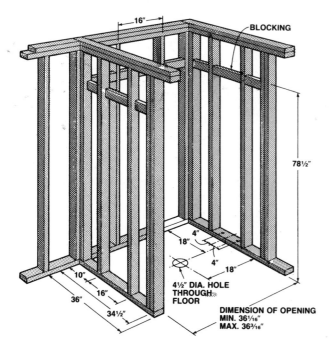

Shower framing in alcove including blocking for shower stall.

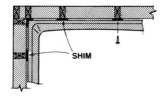

Top view showing shimming and fastening of back and sides of shower.

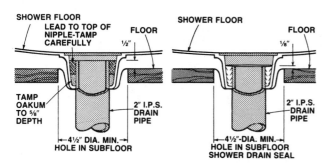

Sealing shower drain (check local codes for allowed methods).

This should be installed now if it conforms with the local code. Apply the snap-in strips to the shallow channels surrounding the fastening screws and hide them. Put green wallboard over the shower and then finish the shower plumbing.

It's all downhill in the bathroom now. Rough in the fan/light combinations—one in the shower ceiling and the other in the bathroom ceiling. Route both of the discharge hoses to outside.

Finish all the wallboard in the bathroom now, taping and jointing to prepare for the tile and wallcovering that follows shortly. When the compound is completely dry and sanded or sponged smooth, seal the entire surface with a coat of paint. White is a good choice.

If you haven't fitted the bathroom entrance door and jamb before this, do it now. This is necessary so that you can set case molding in place on the jambs (both sauna and bathroom) and mark the width that they occupy on adjacent wallboard. While you're marking, place the sink cabinet temporarily in position and pencil its limits on the wallboard, near the floor. This allows you to set the base tile and stop it at these marks.

Local tile shops sell mastic, trowels, nippers (carbide-tipped) and can rent or sell you a tile cutter. The cutter is used for straight work and the nippers for trimming irregular shapes. The general-purpose mastic works on wallboard, concrete and plywood substrates. When using this mastic, press it with a twisting hand motion. Tiles are set best by cutting and fitting them dry, before applying mastic to the substrate. In this way, you're not under any time pressure. Set the tiles over the shower, around the

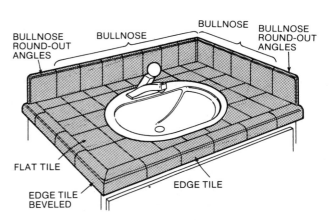

Tile vanity top and backsplash.

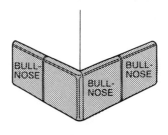

The arrangement at external corner.

room perimeter (up to the marks) and on the floor and marble sills. Use bullnose for the outer edge of the shower tile and the base border.

Cut a plywood top for the sink cabinet and saw out a hole for the sink using the pattern provided. Tile the top; use edge tile on the outer border and flat tile for the field.

When all the tile has set, it's time to grout. This is a job that requires floating the thick, creamy material to fill all cracks. Wipe off with a squeegee, then damp-clean and dry with burlap. The final drying is more like a polishing action that gets rid of the haze formed by the drying of the cement residue. For a more damp-resistant finish, substitute latex grout additive for the water. It's slightly tougher to clean but the results are well worth the effort.

Refit the sink cabinet and lock it to the wall. Then screw the top down to the cabinet and install the lavatory with

sealer under the rim. Let this set. While you're waiting, fit and install the prefinished case molding.

There's another area left to tile: the bullnose backsplash around the sink top. The same procedure applies, but the end tiles are double bulls (tiles with two flat edges and two rounded edges). As soon as the faucet is installed, hook up the plumbing—that is, the hot-and cold-water supplies, the waste and the *P*-trap.

All that's left to do now is to apply the wall covering, to install the toilet and the glass enclosure for the shower (it's a steam bath), and to hang the bathroom door and mirror.

Mount the toilet with its wax seal, cold-water supply, and the anchor bolts that come up from the closet flange. Any slight gaps between the bottom of the toilet and the tile floor can be filled with grout. Actually, it's best to dry-fit the toilet, spot the gaps, then remove the toilet and set it back over both the wax seal and a light bed of grout in the trouble areas.

Included in the electrical work are: lights for the sauna, mounting of the bulb sensor part of the sauna control, light/fan switches, sauna control, sink light switch, outlet, panel breakers for the sauna heater and Thermasol unit and the valance light fixture and plates.

Now a quick check of proper operation is in order for both the electrical and plumbing items.

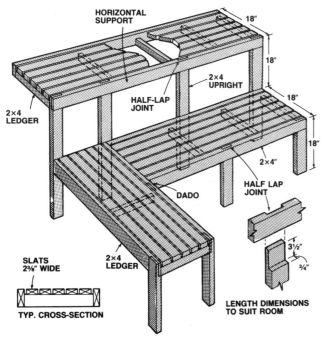

Bench detail.

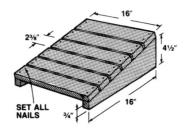

Headrest (1″ redwood stock).

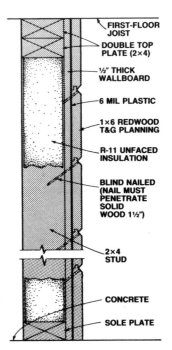

Typical wall cross section in sauna.

Part IV

Kitchen

17

Revolving Pantry

Food storage space is at a premium in every kitchen, and the typical pantry shelf is so jam-packed that you soon forget what's in back—and getting to it. A simple conversion of a pantry or closet to revolving-type shelving plus door-back adjustable shelving corrects this common problem and puts everything in easy reach with the rotation of a shelf.

If you have a closet or pantry that measures 23"×3" minimum inside dimension, what you can do in two hours will return you years of convenience.

How the System Works

The system is called Pantry Pak and is manufactured by the Amerock Corporation of Rockford, Ill. The parts may be purchased from kitchen cabinet dealers, hardware stores and lumberyards who handle the Amerock line.

The spin shelves are circular with a flat section that faces the door so the door can be closed when the door shelves are installed. Each shelf rests on the central post and is supported by a stationary cam that can be locked in any position along the length of the post, so shelf position is infinitely variable.

The door-back shelf standards are notched throughout their entire length, providing adjustable positioning. Since the rectangular shelves are available in 8", 12" and 18" widths, the system is applicable to various size single doors as well as double-door arrangements. The standards come in three lengths so that you can vary the number of door shelves to suit your needs.

How to Install the System

Make sure that the closet shelf (if you are using an existing closet) extends at least 14" out from the back wall. Measure the vertical distance from the closet floor to

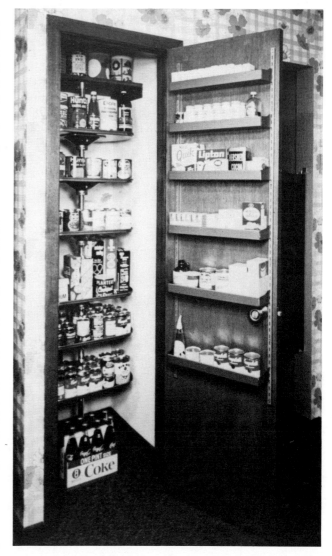

Former broom closet is now a modern pantry with shelves that revolve on a center post.

the shelf bottom side and cut the post ¼″ less than this dimension. Center the template supplied by the manufacturer relative to the door opening, and punchmark the screw locations for the upper and lower post mounting brackets on the bottom side of shelf and the floor. Screw in the upper and lower post mounting brackets. Now install the Pantry Pak circular shelves on the post with a stationary cam support under each shelf, cam-side up. Place the post and shelf assembly in the brackets. Put on the bracket caps, install them with screws, and lock the cams and shelves in the desired positions.

With the inside of the closet complete, installation of the door-back shelves is simple. Lay out the positions for the shelf standards on the door back and screw them in place. Hang the rectangular Pantry Pak door shelves on the standard notches. If you have the typical hollow-core door that is too flimsy to hold the shelf mounting standard screws securely, cut some ¼″ plywood strips 3″ wide and epoxy them to the door back where the standards are to be mounted.

This spin-shelf system also is adaptable to both tall and short closets or cabinets as well as single or double-door arrangements. If you wish to convert a kitchen cabinet, where the bottom shelf is usually 4″ above the room floor, an adjustable support bracket is available to transfer the weight from the cabinet floor to the room floor.

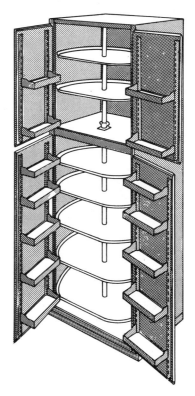

Flat side of circular shelves face front, allowing for door-back shelves.

18

Luminous Ceiling

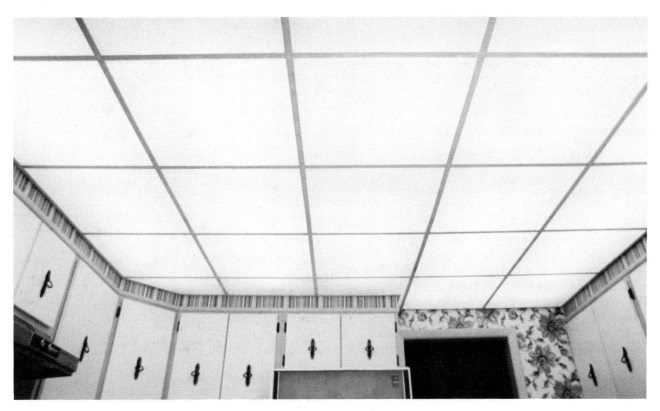

You'll have soft, shadowless lighting and a ceiling that can be cleaned in the kitchen sink.

One way to cure a poorly lighted kitchen is with a luminous ceiling. A weekend's work will do the trick.

A suspended T-bar ceiling system consists of wall angle, main tees, cross tees, suspension wires and panels. The wall angle runs horizontally around the perimeter of the room at a predetermined height, fastened to the studs with nails. The wall angle supports the ends of main tees and border cross tees and diffusing panels.

The main tees, which form the backbone of the structure, are supported by suspension wires attached to the ceiling. Cross tees span the spaces between the main tees or the spaces between other cross tees and connect with locking tabs that insert into mating slots.

You must plan the overall system so the lights do not end up partly covered by main tees or cross tees running parallel to the main tees. If you're using 2′×2′ diffusing panels (usually preferred for small- or average-size

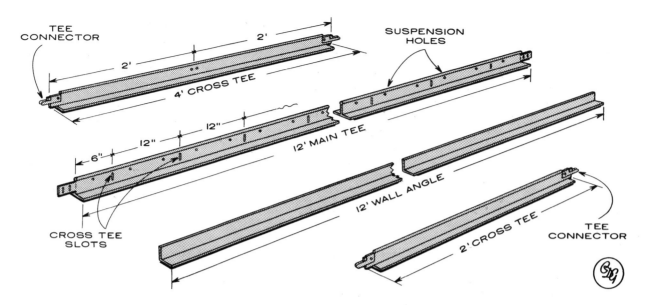

Components of metal grid that holds diffusing panels. Support wires omitted.

rooms), this is easy, because you're running the light fixtures right down the center of the panels. The same is true if you're using 2'×4' panels and running light fixtures parallel to the long edge. If, however, you wish to run the light fixtures perpendicular to the long edge, you must space more carefully.

Begin by measuring your ceiling. Only with accurate measurements can you plan the width of the border panels and thereby balance the ceiling. And only when you have made the plan, can you locate the fixtures.

Measure length and width of the room. Divide the length by the length of the panels you're using. You'll get a number and a remainder. Add the panel size to the remainder and divide the sum by two. This number is the width of the border panels. Example: Measure a length of 136″. Divide this by 48″ (chosen panel edge the way you plan to use it) and get 2 plus 40″. Add 48″ and 40″ and get 88″. Divide 88″ by 2 and get 44″, the width of the border panels (meaning you must trim 4″ from each of two 48″ border panels). Repeat the calculation for the room width.

Main tees should run perpendicular to the ceiling joists, so that you'll be able to suspend the support wires from these joists every 4' to hold up the main tees.

The 200-square foot kitchen ceiling shown has 800 watts of fluorescent light, provided by 20, 4' area lighting fixtures, each equipped with a single 48″, 40-watt cool-white tube. The fixtures are primarily arranged in parallel rows at the panel centerlines, with the fixture ends as close together as possible.

After you have drawn up plans, you're ready for the electrical work.

Light Installation

If you want to control the lighting level in the room—for example, lighting only certain working areas and split-

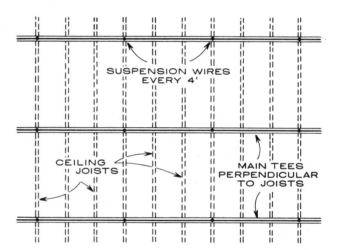

With main tees perpendicular to joists, support wires can be anchored every 4'.

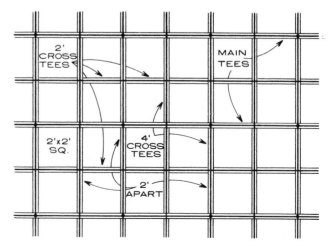

Setup for 2×2 panels has main tees joined by 4″ cross tees, connected by 2' tees.

ting up the remaining lights by using separate switches—you'll have to put in extra outlet boxes and switches. However, the fluorescent fixtures must be installed first.

Begin by snapping chalk lines indicating the fixture centerlines on the ceiling, according to your drawing. Remove the fixture covers and surface-mount the fixtures in straight runs along the chalk lines, with wood screws into the joists or toggle bolts or mollys into the drywall

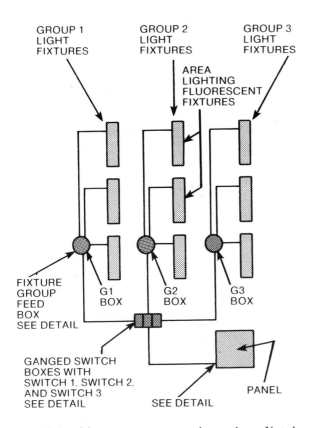

General light wiring arrangements are shown above. Note how light groups are controlled by separate switches.

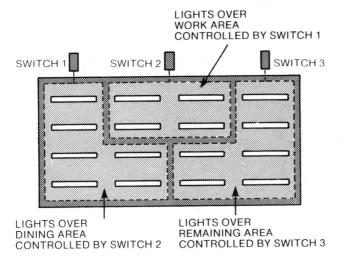

In split setup, at left, Switch 1 controls work area; switches 2 and 3 each control half the rest of room.

ceiling. Make sure the existing outlet boxes remain accessible.

One way to handle fixtures is to lock them together with conduit nipples—then you can run THHN or equivalent wire straight through the line of fixtures. Another way is to separate each fixture slightly and feed power into it from an approved outlet box; here, feed wires running inside fixtures must not pass the ballast unless they are heat-resistant THHN or equivalent.

Metal boxes pose a special problem. The National Electrical Code (NEC) requires that a certain number of cubic inches of volume be assigned to components housed within a box (current-carrying wires, grounds, pairs of clamps, straps with switches or other devices). Example: Four cables enter a box, locked in by a pair of clamps, no devices. Therefore, you must accommodate eight wires, one pair of clamps, one for all the grounds for a total of ten. Multiply ten by the wire-gauge factor established by NEC (2.25 for 12 gauge) and get a box-volume requirement of 22.5 cubic inches. A normal 4″ octagon box, 2⅛″ deep is 21.5 cubic inches. That is not enough, so add a raised cover to the box, increasing its volume, or use a 4″

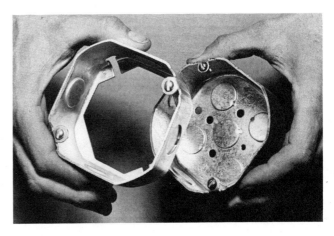

Volume of metal box like 4″ octagon shown below, left, can be increased by adding a raised cover.

Various boxes are used in splicing wires. Below, right, strut-mounted 4″ octagon, nailed between joists.

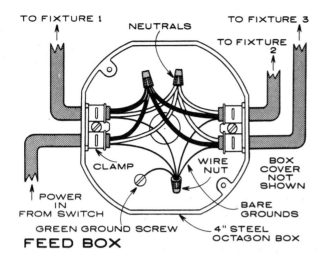

FEED BOX

Fixture group feed-box detail, left, shows grounding, power from switch, fixture feeds.

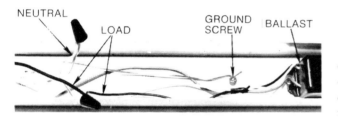

Wiring details are shown above. Do not pass ballast on way to connects unless inside feed wires are THHN or equivalent.

square, 1½″ deep box that has 22.6 cubic inches of volume.

Shut off breakers controlling existing outlet boxes before adding the raised cover. After wiring into light fixtures, install blank covers over raised ones to close the boxes.

If you need more boxes and switches, this is the time to install them. Nail up the boxes—side, strut or surface mounted. Next, route 12-gauge approved cable from the service panel to the switch box. As a safety precaution, don't connect this cable and its breaker to the panel until all wiring is complete. Then, route cable between the outlet and switch boxes and gang-mount the switch boxes. Now wire between the outlet boxes and the fixtures. Connect in boxes, switches and fixtures. Finally, wire in the breaker at the panel. Install tubes, test and remove tubes.

Ceiling Installation

In a standard-height room, locate the wall angle 8″ down from the ceiling. Stretch a chalk cord at this point, check horizontal accuracy with a line level and snap a chalk line. Next, cut the wall angle to size, and fasten to the wall studs with drywall nails, so its horizontal flange lines up with the chalk lines. Cut metal components with snips.

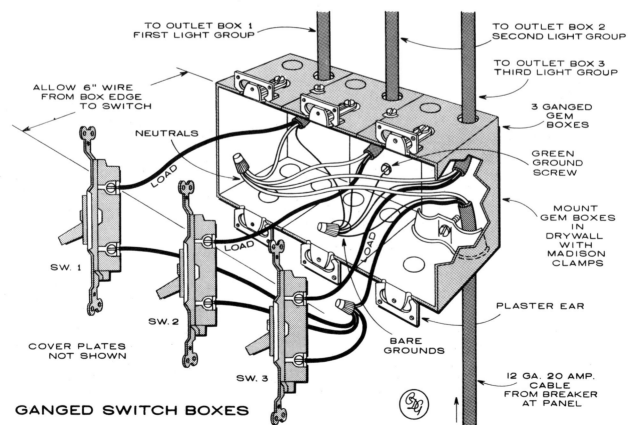

GANGED SWITCH BOXES

Switches go between breaker and feed cables to ganged boxes, mounted with clamps.

Again, refer to your plan, and snap chalk lines on the ceiling over the locations of the main tees. Install either screweyes or partly driven roofing nails every 4' along these chalk lines (into the joists) to hold the support wires. Twist a 12" piece of 18-gauge suspension wire onto each nail or screweye.

Measure the wall-to-wall distance for the main tees as a check against the diagram and subtract ⅛" for wall-angle clearance. Because main tees are usually 12' long, one piece will usually do in rooms less than 12', and these main tees may be quickly spliced to handle rooms longer than 12'. The main tees are slotted every 6" or 12" along their length to receive the cross-tee locking tabs. (Generally, pieces of one manufacturer are not interchangeable with those of another). Use these tab slots as an index when cutting main tees to fit a border as calculated in your plan. This distance from the wall to the first cross tee is the border panel size, less ⅛" for wall-angle clearance.

After trimming one end to border panel size, rest this end of the main tee on the wall angle and insert the support wires in the appropriate holes. If necessary, cut the remainder of this main tee from another full-length main tee and make the splice. Now, stretch a cord across

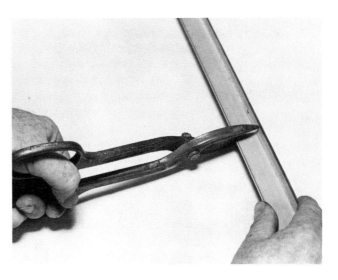

Cut all metal parts—wall angle, main and cross tees, suspension wires—with a tin snips as shown above.

Two sections of a main tee, spliced and supported near the joint by a suspension wire. Note cross tee locked into main tee.

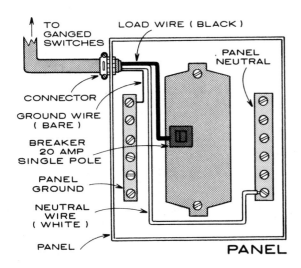

Hook up breaker as shown. Always wire from farthest point back to the panel, with the power off. Power is last.

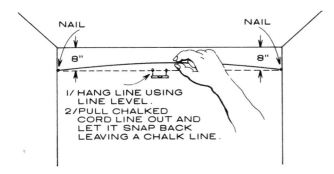

Mark wall 8" down from ceiling; test for accuracy; then snap chalk line for wall angle.

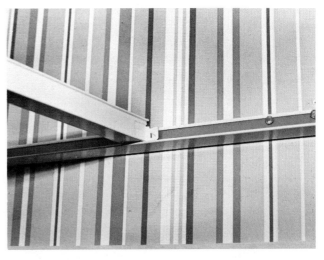

Nailed in place, wall angle supports border cross tees (below), main-tee ends, panels.

the room between opposite wall angles, parallel to the main tee, and adjust the support wires, so the main tee is truly level with the cord. Repeat this operation as you install the remaining main tees. Now insert a couple of cross tees in a corner and check the grid for "out-of-square" condition with a rafter square. Correct any minor discrepancies by nipping a bit off the proper main tees until the grid squares up. Insert the remaining cross tees, cutting to length at the borders. Refit the fluorescent tubes.

Finish Work

Light-diffusing panels generally come in 2'×4' pieces (actually 23⅞×47⅞). They can be clear or white in color, and prismatic, beaded, egg-crate or flat in surface design. The best choice for this job is the flat, milk-white panel, such as the one shown in the photo. This distributes the intensity and gives a soft, even, shadowless light.

Count the number of full-size panels and install any 2'×4' pieces as is. If you're using a 2'×2' design, you must cut 23⅞×23⅞" pieces from 2×4 panel, using one of these methods: (1) table saw with plastic blade; (2) jigsaw with metal cutting blade; (3) scoring with utility knife and steel edge, then cracking over an edge. If the saw blade leaves a flash or residue at the cut, carefully remove it with a utility knife. Complete cutting and fitting all border panels and make sure they're all seated in the grid.

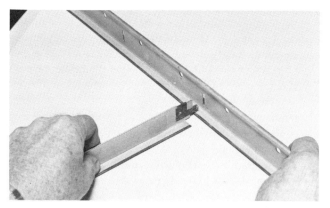

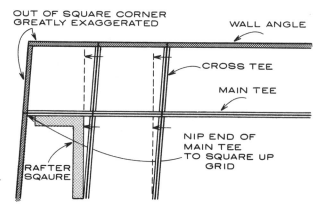

Cross tees have locking tab inserts that engage in indexed slots, either in the main or 4' cross tees.

Check grid at a corner, using a rafter square. Correct out-of-square condition by trimming mains, adjusting cross tees.

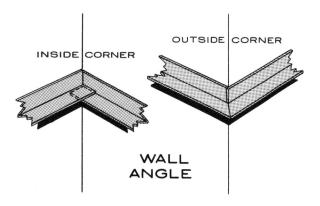

Cut angle at internal corners (one piece laps over other), 45° miter at outer ones.

For smooth-edged panels, use jigsaw with a metal cutting blade.

19

Kitchen Vent Fan

I f not cleared out by some form of venting, kitchens will build up various forms of pollution due to cooking. These include heat, steam, grease, smoke and smells. Various forms of fans available to handle this problem include: (1) the ductless range hood and fan, (2) the ducted range hood and fan which exists to the outside, (3) wall fans and (4) ceiling fans vented to the outside.

The ductless type will not totally handle the problem, especially with heavy cooking. Many times it isn't practical to retrofit a ducted hood or ceiling unit. One practical approach is to install a wall fan.

According to our best sources, it's best to figure on changing the kitchen air about 15 times in an hour, so to get the correct fan for the job, we multiplied the length of the room by the width by the height. This gives the volume, which you multiply by 15 (for the changes) and divide by 60 to get the fan capacity in CFM (cubic feet per minute). A quicker "rule-of-thumb" is to just figure your floor area, double it, and that's your fan requirement in CFM.

Completed installation of vent fan.

Preparation and Installation

We found the installation quite easy. Routing the electrical cable ended up being the hardest part. The job consists of picking a location, making a hole in both the interior and exterior walls, mounting a wall switch, pulling some house electrical power and joining everything together electrically. This routing would generally be easier if your home has an accessible basement.

The tools we needed for the job included a drill, jigsaw, hammer, screwdriver and drywall saw. We also needed a wire stripper. (If you're in an area that demands BX, a hacksaw is a must.) You must make sure that you do all electrical work with the power off.

After you decide on the best location, chalk or pencil in the fan housing sleeve outline and test for any studs or

plumbing that might be in the way, with a hammer and awl. Then enlarge the holes at the edge of the circle and insert a keyhole or jigsaw as shown. Saw out the waste disc, keeping any errors to the inside edge of the outline.

To locate the circle on the exterior wall, rest a long drill bit on the edge of the cutout. Drill, as shown, through the sheathing and siding at four places. Using the outer sleeve as a template, mark the circle with the drilled holes as reference points. Saw out the waste as before and temporarily fit the inner and outer sleeves.

Next, choose a convenient place on the wall to mount the switch. Then, using the gem box as a template, mark the box outline centered at the 48″ level. Cut out the waste drywall with saw. If the wall is plaster, you can drill holes

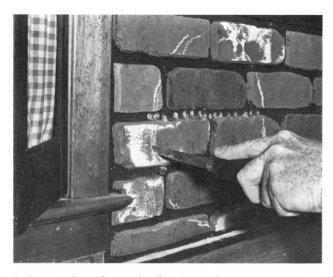

Inside location, after testing for obstructions, is sawn out with keyhole saw for fan housing.

After mounting and wiring wall switch, inner and outer sleeves are inserted and fastened.

Method used to transfer circumference of circle from the inside of wall to exterior wall.

Next an electrical connector is installed in fan outlet junction box, and cable is connected.

Outer sleeve housing is used as template on exterior wall using drill holes as guide.

Fan outlet is hooked up, cover is screwed down and fan is remounted to inner sleeve.

at the corners and join them by sawing between with a hacksaw or similar blade.

From below, drill upward through the subfloor and the sole (bottom) plate with a spade bit and extension. (We located this hole using a basement window as a reference point. Then, we inserted a light in the box hole, and were able to see if we were properly lined up.)

Now snake the electrical cable (not supplied) up from the drilled hole to the box, strip back the outer insulation and lock the cable to the box in the connector so that the wires protrude out about 6″. Strip the insulation back from the wire ends and ground the box by fastening the bare wire under a green ground screw driven into the tapped hole in the box back.

The box is fixed in the hole with metal retainers (madison clamps). Wire in the switch, mount it and then the cover plate and knob.

The fan assembly is removed from the inner sleeve and the sleeve is pushed through the rough opening, while a helper pushes the outer sleeve onto it from the outside. Screw the sleeves together, as shown in the photos. The next job is to apply caulking under the flanges of the outer sleeve before compressing the two sleeves home and tightening the three screws. The screws lock the outer sleeve to the wall. Next, as shown in the photos, an electrical connector is installed in the fan outlet junction box. Connect in the electrical cable as before and screw down the junction box to the housing.

Hook up the fan outlet and screw the cover down. Remount the fan to the inner sleeve. Plug the fan into the outlet and install grille and filter. The last step in the job is turning on the power and testing the unit. Maintenance note: The aluminum mesh filter condenses a lot of the airborne pollutants and may be quickly removed for cleaning at intervals found suitable for your particular kitchen.

Part V

Garden

20

Free-Form Deck

Three-level, free-form deck descends to ground level with diamond-shaped deck around tree.

W e'd wanted to add a deck to our home for some time, but we wanted something other than the usual rectangular shape. We decided to build one of those multileveled decks that extends your living out into the garden.

After some trial and error on paper, we came up with a free-form design that looked interesting. We enlarged it to include a diamond-shaped area around a tree at ground level. For color, we designed planters into the bench ends and added a light-and-sound post on the bench nearest the steps. This illuminates the area, adds a glamorous nighttime effect and makes possible low-level background music. For a cool touch, we penciled in a fountain/pool, which could easily double as a bed for flowers brought in from the garden.

We didn't want maintenance problems, so for all posts, joists and decking, we used pressure-treated lumber. The wood we chose is a fir that was treated with special protective salts to make it virtually impervious to attack from insects and moisture, even when in direct ground contact. You've probably seen similarly treated wood used for sills in new construction. This wood starts out a yellowish-green, but in a year or so turns a pleasing ashen gray. As a final shot at eliminating maintenance, we decided to use hot-dipped galvanized hardware throughout—surely worth the slight extra cost.

Our deck is supported by 2×8 joists. The main joists are bolted and scabbed (discussed in detail later) to the piers and the ledger joist is lag-bolted to the house wall (to the studs if high or into the masonry with lead anchors if low). Most of the remaining joists are hung between the main joists on 2×4 ribbon cleats or, if you prefer, metal joist hangers. The ledger joist and the first main joist nearest the house are set up so that the deck top will be at the same level as the adjacent house floor.

If you'd like to follow this general design (not necessarily the same shape), draw your plans and check with your local building department for the legal joist span and spacing. Then order what you need.

Starting the Deck

Space and dig the postholes for the piers down to the frost line. Imbed the piers in concrete over drainage stone. In most cases, you'll find it's easiest to use prepackaged gravel mix. Make sure you set the piers plumb by placing a level against two adjacent pier faces, correcting as necessary. The piers will be higher than the joists, but you'll cut them down later.

To assure a horizontal deck, set up a mason's cord and line level when installing main and ledger joists. With the piers plumb and the joists level, the critical part of the job's over. Where the main joists form a sandwich around the piers supporting them, install 2×4 filler blocks to eliminate possible gaps under planks.

Add in the border joists (plus any additional joists required to get within 6″ to 8″ of the proposed deck

Ideas you can use on any deck: Diamond-shaped deck around tree (top); post and planter bench (center); fountain/pool that doubles as flower bed (bottom).

With the line level—and the bubble centered on a taut mason's cord—whatever it is you are checking is dead level (horizontal).

All the main joists except the first one are doubled around the 4×4 piers. A 2×4 filler block is installed between the 2×8s.

To set piers vertically, tamp the concrete and check the pier faces on adjacent sides. Adjust by tapping the pier sideways.

Nail the 2×4 ribbon cleats to the main joists, then lay the precut short joists between the main joists; mark for the notches.

The 2×6 over the 2×8 on the first main joist provides the riser for the step between the top and the main deck levels.

After notches have been cut on the short joists, set them between the main joists on ribbon cleats. Toenail them 24″ on center.

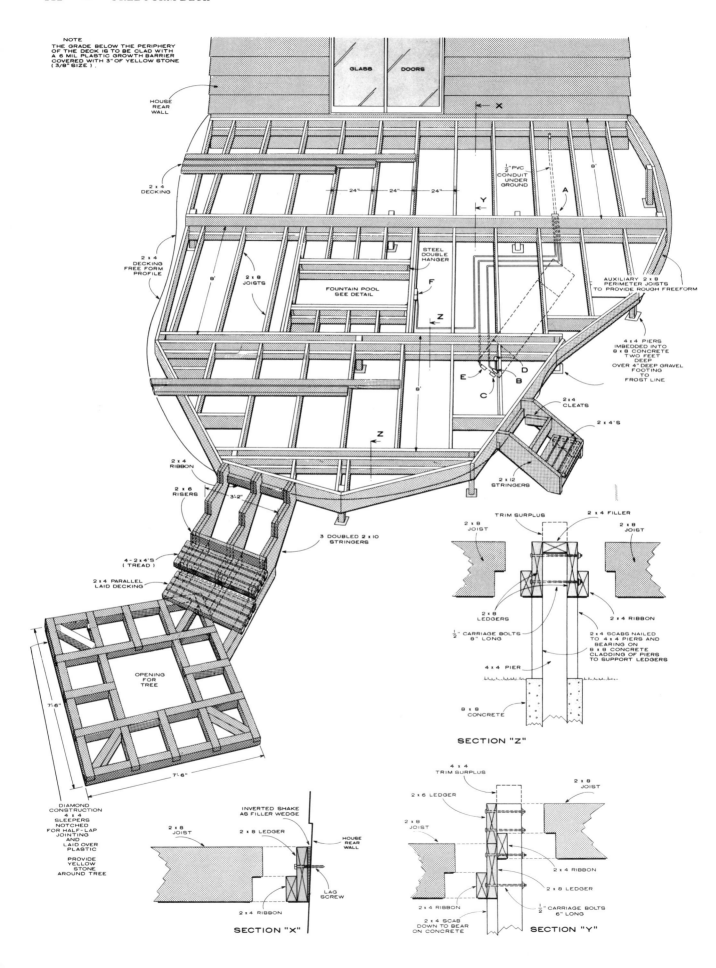

NOTE
THE GRADE BELOW THE PERIPHERY
OF THE DECK IS TO BE CLAD WITH
A 6 MIL PLASTIC GROWTH BARRIER
COVERED WITH 3" OF YELLOW STONE
(3/8" SIZE).

GLASS DOORS

HOUSE
REAR
WALL

X

2 x 4
DECKING

2 x 4
DECKING
FREE FORM
PROFILE

2 x 8
JOISTS

FOUNTAIN POOL
SEE DETAIL

STEEL
DOUBLE
HANGER

F

½" PVC
CONDUIT
UNDER
GROUND

A

8'

Y

24" 24" 24"

8'

Z

AUXILIARY 2 x 8
PERIMETER JOISTS
TO PROVIDE ROUGH FREEFORM

4 x 4 PIERS
IMBEDDED INTO
8 x 8 CONCRETE
TWO FEET
DEEP
OVER 4" DEEP GRAVEL
FOOTING
TO
FROST LINE

E D
B
C

8'

Z

2 x 4
CLEATS

2 x 4'S

2 x 4
RIBBON

2 x 6
RISERS

3½"

4 - 2 x 4'S
(TREAD)

2 x 4 PARALLEL
LAID DECKING

3 DOUBLED 2 x 10
STRINGERS

2 x 12
STRINGERS

OPENING
FOR
TREE

7'6"

7'6"

DIAMOND
CONSTRUCTION
4 x 4
SLEEPERS
NOTCHED
FOR HALF-LAP
JOINTING
AND
LAID OVER
PLASTIC

PROVIDE
YELLOW
STONE
AROUND TREE

SECTION "Z"

2 x 8
JOIST

TRIM SURPLUS

2 x 4 FILLER

2 x 8
JOIST

2 x 8
LEDGERS

2 x 4 RIBBON

½" CARRIAGE BOLTS
8" LONG

2 x 4 SCABS NAILED
TO 4 x 4 PIERS AND
BEARING ON
8 x 8 CONCRETE
CLADDING OF PIERS
TO SUPPORT LEDGERS

4 x 4 PIER

8 x 8
CONCRETE

SECTION "X"

2 x 8
JOIST

INVERTED SHAKE
AS FILLER WEDGE

2 x 8 LEDGER

HOUSE
REAR
WALL

LAG
SCREW

2 x 4 RIBBON

SECTION "Y"

4 x 4
TRIM SURPLUS

2 x 6 LEDGER

2 x 8
JOIST

2 x 8
JOIST

2 x 4 RIBBON

2 x 4 RIBBON

2 x 8 LEDGER

½" CARRIAGE BOLTS
6" LONG

2 x 4 SCAB
DOWN TO BEAR
ON CONCRETE

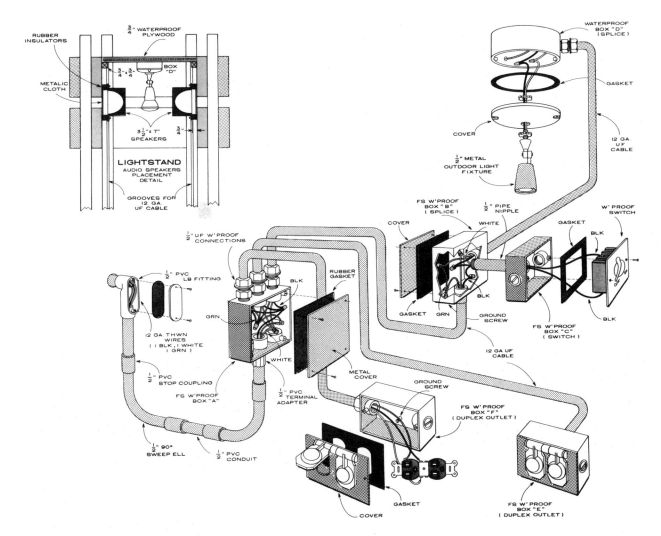

profile, while still maintaining the legal spaces and spans). When fastening border joists (and later, ribbon cleats), use 10d nails aimed slightly downward, so they tend to lock in when a load is applied.

Joists that are nailed to the side faces of piers or other joist ends should have a scab installed. A scab is simply a 2×4 or 2×6 face-nailed vertically to the pier so that it jambs between the concrete pier embedment and the bottom edge of the joist, providing additional reinforcement. Cut the remaining joists to length (between the main joists), drop them in and lay out the notches. Remove these joists and cut out the notches with a jigsaw, then drop them in and toenail them to the main joists.

Next, box in the pool area, toenailing in preassembled pairs of notched joists at both ends. Then, install preassembled pairs of joists (no notches) with metal hangers attached to the end joists along the sides. Add the floor support cleats, the floor, and the support plate for the toilet flush valve (this valve permits you to control the water level with the overflow pipe height, and drain the pool quickly). Nail in the pool sides and drape 4-mil black plastic (available from garden centers) in the pool box. Cut a hole in the plastic somewhat smaller than the sheet metal plate hole and apply bathtub sealer to both top and

bottom plastic surfaces around the hole, then install the valve. Fill the pool with water, trim the overflow pipe to get the desired level and check for leaks. Now, smooth the plastic against the pool surfaces and staple it to the top edge of the pool sides. Cut a small notch in the top edge of one of the sides, place the pump in the pool and run cord through the notch to the outside. Then, fit and nail the pool coaming (the top edging) in place over the cord and the stapled plastic. Trim the plastic. The final step for the pool is the installation of 2×4 vertical ribs between the coaming and the deck planking (so the coaming is strong enough for someone to sit on). This step must wait until the deck planking is down. Now, lay 4- to 6-mil plastic on the ground under the deck to suppress weed and grass growth; then spread some inexpensive stone around to keep the plastic in place.

Notch the sleepers (4×4s laid down on the ground to support planking) for the diamond and short walk. Assemble and nail. Before setting the assembly in place, level the area by removing dirt from the high spots, not by filling in the low spots. This method avoids fresh backfill settling after rain. Make the steps by either of the two methods shown: The first employs cutout stringers to support the treads; the second uses cleats and uncut string-

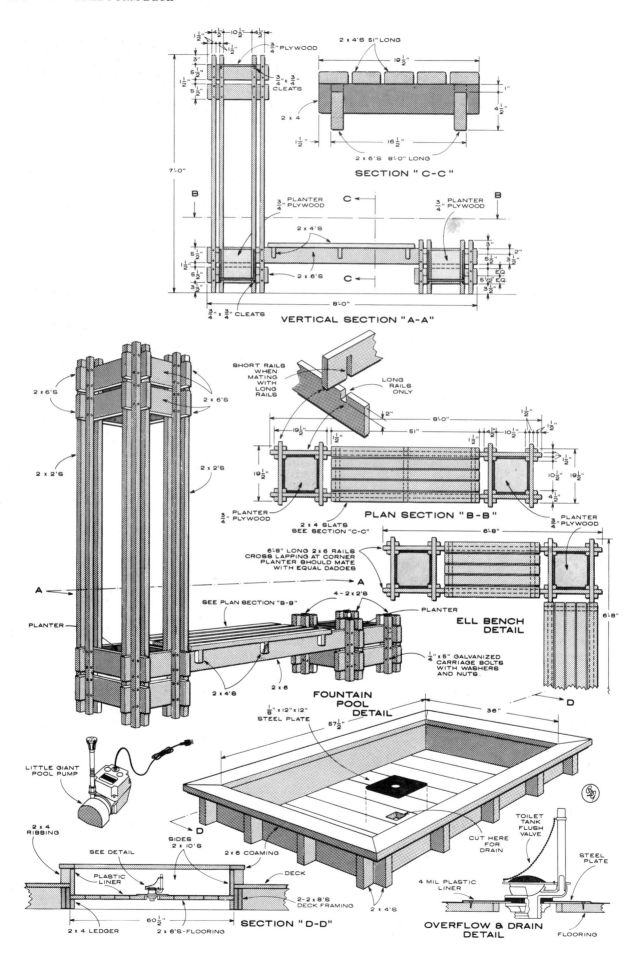

$\frac{3}{4}$" PLYWOOD

$\frac{3}{4}$" x $\frac{3}{4}$" CLEATS

2 x 4'S 51" LONG

2 x 4

2 x 6'S 8'-0" LONG

SECTION "C-C"

7'-0"

B

PLANTER $\frac{3}{4}$" PLYWOOD

C

2 x 4'S

C

PLANTER $\frac{3}{4}$" PLYWOOD

B

2 x 6'S

EQ. EQ.

$\frac{3}{4}$" x $\frac{3}{4}$" CLEATS

8'-0"

VERTICAL SECTION "A-A"

2 x 6'S

2 x 6'S

2 x 2'S

2 x 2'S

SHORT RAILS WHEN MATING WITH LONG RAILS

LONG RAILS ONLY

8'-0"

51"

19$\frac{1}{2}$"

19$\frac{1}{2}$"

$\frac{3}{4}$" PLANTER PLYWOOD

PLAN SECTION "B-B"

2 x 4 SLATS SEE SECTION "C-C"

6'-8" LONG 2 x 6 RAILS CROSS LAPPING AT CORNER PLANTER SHOULD MATE WITH EQUAL DADOES

A

$\frac{3}{4}$" PLANTER PLYWOOD

6'-8"

6'-8"

$\frac{3}{4}$" PLANTER PLYWOOD

ELL BENCH DETAIL

A

PLANTER

A

SEE PLAN SECTION "B-B"

4 - 2 x 2'S

PLANTER

$\frac{1}{4}$" x 5" GALVANIZED CARRIAGE BOLTS WITH WASHERS AND NUTS.

2 x 4'S

2 x 6

D

FOUNTAIN POOL DETAIL

$\frac{1}{8}$" x 12" x 12" STEEL PLATE

36"

57$\frac{1}{2}$"

LITTLE GIANT POOL PUMP

2 x 4 RIBBING

SEE DETAIL

PLASTIC LINER

SIDES 2 x 10'S

2 x 6 COAMING

D

DECK

CUT HERE FOR DRAIN

TOILET TANK FLUSH VALVE

STEEL PLATE

2 - 2 x 8'S DECK FRAMING

2 x 4'S

4 MIL PLASTIC LINER

60$\frac{1}{2}$"

2 x 4 LEDGER

2 x 6'S - FLOORING

SECTION "D-D"

OVERFLOW & DRAIN DETAIL

FLOORING

Position the pool between the first and second main joists. Box it with double 2×8s. The floor is made of 2×6s, over 2×4 support cleats.

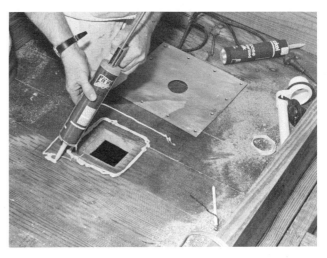

Saw hole in the center plank to serve as a pass-through for plastic toilet flush valve. Caulk and screw down the metal retaining plate.

Light-and-sound post floodlights planter and stairs. Stereo speakers can be installed in top to provide low-level background music at this distance from the house. The planters are designed to take plastic wastebaskets, which serve as flower pots.

ers. In either case, install the steps before starting the planking. The planking overhangs the border joists and it would be difficult to get to these areas out of this sequence.

Follow the electrical drawing, starting with the GFI (ground fault interrupter) breaker. Dig in the PVC conduit 12″ below grade and mount all FS boxes except those that will go on the post lamp. Connect the THWN (Thermoplastic, Heat resistant, Wet location, Nylon jacket) 12-gauge wire from the PVC underground conduit to the UF (Underground Feeder) cable (which is used on the deck intself) at main joist-mounted FS (catalog term for weatherproof box) box. Then, bring the UF branches up to the pool and post lamp areas. After planking, install a duplex receptale by the pool. The remaining electrical work (a duplex receptacle, light switch and post light) is completed when the post light and bench are in place. Make sure that you ground all indicated boxes.

Planking

Saw the 4×4 piers off flush with the joists, then fasten the 2×4 planking perpendicular to the notched joists on

The pump has a removable screen that can be adjusted to 10′.

Approximate the desired free-form profile with piers and border joists, maintaining the allowed spans and the 24″ on-center spacing.

After the 4×4 sleepers (diamond and short walk) are set on plastic, which has been placed over level ground, the stair stringers are nailed.

Understructure shows the main, notched and border joists; ledger; ribbon cleats; pool. Lumber is treated with Koppers Wolman process.

Planking is nailed with 8d common galvanized nails. Space the planks with 10d nails, and wedge them, using a screwdriver for the job.

PVC ½″ conduit from under the deck enters the main, weatherproof electrical box. From here, electricity goes to post light and fountain.

The treads of the side stairs are supported with cleated stringers, while a flat sleeper at the bottom supports the lower stair end.

Planking laid diagonally on the diamond deck parallels the planking on the stairs. The opening around the tree is treated with plastic and stone.

When removing waste stock from the notches with a chisel and hammer, be sure that the flat side of the chisel faces away from the opening.

Use a flexed piece of molding to trace the free-form deck outline. Then you can trim to the line with a reciprocating saw or jigsaw.

When assembling the benches, it helps to put the structure on stands or boxes and to clamp the area you're working on.

Bench notches can be gang-sawed or cut with a jig or bayonet saw. It just takes a little longer for the individual marking and cutting of the notches.

the top and mail levels and diagonally on the diamond using 8d nails. To make sure that your planking comes out properly on the top level, start the planking at the step edge of the top level, and work toward the house wall. Trim the last plank to fit against the wall, if necessary, but leave the next-to-the-last plank out until you've nailed in the last one so you'll be able to nail everything in easily.

Allow the ends of planks to overhang border joists by about 1' after rough sawing the edge. To get a pleasing curve, flex a batten or thin molding to a shape that you like and follow the molding curve with a pencil line. Cut the curve with a good jigsaw or reciprocating saw, and belt-sand any rough spots. *Note:* Depending on the width of the deck at a particular point, you may need two lengths of 2×4 planking to cover the span—if so, trim planks so that each spans at least three joists, and toenail planks at the butt joint to the joist below.

Benches

Cut out and trim to size all component parts at one time, then lay out all notches. Make the necessary crosscuts, and chisel away the waste, completing the notches. Test the fit with the mating pieces and mark the parts for assembly. Use a table saw or power router to make the grooves to accommodate the UF cable that runs up the post light 2×2s. Assemble the benches as shown, drilling and bolting to complete the assembly. Nail on the bench slats and install ½" A-C plywood panels in the planters to support flower containers.

With the exception of the post light and bench, no bolting to the deck is necessary due to the ample weight of the units. You'll want to bolt down the post light and bench unit because of its height and the UF cable running through it from the deck. Use either galvanized angle or steel angle sprayed with cold galvanizing compound (1½"×1½"×⅛" plus 2" carriage bolts and 1½" lags for attachment to the deck work well).

Finish by spreading a couple of tons of small, colored stones around the edges and slightly underneath the deck. We used ⅜" yellow stone over the plastic ground cover.

Pool serves as focal point on second level of deck. Unique post light and planter benches add interest to broad expanse of deck.

21

Kid's Wonder Gym

"**W**hat's there to do?" If you have kids between 4 and 10, you probably heard that question over and over this past summer. To make sure you don't hear it quite as often next summer, you can start building our outdoor Wonder Gym right now in your own backyard.

Outdoor gym sets are just plain fun for kids, while helping to develop their physical skills and coordination. And the best part is that you know where the kids are.

Two basic commercial types are in general use today: (1) pipe assemblies with bipod leg supports and (2) wooden combination climbers typically sold in kit form by mail order. The pipe units provide limited activities and are prone to weather and rust problems. Wooden kits, on the other hand, are more versatile but come with a heavy price tag.

The outdoor Wonder Gym shown here provides a wide range of activities and offers safe and simple construction for years of trouble-free fun. With the exception of a few exterior grade A-C plywood panels, all lumber is dimensioned Wolmanized®, pressure-treated wood and the hardware is hot-dipped galvanized.

Tool requirements are minimal. You probably have almost everything necessary to do the job. With three or four weekends and a minimal cash outlay, you'll come out with a play center worth much more.

Assembly

You can get started by preparing all 2×4s for the ladders, braces, arms and supports. Smooth all four edges of each piece using a power router and a rounding-over bit. Because a large part of the design is merely assembling the ladders, it's best to make them up now. Cut the rungs to length from 1⅛" closet pole. Cut them to 17½" for all ladders, except the long horizontal and short "tree house" access ladder, which are 14½". Discard any cracked or heavily splintered rungs. Then sand the good rungs and finish them with two coats of urethane, sanding between coats. At the same time, finish six lengths of ¾″×36″ dowel. These will tie the ladders together at the house end of the structure.

While the rungs and dowels are drying, set out the ladder sides in pairs and mark off the rung centers about 11″ apart. Now attach a drill with a ⅜″, 24-thread shaft to a drilling guide. Chuck up a 1⅛″-diameter spade bit and set the lock collar for a cut depth of ¾″. When you drill the rung holes with this setup, you'll get flat-bottomed holes, drilled in at 90° to the faces of the ladder sides, making for accurate assembly.

Lay one side of each ladder down on a flat surface with the holes facing up. Then tap in the rungs. Place the matching side over the erect rungs, holes facing down and tap down, driving the rungs home in their seats. Complete this work on all ladders and check that the narrow ladders will just fit between the sides of the wider ladders. To lock the rungs, first drill a ⅛″-diameter hole through the edge of the ladder side at each rung position and then drive in a shake nail through the rung to pin it.

As you can see, the slides form an integral part of the bracing, so make them up before starting the major assembly. Each slide requires a pair of 2×4 sides, a plywood center, two pieces of half-round molding and some 20″-

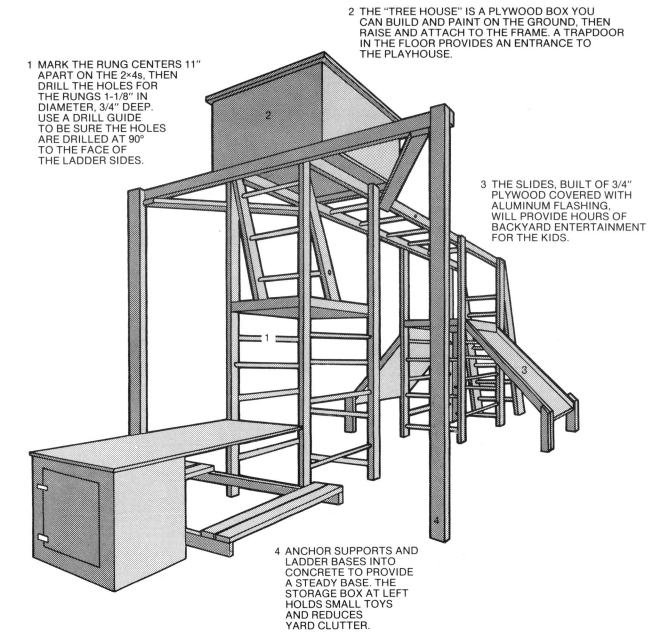

2 THE "TREE HOUSE" IS A PLYWOOD BOX YOU CAN BUILD AND PAINT ON THE GROUND, THEN RAISE AND ATTACH TO THE FRAME. A TRAPDOOR IN THE FLOOR PROVIDES AN ENTRANCE TO THE PLAYHOUSE.

1 MARK THE RUNG CENTERS 11″ APART ON THE 2×4s, THEN DRILL THE HOLES FOR THE RUNGS 1-1/8″ IN DIAMETER, 3/4″ DEEP. USE A DRILL GUIDE TO BE SURE THE HOLES ARE DRILLED AT 90° TO THE FACE OF THE LADDER SIDES.

3 THE SLIDES, BUILT OF 3/4″ PLYWOOD COVERED WITH ALUMINUM FLASHING, WILL PROVIDE HOURS OF BACKYARD ENTERTAINMENT FOR THE KIDS.

4 ANCHOR SUPPORTS AND LADDER BASES INTO CONCRETE TO PROVIDE A STEADY BASE. THE STORAGE BOX AT LEFT HOLDS SMALL TOYS AND REDUCES YARD CLUTTER.

Build it in four easy steps: The Wonder Gym is made up of a combination of ladders, framework, boxes and slides. You build the separate components separately, then bolt it all together.

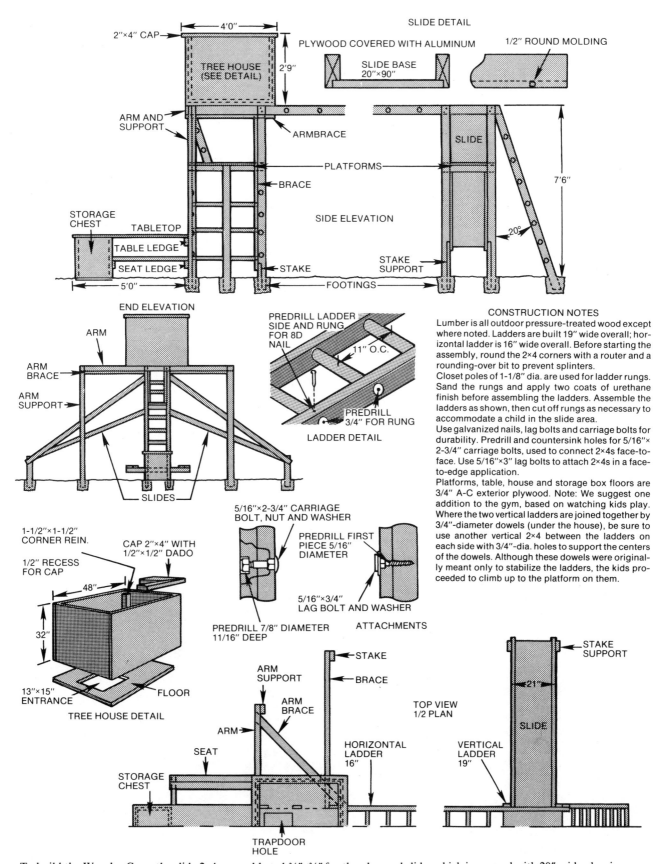

SLIDE DETAIL

2"×4" CAP

4'0"

TREE HOUSE (SEE DETAIL)

2'9"

PLYWOOD COVERED WITH ALUMINUM

SLIDE BASE 20"×90"

1/2" ROUND MOLDING

ARM AND SUPPORT

ARMBRACE

PLATFORMS

BRACE

SLIDE

SIDE ELEVATION

7'6"

STORAGE CHEST

TABLETOP

TABLE LEDGE

SEAT LEDGE

STAKE

STAKE SUPPORT

20°

5'0"

FOOTINGS

END ELEVATION

ARM

ARM BRACE

ARM SUPPORT

SLIDES

PREDRILL LADDER SIDE AND RUNG FOR 8D NAIL

11" O.C.

PREDRILL 3/4" FOR RUNG

LADDER DETAIL

CONSTRUCTION NOTES

Lumber is all outdoor pressure-treated wood except where noted. Ladders are built 19" wide overall; horizontal ladder is 16" wide overall. Before starting the assembly, round the 2×4 corners with a router and a rounding-over bit to prevent splinters.

Closet poles of 1-1/8" dia. are used for ladder rungs. Sand the rungs and apply two coats of urethane finish before assembling the ladders. Assemble the ladders as shown, then cut off rungs as necessary to accommodate a child in the slide area.

Use galvanized nails, lag bolts and carriage bolts for durability. Predrill and countersink holes for 5/16"× 2-3/4" carriage bolts, used to connect 2×4s face-to-face. Use 5/16"×3" lag bolts to attach 2×4s in a face-to-edge application.

Platforms, table, house and storage box floors are 3/4" A-C exterior plywood. Note: We suggest one addition to the gym, based on watching kids play. Where the two vertical ladders are joined together by 3/4"-diameter dowels (under the house), be sure to use another vertical 2×4 between the ladders on each side with 3/4"-dia. holes to support the centers of the dowels. Although these dowels were originally meant only to stabilize the ladders, the kids proceeded to climb up to the platform on them.

1-1/2"×1-1/2" CORNER REIN.

1/2" RECESS FOR CAP

CAP 2"×4" WITH 1/2"×1/2" DADO

48"

32"

13"×15" ENTRANCE

FLOOR

TREE HOUSE DETAIL

5/16"×2-3/4" CARRIAGE BOLT, NUT AND WASHER

PREDRILL FIRST PIECE 5/16" DIAMETER

5/16"×3/4" LAG BOLT AND WASHER

PREDRILL 7/8" DIAMETER 11/16" DEEP

ATTACHMENTS

STAKE

ARM SUPPORT

ARM BRACE

BRACE

ARM

SEAT

STORAGE CHEST

TRAPDOOR HOLE

HORIZONTAL LADDER 16"

TOP VIEW 1/2 PLAN

STAKE SUPPORT

21"

SLIDE

VERTICAL LADDER 19"

To build the Wonder Gym, the slide 2×4s are rabbeted ¾"×¾" for the plywood slide, which is covered with 20"-wide aluminum flashing. A ½"-round molding at the top of the slide permits aluminum to be formed around the end and nailed from the bottom so nails are concealed. Anchor 2×4 braces, supports and ladders 6" into the ground. The tree house and storage box are of ½" sides, ¾" plywood floors. Corner reinforcing is 2×2s.

wide aluminum flashing. First rout or saw-in the rabbets on the sides. Then nail a piece of molding to each end of the plywood. Roll a fitted piece of flashing over these rounded ends and nail them fast at the bottom. Be sure to nail the flat part of the flashing to the plywood on the top, very near the edge. This will make sure that these nails will be hidden by the shoulder of the rabbet in the sides. Finish the slides by nailing the aluminum sheathed plywood center to sides from the bottom.

Next drill the ¾″-diameter holes 1″ deep into the edges of the ladders that support the house. These holes will accept the ¾″-diameter dowels that you have already

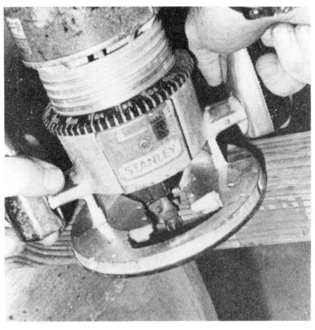

All 2×4s should have all edges smoothed by running a router over them with a rounding-over bit. This eliminates splinters.

Use an angle drive on your drill when making the recessed bores in the horizontal ladder sides. Space here is limited.

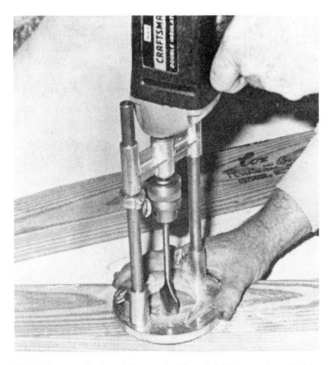

Make the rung holes with a spade bit and drill motor installed in a drilling jig. Hole will be 90° to face.

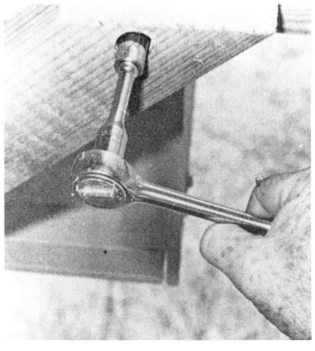

The ⅞″-diameter hole drilled in previous photo is ideal for pocketing the nut, washer and bolt shank. A socket wrench works well.

finished and add greater strength to the ladder pair. Lock these dowels as you did the rungs, and you're ready to start the major assembly.

Use the carriage bolts to attach all the vertical ladders and the angled ladder at the end to the main horizontal ladder (two bolts at each joint). So that no bolts protrude

Use temporary bracing to align. Level and plumb the structure before putting in the concrete footing.

After "tree house" is assembled on the ground, it's painted, then placed into position and attached.

from the structure, use the following method to drill and fasten the members once they're clamped in position. Drill a ⅞"-diameter hole from one side to a depth of 11/16" with a spade bit. Then use the pilot hole of the spade bit as the drill center for a 5/16"-diameter bit to run the bolt hole through to the outer face of the second member. When you insert the carriage bolt from the side opposite the spade bit hole, you'll be able to install the washer and nut completely below the wood surface.

Try to get a helping hand at this point because the project will grow larger and heavier very rapidly. The major assembly can be bolted together either on its side or in an inverted position with the vertical ladders sticking up. Mark out the locations for the four vertical ladders on the long horizontal ladder. But be sure to allow 21½" between the ladders that hold the slides and enough room at the end for the angled ladder that will be attached later. Make sure that you insert a carpenter's or rafter square at the junction formed by the horizontal and vertical ladders to get 90° angles.

Placement

When the basic bolting has been completed, set the assembly upright and nail on some scrap bracing to keep things from getting out of hand. Because the vertical ladders are 8' high, you'll be able to set about 6" of the ladder sides into a concrete base and still have a height of about 7'6" at the top of the horizontal ladder. Use pre-mixed dry aggregate in bags (80 pounds dry weight will make 0.6 cubic feet of wet concrete) since only a small volume will be required.

Tilt the assembly to one side to dig out the footing holes on the other side, then reverse the procedure. Install the angled end ladder at this time and dig its footing holes. The slides, side braces and their stakes should be installed now as well. The upper ends of the slides and braces attach to their respective ladder sides in a face surface-to-edge surface manner, so for all such joints, use 5/16"-diameter, 3"-long lag bolts with washers. Remember to recess the heads as before.

Adjust your scrap bracing so that the horizontal ladder is level and the vertical ladders are plumb on two adjacent faces when checked with a 4' level. Mix and pour concrete into all the holes. Then allow the concrete to cure for 72 hours, sprinkling with water occasionally during the period.

When the concrete has cured, add the arm, arm supports and horizontal arm braces. Then imbed the arm supports in concrete just as before.

Cut the two platforms (between the slides and underneath the house) from ¾" A-C plywood. Notch the corners to clear the ladder sides; sand and paint them. When the paint and concrete are dry, nail in the platforms and their supports.

Adding the latch to the storage box door with seats, tabletop and their ledgers already installed. The arms, braces and slides are visible.

The swings, ropes, climbers and rings complete the Wonder Gym. These items are available at discount stores or at your local home center.

Finish Work

Both the "tree house" and storage box are constructed from plywood reinforced at the corners with 2×2s (1½"×1½") ripped from 2×4s. Make the floor of the house, tabletop and storage box from ¾" and the house sides from ½" A.C. plywood. Assemble the house on the ground, paint it and place it in position. Bolt it to the arm and horizontal ladder with lag bolts recessing the heads as usual.

Cut an access hole about 13"×15" in the floor of the house and make a two-layered cover for the hole (one piece inserts to locate the cover and the top layer overlaps the hole). Rout or saw a ½" square dado in the bottom side of the house side cap 2×6s. Miter the corners and install them with nails. Finish off the house area by installing the short access ladder between the platform and the access hole.

The height of the tabletop, storage box and seat depend on the size of your kids, so do a little test seating to determine this dimension before bolting the seat and tabletop ledgers in place. (You can change this height later on as the kids grow.) Mount the storage box on 2×4 sleepers (direct ground contact supports), bolt the ledgers onto the ladder edges and the box side, then install the seats and tabletop. Paint the box and tabletop, then hinge the door and install a latch.

Now make a trip to the store to buy a variety of swings, ropes, climbers, and rings. Suspend the apparatus from the arm and horizontal ladder lower edges with 5/16" screw-eyes and "S" hooks. You'll be able to easily remove everything for winter storage, or when you go on vacation. Final tip: By bolting the major assemblies, you make it easier to move the gym when you change homes.

22

Garden Shed/Greenhouse

The garden shed/greenhouse is built on an 8'×12' floor plan. The greenhouse end (top) occupies about one-third of the area. The garden shed portion (above) has a wide door and ramp for parking your garden tractor. The structure sits on a network of several 6"×6" railroad ties.

The greening of lawns and the flowering of houses and grounds are two earthly pleasures many home-owners delight in but, alas, usually without the advantages and usefulness of a special place for centering these activities. All too often, the garden tractor is pinned by the car's bumper in the garage and potting tools are jumbled in a plastic carryall on top of a garbage can filled with soil mix.

All of these things can be put right for you, here and now, with a little structure for the backyard that will capture the heart of anyone who has ever put thumb to dirt. It is our garden shed/greenhouse...great to look at, delightful for puttering and potting and tremendously useful as a home for all the tools, equipment and needs of lawn and garden care. The garden shed/greenhouse also is a project you and yours can build yourselves.

The construction is sound. There are few frills, therefore natural good looks. The materials you need all come straight from a local lumberyard and a home-center store. The building's plan is an example of clear-and-simple thinking. And the shed/greenhouse is manageable—built on an 8'×12' floor plan, just about the area of the average livingroom rug.

The floor is supported by a network of 6"×6" railroad-tie sleepers. They're lap-joined with a chain saw, hammered, chiseled, then fastened together with ⅜"×12" spikes.

We drilled through the ties and staked them to the ground with lengths of concrete reinforcing rods driven 2' down. The ties are carefully dug into the ground to assure a square and level foundation. Apply creosote to cut laps.

The floor (marine plywood is preferable) consists of three 4'×8' sheets nailed to the ties. A full sheet, incidentally, can be used as an excellent squaring gauge or guide.

We decided to use precut studs for the wall framing—92⅝" long. When used with a sole plate and a double top plate, you get a wall just a hair over 97" high. These saved cutting times. You can save additional time by using 4×4s at the corners instead of the usual three-ganged 2×4s (typically used to provide structural strength and to serve as nailers for interior drywall surfacing). Whenever possible, use full length 2×stock for the plates for the additional strength and time savings.

A good method for laying out the walls is to nail the sole plates in their places right away. Then, nail the top plates for a wall together, staggering them the width of a 2×4 (3½") at each end (for lap-joining the walls later).

Next, temporarily tack the assembled top plate upside down to the sole plate. Mark off the 16" centers and carry these marks across and down. This guarantees parallel studding. The precuts assure parallel plates; the use of a level and diagonal bracing assures a square structure.

With the marking complete, remove the top-plate assembly from the sole plate, lay it down and toenail all of the required studs to it (with the exception of trimmers and cripples, which support the headers over window and door openings). *Note:* The door headers are two 2×8s with a piece of ½" CDX sandwiched between, and the window headers are two 2×6s with ½" CDX. This brings them to the face dimension of the 2×4. Complete the framing in these areas.

Then, with a couple of helpers, erect the partially complete wall over the sole plate and toenail the studs in place. Brace the wall and go on to the next walls in order, lap-joining the corners as you proceed.

Add the trimmers, heads, cripples and rough sills to all walls and install the stud blocking in the greenhouse area. This is the highest point for the sheathing at this end. Next, mark the locations of the joists and rafters on the top surfaces of the top plates on the two long walls.

Set up your rafter square for a 6 (rise)/12 (run) roof angle with screw-on angle guides and lay out the rafters and joist ends. Note that each of the rafters has a bird's-mouth (notch) that fits the top plates and a tail that extends 1' beyond the walls.

Follow the step-off rafter layout in the drawing and then cut out one pair, to test for accuracy, before cutting the remaining rafters. Don't dismantle the guides from the square—you need the setup again for the gable fascias.

Figure the height of the ridge board and brace it in position so you can get the rafters on accurately. Nail the joists on at the same time—to the top plates and to the

The floor consists of three 4×8 sheets of marine plywood nailed to railroad ties. The framing is conventional throughout. Here, the roof sheathing is nailed to the roof rafters.

Sheathing is applied to the wall studs. Note the blocking between the studs delineating the greenhouse end. Note, too, how the rafter ends are notched in a bird-mouth pattern.

The greenhouse wall is sheathed to the blocking; the sheathing is covered with felt paper. Framing for the entry door is trimmed later with fluted casing and bull's-eyes.

Felt paper is applied to the roof sheathing (with a hammer-tacker for speedy installation) and to the ridge portion that extends over the greenhouse. Scaffolding is convenient.

Vertical corner trim is applied, clearing the way for installation of the finished clapboard siding. To avoid damage to the clapboard, predrill the holes, then drive the nails.

rafters (the rafters are on 24″ centers and the joists are on 16″ and will only meet at the 48″ and 96″ points, except for the joists in the 4′ greenhouse area). Install the 2×6 blocking between the rafters in the greenhouse area. These provide support for the plastic roof that is installed later.

Use joist cutoffs to fill the small triangular gaps on the rafter tails; these give you a full, horizontal nailing surface for the soffits. Fill in the gable with studding at the storage end, but leave a space for the installation of the exhaust fan and its exterior vent.

Apply sheathing to the sides and roof and to the roof portion extending out from the greenhouse end. This portion of roof sheathing goes down only to the top rafter blockings. Don't nail the top edge of the lower-section sheathing to the stud blocking yet, because the plastic roof portion gets tucked in behind.

Install felt paper to both the roof and the sides with a hammer-tacker or with roofing nails. According to the procedure, you don't have to put paper behind horizontal siding, but if you have enough left over from the roll after doing the roof, it won't hurt.

Next, install ¾″-thick jambs in both of the door openings.

Build the window boxes and struts, then machine the dentil strips and window and door casings. Cut the sills, battens, fascias and fascia trim. Incidentally, the rake fascias and trim need the rafter-square step-off to get the end angles correct. Make the doors and shutters, then start painting.

The stock windows have to be carefully stripped of their casings to receive the Victorian-style casings. Use a router with core-box bit and edge guide to make the evenly spaced four flutes. Then a circle cutter on a drill press is used to make a concentric circle of the bull's-eye. Enlarge the circle-cutter pilot hole for hardwood button in the bull's-eye. A saw kerf gives square-block appearance around the bull's-eye. Assemble the casings.

Now, back at the building, nail the ledger (to be used as a nailer for the soffit) in the storage area. You can't use an equivalent nailer in the greenhouse area because it must be installed over a vertical plastic surface. Next is the installation of the plastic.

We used 4′-wide Solar-Gro, manufactured by Filon. The best way to lay it out is with a felt marker, noting the labels indicating outside surface.

Some people like to scribe, then snap this material, but sharp snips do the cutting just fine. Special aluminum nails with weatherproof neoprene washers are the proper fasteners to use and be sure to drive them where you want them.

Many lumberyards tell you that you must predrill for the nails, but we found this unnecessary. However, if you experience any crazing or cracking without drilling, the solution is predrilling. Caulk thoroughly at joints; it is covered later by the trim.

Fit all the plastic in the greenhouse area except the soffit pieces. Then nail the ledger over both side (vertical)

The interior of the garden shed/greenhouse is surprisingly spacious, allowing ample floor space for tractor parking, maintenance walk-around, potting table and plant displays. The walls have pegboards with hooks for garden tool storage. Ceiling joists are unsheathed which makes them ideal for hanging a variety of plants. You can alter the interior arrangement of your structure if more greenhouse and less storage area is needed; if so, simply extend the greenhouse roof back toward the midpoint.

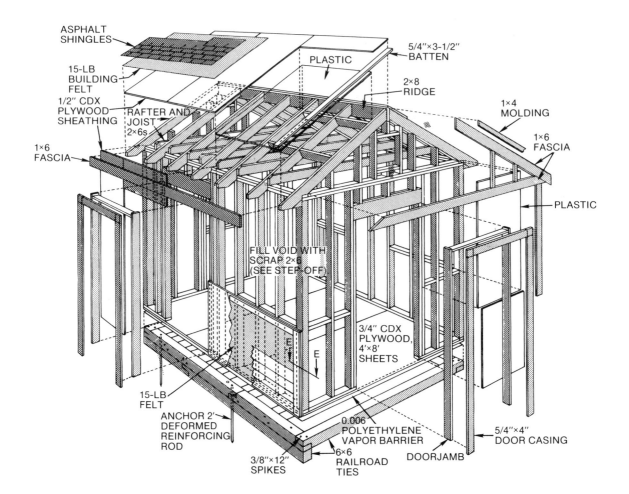

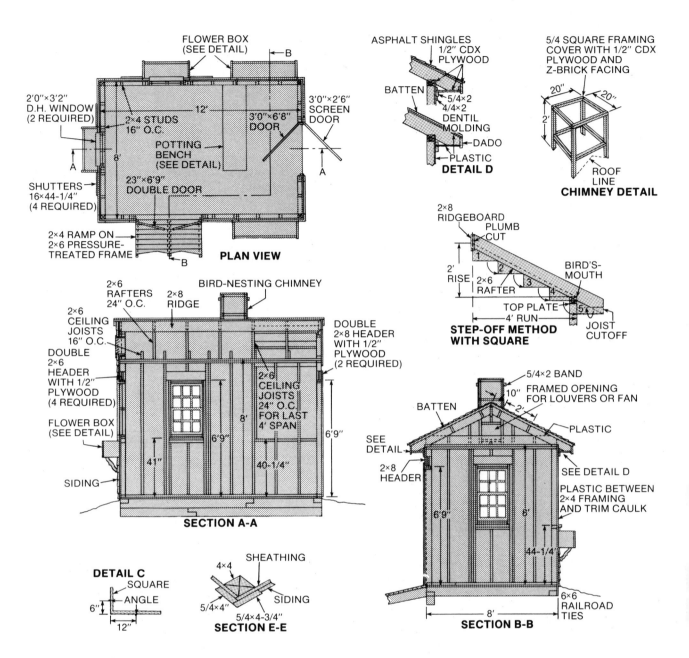

PLAN VIEW

FLOWER BOX (SEE DETAIL)
2'0"×3'2" D.H. WINDOW (2 REQUIRED)
2×4 STUDS 16" O.C.
POTTING BENCH (SEE DETAIL)
3'0"×6'8" DOORS
3'0"×2'6" SCREEN DOOR
12'
8'
SHUTTERS 16×44-1/4" (4 REQUIRED)
23"×6'9" DOUBLE DOOR
2×4 RAMP ON 2×6 PRESSURE-TREATED FRAME

ASPHALT SHINGLES
1/2" CDX PLYWOOD
BATTEN
5/4×2
4/4×2
DENTIL MOLDING
DADO
PLASTIC
DETAIL D

5/4 SQUARE FRAMING COVER WITH 1/2" CDX PLYWOOD AND Z-BRICK FACING
20"
20"
2'
ROOF LINE
CHIMNEY DETAIL

SECTION A-A

2×6 RAFTERS 24" O.C.
2×8 RIDGE
BIRD-NESTING CHIMNEY
2×6 CEILING JOISTS 16" O.C.
DOUBLE 2×6 HEADER WITH 1/2" PLYWOOD (4 REQUIRED)
FLOWER BOX (SEE DETAIL)
SIDING
DOUBLE 2×8 HEADER WITH 1/2" PLYWOOD (2 REQUIRED)
2×6 CEILING JOISTS 24" O.C. FOR LAST 4' SPAN
8'
6'9"
41"
40-1/4"

2×8 RIDGEBOARD
PLUMB CUT
2' RISE
2×6 RAFTER
BIRD'S-MOUTH
TOP PLATE
4' RUN
JOIST CUTOFF
STEP-OFF METHOD WITH SQUARE

DETAIL C
SQUARE
ANGLE
6"
12"

SECTION E-E
SHEATHING
4×4
5/4×4"
5/4×4-3/4"
SIDING

SECTION B-B
5/4×2 BAND
FRAMED OPENING FOR LOUVERS OR FAN
10"
BATTEN
SEE DETAIL
2×8 HEADER
PLASTIC
SEE DETAIL D
PLASTIC BETWEEN 2×4 FRAMING AND TRIM CAULK
6'9"
6'
44-1/4"
8'
6×6 RAILROAD TIES

plastic surfaces, followed by the plastic soffit. Install the greenhouse vent.

The fascias attach to the rafter tails and are divided into two parts for each side. One part is about 8' long and covers the storage area. The other, about 4' long, is for the greenhouse area. That 4'-long fascia is kerfed on its inner face to pocket the outer edge of the plastic soffit. Of course, the top edges of all fascias attached to rafter tails must be bevel-cut to the roof angle. Nail on all remaining soffits, fascia and frieze (ornamented) boards.

Assemble all of the 5/4 corners into "L"-shaped assemblies before installing them on the structure. While you're at it, make sure the bottom edges of all corners are in the same vertical position so the siding is level afterward. Note that the sill in the greenhouse area provides a vertical break for the transition from sheathing to plastic; caulk it well.

After nailing in the windows, install the fascias and trim pieces on both gable ends as well as on the surrounds for the vents. At the storage-gable end, join the vertical corners to the rake fascia with trim. At the greenhouse gable, nail on the horizontal trim covering the double top plates and blend them into the rake fascias. Install the door casings and trim the perimeter of the plastic at this time. Add the remaining vertical and roof battens at your convenience. Start the roofing now.

When roofing, note the following: (1) A starter strip made from shingles must be installed at the lower edge of the roof. The starter shingles are inverted to fill the tab slots under the first shingle row and to continue the shingle rake to the edge of the roof. (2) Stagger adjacent rows of shingles to line up the keys and to alternate the joints. (3) Line up adjacent rows of shingles with chalk lines snapped on the felt paper.

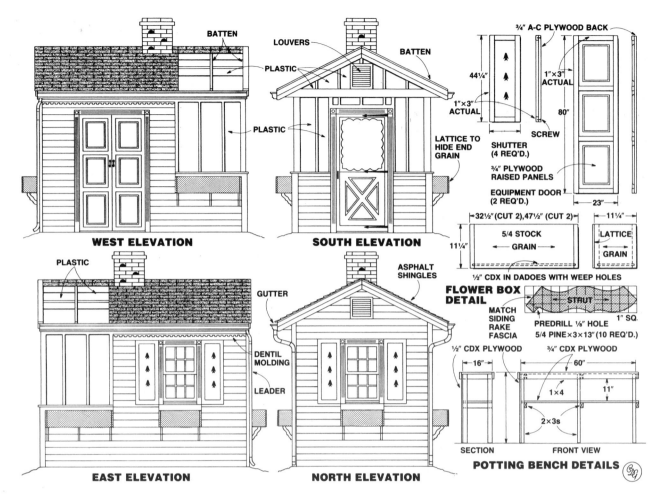

WEST ELEVATION

SOUTH ELEVATION

EAST ELEVATION

NORTH ELEVATION

BATTEN
LOUVERS
PLASTIC
BATTEN
PLASTIC
PLASTIC
LATTICE TO HIDE END GRAIN
PLASTIC
GUTTER
DENTIL MOLDING
LEADER
ASPHALT SHINGLES

¾" A-C PLYWOOD BACK
1"×3" ACTUAL
44¼"
1"×3" ACTUAL
80"
SCREW
SHUTTER (4 REQ'D.)
¾" PLYWOOD RAISED PANELS
EQUIPMENT DOOR (2 REQ'D.)
23"
11¼"
LATTICE
GRAIN
32½" (CUT 2), 47½" (CUT 2)
5/4 STOCK
GRAIN
11¼"
½" CDX IN DADOES WITH WEEP HOLES

FLOWER BOX DETAIL
MATCH SIDING RAKE FASCIA
STRUT
1" SQ.
PREDRILL ⅛" HOLE
5/4 PINE×3×13" (10 REQ'D.)
½" CDX PLYWOOD
¾" CDX PLYWOOD
16"
60"
11"
1×4
2×3s
SECTION
FRONT VIEW
POTTING BENCH DETAILS

(4) Cover the hip with shingle pieces (three from each shingle) after both sides of the roof have been shingled. (5) Use four roofing nails per shingle in the main field.

Saw off all overhanging roof trims and complete all the trim installation. Mount the flower boxes but not their struts. They go on after the siding, as do the shutters and dentil moldings. Nail on the gutters but not the leaders because the leader hooks may interfere with the siding in those areas. Install drip moldings over doors and windows.

Before cutting any siding, determine how many rows from the bottom are needed to cover the wall using a weather exposure of 4½" to 4⅝" (for 6" bevel siding). Provide a starter strip about ¼" thick around the wall bottom so the last siding piece has a rake angle.

When cutting the siding, work to avoid joints. Use a veneer blade to cut through the reverse side.

When installing the siding, predrill it to prevent the shake nails from splitting the wood. The installation is much easier if you have several combination squares set up for the weather exposure, especially when handling long pieces. When nailing, don't hit too hard—it's not necessary and may split the wood. You can notch around obstacles such as windows quite easily by cutting with a fine-tooth saw, removing the waste with a utility knife. All nails should go into studs. Driving nails into the bottom edge of siding (through the top edge of the piece below it), results in patching.

We used another technique. We nailed near the top of each piece so that the higher piece would conceal the nails. When the siding is installed, bead caulk at siding ends and on all corners, windows, window boxes and trim.

Because dentil molding is very fragile to stock, I found I had to make it. Use either 1×2 or 1×3 pine stock for molding. To set up jig as shown, first install dado blades and remove the guard. Position the dado insert and adjust the height of the blades to ¾". Attach the backup from scrap to the miter head. Measure ¾" to the right of the blade set and clamp a guide in place. Check that guide is parallel to the blades.

Start at the right edge of the workpiece and hold it against the backup; make the cut. Reposition the work-piece so that the first cut rides over the guide; bring the miter head up and push through dado for the second cut. Continue making parallel cuts.

Nail on the dentil molding, shutters, window box struts, leaders, doors and pegboards for tools. Make a potting bench of several 2×3 A-frames, 1×3s and plywood. Spread stone around the shed perimeter to soften the edges, and you're ready for some serious greening and growing.

23

Masonry Planter

T he appearance of our 40'-long asphalt driveway was marred when a pair of huge oak trees suddenly cropped out along one edge. So we decided to conceal this by constructing a shapely masonry divider-planter to divert attention from it.

Planning and Choosing Materials

Initially our choice of materials included brick of various shapes and colors, stone, slate and flagstone. However, one day, while browsing through some products in a local fireplace store, we came across a material called cultured veneer-stone. Lightweight and attractive, we decided it was the most practical material for the main surface of the divider-planter. Cast, cultured veneer-stone is considerably lighter than stone, cuts very easily and is handled with standard masonry techniques.

Veneer-stone is available in a variety of shapes (simulating different stones) and colors. The manufacturer even makes an ell-shape corner piece in a number of thicknesses. The cultured type is manufactured by Stucco-Stone of California and is sold throughout the country. Its price varies regionally.

Working with actual stone requires both skill and muscle. In discussing our divider/planter with the owner of the local fireplace store, he suggested that for an exterior wall application the job would be easier if the top edges were covered with a brick cap. Also, the brick cap would bring out the beauty of the curved shape.

The skills required to build this planter are modest. Breaking block, more or less to the size you need, is one requirement and laying brick or block is the other. The remainder of the work involves shaping the blocks, mixing mortar and moving things around.

Preparing and Laying Block

We started by cutting away the grass between two parallel but curved lines. Next, we trenched out the dirt to the depth of the frost line. Check your local codes for the required depth. For the concrete, we used an instant-mix

truck, some rakes and a come-along to drag the mix. We pushed down the aggregate from the surface, generally leveling the top. Then we waited until the water rose and fell before floating the concrete again.

Our basic planter design was serpentine, divided into a number of compartments formed by bridging between the walls. Each compartment is leveled across its top. The levels gradually step down from the center out to each end. After allowing the concrete to cure for three days, we mixed the mortar. Following the outline of the foundation, we then laid in the block.

All the block, laid at the foundation level as 8″ wide, be it 4″ or 8″ thick. By laying the 4″ block on its side at the foundation, it's easy to make the weep holes for draining the water from the planter. To make straight block fit the curve, we knocked the ears off some of the stretcher blocks and broke others apart by scoring them completely around a break line and then cracking them apart. Compartment levels differing by 4″ can be achieved by using 4″ block in one compartment and 8″ block in the next. If you wish an 8″ difference in height, simply use one less course of 8″ block in the lower compartment.

The final trick is to keep a level run of block where the foundation slopes. For this, we used broken block chips and mortar to wedge under a full block as the foundation fell away. However, this is required only between the foundation and the first block course. As the walls begin to take shape, check frequently for plumb with your level, and make sure that both walls are even and parallel.

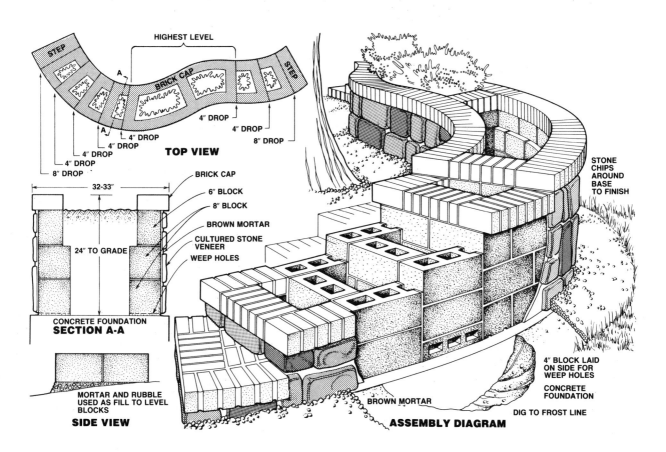

Rakes and a come-along are used to drag the mix.

To lay block, throw two ribbons of mortar on the block or concrete base.

Aggregate is pushed down and the top is leveled.

Butter the end of the next block and position it.

Our lawn and foundation slopes away so different thicknesses of block plus some mortar keep the different heights level.

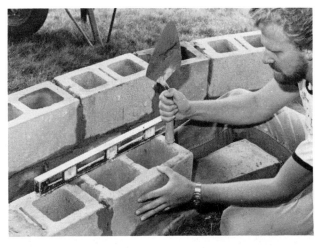

Set and level the blocks.

Laying the block itself isn't difficult. Throw or place two ribbons of mortar onto the block or concrete below. These contact the bottom edges of the block to be laid. Before setting the new block in place, butter the ends with mortar. Don't allow the mortar to drop out while the block is being positioned. Level the block along its top in both directions. Scrape or strike off the excess mortar at the joint with the trowel. Also try to bond the blocks as much as possible in a running bond for strength. This means that joints of one course don't line up over joints in the course below. As you come to the top course, switch over to 6″ block to allow for wider compartments. When all the block has been laid, eliminate high and low spots in the curving of the wall surface by filling and feathering with mortar. Fill in the cavities in the top block course with rubble and mortar. This makes for a good gripping surface for the brick cap.

In order to keep the wall surface clean, the brick cap was set before the stone veneering. The curves here were

To make a straight block fit the curve, break it by scoring it completely around a break line then cracking it apart.

Scrape off the excess mortar at the joints with a trowel.

Eliminate high and low spots in the curving of the wall surface by filling and feathering with mortar.

When working two walls, constantly check the level between them.

Lay out the brick for the tread dry first, then check to see if any cutting is necessary.

Be sure to point the mortar in the brick joints, especially on the outer edges.

Press the stone in place with a twisting motion.

Use a farrier's hoof nipper to cut stone veneer pieces to size. You can also use an axe or masonry hammer.

Be sure to check the alignment of the stone from time to time.

Trowel on enough brown mortar at one time to cover 6 to 8 square feet.

handled by varying the mortar joints from straight to wedge, while the compartments were outlined by capping over the bridges between the wall. Butter the bottom edges and the adjacent faces of the bricks with mortar, using the same leveling procedure described for the blocks. Make sure that the brick cap overhangs the block edge by the width of the stone plus an additional ⅜″ minimum for mortar. Make sure to point the mortar in the brick joints, especially on the outer edges.

Brown mortar is a very light powdery material that mixes with water in a mortar box or pan in a strange manner. It remains powdery throughout most of the mixing time and then suddenly turns to a cohesive muck. Use to cement the stone.

Try to plan the stone pattern on the wall every few feet, so all the fitting and cutting can be for that section. We bought a hoof nipper, which is a long-handle pincer with wide cutting edges for the stone. We found the pieces fit better if the smaller or vertically placed stones are used over the tighter-radius convex curves. The thicker pieces are placed near the bottom and the various-size corner pieces made for an easy transition at the wall ends.

Trowel on enough brown mortar at one time to cover 6 to 8 square feet. Use a pointing trowel to get into the awkward areas and corners. Get on a good thick coat, say ⅜″ to ½″ because the stone sets in a bit. Also, because of the nonuniform surface on the reverse side of the stone, you want plenty of mortar to squeeze in and grip solidly.

When you set the stone, press it in place with a twisting motion, similar to working wall tile on solvent mastic. Be sure to step back a few feet from time to time to view the alignment. Pieces can be shifted slightly if moved quickly after the initial setting. Avoid getting the brown mortar on the stone because it's tough to remove. Instead, remove the stained piece from the wall, clean it right away with a hose and reset.

When the mortar has set completely, fill the planter compartments with dirt from the excavation. Then plant shrubs and flowers. Place stone chips around the base to finish the ground.

24

Barbecue

For the family that enjoys entertaining and cooking outdoors, our old-fashioned brick barbecue will be as functional as it is appealing. We built it to use charcoal, but the same dimensions accommodate a drop-in unit that can operate on either natural or LP gas.

Our barbecue has several other special features. The removable drop-in unit can serve as a grill, a spit, a griddle and a smoker. The brick barbecue itself has two huge storage areas with access through a pair of steel doors for stowing utensils or whatever you wish. The barbecue's tiled top surface is about 25 square feet. Add to this the 12 square feet of the pier tops and the slatted redwood bench/counters that span the piers and the main barbecue area and you have more work space than you ever dreamed possible. The slatted bench/counters are designed for extra seating.

What's more, the picnic table folds up into a compact bench. The end pieces come as a kit, to which you add redwood 2×4s to assemble the bench/table. The mechanism is a flip-and-lock device.

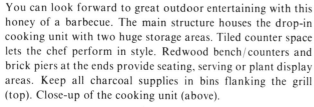

You can look forward to great outdoor entertaining with this honey of a barbecue. The main structure houses the drop-in cooking unit with two huge storage areas. Tiled counter space lets the chef perform in style. Redwood bench/counters and brick piers at the ends provide seating, serving or plant display areas. Keep all charcoal supplies in bins flanking the grill (top). Close-up of the cooking unit (above).

Base kits and 2× 4 redwood allow you to quickly and easily put together this convertible bench/table. With a simple flip you can convert the bench to either a one-bench or two-bench picnic table. It can be flipped back to a bench when not in use for extra seating outdoors.

Establishing the barbecue foundation is the first step toward a fabulous summer of outdoor entertaining. Lay out the dimensions for the three foundations and mark them, using a flat spade. The two-pier digs are merely rectangles, but the hole for the main section is a rectangular trench with the dirt left in the middle. Remove enough dirt from the center dirt island to allow a 6"-deep slab to cover the entire main section. Carry all excavation down to the frost line, as specified by the local codes in your area.

If available, the best way to handle the concrete foundations is with a truck that mixes your concrete right on the spot. That way you get only as much concrete as you need; in addition, the mix is fresh and the strength of the concrete (and its workability) is readily adjustable.

We found a neat way of transporting the concrete from the truck to the excavation—with a Georgia buggy. This cart has two large wheels that balance the load over the axles. It also can carry three times the quantity of a large wheelbarrow. When you plan to pour, have enough help on hand so nobody gets pooped out. Wet concrete is mighty heavy. Also, the use of a come-along (a long-handled blade that looks like a solid rake) is recommended. It gets the concrete out of the buggy into the excavation and, once there, pushes it around very easily.

Make sure that the surface of the concrete is roughly level so that the first brick course can go in without any problem. Push down the aggregate right away, allowing the water to rise and drop again. Use a wood float to smooth the surface. Allow the concrete to cure for three days before beginning the brickwork.

The bricks are bonded together with mortar, and you have some choices concerning which mortar to use. You can buy mortar mix by the bag, add water and mix it, or

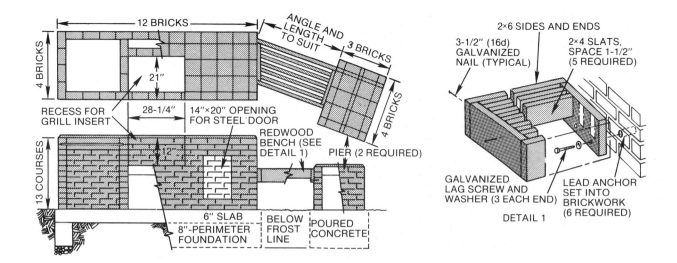

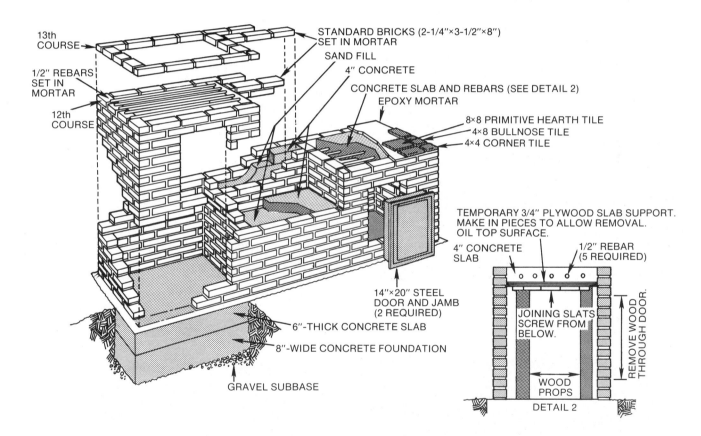

you can buy the ingredients and mix them together with water. The premixed bags make for a neater operation, but the resulting mortar won't shear as well. This means it won't throw as easily, butter the bricks as easily, compress down to form a joint as easily or strike off as easily. It's also more expensive, but it's a lot less mess and you can keep up with the amount of mortar mixed, as opposed to mixing the separate ingredients. It's better to mix the dry bags and water in a pan or mortar box, as we did. However, for those who choose to mix from scratch, the formula is: 1 bag of cement to 3 shovels of lime and 15 shovels of sand.

Mix your mortar and lay a course of 12 bricks to form the start of the back wall. After setting the first brick in place, butter the end of all subsequent bricks in the row. Complete the first course of the back wall.

Then, turn the corners for both 4-brick-long side walls and start the front wall. As you're setting the bricks in place, tap and adjust them so that the course as a whole is level and that each brick is level within the course. As you get into subsequent courses, check frequently that the walls are going up plumb by using your level.

Keep the steel doors handy, because the openings for them start in the third brick course. As you raise the

Rent a Georgia buggy to transport the concrete to the site. It's balanced over the wheels and carries about three wheelbarrow loads of concrete at once.

Once the first course of brick is level on the foundation, build up the corners and fill the rows in between. On a bed of mortar set a brick. Butter adjacent brick ends with mortar.

Check the level of the foundation with a transit or level, then set up stakes and mason's cord to guide the first brick course.

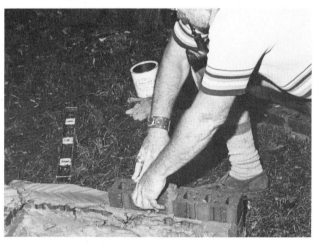

Set buttered bricks, and level them on both long and short edges. Also check for plumb.

Cut bricks to size by scoring all four sides and striking with a masonry hammer and chisel.

For building up the opposite corner several sizes of straight 2×4 are handy. Use a long 4' or 6' level frequently.

courses, keep trial-fitting the doors to ensure a clean, rough opening. Begin at the corners, building up as a triangular echelon (stepped) for the starts of the adjacent walls. Do this at all four corners. Fill in the courses between the built-up corners. To keep these courses level and straight, use a couple of nails stuck into the mortar at the corners with a piece of mason's cord stretched between them or a straight length of 2×4, whichever is more convenient.

The joints can be bevel-tooled with the trowel, set back using a jointing tool, struck off flush or left to ooze out mortar in a bleeding-mortar manner. This is a matter of personal taste. Striking off can be done almost immediately, but wait to joint-tool until the mortar is partially set.

Note that there are three interior walls outlining the notch for the grill insert. These start right at the founda-

tion and work their way up to the maximum height at the thirteenth course.

Therefore, lay out the notch dimensions at the first course, along with the exterior walls. The front-wall notch for the face of the grill begins at the top of the eighth course.

When you're ready, install the steel doors into the rough masonry openings, filling them with mortar for a tight fit. Again, as with the steel doors, trial-fit the insert as you build up the course. However, leave a slight gap between the notch and the insert, because the insert is removable for the winter.

When you've laid the twelfth course, set ½"-diameter rebars (reinforcement bars) on top of this course and over the two open-box structures on the ends of the barbecue. These bars run from left to right and are evenly spaced to reinforce the concrete slab that is to come. After laying

Test-fit the doors often to assure easy installation. The wide embossed flanges are held by mortar, although there are pre-drilled holes for screws, if necessary.

Tool the joints to strengthen them after the mortar has set a bit.

Start another corner buildup. First, put down a mortar bed, then set the bricks, checking that they're level and plumb. Finally, strike off the mortar joint.

The doors are installed, but continue to check the fit of the cooking unit.

Rebars (½″ reinforcing bars) span between the end walls and notch walls. They'll reinforce the concrete slab in the opening over the doors. While curing, the slab is supported by a plywood form.

Cut and assemble the redwood slats to span the distance between the main brick structure and the piers.

Pour and float the concrete slabs to level and push down the aggregate. When the water rises and falls, float the surface again.

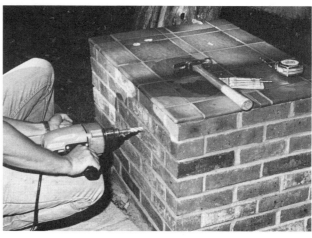

Predrill holes through the sides of the redwood bench/counters, place them in position and mark the location for the anchors and lag bolts. Remove the bench/counter and drill holes with a carbide-tipped masonry bit. Tap in the lead anchors, reposition the bench/counters and bolt in place.

Mix thinset mortar with water, and trowel onto the concrete and brick surface in broad sweeping strokes. Note the tiles that have been dry-fit and precut for quick and easy assembly.

Benches between the barbecue and piers are redwood 2×4s, framed by 2×6s.

the thirteenth course, set up a temporary support below the bars. This support is made from two pieces of plywood screwed together from underneath by a pair of joining slats, then held in place by wood props. The idea is to remove it later through the steel doors. To ease the removal, oil the top surface of the plywood. Complete the brickwork on the piers, using the same masonry techniques.

Fill the opening directly behind the notch with sand from the foundation to within 4″ of the top of the thirteenth course and tamp this sand until solid. Next, mix up enough aggregate concrete (also available in dry mix) to top off this opening, as well as the two reinforced openings. Shovel the concrete into them and then run a 2×4 screed across the fresh concrete in all three locations as you push down any stones appearing on the surface. Wait for the water to rise and fall again. Use a wood float to smooth the surfaces. These surfaces, along with the top of the thirteenth course, serve as a tile base.

Allow a few days for the concrete to cure and then remove the plywood supports. Dry-fit the tiles, using bullnose 4×8s on the edges, 4×4 corners and 8×8s in the field. This material is really hard, but it can be scored and cracked with a hand-operated tile machine. If you can't locate a tile cutter, either accurately mark the tiles to be cut and have them wet-sawn by a tile contractor or rent a wet saw and do it.

Thinset mortar is used for the tile setting. There is a defined curing time for its use, so mix only what you can use. Spread the mortar on the surface, using a ¼″ square-notched trowel. The mortar cusps formed should stand up—not sag. Lay out the precut tile in aligned rows and beat them in with a flat board and hammer. Make any minor joint-alignment corrections. The beating locks down the tiles and gives you a level surface. Allow the mortar to set up at least 24 hours.

Mix the grout to a creamy consistency and work it into all the joints with a rubber-platen grouting trowel. Remove the excess grout with a rubber squeegee. Sprinkle sawdust on the surface and rub it out with natural burlap. When dry, there will be a haze, so rub it again using damp sawdust.

The benches between the main barbecue and the piers are redwood 2×4s, framed by 2×6s. Cut and assemble them, using aluminum or stainless-steel nails, so that they just fit into the spans between the masonry. Then, drill the redwood ends with the benches in place and make pilot marks on the brickwork. Make sure that the benches are level during the operation. With a carbide drill, make holes for lead anchors and set these anchors in place. Now, bolt the benches in position using galvanized lags and washers. (Refer to the bench detail.)

Clean up the area, backfill a bit around the masonry foundation and you're ready to cook.

25

Garden Lights

If your backyard is part of your leisure living space, you can give it the convenience of the indoors with electric power. A 20-amp branch circuit, the most practical choice, not only means lights for your garden, patio or deck, but also outdoor outlets for appliances, TV, stereo and other equipment normally confined to the house.

The wiring and conduit are routed underground primarily, so you must use a method of installation that is safe, and in accord with local electrical codes—they are normally based on the National Electrical Code (NEC)—and within reasonable cost limits. A GFI (ground fault interrupter) breaker at the panel; 12-gauge, 20-amp wire;

and ½" PVC rigid nonmetallic conduit buried 12" below grade are typical components of such a system that will meet the safety, practical, legal and cost criteria.

Planning the Job

First, choose the light fixture/receptacle locations (stations) in the garden, avoiding large tree roots where possible throughout the underground run.

The 20-amp circuit that you'll be using shouldn't be loaded to more than 80% of its capacity (16 amps), so if you figure each light fixture/outlet as 1½ amps, you'll have ten on the circuit for a total of 15 amps. If your design requires more than 10 stations, start another branch circuit from a separate GFI at the panel. Finally, decide where your branch circuit will exit the house and enter the ground. Draw up your design in plan view and you'll easily be able to determine the bill of materials.

(A) Fixed pagoda tier light illuminates pachysandra, mountain laurel and rhododendrons. (B) A mushroom among Mugho pines will beautifully light up these little trees for a festive garden party. (C) FS weatherproof box supporting a mushroom provides power for auxiliary stake lights or appliances. (D) Portable spike light fixtures with colored outdoor lamps can be placed anywhere within reach of an outlet.

Getting Started

Lay out a garden hose as a guide and trench out the entire underground run, either by hand or with a rental machine. Indicate the station locations with small stakes.

Build up the required number of metal stations, but note that the legs are of different length to permit their assembly to the FS box. Install the shorter leg first and you'll have no problem. Place the metal station assemblies in the positions marked by the stakes and dry-fit all

the PVC conduit and components. Note that, because the FS boxes will be used as pull boxes for the wires, don't allow more than 360° of angle change between adjacent FS boxes. Pulling the wires through five 90° ells would involve a total angle change of 450°, a very difficult job.

If all looks well at this point, cement all conduit to the terminal adapters at the stations, taking care to keep the stations erect. Note that the last station in the line has no wires in its final leg, required for mechanical support.

A

B

FS WEATHERPROOF BOX (T-BOX)

1/2" GALVANIZED NIPPLE 8" LONG

1/2" GALVANIZED NIPPLE 6" LONG

1/2" PVC TERMINAL ADAPTER

1/2" GALVANIZED COUPLING

1/2" PVC CONDUIT

90 DEGREE SWEEP ELL 1/2" GALVANIZED

C

(A) The ½″ PVC conduit is buried in a 1'-deep trench. You can cement lengths of conduit together for long, straight runs, or curve it gently to avoid obstacles. To change directions, 30°, 45° and 90° ells are available. (B) Try to avoid areas that are heavily rooted; if you can't drive a plumbing pipe through the soil in these areas, and then push conduit through with the ends taped so dirt won't get inside. (C) Assemble these metal stations to provide mechanical support for the FS weatherproof boxes and fixtures.

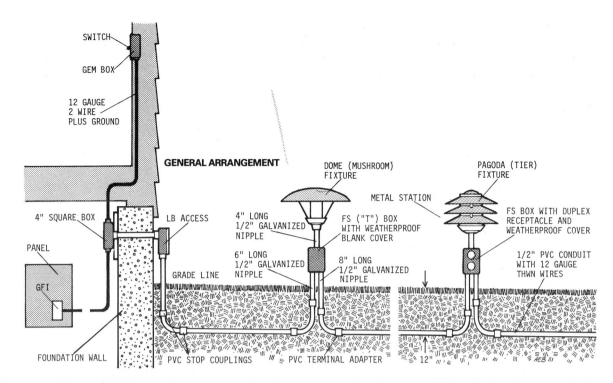

GENERAL ARRANGEMENT

The garden light branch circuit starts with a ground fault interrupter breaker (known as a GFI breaker) at the service panel and then continues to a box that is mounted inside of the foundation wall. The cable for the switch box and the wiring for the underground section also enter this box. The underground wiring goes through the wall via PVC conduit and an LB access, and then is routed into the ground, encased in PVC conduit, joining light fixture/receptacle stations in continuous run.

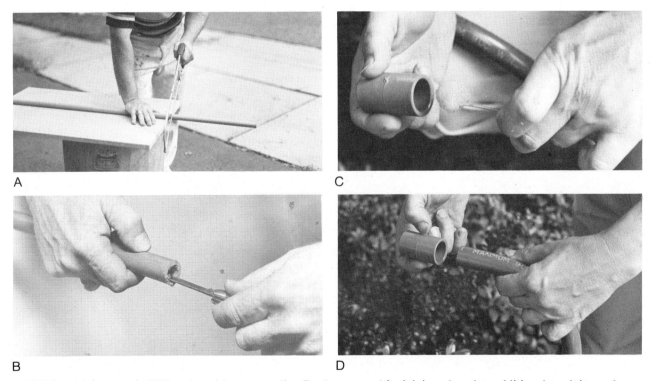

(A) PVC conduit comes in 10′ lengths, with stop coupling fixed to one end for joining a length to additional conduit or other components. You can cut conduit easily with a fine-toothed hacksaw blade. (B) Deburr conduit (remove flash) from both inside and outside with a penknife before cementing to other components. Figure ¾″ for insertion into the female ends of parts. (C) Cement is being applied for joining a 90° sweep ell to a stop coupling. Cement is applied sparingly with dauber to either of the components (in this case, the stop coupling). Excess cement may creep inside surface of the joint and leave a sticky deposit, making wire pulling difficult. (D) If you move swiftly you can change the orientation of joined parts before the cement sets.

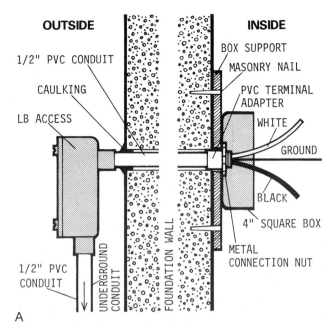

OUTSIDE

1/2" PVC CONDUIT

CAULKING

LB ACCESS

1/2" PVC CONDUIT

UNDERGROUND CONDUIT

FOUNDATION WALL

INSIDE

BOX SUPPORT

MASONRY NAIL

PVC TERMINAL ADAPTER

WHITE

GROUND

BLACK

4" SQUARE BOX

METAL CONNECTION NUT

A

Route the conduit from the ground, up through the PVC LB access into the house and into the 4" square box. It's best to run the conduit into the foundation wall above the grade line, and caulk around the conduit to avoid any leaks.

Now, replace the dirt and sod, and tamp it down. It will take a couple of rains to return the backfill to its original grade. Thread 4" nipples and the fixtures onto the FS boxes.

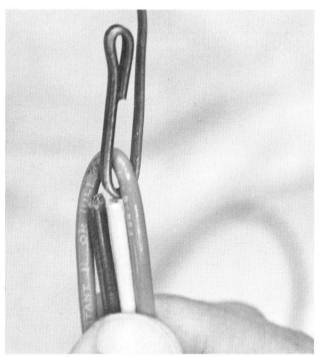

(A) Cross section at wall shows 4" square box mounted to wood support on inside of foundation wall. PVC terminal adapter, locked to box with connector nut, starts PVC conduit into a hole punched through wall. The PVC LB access changes conduit direction, provides easy routing of wires. (B) An LB access, with removable cover, seen from outside. Conduit hole should be caulked.

Three wires (black load, white neutral and green ground, all 12-gauge THWN for wet locations) are pulled from station to station, through the LB access and into the 4" square box inside foundation wall. Insert fish tape (electrical snake) down one FS box leg; keep pushing it, occasionally using a twisting or back-and-forth motion, until it emerges at adjacent box. Attach wires as shown and apply electrician's tape. Have helper feed in the wires from the second box as you pull both the fish tape and wires back into the first box.

Wiring the Job

Wire between the stations and into the 4″ square box, leaving about 8″ of wiring protruding out at each box. Next, route a two-wire plus ground 12-gauge cable (BX or Romex according to the local code) from the 4″ box to the panel, but don't connect anything yet.

Now install a Gem (switch) box at a convenient indoor location, and run another two-wire plus ground 20-amp cable from the Gem to the 4″ box.

Wire up the FS boxes with lights only, and those with both lights and receptacles. Install 25-watt, low-energy

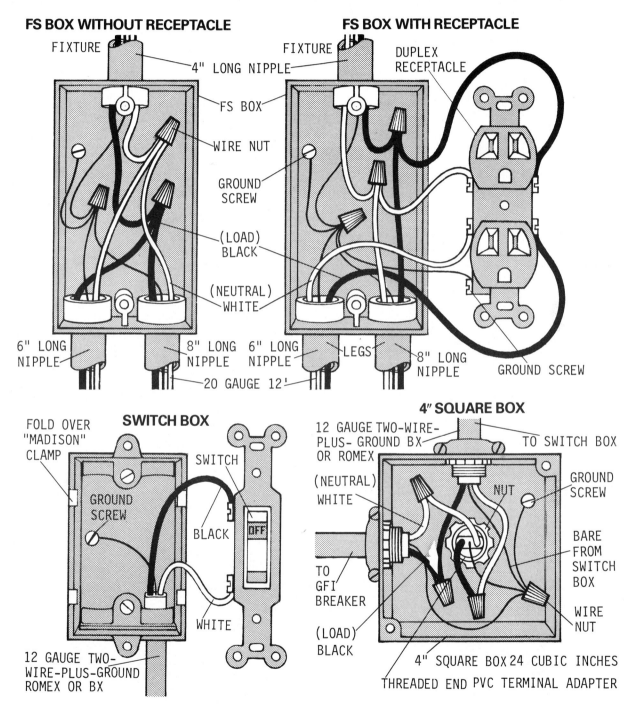

Note that all boxes are grounded with ground wire and green ground screws (terminals optional). All receptacles are grounded by connections to their own green screws. Select the wire nuts according to their capacity to contain a given number of wires of a specific gauge (shown on the wire nut packaging). After making the Gem box cutout in the wall, lock the box in the hole by installing "Madison" clamps. Note that the switch in the Gem box simply breaks the load wire "loop" when open and completes the circuit when closed. The nut locking the PVC terminal adapter to the 4″ square box is from a ⅜″ Romex or Bx connector. In the interest of clarity, the built-in nut plates which retain receptacles in the FS boxes have been omitted here.

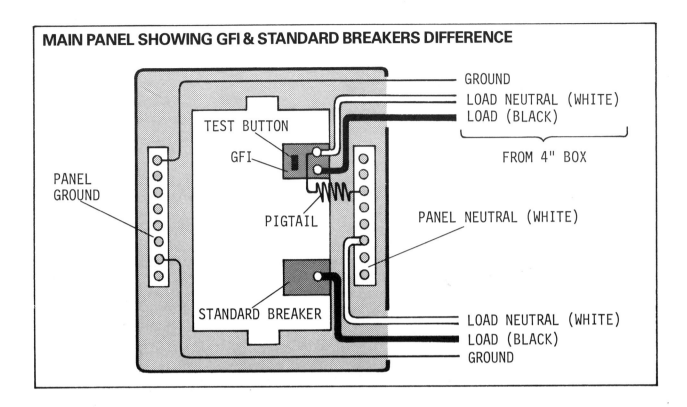

MAIN PANEL SHOWING GFI & STANDARD BREAKERS DIFFERENCE

lamps in the fixtures, and weatherproof covers on all outside boxes.

At the panel, take the precaution of shutting off the main breaker and run the cable from the 4″ box into the panel through a connector. Wire in the GFI breaker, noting the difference in wiring compared with the standard breaker. Operate the GFI breaker "test" button according to the instructions in the packaging, then check out the receptacles and lights. That's it—you're ready for your next backyard picnic.

Part VI

Garage

26

Garage Add-On Workshop

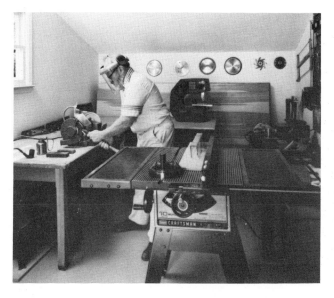

A compact woodworking shop (left) that is not in a basement but added on to a garage has ample space for doing home-improvement projects. Add-on matches house and garage lines (right).

There are sometimes very good reasons why your basement cannot be the place for a home workshop—so you must find an alternative location. We think we've found a terrific one with our workshop add-on to a garage.

The advantages of this add-on are many. First there's the convenience of a workshop that has a good portion of space over 8' high. (This is handy when dealing with 4'×8' sheets and other lumber over 8' long.) Another advantage is that the garage's concrete floor joins the concrete floor of the workshop—making for uniformity and less work. The shop addition is compact—about 120 square feet of

floor space—and its cost per square foot is reasonable. Finally, this addition is built against the house wall, making for clean architectural lines and allowing no one to guess that it wasn't part of the original design.

Clearing and Pouring Foundation

To start, clear away shrubbery, sprinkler lines, garden-line conduit or other obstructions from the area. Next, mark the outline of the new foundation with mason's line and stakes, bringing the addition right up to the house wall adjacent to the garage.

There are only two critical measurements to make before you lay the foundation and build the structure. The first is to strip back the siding from the exterior corner of the garage so that you can determine the top line of the concrete blocks, and can thereby measure to determine the location of the concrete footing below grade. The second critical measurement is to match the pitch of the garage roof with that of the addition, but this measurement is not performed until much later.

Dig the 22′ of trench down to the frost line, conforming to your local building code for foundations. Have the concrete delivered by a metered instant-mix truck. Then, with several helpers and wheelbarrows, pour, rake and level the concrete footing up to the determined point— where the poured-concrete portion of the house foundation begins. Allow the concrete to cure for about three days.

Use a mason's cord and a level to check that the corners are in a level position.

Building the Structure

With the concrete foundation dry, mix mortar in a pan or wheelbarrow and start laying the block at the corners. Except for a generous mortar bed at the concrete/block interface, keep joints about ⅜″ thick while lapping the corner blocks for strength. Check that the corners are in a leveled position by making certain the garage and house walls are plumb and square at the corner, that each block face is plumb, within its own row, and that each block is level across its long top edge. Using either a stretched piece of mason's cord or a straight 2×4 plus a level, fill in the block in the rows between.

When the mortar has set, add the anchor bolts, which lock the sill plates down to the block. Also coat the outer block-wall face with a sand-mix concrete that has been spiked with a latex bonding agent. To do this easily, roll a coat of bonding agent on the block wall as well, and work in reverse order by troweling the mix onto the block first; then roughen slightly with a wood float. When dry, drill the pressure-treated sill plates to match the anchor bolts and install the plates over either a mortar- or sill-sealer bedding. This fills any minor discrepancies and keeps out bugs or drafts. Note also that the plates are located on the block wall so that the sheathing and finish wall come out flush with the existing garage wall. With the plates locked down, start the short-end stud wall.

When the mortar has set, add the anchor bolts.

To match the roof pitches, check the rise in inches per foot of the run of the existing roof. As an additional check, sight along the house wall to the existing roof. This establishes the top of the roof shingles at the short-end wall. Mark this line on the house wall using a snapped chalk line. Next cut one rafter completely and tack it up on the wall temporarily, allowing for the thickness of both sheathing and roof shingles between the snapped line and the top edge of the rafter. In this way you'll instantly obtain the actual height of the top plate of the short-end stud wall.

Coat the outer block-wall face with a sand-mix concrete.

Drill the sill plates to match the anchor bolts and install over either a mortar- or sill-sealer bedding.

The end wall with doubled top plates is toenailed to the sill plates and propped level with a brace.

Trim the studs to length, double-plate them at the top and toenail the assembly in-place on 16″ centers to the sill plates of the end wall. To get flush to the house wall, strip away the existing shingles and refit them at the end of the job. As you strip shingles, continue to remove all of them on the garage-wall end and on the house wall up to the snapped line. Trim the line evenly with a saw. Before continuing, place a temporary brace on the end stud wall to assure that it's plumb. Strip away all gutters, fascia and trim from the existing garage wall, and replace them with a 2×8 ledger board to serve as an anchoring point for the rafters.

Use the temporary rafter as a pattern to cut the remaining rafters and proceed to install them on 16″ centers. Complete the framing by filling the gable wall with studding, which includes roughing out the window. It's easier to do by first nailing up a top plate to the underside of the end rafter, then nailing the top ends of bevel-cut studding

to this. Sheath the addition with ½″ CDX plywood. Continue to staple on the felt paper, adding the new fascias, trims and spacers. (The spacers allow the top shingle row to be tucked under the fascia board for instant weatherproofing.) Install the window.

Cut all rafters from a sample rafter and install and toenail them between the ledger and the end-wall top plates.

Skin the addition with CDX plywood first, then the roof will be ready for felt paper and shingles in short order.

Apply step-flashing over the shingles where the roof meets the house wall. (Step-flashing is aluminum folded at right angles and laid over one row of shingles while lapped under the shingles in the row above. The second flange of the right angle is tucked up under the existing wall siding and the building paper.) If you can't match the new shingles to those of the existing roof, continue the new shingles over the existing hip of the garage.

We used 18″-long striated cedar shakes, double-coursed to match the existing building, and lined them up for a perfect fit. At the bottom, use a starter strip (lattice or scrap plywood) to rake the shake out from the wall. Next

Apply step-flashing where the roof meets the house wall.

If you can't match the new shingles to those of the existing roof, continue the new shingles over the hip of the garage.

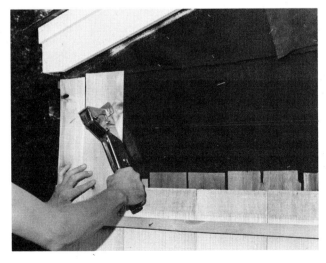

Striated cedar shakes, 18″ long, double-coursed to match the existing building, were lined up for a perfect fit.

install a row of the rougher, cheaper undercourse shakes with their butt (thick) ends face-nailed to the starter strip. Over this and dropped ½″, face-nail the bottom row of finished shakes. Face-nail the second undercourse, keeping the weather (exposed) height plus ½″ to allow for the finish drop. In this manner, proceed up the wall, keeping a maximum 14″ weather height for this shingle size. To keep the rows neat, use a batten temporarily nailed in place under the butt ends. Also, to prevent staining and rust drips, use aluminum or galvanized shake nails. At the exterior corner, alternate the lapping from one wall to another; while at the window, cut as accurately as possible to minimize caulking. A utility knife and a small block plane accomplish this job quickly. On the outside, caulk, paint and hang the gutter/leader.

Create an opening between the addition and the garage proper. Laminate a header of two 2×6s or 2×8s (depending upon the size of the opening between existing studs) with a piece of ½″-thick plywood in between, and cap it on the bottom with a 2×4 laid flat. Along a straight line, cut through the existing wall studs where you want the top of the header to rest. Remove the lower portion of these studs and nail the header in place. From a pair of the removed lower studs, cut a pair of trimmers to length so that they just fit in underneath the ends of the head, and nail them in place. Finish the rough opening by trimming away the sheathing within the outline bounded by the bottom of the header and the trimmers. Do the floor now, and save the trimming of base, case, jambs, window stool, apron, stops, insulation and drywall for the end.

Knock down any existing block at the bottom of the opening between the garage and the addition below the concrete-floor level, clean the dirt within the addition down to subgrade (about 4″ below the existing garage floor), and tamp to compress it. To float the floor, use a couple of 2×4s temporary joined, parallel and set on edge. Then, starting from the existing floor and reaching out to the end wall, set these leveling boards so that their top edges are where you want the floor surface to be.

Before pouring the concrete, have enough help on hand. Also have a couple of wheelbarrows, some screeding boards, rubber boots or galoshes, heavy-duty gloves, trowel, wood float, bull-float rake, shovel and a jitterbug to knock the aggregate below the surface and allow you to screed properly to a smooth surface. You need boots because you'll stand in the wet concrete; it is caustic, and if it gets trapped in your shoes, you might be burned. In addition, use a pair of 12″×18″ plywood kneeboards to support your weight during the later work.

Divide the floor into three sections with 2×4s. Pour the concrete and rough-level it with a rake or screed board, working the jitterbug around as quickly as possible. Then level the concrete by pulling the screed board gradually over the leveling boards with a back-and-forth sawing motion, slowly working toward the existing garage floor. Use a bull float to get a relatively smooth surface. After a

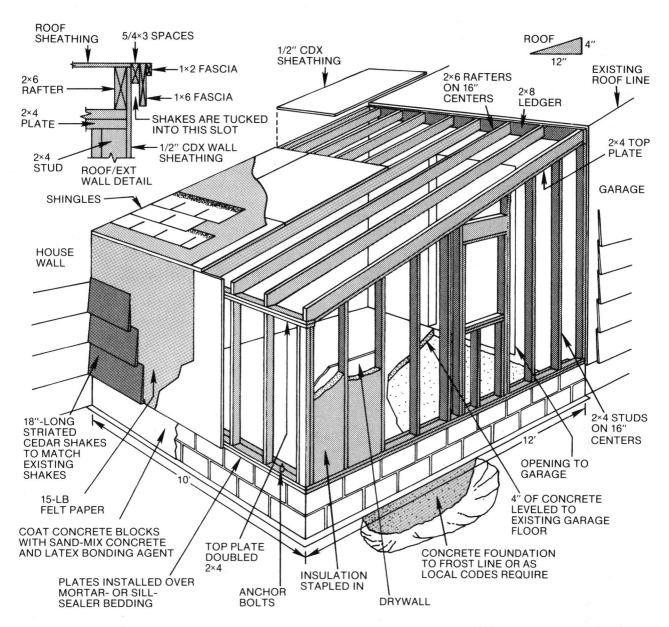

ROOF SHEATHING

5/4×3 SPACES

1×2 FASCIA

1/2" CDX SHEATHING

2×6 RAFTERS ON 16" CENTERS

2×8 LEDGER

ROOF 4" / 12"

EXISTING ROOF LINE

2×6 RAFTER

1×6 FASCIA

2×4 PLATE

SHAKES ARE TUCKED INTO THIS SLOT

2×4 TOP PLATE

2×4 STUD

1/2" CDX WALL SHEATHING

GARAGE

ROOF/EXT WALL DETAIL

SHINGLES

HOUSE WALL

18"-LONG STRIATED CEDAR SHAKES TO MATCH EXISTING SHAKES

15-LB FELT PAPER

2×4 STUDS ON 16" CENTERS

12'

OPENING TO GARAGE

COAT CONCRETE BLOCKS WITH SAND-MIX CONCRETE AND LATEX BONDING AGENT

10'

TOP PLATE DOUBLED 2×4

4" OF CONCRETE LEVELED TO EXISTING GARAGE FLOOR

PLATES INSTALLED OVER MORTAR- OR SILL-SEALER BEDDING

ANCHOR BOLTS

INSULATION STAPLED IN

CONCRETE FOUNDATION TO FROST LINE OR AS LOCAL CODES REQUIRE

DRYWALL

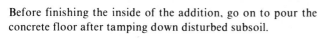

Before finishing the inside of the addition, go on to pour the concrete floor after tamping down disturbed subsoil.

When you can safely walk on the floor, staple in the insulation.

half-hour to an hour and a half, depending upon the temperature and the mix, pull out the leveling boards and fill in the depressions with concrete stored in the wheelbarrows. Float the concrete to remove the discrepancies. When the surface has cured a little to the point where it supports you on the kneeboard but still is slightly workable, hand-float and trowel for a very smooth surface. Let the floor cure for a few days.

When you can safely walk on the floor, staple in the insulation and install drywall nailers, if necessary. Nail up the drywall, then tape and joint as required. Install the jamb in the wall opening, and trim out the window, doorway and floor-wall joints.

For electricals, surface-mount for light and power as required. You may choose to hang up pegboard, such as we did here, or have cabinets or shelves for tool storage.

27

Horizontal Garage Storage

Are paint cans, lawn furniture, garden fertilizer and other such items eating up your garage floor space? You can clear the floor in a weekend's time by building an over-the-hood deck, shelves and cabinet that will give you about 60 square feet of storage. The construction is basic and the required tools are minimal.

Measuring and Preparing

Drive your car into the garage in its normal parking location and measure: (1) The height of the engine hood (and possibly part of the windshield) at a point 6½' to 7' out from the wall facing your front bumper. (2) The location for a 2×4, which, when placed on the floor before the front wheels, will stop the car's forward progress. (3) The maximum width the storage deck can extend out from the garage side wall. (4) The width of your car. Make your deck 24″ wider, so you can get in and out easily. The storage deck shown was installed in a two-car garage and extends from a side wall to the door that connects the house and garage.

Snap a chalk line a few inches above hood height on the wall in front of the car and on the adjacent side wall. This line marks the bottom edge of the wall ledgers. Next, locate the studs (this should be easy, since most builders don't hide the slightly recessed drywall nails under joint compound) and mark their locations just below the chalk lines.

Beginning Construction

The basic structure consists of wall ledgers, joists, joist headers and a corner ladder. Start construction by trimming a ledger to 7'10½″ and nailing or lag bolting it to the side wall so it butts against the front wall. Then trim another ledger 3″ shorter than the actual long dimension

of the deck (in our case, 9'3″) and fasten it to the front wall, butting it against the side wall ledger.

Set up a ladder at the external corner of the deck for a temporary support. Then, cut and toenail a joist header, the same length as the front wall ledger, to the side wall ledger, flush with its end, and rest the other end of the header on the ladder. Trim a joist, equal in length to the side wall ledger and nail it to both the front wall ledger and the joist header. Now, nail the doubler to the header, making sure that it butts against the wall and is flush with the joist at the opposite end.

The ladder not only provides access to the deck, but also serves as permanent support for the external corner of the structure. Note that the garage floor slopes downward as it approaches the doors, so take this into consideration when you cut the ladder sides (the side nearest the garage doors may be slightly shorter than the other side.) Therefore, measure and mark the spacing of the tread dadoes from the tops of the ladder sides so they'll be level.

Make the ½"-deep tread dado crosscuts with your portable saw (adjust platen accordingly) and then knock out the waste between the cuts with a butt or firmer chisel. Cut the treads to length and nail the ladder together.

Erect the ladder temporarily at the corner and mark the notches on the sides to hold the deck joist. Place angle irons in position on the floor at the inside faces of the ladder sides and mark the hole locations on the floor and ladder sides. Remove the ladder and cut and chisel the notches. Drill the holes in the ladder side.

Set up your drill with a carbide-tipped bit and drill holes in the concrete for the lead anchors. While you have

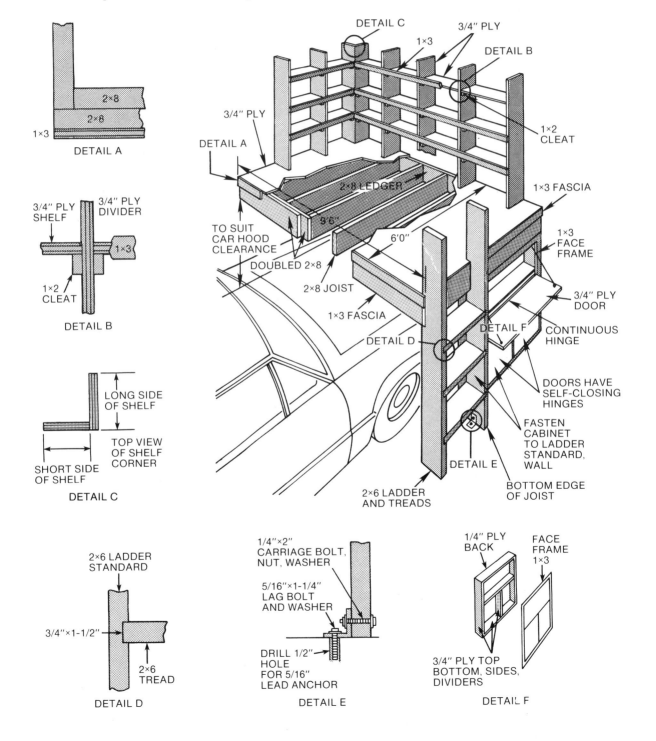

your drill in action, also make holes for the mounting bolts that will retain the 2×4 wheel stop. Insert the lead anchors into all holes, flush with the floor.

Attach the angle irons to the ladder sides with carriage bolts, nuts and washers, then position the ladder over the angle iron lead anchors with the joist resting in the notches. Finish the corner work by running lag bolts with washers through the angle irons into the anchors, and toenail the ladder to the joist.

Starting from the side wall, mark off the exposed faces of both the front ledger and the joist header at 16″ intervals for placement of the remaining joists. Trim the joists to length at these marks and toenail them in place, keeping the 16″ on center spacing.

Now nail on the plywood deck, making sure that all plywood joints parallel to the joists are squarely over the joist edges. You'll have to do a little fitting and notching around the ladder sides, but it's no problem. Complete the deck by nailing the fascias in place and painting it.

Shelving, Cabinets and Finish Work

The shelves are built in two modules, then joined together on the deck to form an "ell" against the front and side walls. Cut the shelves, dividers and ends for both the long and short legs of the "ell" from ¾″ plywood. They should all be 9″ deep, but the height depends on the distance between your deck and ceiling. Mark all cleat locations on the dividers and ends and nail or screw the cleats in place. Insert and fasten in the shelves, working from the bottom shelf up for ease of assembly.

Paint the shelf modules, and when dry, place them on the deck. Then join the ends together to form the "ell," nail the shelves to the deck and fasten the upper parts to the walls with metal brackets.

Start the cabinet by making a box frame with a center shelf and lower divider. This should be sized so that it fits between the ladder side and the front wall of the garage, and high enough so that when the top touches the bottom edge of the joist, there's about a 6″ clearance from the floor. This clearance will be handy later, when you sweep, hose or paint the garage floor.

Add a plywood back to the box frame and then make up and install a face frame from 1×3 stock to hold the flap door and lower hinged doors. Cut all doors to size. Then fit a length of continuous hinge to the flap door and self-closing hinges and pulls to the lower doors. Paint the cabinet and doors. When everything's dry, mount the cabinet and install all doors. Provide screweyes and chains to support the door in a horizontal position and a gate hook and eye to hold it closed. Lag bolt the wheel stop in place and you're done.

Shelves should be 9″ deep.

The cabinet fits between the ladder side and the front wall

28

Vertical Garage Storage

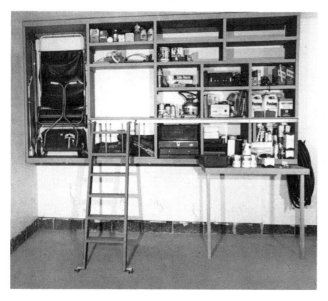

Completed over-the-hood garage storage system showing firewood storage, sliding ladder, and worktable loaded with equipment to change oil in owner's car.

The wall system, a popular shelving arrangement for the rec room, also is an ideal way to clean up the clutter in your garage. Here's one with a sliding detachable ladder, firewood storage, a convertible worktable and planned storage integrated into a sturdy structure that fits neatly into some of those unused cubic feet over the hood of your car.

The construction is primarily of plywood and dimensioned lumber, with some inexpensive garage door hardware to handle the sliding ladder. You may wish to modify some of the spaces to fit a particular requirement.

Making the Cabinet

Cut all plywood parts according to the cutting schedule. If you don't own a table saw, you can speed up the work by paying the lumberyard a few extra dollars to do it for you. The object is to make the top, bottom, sides and the longest vertical dividers in subassemblies and join these together into a large open-box structure on the ground. Then scribe a horizontal line 75″ down from the ceiling and mount the 2×4 ledger. This will allow about an 1″ of space between the cabinet top and ceiling for ease of installation, assuming a 10′ garage ceiling.

After that, two people lift the partially completed system onto the ledger, while a third person holds it against the wall with a 2×4. While it's being held there, drive screws through the nailing cleat at the top into the 2×4 wall studs. The rest of the work is finished in place.

Lay the two half tops and two half bottoms with their splices on the floor. Glue and fasten these subassemblies with 1¼″ screws and allow the glue to set. Next, glue and screw the 1×2 stiffener and the 1×3 nailing cleat to the upper front and lower rear edges, respectively, of the top. Set this section aside. Glue and screw the two 1×2 stiffeners to underside front and rear edges of the bottom piece. While these are drying, cut all the short cleats to 15⅞″ and glue and screw them to all sides and dividers as shown.

Now, cut the notches to accommodate the 1×3 nailing cleat in the upper back corners of dividers 6, 7 and 14. Build the box structure on the ground, including the notched No. 14 divider, again fastening with glue and screws. Use the longer screws, driving from the rear to lock the nailing cleat to each of the dividers. Note that the nailing cleat will just fit inside the side pieces, so drive in some screws through the side faces into the ends of the cleat.

Scribe that horizontal line for the ledger, and then locate and mark the wall stud centers just below this line. To locate exact stud centers, probe the sheetrock with an awl or similar tool. Transfer these marks to the ledger and drill through the center of the ledger face at the marks with a ¼" bit.

With the ledger held temporarily in its proper place, run this same bit through the holes into the wall. Now, drill through the ledger alone with a ⅜" bit (for bolt clearance) and mount the ledger with the large lag bolts and washers. Locate the wall studs at least 4" down from the ceiling (to eliminate the top plates), and mark the locations at least 6" down, so you'll see them when the cabinet is in place and the nailing cleat hides the punch marks.

Lift the assembly up onto the ledger and hold it as described before. Drive screws through the nailing cleat at the locations marked. Lock in the cabinet bottom by driving screws through piece No. 15 into the studs just above the ledger mounting bolts.

Screw in the remaining dividers and shelves. Make up the firewood storage grille and install it as shown. Nail or screw on all remaining 1×2 and 1×3 trim pieces at this time, giving special attention to piece No. 18, which is the garage track support. The four 10" high shelves in the upper right section may be used for tire storage, but if you have a larger car, increase the depth of shelves Nos. 8 and 9 by 4".

Ladder and Table

Place the metal garage door track over piece No. 18, and mark the track in the center of each divider. Take it down, and drill and countersink holes with a No. 21 bit after punch marking. Make sure that you have countersunk sufficiently for a No. 8 flathead screw to fit flush in the countersink or it may interfere with the ladder roller. Screw the track to piece No. 18.

Make the two ladder stringers and treads. Cut the ends and tread dadoes on the inside faces of the stringers as indicated in the drawing (one left, one right).

Assemble the ladder and drive screws through the stringer faces into the tread ends. Slip the roller axles into the bracket holes, leaving enough room on the ends opposite the rollers for a washer and cotter pin. Punch-mark the axle, then drill a 1/16" hole through it, and install the washer and pin to retain it in the bracket. Remember, there are left and right brackets—don't mix them up.

Place the top of the ladder against the metal track at the correct angle and temporarily clamp a bracket and roller to each of the ladder stringers near the bottom. Adjust the brackets so that the bottom edges of the stringers clear the floor by at least ½", so the ladder can roll sideways. Mark the stringer faces at the center of the bracket mounting slots and drill ¼" carriage hardware. Carry out the same operation at the top of the ladder, making sure that the roller is cleanly in the track and that the stringer tops are clear. Trim the stringers if necessary.

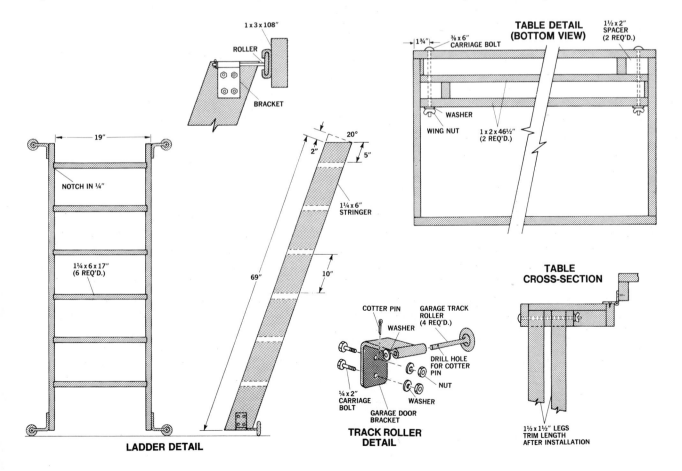

LADDER DETAIL

TRACK ROLLER DETAIL

TABLE DETAIL (BOTTOM VIEW)

TABLE CROSS-SECTION

Cut the tabletop from ¾″ plywood to the dimension shown and edge it with 1×3 common pine. Cut the 8′ length of 2×2 into two pieces 42″ long. Next, fit these "legs" into the underside of the table along with two pieces of 1×3 (the 1×3 will stick out but will be trimmed down), which form hollow boxes for the legs. Slide each leg so that its top end butts against the 1×3 end piece (one leg to the left and one to the right).

Make up spacer blocks from the scrap 2×2 and insert them in the hollow box areas next to the foot of each leg. Leave about ½″ gap next to the feet so you'll be able to pull the legs down. Clamp the sandwich of legs and 1×3 near both ends.

Drill through the complete sandwich 1½″ from each table end and ⅞″ from the bottom edge. Mark all components and disassemble them. Round off the leg tops so that they will be able to turn freely on the ⅜″ bolts to the

installed. This may require a little fitting. Cut the 1×3 down to 1¾″ width, and taper the legs slightly by sanding. Assemble all parts with the carriage bolts, washers and wing nuts. Adjust friction to suit. Note how the spacer blocks hold the cut-down 1×3 and legs in position, allowing tightening of the carriage bolts.

Mount the table to the lowest 1×3 trim piece on the cabinet, placing the 3×3 butts so that the hinge pin fits just below the bottom edge of the 1×3. Trim both legs as required to level the table. Add the hooks and eyes to hold the table in the folded-up position.

The exposed right side of the wall unit is a convenient surface for hose, extension cord, and tool holders. This wall unit will accommodate all the things that may be misplaced around the garage, and also provide room for future acquisitions.

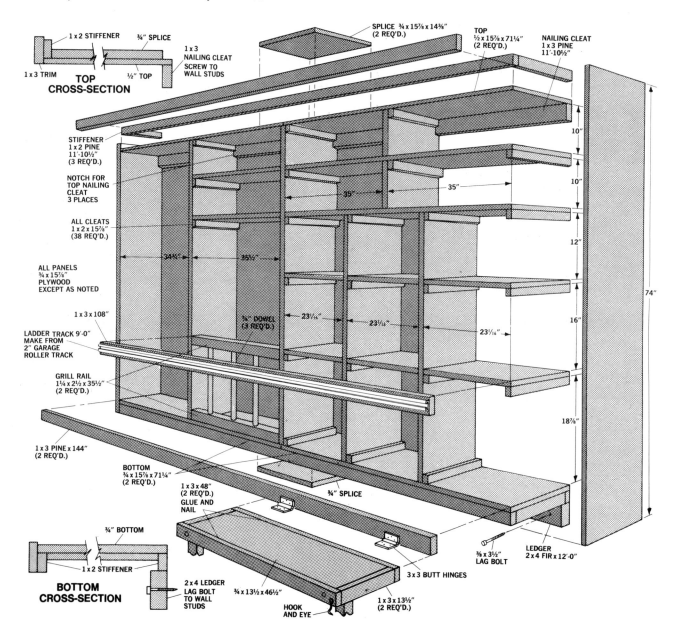

29

Automatic Garage Door Installation

Y ou can add quiet convenience as well as extra security to the overhead garage-door entrance of your home with a new opening system. The systems presently on the market are much less noisy than the usual bicycle-chain arrangement. The garage-door opener system that we chose to install owes its quiet glide to a perforated drive tape of a new elastomeric material. When the system is properly adjusted, the closed garage door cannot be raised manually from the outside. A combination of pushbutton and transmitter controls eliminates fumbling for the key in darkness or inclement weather. And installation takes just a few hours.

First, check your overhead garage door for proper manual operation. Make any needed adjustments. Lubricate the door rollers and track. Inspect the hinges and the brackets connecting door sections.

Beginning Installation

The installation starts with the assembly of the rail, drive tape, inner slide, carriage, release, power unit and limit switches. This primary assembly is then centered over the door and mounted from the ceiling at the correct height. Then the door arm is attached, limit switches set and the control pushbutton installed.

You need to provide a 120V AC receptacle in the ceiling area, approximately 12' to 14' back from the garage door opening. Also, set up a long plank or a couple of narrow benches to support the assembly as you work on it.

Line up the three extruded aluminum rail sections with the stamped Xs all on the same side. Note that the three different sections must be assembled in the proper order. There are two channels inside these sections, near the bottom flange, that accept the drive tape. Uncoil the perforated tape coming from the power unit and insert the top drive tape into the upper channel of the first rail

section. Next, the inner slide is indexed to the last five perforations in the bottom drive tape and inserted into the lower channel of the first section. The first rail section is then inserted into the slot at the top of the power unit where it is locked in place with the hardware provided.

Continue to feed the tape through the upper channels of the second and third rail sections and splice them together using the rail clamps and hardware provided. There are bushings with the rail-splicing hardware to assure a straight run. Check the rail to make certain it is straight. The carriage, with the release cord and knob, is then inserted, knob end first, into the far end of the third rail section. Slide the carriage toward the power unit until

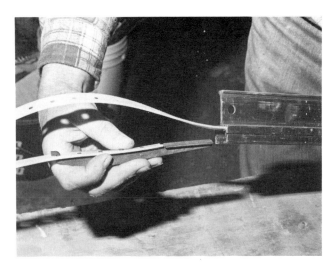

Insert inner slide and bottom drive tape into the bottom channel of the first rail.

Snap on Up and Down limit switches on rail top with actuating arms hanging down.

Insert the first channel into the slot on the power unit and lock it in place with bushings, nuts and bolts.

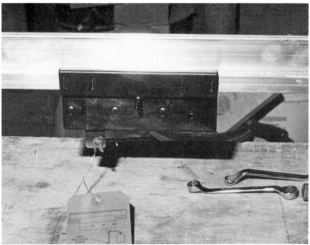

Mount carriage, tag, release cord and knob to rail bottom; slide them along rail.

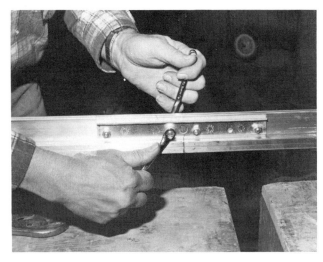

Connect the rail sections with plates, bushings, nuts and bolts. Check that the assembly is straight.

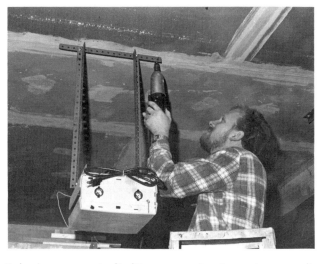

Raise door, support rail with scrap wood and mount power unit to ceiling with lengths of angle iron cut to size.

it engages the tape. Snap the Up and Down limit switches onto the rail top so that their actuating rods are on opposite sides. The Down switch should be near the door end and the Up switch near the power-unit end of the rail. We left off the wires between the switches and the terminals on the power unit, to be connected after the main assembly had been mounted.

There are several possible door types to be reckoned with (they're all covered in the manufacturer's manual). The sectional door with the curved track is most popular—and the one we chose. The header bracket, which supports the door end of the rail, can be mounted directly on the wall if the header over the door opening goes up high enough. If not, a ledger should be nailed horizontally across the header and the studs above it. The safest bet is to use a ledger. To locate the header bracket both horizontally and vertically, raise the top section of the door to its highest point. With the aid of a level, mark the wall at the same height on the vertical centerline of the door. Lower the door and nail the ledger with its bottom edge on the mark. Using the lag bolts provided, install the header bracket 2½″ above the bottom edge of the ledger and on the vertical centerline of the door.

To install the completed primary assembly, you need the materials described in the manual. We prefer the angle-iron approach, although conduit or wood may be used as well.

First, position a ladder to support the power-unit end of the assembly temporarily. Attach the front end of the rail to the header bracket on the ledger, then raise the door to the Up position. Place some scrap blocking between the door and the rail to provide the necessary operating space. With the power unit and rail propped up in this manner and aligned with the centerline of the door, measure from the garage ceiling to the perforated bars on the top of the power unit.

Next, hacksaw three pieces of angle iron, one of which fits flush to the ceiling and is lagged to the joists. The two vertical irons are attached to the iron at the ceiling and to the two perforated bars on the power unit. Remove the blocking between door and rail, then lower the door to the Down position.

The two pieces of the door arm have multiple holes in order that the length, when they are bolted together, can be varied if required. An average length would be 18″ but installations may differ. The connections at both the carriage and the door-bracket ends employ clevis and cotter pins. The door bracket will be carriage-bolted to the door near the top on the vertical centerline. Because of this, metal or fiberglass doors may require some wood reinforcement, as shown in the manual.

With the door arm assembled and pinned to both carriage and bracket, and the door in the Down position, pull the release knob. This disengages the carriage from the tape, allowing the carriage to be manually advanced toward the door. Move the carriage forward until the clevis

Connect door arms to carriage and door bracket with clevis pins. Carriage-bolt bracket to door.

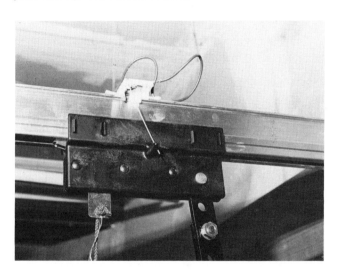

View of Down limit switch; carriage, release and arm from below.

pin at the carriage and the clevis pin at the bracket are separated by a minimum horizontal distance of 6″, with the bracket held flush against the door.

Mark the bracket holes at this location on the door and drill them through. Fasten the bracket to the door with the carriage bolts, locating the the bolt heads on the outside.

Now install the wires to the Up and Down limit switches and from the Up limit switch to terminal No. 3 on the power unit. Secure the wire in the switch-loop retainers and in the groove along the rail top. Roughly position the limit switches as follows. With the door fully raised manually, move the Up limit switch until the actuator arm (the thin rod) is 3″ from the carriage switch actuator (the horizontal pin). With the door manually placed in the Down position, move the Down limit switch to provide a 1″ space between the arm and the actuator.

Finishing and Testing

Connect one end of the bell wire to the pushbutton switch, the other end to terminal Nos. 1 and 2 of the power unit. The preferred location for the pushbutton is on the garage wall next to the door. Staples are provided to hold the bell wire in place. Install the four 40-watt bulbs (maximum) in the power-unit sockets, then secure the lenses. Plug the power cord into the receptacle.

Make sure the vacation switch (the On/Off toggle at the rear of the power unit) is On. Pull the release cord and let it go. Move the door to the Open position manually until the carriage is 2″ from, but not touching, the Up limit arm. Hit the button once for Up. Lights go on and the motor runs briefly and stops, but the door won't move. Then hit the button twice, for Down. The motor starts and the door comes down. You should also check the instant safety-reversing feature. Raise the door and then lower it electrically while applying upward pressure to the bottom of the door. If the door doesn't reverse direction, loosen the clutch-screw adjustment at the power unit (with the power disconnected) as described in the manual. Complete your check and give the door opener a trial run—from outside—using the radio controls.

30

Fixing Overhead Garage Doors

The typical single-width overhead garage door stands 7′ high and spans 8′ or 9′ jamb to jamb. It's made up of four or five sections hinged together, and its weight is counterbalanced by a pair of long coil-extension springs. A less typical type of overhead door is the double-width door or doors equipped with torsion-type springs. Work on torsion springs is best left, for safety reasons, to the professional. However, doors with extension springs can be easily fixed by the average DIY homeowner.

First, let's take a closer look at the overhead garage door system. You can clearly see in the diagram that the hinged sections, in proper working order, move as a unit on a pair of tracks (an inverted "L" on each side of the garage door opening). This means that the rollers ride in the tracks, their axles sitting in the brackets or hinges bolted to the edges of the door sections.

The tracks have mounting brackets that are lag-bolted to 2×6 vertical pads on either side of the door opening, as

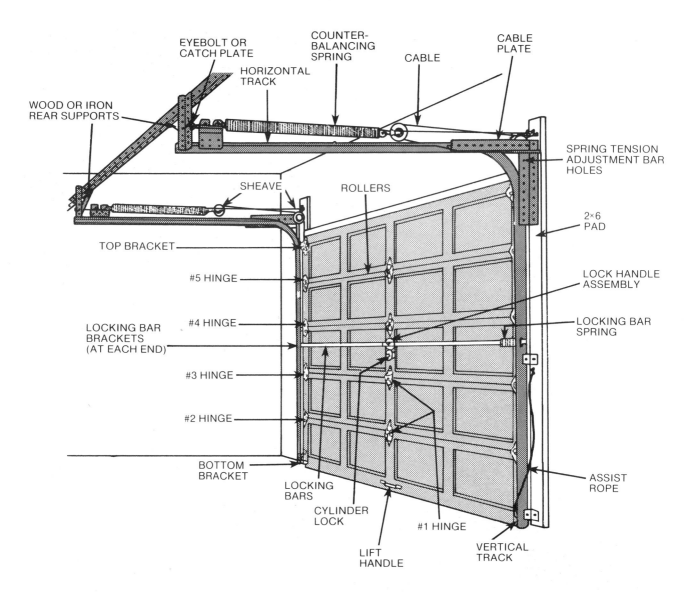

well as to the garage's ceiling joists, by angle irons. In addition to supporting the door and providing a track for the rollers, the tracks also control the lateral position and slope (free play) of the door.

Note that the vertical sections of the track near the front of the garage are not truly vertical. Instead, they are raked back slightly at the top, creating a wedge opening between the tracks and the profile of the door in the Down position. Also, the roller hinges or brackets are graduated in size from bottom to top, thereby increasing the space between the door sections and the roller axles toward the top of the door. This provides a good, running fit between the door and the doorstops, while the door is in motion, and achieves a tight fit against the stops when in the full Down position.

Linkage consists of coil springs, anchors, S-hooks, cable sheaves (pulleys), cable plates, spring-tension adjustment bars and bottom brackets (which are attached to the lower corners of the door's bottom section and connect the system to counterbalance the weight of the door). You

may find alternate hardware such as screw eyes or eyebolts at terminal points on the linkage in your particular door system. The springs themselves are sized by diameter and gauge for the approximate door weight, and the tension should be fine-tuned to achieve the balance required.

In addition to the lift handles to be found on both faces of the bottom section, the middle section is equipped with a lock, lock handle, locking bars, return springs and locking-bar guide brackets. These bars move more or less horizontally into rectangular openings in the vertical tracks to lock the door in the Down position and should snap back smartly when released, either by the key from the outside or the latch from the inside.

Common problems that do occur in overhead garage doors include the door slamming down; difficult lifting; sluggish rolling; sticking locking bars; broken, missing or deteriorated hinges; broken or fatigued springs; broken or frayed cables; rotted panels; broken glass and inoperative lock cylinders.

While some of the tracking problems are caused by misalignments due to faulty installation, others such as sluggish rolling are caused by lack of lubrication or worn-out sheaves and rollers. Still another cause of sluggish rolling is the installation of cheaper, non-ball-bearing sheaves or rollers. Cheap parts also may account for the rapid deterioration of hinges and brackets, especially when the gauge of the metal used is inadequate.

Rotting panels, mostly near the bottom, may be caused by water damage due to improper grading of the concrete apron at the garage front, which traps rainwater in the area. Springs and cables suffer fatigue and failure, given enough time and usage, while broken lights or panes usually are the result of errant baseballs or excessive door slamming.

Let's look at some cures or preventive measures you can take to guarantee a well-running overhead system. Lubrication of the moving parts is the simplest solution to tracking or motion problems, assuming that the moving parts are of good quality, in working condition and that the door and tracks are aligned. Apply lightweight oil to the tracks, rollers, sheaves and locking mechanisms. Nev-

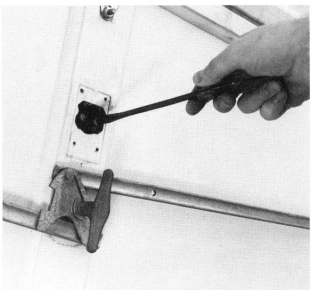

Before installing overhead door, provide all necessary jambs.

Fasten all hardware to door sections.

Fasten the lower track to the back jamb with lag screws.

Check the door lock mechanism to be sure it works properly.

er use grease on the tracks, because the accumulation of dirt and dust forms a scum that gradually slows the roller movement.

To replace a broken or fatigued spring (one spring usually is longer than the other when not under tension), proceed as follows: First, raise the door high enough to relieve the spring tension, and lock the door in that position by clamping a pair of locking pliers onto the tracks just under the bottom door section.

Remove the spring by releasing the S-hook at the front of the cable, then unhook the rear end of the spring from its bolt or catch plate. Complete the removal by releasing

the sheave at the front end of the spring. Reverse this procedure to install the new spring. Always replace pairs of springs—not just one. This ensures even tension. In some cases, the sheave may have a bolt-type axle with a nut that must be unscrewed to remove the sheave from the front of the spring.

Note that the S-hook, at the front of the cable near the garage front, joins the front of the cable plate to the holes in the spring-tension adjustment bar. The S-hook occupies one of the three plate holes, and the cable ties the remaining two. If you move the S-hook forward to the front of the garage, the spring tension increases. Moving

After installing rollers, insert the first door section in the track.

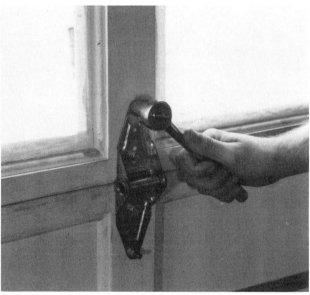

Sections can be fastened together by bolting hinge hardware.

Once first section is level, all others can be inserted in track.

Fasten stop around the door to prevent drafts.

The completed door. The door should ride along the track.

the hook toward the rear of the garage lessens tension. This fine-tuning adjustment must be done with the door held in the Up position.

To change the cables (again, as for the changing springs), lock the door in the Up position and release the spring tension. Remove the old cable from its attachment at the bottom corner bracket and at the S-hook and cable plate. Then simply route and attach the new one. Check and adjust the spring tension if necessary.

The best cables to buy are the stainless-steel aircraft type. These are somewhat harder to work with and cut, but they'll last a lot longer. Cable sheaves can be changed easily while the door is locked in the Up position and the tension released. Make sure that the replacement sheaves are the ball-bearing type. They last longer and work better.

While you're up there, install safety wires through the springs. These can be anchored at the ends with standard hardware such as eyebolts or screw eyes, and they're well worth the trouble. When a garage door spring fails, it can travel 20′ and still have enough punch to dent a wall or your body. When the springs fail with the safety wires installed, there's just a banging noise and some rattling along the wire.

If you've got just one panel to replace and the section is in good shape, chisel away and plane smooth the inner molding edge retaining the panel. Insert a piece of tem-pered Masonite, holding it in place with bead molding and brads. On the other hand, if there are a number of panels to replace and the condition of the section is questionable, consider replacing the section as a unit. It's usually the bottom section; new sections can be obtained from a local door manufacturer if you give him the specs.

When doing the replacement, be sure to lock the door in the Up position, as if working on springs or cables, and release the spring tension. If you have to remove the bottom of any intermediate section, be sure to control the weight of all sections above the replacement before disconnecting any hinges or brackets. Always replace hinges or brackets with the heaviest-duty ones available and install them with carriage bolts, drilling completely through the door to mount them. Again, lock the door in the Up position and control the weight of the section and release the spring tension.

Remember that the hinges and brackets on the door edges are graduated and numbered accordingly. The higher up the hinge or bracket, the farther away from the door plane the roller axles are located, and the larger the number of the hinge or bracket that is toward the top (1, 2, 3, etc., in the diagram).

As mentioned before, part of the function of the tracks, rollers, brackets and hinges is to locate the door's lateral position and control its side play. The brackets and hinges are, of course, fixed to the door sections, but the roller axles can move laterally. Their movement toward the center of the door is controlled by contact between the axle shoulders and the hinges or brackets, while movement away from the center of the door is constrained by the rollers against the tracks.

Therefore, set up the track brackets and hinges relative to their 2×6 pads on one side of the door so that the door edge is aligned with the door opening on that side and the roller shoulders are about 8″ out from their respective brackets or rollers. This adjustment can be made by loosening the track bracket lag bolts slightly and tapping the track to the desired position. When this is done, repeat the adjustment on the opposite side of the door.

To adjust locking bars, simply reposition the guide brackets vertically. Then make sure that the locking bars return smartly when the latch is released and, if necessary, replace the locking-bar return spring.

From the inside face of the door section, which has the locking handle, remove the latch-plate retaining screws and the latch plate. Then, from the outside, pull out the lock with its bezel or ring. To install the new lock, reverse the procedure and mate the lock tongue with the corresponding slot in the latch plate.

Part VII

Projects for
Better Living

31

Entryway

If you want to spruce up the look of your house without major alterations, consider building a new front entryway. I redesigned the facade of my home by replacing my old double front door with a single door and sidelights. A columned roof extension over the door embellishes the face and helps protect callers from the weather.

The project has two stages. Replace the old doors, jambs and storm doors with a new jamb, door, sidelights and storm door. Then build a post-supported shelter,

complete with decorative side-fencing and a convenient bench.

My plans called for a new jamb assembly with a single 3'-wide exterior door and a pair of 1'-wide sidelights. Both the sidelights and door would be steel-clad and insulated to provide energy savings as well as beauty.

The rough opening of the existing double door and its jamb was just a touch wider than the width of the new combination and its jamb. This meant the existing header could be left in place—a real time-saver.

If you are replacing a single exterior door and jamb with a similar combination, you will have to install a longer header and support trimmers. The header can be made from a pair of 2×10s with a piece of ½"-thick plywood sandwiched between them—plus a 2×4 bottom plate laid flat. From that point on, both jobs are the same.

To start the project, first rip the new jamb parts from 5/4×6 stock (actually 1⅛"×5½") to a width of 4 9/16". After trimming the pieces to length, identify and machine them. Note that the rabbets that receive the door are the standard ½"×1¾" size, while those that receive the sidelights are 2" deep. This extra depth allows enough space on the inner side of the 1½"-thick sidelights to install ¾" quarter-round molding.

Assemble the jamb parts with screws (including the doubled inner jambs) and then install the sidelights complete with their sweeps at the bottom. This is necessary because the sidelights are about ¾" shorter than the door (which comes with a threshold). Make sure to caulk the rabbet when inserting the sidelights and sweeps. Sidelights have wrap-around metal edges, so calculate their position on the side jambs, mark them, drill screw holes and screw them in place.

Trial-fit the door in the jamb, noting the height of the threshold on the inside. When you install the jamb assembly with its sidelights, you can adjust its height by adding or removing spacers under the sill. Note that the threshold itself has height adjustment screws. Also, make sure the double inner jambs are at least as wide as the door flanges. This eliminates any problem in applying interior molding later.

Remove the existing doors and jamb and then level, plumb and square the new jamb assembly within the rough opening. Tapered shims (undercourse shakes) can be inserted in pairs from both jamb sides as the fascias are added later. With all corrections made, nail the jamb in place so the nails are hidden by the moldings. Trim any shim excess flush with the moldings.

Add flat shims (provided with the door) to the jamb rabbet faces, as required, at the hinge and other recommended locations. Then insert and square the door and its steel jamb within the rabbet of the wooden jamb. Use caulking under the threshold. Lock the door in place by hammering the drive nails provided through the rear metal flanges, into the wooden jambs.

Remove the shipping hardware and lock the latch side of the door to the metal jamb. Drive the security screws, but avoid overtightening them because you might distort the metal jamb. Add the locks and strikes and fit the weatherstrip/stop. Tack it in place until you're sure the closure is snug; then drive the nails home.

Finish all exterior work first so the house can be made weathertight as quickly as possible. Leave the inside trim for later. Add the 5/4×2 fascias to the jamb head and to the outer and inner side jambs. Set the fascias on the inner side jambs so they'll fit the width of the storm door, if any.

The header can be made from a pair of 2×10s.

Rip the new jamb parts from 5/4×6 stock.

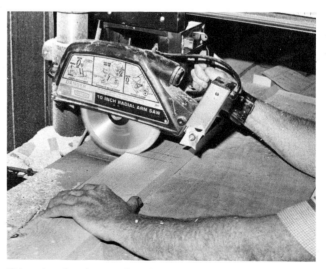

Trimming the pieces to length.

Assembling the jamb parts.

Fit the prehung door into the space between the sidelights. Make sure it's plumb and level before securing flanges.

Entry framework, which includes factory-installed sidelights, is positioned in the rough opening.

Install the head and side weatherstrip stops.

Check for square. If out of square, shim where necessary to correct.

Stanley Tools, Inc., cautions that the heat buildup between a storm door with thermal breaks and their insulated door is enough to distort the plastic breaks.

In my case, the door will be used with the screen only, for ventilation, so this doesn't apply. Refit the sheathing, building paper, undercourse and finish shakes to the outer jamb fascia. Caulk everything. The steel door and sidelights are factory primed, so you need only to prime the jamb and its fascia. Your home is now safe from the weather.

Begin the entryway roof by outlining a 5¾"×7' rectangle on the shakes, centered over the door 8' above the sill. Saw through the finish and undercourse shakes on the outline and mount the 2'×6'×6'9" lower ledger in the recess, nailing into the studs.

Next, cut to length and assemble the 2×6s for the "C"-shaped lower structure. Then, with the aid of a support,

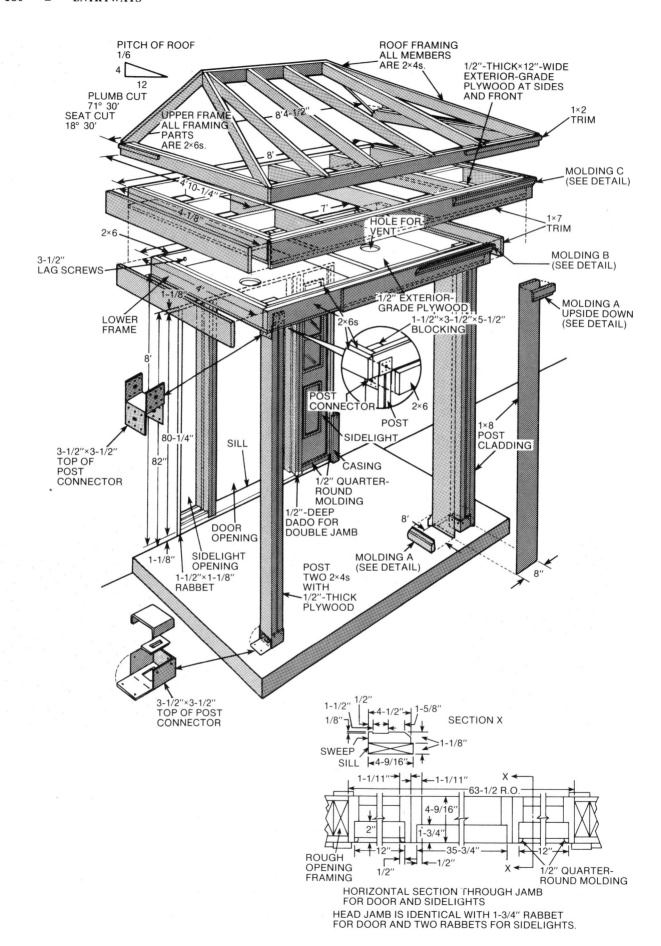

PITCH OF ROOF
1/6

4
12

PLUMB CUT
71° 30'
SEAT CUT
18° 30'

ROOF FRAMING
ALL MEMBERS
ARE 2×4s.

1/2''-THICK×12''-WIDE
EXTERIOR-GRADE
PLYWOOD AT SIDES
AND FRONT

UPPER FRAME
ALL FRAMING
PARTS
ARE 2×6s.

8'4-1/2''

8'

1×2
TRIM

MOLDING C
(SEE DETAIL)

4'10-1/4''

4-1/8''

7'

1×7
TRIM

2×6

HOLE FOR
VENT

MOLDING B
(SEE DETAIL)

3-1/2''
LAG SCREWS

1-1/8''

LOWER
FRAME

1/2'' EXTERIOR-
GRADE PLYWOOD

MOLDING A
UPSIDE DOWN
(SEE DETAIL)

2×6s

1-1/2''×3-1/2''×5-1/2''
BLOCKING

POST
CONNECTOR

POST

2×6

8'

3-1/2''×3-1/2''
TOP OF
POST
CONNECTOR

80-1/4''

82''

SILL

SIDELIGHT

CASING

1/2'' QUARTER-
ROUND
MOLDING

1/2''-DEEP
DADO FOR
DOUBLE JAMB

1×8
POST
CLADDING

DOOR
OPENING

SIDELIGHT
OPENING

1-1/2''×1-1/8''
RABBET

1-1/8''

POST
TWO 2×4s
WITH
1/2''-THICK
PLYWOOD

8'

MOLDING A
(SEE DETAIL)

8''

3-1/2''×3-1/2''
TOP OF POST
CONNECTOR

SECTION X

1-1/2''
1/2''
4-1/2''
1-5/8''

1/8''

1-1/8''

SWEEP
SILL

4-9/16''

1-1/11''
1-1/11''

63-1/2 R.O.

X

4-9/16''

2''

1-3/4''

35-3/4''

12''

12''

ROUGH
OPENING
FRAMING

1/2''
1/2''

X

1/2'' QUARTER-
ROUND MOLDING

HORIZONTAL SECTION THROUGH JAMB
FOR DOOR AND SIDELIGHTS

HEAD JAMB IS IDENTICAL WITH 1-3/4'' RABBET
FOR DOOR AND TWO RABBETS FOR SIDELIGHTS.

attach the "C" to the ledger. The ends of the side pieces should cap the ledger ends, making the structure width 7'.

Make up the piers, calculate their height (including the post connectors at both top and bottom) and trim to length. Plumb the piers and install them. Because the rectangle (formed by the "C" and the lower ledger) can still be forced out of square, nail ½"-thick exterior plywood to the underside of the rectangle with rosin-coated nails. Now the structure is totally stable.

Nail the upper ledger directly above the lower one, over the shakes. Insert inverted shakes between the wall and the ledger to plumb the ledger face and drive the nails into the studs. This 2×6 ledger, which is 7'9" long, should be centered over the lower one.

Now nail three 2×6 joists to the ledger on the house end and toenail them to the top edges at the front of the "C"

structure, allowing them to protrude 6". Add the inner layer of the upper structure to the ends of these joists and tie them in at the upper ledger. Nail the outer layer to the 2×6 at the front and to the ends of the upper ledger, capping over the top row of roof shingles, weatherproofing the structure.

Nail on 2×4 ledgers in the shape of the roof/wall line. Then cut and nail the 2×4 rafters. Note that the hip rafters going to the corners at the front must be double-beveled (where two roof planes meet). Add the 2×4 boards to the rafter tails and sheathe the roof. The structure is complete, except for the roofing and trim.

Staple the felt or building paper so that upper pieces overlap lower pieces. Nail upside down on the starter row of shingles. This provides a granular surface in the keys of the first row and creates a slight rake. Continue the shin-

Nail up the entryway lower ledger after cutting and removing the existing shakes from the siding. Allow space at both ends for the attachment of the roof framework.

The piers (pairs of 2×4s with ½"-thick plywood inserts) are mounted with connectors.

Basic E-frame is nailed to the ledger. You will need a temporary vertical brace like the one shown to stabilize the frame while securing it.

The upper ledger is bolted on, and the box header and ends are doubled.

Tuck aluminum flashing up under the shingles surrounding the roof outline. The bottom half of this flashing goes over the top row of roof shingles later. Then nail up ledgers inside the outline.

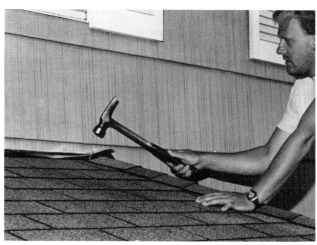

After this, staple on felt paper and secure the roof shingles.

Nail up four 2×4 common rafters on 24″ centers. Nail two hip rafters at the corners. Nail one rafter on each side into the hip rafter. Face off the tail ends of the rafters with 2×4s.

Square columns are made up of four 1×8s each. Two of the four boards are nailed to a pair of 2×4s; the remaining two boards are edge-nailed.

Fit the CDX ½″ roof sheathing and nail it down with rosin-coated box nails.

Nail up fascia; then add the trim and moldings.

gles, allowing a 5″ weather exposure. The rows from the small sides do not align, but this won't be noticeable at ground level.

Complete the roof by cutting the hip pieces from 3-tab butt shingles (three per shingle) and nailing them over the hip joint, starting at the bottom. Apply some roof mastic under the flashing, driving in a few roofing nails to keep it flat if necessary. Be sure to mastic these nails and holes.

Make up the columns from 1×8s, nailing face-to-edge at each corner. Nail two adjacent column faces to the cor-

responding faces of the piers (for strength) and trim the tops and bottoms of these columns with base or stop molding. Apply 1″ face boards to each horizontal surface; add the trim to the upper face board and add cove molding to both horizontal, inside corners. Set all nails, fill holes and defects with putty, sand lightly and apply a prime coat.

Make up the fences. The chamfers should be ripped off from the 2×4 stock used for the fences. Then the pieces should be trimmed to size and the half-notches machined.

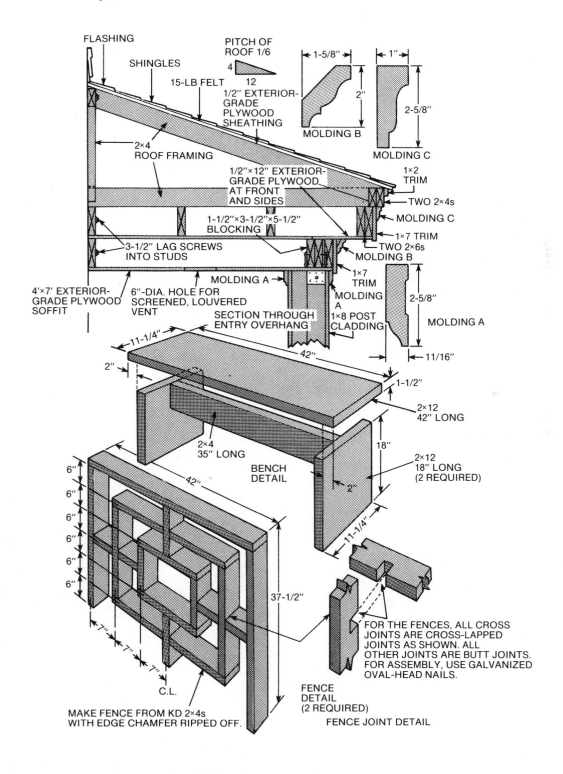

32

Intercom

This intercom system carries the sound of electronic door chimes throughout the house by means of remote speakers. From any station, you can talk to a caller, or to all other stations in the house. The system can have as many as ten remote speakers and two door speakers, or nine remote speakers and three door speakers. By leaving any inside speaker locked in the "talk" position, you can monitor the area from all other stations.

How It Works

A complete system, consisting of amplifier, transformers, inside and outside speakers, and an electronic chime, is shown in an accompanying diagram. The amplifier (the heart of the system) and the chime are each powered by a transformer, and all remote speakers hook into the amplifier, allowing speaking and listening be-

A 516 system inside speaker, mounted right above phone, provides inside and outside communication in one area.

A re you tired of running up and down stairs to answer the doorbell? Hoarse from screaming from the second floor to someone in the basement? Apprehensive about leaving the baby alone in the nursery while you attend to chores elsewhere in the house? If so, you need an intercom system. It will take you just one weekend to install such a system in your house.

The intercom shown here is a no frills system—just security and convenience, with good station-to-station performance.

tween all stations. Transformer power is carried to the amplifier on 18/2 bell wire, and all speakers are linked to the amplifier either by IW-6 (three twisted pairs) or IW-2 (one twisted pair) wire cable.

Inside speakers have a volume control, "talk" button, and outside-speaker cut-in control; outside speakers require no controls. The electronic chimes are always operative to alert you at any of the inside remote stations.

Planning the Job

In planning your system, take a little time to consider where you wish to place the inside speakers. Bedrooms, nursery, basement, kitchen and laundry rooms are good

bets, because your family members spend a lot of time there. Choosing locations for such other elements as the door chimes and outside speaker should be easier.

Once you have decided where to put things, the work consists of making cutouts for the remotes, routing the various wires and tying the system together. Final wiring is easy, thanks to the excellent labeling of the unit terminals and the color-coded wiring. Here are some things to keep in mind as your plans develop:

- For a good-looking installation, surface-mount the outside door speakers and flush-mount the inside ones.
- Locate the amplifier and transformers close to a 115/120-volt power source (usually in the basement).

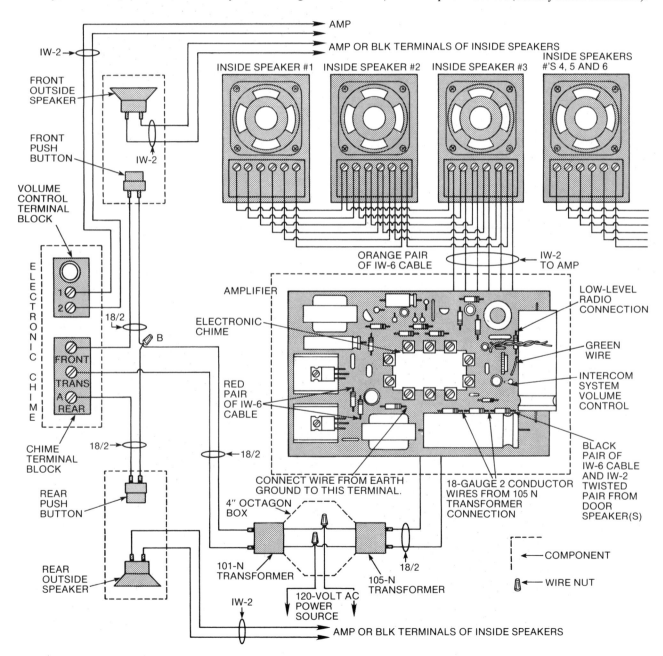

Complete wiring of system from power to outside speakers. If you use only one bell, eliminate wiring between A and B.

- Generally, it's best to mount both the 101-N transformer (for the chime) and the 105-N (for the amplifier) on a 4″ octagon box that will supply power for them.
- Except for the outside speakers, don't route wires through, or mount equipment on, exterior walls. That way, you avoid fighting through insulation and tearing vapor barriers found there. Besides, exterior mountings are subject to moisture damage. Wherever possible, route wiring within interior walls to the stations.
- Keep intercom wires at least 12″ away from AC power wiring to eliminate buzzing or humming in the system.
- The allowable length of wire to one speaker is 500′; to two speakers hooked together, 250′; to three speakers hooked together, 150′.
- Try to take the shortest route between components.
- To avoid feedback, never mount speakers back-to-back on a common wall.
- No more than three speakers can be connected on a single run of wire.

It's easiest to mount both transformers on one box and supply low-voltage power to chimes and amplifier this way.

Drilling Holes, Routing Wires

In a one-story home with a basement, it's easiest to run the speaker wires to the wall locations directly from the basement. In a one-story house built on a concrete slab, the wall locations are best reached by running wire up into the attic and then dropping it down inside walls where required. A two-story home with a basement can be wired by using a combination of methods: Wire first-floor locations from the basement; second-floor locations from the attic. In split level homes, wire the first or lower floor(s) from the basement, the upper rooms from the attic and the intermediate levels using one or more of these methods.

- Run wires horizontally between joists, behind base moldings or in the space between the head jamb and header over a doorway.
- Run wires vertically in the space between the side jamb and 2×4 trimmer in doorways. To do this, you have to pull moldings or casings; to prevent paint from pulling off with them, first score the paint joints where the millwork touches walls or jambs.
- Run wires horizontally and/or vertically inside closets.

Begin work by outlining the inside speaker rough-in holes. Before cutting a hole, make a small opening in the center and fish around inside for a possible obstruction. If all's clear, cut the hole with a wallboard saw, keyhole saw or jigsaw. To avoid excessive cracking in plaster walls, prior to sawing, deeply score the outline with a utility knife, awl or chisel; if the plaster is mounted on metal lath, cut the lath with a tin snips after removing the plaster.

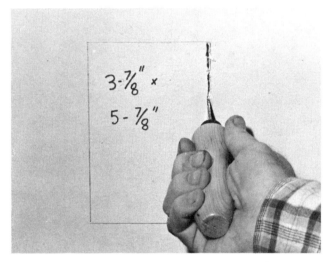

Make the cutouts for the inside speakers by cutting through plasterboard with plasterboard saw, keyhole saw or jigsaw.

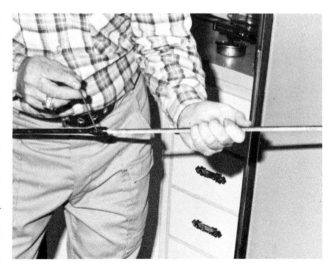

For those awkward spots, make up a long drill by locking extensions on to a bell-hangers or other type bit.

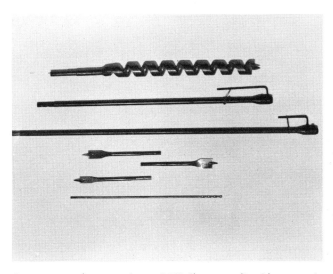

Auger, extensions, spades and ⅛"-diameter pilot bit are tools that make wire routing a no-problem job.

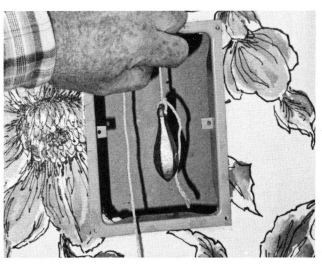

Fishing sinker tied to end of a length of mason's cord is handy for probing and snaking wires to hole below.

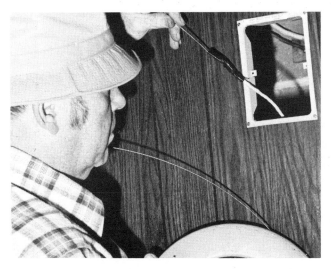

After running fishtape through hidden area, attach the wires to the loop and pull both fishtape and wires back.

Once you reach the lower hole, tie wires to end of the mason's cord and pull both back to access hole.

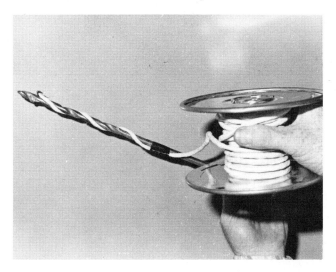

Use the tip hole in the bell-hangers bit to attach wires. Then route the wires using this bit with extensions.

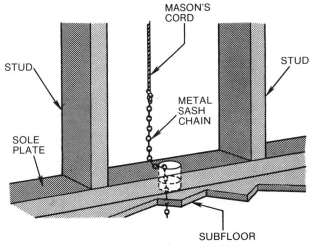

Old-timers use piece of metal sash chain attached to mason's cord. When chain enters hole, it drags the rest along.

Once rough-in holes are cut, drill wire-routing holes through either top or sole (bottom) plates, using one of these methods:

1. Locate the center of the correct stud bay by measuring and then drill through plates from above or below as required.
2. Temporarily pull the base molding away from the wall, drill a ⅛" diameter pilot hole down through the floor, and then go below to locate the stud bay center from the protruding bit. This technique may also be used at the wall-ceiling joint to locate the center of the top plates from above, after which the small hole may be spackled.

If you run into a firestop (a horizontal 2×4 nailed between adjacent studs), open a hole in it by inserting a drill bit and the necessary extensions with a ¼" drill motor. You might also use this method to go through plates.

To go from basement to attic, try to find, and run the wires alongside the main stack (plumbing), pipes or air ducts (there is usually extra space). In a two-story house, you can run wires up through a closet-over-closet construction.

There are a number of ways to route wires:

- Work fishtape (electrical snake) along the run, from one accessible spot to the next.
- Fasten the wires or a length of mason's cord to the tip hole in the end of a bell hangers drill (add extensions as necessary); insert into the hidden areas; probe for the exit hole; and pull out the wires or cord at the next accessible area. If the run is made with cord, attach the wires to either end and pull them through; if you started with the wires, you're all set.
- Suspend a fishing weight from a length of mason's cord and tease the weight through a hole located below.
- Add a foot or so of metal sash chain to a length of mason's cord, suspend the combination and fish for the hole. Once the chain finds the hole, it will pull the rest through, link by link.

Mechanical Work

Cut off the power to the octagon box, where you're going to mount both transformers, and lock these transformers into two of the box holes. Next, at the outside doorspeaker location(s), outline the rough-in plate on the siding and drill a 1½" diameter hole in the center. Caulk and screw the plate to the siding. Then pull both an IW-2 and an 18/2 cable through the hole from the wall. The IW-2 will go from the speaker terminals to the amplifier and the 18/2 cable will go from the pushbutton to the chime terminal block and the 101-N transformer.

Install the IR-3 inside speaker rough-in plates, either with small screws or even better, with five-minute epoxy, pulling the IW-6 cables through the holes in the plates.

The amplifier, with the cover removed shows both 18/2 and IW wires coming into the electronic component board.

Electronic chime, with cover removed, shows volume-control terminal block (top) and chime terminal block (center).

Outside speaker, showing 18/2 and IW-2 wires coming out of hole in plate, connected to speaker, bell pushbutton.

Outside door speaker and pushbutton when covered. Button is always operative; speaker is controlled indoors.

Mount the amplifier in a convenient spot so that it can be wired and serviced.

Finishing Up

Connect the pair of 18/2 wires between the 105-N transformer and the amplifier. Connect the 18/2 wires between the 101-N transformer, pushbuttons and the chime terminal board. If you plan to use only one outside speaker and pushbutton, eliminate the 18/2 wire between points A and B in the system diagram (rear terminal on board and junction).

Connect the IW-2 coming from the chime volume-control board to the appropriate terminal of the amplifier. Connect the IW-2 wires coming from the outside speakers either to the appropriate amplifier terminals or to the black terminals of an inside speaker. Grouped inside speakers should be parallel wired as shown, with

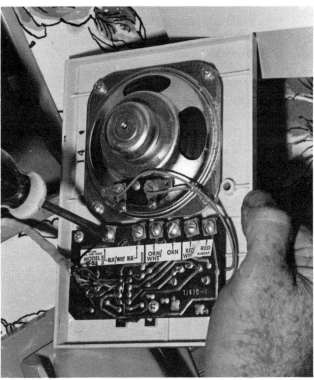

Business end of inside speaker shows wires of IW-6 cable connected to a very well marked terminal board.

the IW-6 harness from the nearest inside speaker connected directly to the amplifier.

Wire all speakers and mount them to the rough-in plates using the screws provided.

Turn the breaker on to provide power for the transformers, amplifier and electronic chime. Set all inside speaker volume controls at maximum, then set the master volume control at the amplifier to eliminate distortion. Reset the speaker volume controls, and the system is ready to go.

33

Central Vac System

You can put an end to struggling up and down stairs with noisy upright or canister portable vacuum cleaners by installing a central vacuum system yourself. The cost is moderate, the system adds more than its cost to the value of your house and with some advance planning, it's not a difficult job.

How It Works

One system we installed is a gigantic two-port power unit that provides better suction at the business end than the smaller portable types. You still have to dispose of bags (accomplished by opening two retaining clips and removing the lower canister from the power unit) but only a few times a year.

An outlet port exhausts air and excess dust to the outside of the house. The vacuum port connects to a tube, the main trunk, which goes to the service hose inlet at the location farthest from the power unit. Branch tubes run off the main trunk to the rest of the inlets, located at strategic spots throughout the house. An average house requires three or four inlets.

Both main trunk and branch tubing are 2″ O.D. PVC cemented to a variety of PVC plumbing fittings, mostly tees, wyes, ells, stop couplings and flanged ells. Eighteen-gauge wire (routed along with the tubing) connects the inlets to the low-voltage circuit at the power unit to provide remote control startup from each inlet.

The service hose, either 23′ or 32′ long, comes with an electrical cord to run the power beater.

Planning the System

First, decide where to put the power unit. For the quietest operation, it should be away from the general living area, in the basement, garage or closet. But it should be near a household electrical outlet.

Plan the mounting on or near an exterior wall so that you can punch a hole through that wall to vent the unit, preferably through a muffler. There must be 12″ of free space above the unit and 18″ below to allow access to the motor reset button, motor service and lower canister.

The service hose inlets are usually placed in the walls, but can be installed in the floor as well, depending upon

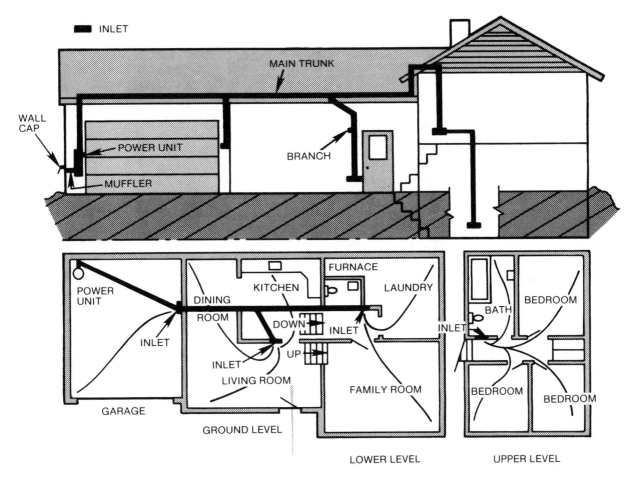

INLET

MAIN TRUNK

WALL CAP

POWER UNIT

BRANCH

MUFFLER

POWER UNIT

KITCHEN

FURNACE

DINING ROOM

LAUNDRY

DOWN

INLET

BATH

BEDROOM

INLET

INLET

UP

INLET

LIVING ROOM

FAMILY ROOM

BEDROOM

BEDROOM

GARAGE

GROUND LEVEL

LOWER LEVEL

UPPER LEVEL

Typical split-level home equipped with four-inlet central vacuum system with power unit in garage. System offers better suction, twice-a-year bag disposal.

the construction of your house. These inlet locations should be chosen so that the service hose will be used to best advantage. Spend some time with a piece of string and tack to determine the best possible inlet locations. Tack one end of the string to the base molding at the proposed inlet locations. With some experimentation, you'll be able to cover the entire floor area with the minimum number of inlets.

Keep in mind that the inlets should not be blocked by doors, furniture, electrical or plumbing devices. Finally, they should be located within 6' of a household electrical outlet so you can plug in the beater cord.

Tubing and Wiring

Routing the tubing and wiring can be tricky, but it doesn't have to be. If you have a one-story house with a basement, routing and installing the tubing and wiring is a snap. The power unit goes in the basement and the tubing with the wiring is routed directly through the subfloor into the sole plates of the interior walls.

However, if you have a one-story without a basement, a colonial or other multilevel, don't give up the idea. For

the house lacking a basement, you can locate the power unit in the garage or a closet. Route the tubing up to the attic, branch as necessary, and drop down through the wall top plates to the inlets.

Colonial installation usually starts with the power unit in the basement. Run the main trunk up to the attic, branch as necessary and drop down through the second story wall inlets. Most colonials have closet-over-closet construction, which will permit you to make the basement-to-attic run inside the closets. First floor inlets in a colonial are handled in the same way as the one-story home with basement.

In some multilevel houses, it's easier to place the power unit in the garage and get the tubing into the walls from there. Or you might run tubing from the basement to the attic as I did in my split ranch, through the forced air return duct. Removing panels is another way of routing tubing vertically. However, if you must open a wall (a rare situation), do it in a closet, behind cloth-backed wall covering or in an area where the drywall repair will be hidden.

Routing the tubing and 18-gauge low-voltage wire will require drilling large holes (about 2½" diameter) with a

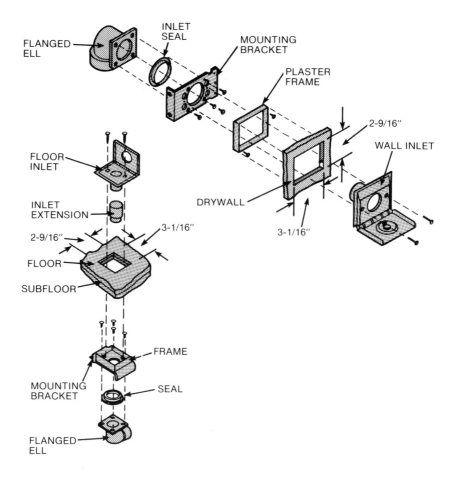

Locate center of wall for drilling large hole by calculating from a pilot hole drilled at base molding. As seen from the basement, photo shows large hole bored. Note the dowel sticking through.

Tape low-voltage wiring to the tube at least 1″ from the end of the tube. This allows for ¾″ of tube to be inserted into the fitting.

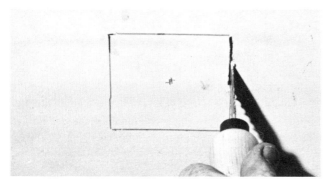

Cut out rectangular opening in the wall above pilot hole after checking inside wall for interference.

Flanged ell has been cemented to tube, bracket screwed to flange.

½″ drill and a 2⁹/₁₆ multi-spur bit or equivalent typically used by plumbers. If you run into construction nails, just drill a series of smaller holes in a circular or rectangular pattern and knock out the waste material in the middle.

Wall Inlets

Once you've decided on the inlet locations and tube routing, pull the base or shoe molding away from the wall directly below the proposed inlet.

Now drill down through the subfloor using a ⅛″ extra-long bit. Remove the bit and insert a ⅛″ dowel into this pilot hole so that it protrudes into the basement. From the basement, find the center of the wall sole plate using the dowel as a guide as shown, and drill 2½″ holes upward. Inspect the inside of the wall for any interference with a flashlight.

If the area is clear, go back upstairs and cut a 3 ¹/₁₆″×2⁹/₁₆″ hole in the wall about 18″ above the floor. Then have a helper insert a length of tube, with the low voltage wire taped on, up into the hole in the subfloor and sole plate from the basement. Insert a 90° flanged ell into the wall cutout and cement the ell to the top end of the tube. Center the ell in the cutout and have your helper cut off the tube to length, from below.

Next insert an inlet bracket through the cutout and fasten it to the ell with the screws provided, making sure

not to dislodge the inlet seal. Pull the free end (about 6″ from where it's taped to the tube) of the low-voltage wire through one of the small access holes in the bracket, and attach the stripped wire ends to the terminals on the inlet base.

Moisten the inside of the inlet seal and insert the tube end of the inlet base into the gasket with a slight twisting motion. Fasten the base to the bracket with the long screws provided, tucking the excess low-voltage wire back through the access hole as you drive the screws home. Check the diagram for correct assembly.

From the attic, installation of a wall inlet is basically the same. Calculate the center for the large hole in the doubled top plates of the wall, from a dowel inserted in a pilot hole drilled into the ceiling very close to the wall. Bore the large hole from the attic, check for any interference, make the drywall cutout and drop a tube down from the attic. Complete the mechanical and electrical work on the inlet.

Study the diagram for a back-to-back to wall installation, and note that if the wall is thin, the inlet base tubes may get too close together, blocking the passage. If this is the case, trim back the tubes somewhat, with a hacksaw.

A diagram is also shown here for a floor inlet installation. Note the use of the extension sleeve to take up the space.

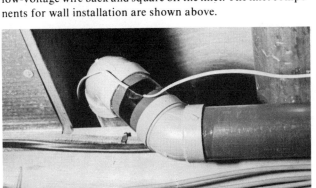

As you drive home the inlet screws into the bracket, tuck the low-voltage wire back and square off the inlet. The inlet components for wall installation are shown above.

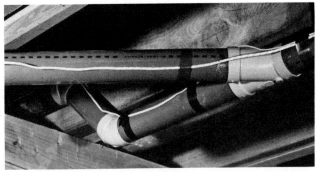

The branch is entering the main through a 45° ell, tube and 45° wye. Note that the wye is one-directional only, toward right.

Branch level and direction have been changed by the use of two 45° ells and a short length of tube. Note low-voltage wire.

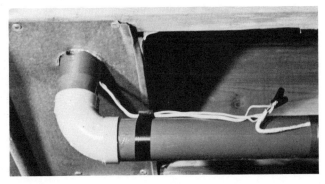

This is main trunk heading up to the attic where it will branch and drop to the inlets. It's going inside of a return duct.

Installing Tubing

Begin the power unit installation by mounting a ¾"×15"×20" piece of plywood firmly on or near an exterior wall. Using the power unit mounting bracket for a template, locate and drive in the mounting bolts and hang the unit as shown. Bring the branch tubes into the main trunk and head the trunk toward the vacuum (lower) port of the unit.

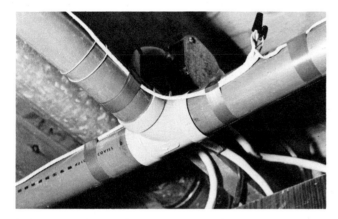

Branch enters main through a one-directional 90° tee. Note hanger at left and low-voltage wire nut junction at right.

Horizontal tube is main trunk going toward vacuum port and 45° angled tube has left the muffler going to the wall cap.

Exhaust port (top), rubber hose, tube, ell and muffler. Vacuum port (bottom), rubber hose, ell and main trunk at power unit.

Note that all branches should come into the main trunk on the same level or from above the main trunk. Connect the trunk to the vacuum port with the rubber hose and clamps provided.

Test-fit the tubing and fittings of the exhaust branch, including the muffler (optional, but well worth it), so that it will fit neatly between the exhaust (upper) port and the outside of the exterior wall. Drill a small hole through the wall from the inside at this exit point. Then backdrill the large hole from the outside to avoid splintering the siding. Complete the exhaust by connecting the tubes and fittings from the exhaust port to the wall cap on the outside. Caulk the rear face of the wall cap as shown.

Complete the low-voltage circuit by connecting the two 18-gauge wire leads to the terminal screws on the low-voltage terminal block at the power unit.

Finishing Up

Plug the power cord of the unit into the nearest household electrical outlet, remove the lower canister, take out the extra disposable bags and replace the canister.

Short across the two screws of the low-voltage terminal block on the power unit and the unit should start. Make

Exhaust ends in wall cap outside of the house. Caulk rear face of cap. The muffler on the inside really quiets this system.

Close-up view of the low-voltage wires attached to the screws on the low-voltage terminal block on power unit near exhaust.

sure each inlet is electrically operative by inserting the service hose into it. Check the diagram of the low-voltage hookup. If you experience poor vacuum at any inlet, check inlet seals and joints for any possible leaks.

Tips on PVC Tubing

Here are some hints that may be handy when working with PVC tube and fittings. The photos show cutting, deburring, cementing and inserting tubes into fittings.

- Once the routing holes are bored in sole or top plates of the wall, you can feed in tube and fittings in tandem, cementing up as you go. Just make sure that tees or wyes or ells are oriented correctly.
- Where angles are involved, such as in joining branches to main trunks or fitting exhaust branches, it's best to cut the tubes and assemble the branch dry before cementing. Allow ¾" of tube for insertion into fittings.
- Some of the plumbing fittings such as tees and wyes are directional. Study the photos.

- Unsupported spans of tubing should be suspended from wires and nails placed at reasonable intervals.
- Loss of vacuum may occur due to obstructions in the service hose or branch, leakage at an inlet or disposable bag full. The latter problem is easily corrected by changing the bag and cleaning the secondary filter above it. Correct leakage at inlets with proper inlet door sealing.
- Test for a clogged hose by inserting it into one of the inlets and checking for good vacuum at the other inlets. If the vacuum is good at the other inlets, insert the service hose into one of these inlets. If the clog remains, it's in the hose and can be cleared by running a length of garden hose through the service hose. If the blockage is not in the hose, but in the branch (determined by inserting the hose in one inlet that appears clogged, and then in a second inlet will work), further service is required.

With proper planning and all the parts on hand, you should be able to complete the installation in a weekend.

PVC tube is easily cut with a hacksaw with fine-toothed blade. Make sure that you cut square to effect the best possible seal.

Apply cement to the outside of the tube covering about the first inch. Use cement sparingly to avoid excess gumming in joint.

Deburr both the inside and the outside edges of the hacksaw cut with a knife. A clean ended tube makes the best seal.

Insert tube with wet cement into fitting with a slight twisting motion and press home. Here, we're using a flanged ell.

Use oval-head galvanized nails for assembly. After a light sanding, prime the fences. Assemble the bench in a similar manner and prime it as well.

At this point all that remains is the finish coat of paint and the light fixture mounting. Screw the fences in place so they can be easily removed for repainting in the future.

Inside the house, build out the moldings on the head and side to allow for the thickness of the jamb moldings on either side of the door. These moldings may require nailing through predrilled holes in the steel flanges beneath them.

Screw the fences in place for easy removal for repainting.

34

Skylight

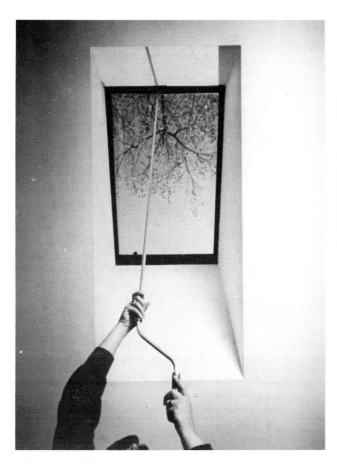

With the installation of a skylight, you get more light and better airflow. An optional feature with this model is the extension handle to operate the crank handle on the window (left). The roof view shows the window open.

W hether your home is a ranch, split or colonial type, you can give any room in it additional light and air by installing a skylight. With a skylight you gain reduced lighting costs, maximum air circulation in the summer as the hotter air escapes, some free heat in the winter because the unit acts as a solar collector (especially true for southern exposures) and streaming sunlight, creating the feeling of a Vermeer canvas.

Installing a typical small skylight takes about 4 to 5 hours in a cathedral ceiling and, more time, 2 to 3 days for a flat ceiling.

The skylight shown here has a one-piece molded-urethane base with predrilled mounting holes, a crank-open top with laminated safety glass and thermal breaks, plus several optional items worth considering. The options are an extension handle to operate the top, a shade screen for the summer and a triple-glazed storm panel for the winter. Both the screen and storm panel fit into a groove with spring loading. The skylight we chose was 30″×46″. Of course, skylights come in various other sizes. If your roof has a pitch of 3″ to 12″ or greater, you can install a small one yourself.

Considerations and Decision Making

Basically, the job entails opening a hole in both the roof and the ceiling of the room just below, except in the case of the cathedral ceiling. These holes are then boxed in, the unit installed on the roof and the space between the openings (the light shaft) framed out to support insulation and finish wall.

Select your room, if possible, so that the sun will be over the skylight for the longest possible time (facing south is the best, as demonstrated by solar collector design). The unit size is dictated by the rafter spacing of your roof. For example, if the rafters are on 16″ centers it's most practical to install a 30″-wide skylight, removing part of only one rafter and thus exposing two rafter bays. On the other hand, if your rafters are on 24″ centers, the best bet is a 22″-wide skylight, which will fit in the bay between two rafters. In both cases, only a couple of pieces of lumber are needed to box out the rough opening on the roof.

Then there's the shape of the light shaft, which may be either rectangular or fan-shaped. The simplest but least efficient is the rectangular shape, which is constructed with all four walls plumb. By keeping two sides and one end plumb and then raking the opposite end, you get a moderate fan effect; if you rake both ends, you get a broad fan effect. The latter is more efficient but requires a lot of ceiling. In our case, we chose the moderate fan-shape, keeping the end nearest the exterior wall (on the low side of the roof opening) plumb and raking the opposite end. It's best to keep the side walls plumb, otherwise you must open a larger hole in the ceiling in the wrong direction; i.e., cut too many joists and placing heads between without additional support.

Tools and Materials

You need a tape, rafter square, hammer, saw, screwdriver (better, a brace and bit snips), utility knife, prybar with a broad flat end (or a fairly brutish putty knife), drill, stapler, caulking gun and trowel. Although a portable circular saw may be used to cut open the roof sheathing, the most efficient combination of cutters are a jigsaw and reciprocating saw. These give you speed, control and easy access to rafters and joists, which are awkward to undercut. Materials needed are enough 2× stock to box in both the roof and ceiling (except for cathedrals), plus the light-shaft framing. You also need drywall, insulation, common, roofing and drywall nails, perhaps a bit of roofing felt, roof mastic, silcone caulking, corner bead, tape and jointing compound.

For the actual installation, I strayed from the manufacturer's instructions, but you may choose to follow them. Begin by cutting out a small hole in the ceiling where the skylight will go, then drilling a reference hole through the roof from this access point. The hole represents a corner of the roof's rough opening, so it should be right next to the rafter that borders the skylight. Also, check the weather report before you start opening the roof unless you really relish working under the gun because the rains have begun.

Preparation

Mark the outline of the rough opening on the roof, starting from the drilled reference hole and following the dimensions on the carton. Don't cut anything yet. Strip back enough shingles (three tab butts are 12″×36″) to completely expose the roofing felt over the opening. To remove the shingles, first separate the overlapping course from those below them, driving a putty knife or prybar end underneath before lifting. Be gentle with a brittle, old roof to avoid cracking it. Work on a real hot day, when the roofing shingles will be most flexible. After separating the shingles, remove the four roofing nails holding each one and set the shingles aside for later refitting and installation.

Mark the rough opening outline again and saw it out. Next trim back the rafters, as necessary, at the correct angle to accommodate either plumb or raked end walls. Start the cuts 1½″ above and below the opening to provide room for the box heading to be nailed between the adjacent rafters and to the cut rafter ends (at the high and low ends of the opening). Make sure that the top edges of the cut rafters are flush with the header, which is flush with the adjacent rafters. Complete the roof rough opening by renailing the roof sheathing to the box-in framing.

Installation

Dry-fit the skylight to the opening, noting that it overhangs it by about ½″ all around the perimeter. This is where the finish material from the shaft walls butts later on. Remove the skylight and apply caulking, as shown in the manufacturer's instructions, both over and under the roofing felt. If the felt was damaged in previous work, replace the bad portions before caulking. Keep the caulking back from the opening edge to avoid a messy installation because the caulking does squeeze out.

Now, realign the skylight (top closed) with the opening; attach with screws through the predrilled holes in the base flange. Complete the roof work by applying mastic to the flange and refitting the shingles. Trim the shingles with a utility knife or snips.

Moving inside, nail the rafters directly to the adjacent joists. This offsets the joists in the ceiling relative to the rafters above them. Therefore, to get the side walls in the light shaft plumb, add a sister joist to the existing joist on the scant side and relocate the joist on the full side after you complete the cutting and heading. The offset is the width of the rafter lumber: 1½″ from the 2× stock.

Start by enlarging the hole in the ceiling to get some working room. Then install temporary supports under

Carefully remove shingles at installation site and mark outline for opening. Use a reciprocating saw to cut out opening after making a small hole to locate a rafter.

Apply a wide bead of mastic or silicone all around the perimeter of opening, leaving the edges clear.

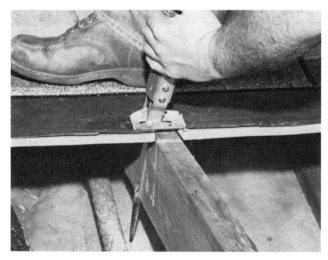

Trim back rafter 1″ to 1½″ by sawing a small notch at the high and low ends.

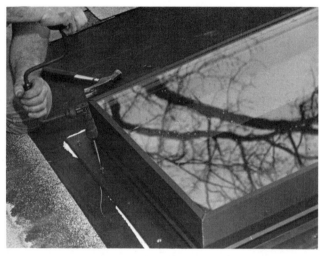

Align skylight with opening and drive screws into predrilled holes. Mastic will squeeze out.

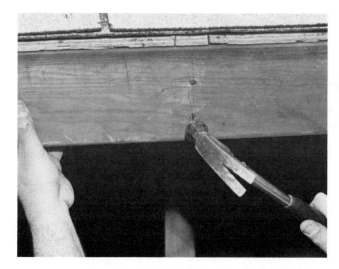

Nail headers to the adjacent rafters to frame opening. Keep all top edges flush.

Complete the roof work by applying mastic to the flange and refitting the shingles.

the ceiling to prevent any cracking until the box-in is done. Cut out both the center and full-side joists (assuming 16″ on center spacing) 3″ longer on each end than the ceiling opening to provide room for the doubled headers that box in the ends. Next, preassemble a double header and install it at the high end, where there's room to get behind it for nailing. On the low end, install the double header one piece at a time. Now measure, fit and install the joists. Double up with the existing joist on the scant side and relocate the joist on the full side, 1½″ away. Both of these joists fit between the heads, adding blocking between the full-side joist and its neighbor to prevent any bellying at the opening. Nail drywall ceiling to the box-in members as needed.

Fit and nail in the cripple studs between the two box-in frames (roof and ceiling) on 16″ centers and be sure to throw in a couple of nailers at the corners for drywall support. Remove the ceiling supports. Staple the insulation to the shaft framing, apply the drywall, corner bead, tape and joint compound. Sand and prime and you're ready to paint.

Mark the ceiling inside with outline of opening and cut it out.

Nail drywall ceiling to the box-in members as needed.

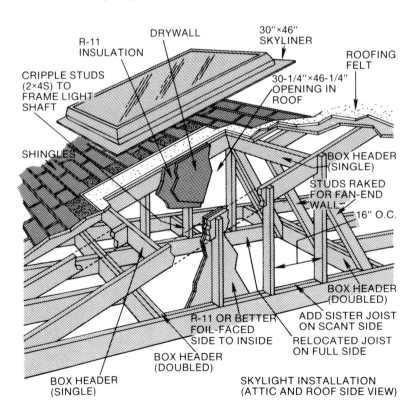

Skylight installation (attic and roof side view).

Part VIII

Basement

35

Basement Shop/Tool Organizer

When the top cabinet is open, tools are visible and easily accessible. Slide-mounted drawers of lower section are used for large tools. Both units are easy to construct and are primarily made of plywood.

Here's a complete tool organizer for your home shop. The system consists of a 30″×60″, wall-mounted cabinet above a cabinet with drawers.

Some of its advantages:

1. The drawer section can be constructed small enough so it takes up no more room than a modest-sized workbench. But, if you have room, it can be made much larger.

2. Although, when it is closed, the box cabinet uses only 10 square feet of wall space, when it is open, it provides 40 square feet of storage—and that's not even counting the front faces.

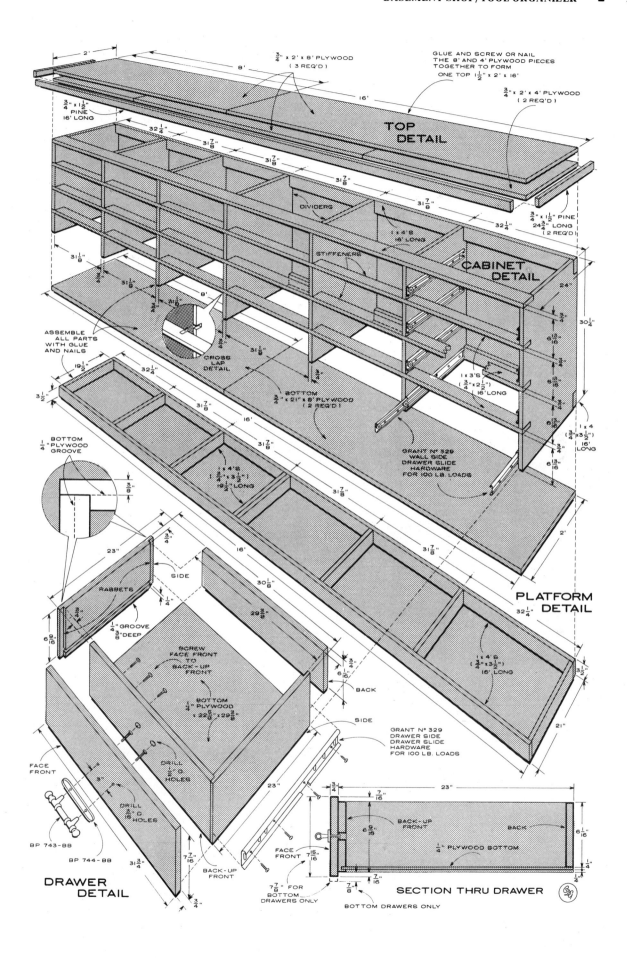

2'

8'

16'

¾" x 2' x 8' PLYWOOD
(3 REQ'D)

GLUE AND SCREW OR NAIL
THE 8' AND 4' PLYWOOD PIECES
TOGETHER TO FORM
ONE TOP 1½" x 2' x 16'

¾" x 2' x 4' PLYWOOD
(2 REQ'D)

TOP
DETAIL

¾" x 1½"
PINE
16' LONG

32¼"

3⅞"

3⅞"

3⅞"

3⅞"

DIVIDERS

31⅞"

32¼"

¾" x 1½" PINE
24¾" LONG
(2 REQ'D)

1 x 4's
16' LONG

CABINET
DETAIL

24"

30¼"

31⅛"

STIFFENERS

8'

CROSS
LAP
DETAIL

ASSEMBLE
ALL PARTS
WITH GLUE
AND NAILS

1 x 3's
(¾" x 2½")
16' LONG

1 x 4
(¾" x 3½")
16'
LONG

6⅝₁₆

3½"

19½"

32¼"

31⅞"

16'

31⅞"

31⅞"

BOTTOM
¾" x 21" x 8' PLYWOOD
(2 REQ'D)

GRANT N° 329
WALL SIDE
DRAWER SLIDE
HARDWARE
FOR 100 LB. LOADS

BOTTOM
¼" PLYWOOD
GROOVE

⅜"

23"

SIDE

16'

30⅛"

31⅞"

PLATFORM
DETAIL

32¼"

RABBETS

¼"

¼" GROOVE
¾" DEEP

6⅝₁₆

¾"

29⅞"

SCREW
FACE FRONT
TO
BACK-UP
FRONT

BOTTOM
¼" PLYWOOD
22⅝" x 29⅝"

¾"

6⅝₁₆

BACK

SIDE

1 x 4's
(¾" x 3½")
16' LONG

3½"

21"

2'

GRANT N° 329
DRAWER SIDE
DRAWER SLIDE
HARDWARE
FOR 100 LB. LOADS

FACE
FRONT

3"

DRILL
⅝" Ø.
HOLES

DRILL
⅜" Ø
HOLES

23"

23"

¾"

7/16"

6⅝₁₆

BACK-UP
FRONT

BACK

¼" PLYWOOD BOTTOM

6⅝₁₆

¼"

BP 743-BB

BP 744-BB

31¾"

7 7/16"

¾"

BACK-UP
FRONT

FACE
FRONT

7 15/16"

7⅞" FOR
BOTTOM
DRAWERS ONLY

7/16"

⅞"

SECTION THRU DRAWER

DRAWER
DETAIL

BOTTOM DRAWERS ONLY

3. Either unit may be mounted separately.
4. Fold-out doors of the box cabinet (it is a modification of a tall kitchen cabinet) can be used to group tools according to the type of work for which they will be used. For example, I devote one entire section to router bits and accessories and another to woodwork measurement.
5. When the cabinet is open, tools are both visible and accessible. When it is closed, the tools are kept clean and dust-free.
6. Somewhat larger tools and bulkier supplies can be stored in the slide-mounted drawers of the lower section.
7. Neither piece is difficult to construct, and both use standard plywood as the basic material.
8. You may build both units at one time or either unit at any time, depending upon your storage requirements and the time you have to devote to the project.

Drawer Cabinets

The drawer sections may be built any length down to a minimum of two drawer widths. The 16'-long drawer unit shown (it was decided upon because enough space was available for it) took two full lengths of plywood.

Each fold-out door can be used to group tools according to work they're used for.

Start by building the platform from 1×4 stock to provide a toe space and a level base for the cabinet. Assemble the box-frame platform, and level. You can do this either by scribing and trimming down the high spots, or by wedging up the low ones with undercourse shakes (these do the job as well as finish shake siding, and they cost a lot less).

Next, cut out the drawer dividers, top and bottom. Then notch the dividers for the 1×3 and 1×4 horizontal stiffeners, but note that the front stiffeners are joined to the dividers with half laps (half the notch in the divider and half in the stiffener).

With a rafter square, carefully lay out the tops and bottoms to receive the dividers—when the drawers are installed with their slides, you should have a ½" space between each drawer side and its respective divider. This will ensure proper sliding action.

Mark off the half lap notches on the front stiffeners, using the top or bottom layout as a pattern. After cutting all notches, assemble the complete drawer sections and mount them to the platform. Apply border trim to the top to hide all raw edges.

Cut out all drawer parts and machine-in the rabbets and grooves with a table saw or router. Assemble the box drawers, except for the face fronts, being careful to keep everything square. Next, lay out the drawer-pull screw holes and drill the large screw clearance holes in the front members. These will provide room for the screwheads, which mount the drawer pulls to the face fronts that will be installed shortly.

Now install the drawer sides according to the manufacturer's instructions. Then line up the face fronts on the drawers, mark their locations on the rear and screw them in place. Mark and drill the face fronts for the No. 10 pull mounting screws. Remove all hardware, identify the drawers and their respective openings and apply your favorite finish. When the finish is dry, install all the hardware and the drawers in their proper places.

Wall-mounted Cabinet

The wall-mounted cabinet is basically a divided box frame with both external and internal doors, continuously hinged. The entire structure is made of ¾" plywood,

with pine edging to cover the raw edges and provide solid screw-mounting surfaces for the doors. There's a little mahogany trim on the outer door edges for cosmetic purposes.

Cut out the pieces, assemble them and add the pine edging. Sand these assemblies and apply your finish. Mount the divided box frame to the wall, using a bottom cleat if no drawer section is to be fitted beneath, or with a 2×4 or 2×6 to raise it off the top if a drawer cabinet is used.

Hinge all doors and mount magnetic latches for the outer doors only. Note that the inner doors can fold out to cover the opposite half of the divided box. Add the mahogany trim to the outer door edges.

Some of the devices shown for storing various tools may suit your purposes, but if not, here's a great chance to let your imagination run freely. Plan the tool panels according to the type of work you do most frequently. Just be careful to place the "thicker" tools where they won't conflict with anything else on the opposing surface when the doors are closed. Spring clips, leather pieces, dowels, slotted wood, ledges, and door sides and bottoms themselves can hold tools. For greatest efficiency, place the cabinet under an existing light or, if necessary, add one.

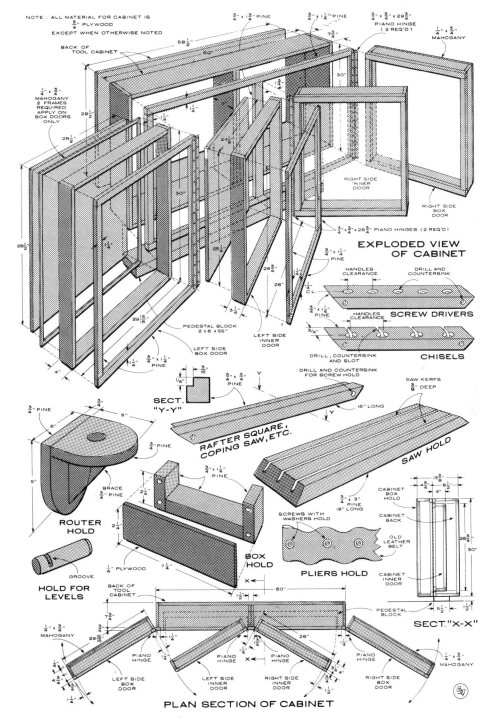

36

Laundry Center

Even at best, a homemaker's close encounters with the basement laundry room are not likely to be the high point in home fun. If the room happens to be dismal and inefficient, those encounters can be awful. The solution: Make your laundry setup as attractive and efficient as possible.

The conversion shown here provides cabinet storage for all cleaning necessities, a folding area for finished laundry and a rolling hamper cabinet. Rich oak panels have been installed over a drywall-reinforced stud wall; electrical outlets, vents and service lines have been neatly positioned for accessibility and appearance.

All cabinets and appliances fit flush against the wall and the room has a suspended ceiling and vinyl tile floor. This project, well within the ability of the average do-it-yourselfer, takes only about a week to complete, but will provide years of satisfaction.

Before starting, decide on the exact location and gather up all the required materials. Begin the job by erecting the stud wall(s); do it right and the rest is downhill. The wall structure (studs top and bottom plates) must be plumb (vertical) and the studs themselves must be parallel and plumb. The bottom plate can be concrete-nailed to the floor and the top plate-nailed to either joists or blocking between the joists. If the joists run perpendicular to the foundation wall where you're working, just pick a line location about 2' in from the foundation. If they run parallel to the foundation, there are two possibilities: (1) Locate the top plate and nail it to the bottom edge of a convenient joist. Or if this isn't feasible, (2) nail in some inter-joist blocking to mount the top wall plate.

Begin by laying out the bottom plates for a single wall and then place the top plates over them. Then, mark off the top plate at 16″ increments and transfer these marks to the bottom plate with a square. This procedure will ensure parallel studs after assembly. Now, nail the top plates to the joists or blocking at the location chosen, using a

Before conversion, the laundry center was nothing more than a washer and the dryer dumped near the necessary outlets in the basement. No counters, no storage cabinets, no amenities. Now appliances are flanked by utility cabinets. There's space for sorting and folding clothes and even a rolling hamper.

stretched or chalked string to give you a good straight run. Then drop a weight (plumb bob or fishing lead) from a string attached to either end of the top plate to locate

and mark the ends of the bottom plate. As before, stretch a string to get a straight run and lay down the bottom plates, but don't nail down these plates yet. You are now assured of a plumb wall. To meet the last requirement (plumb studs), trim to length and nail in one stud between the top and bottom plate with the 16" marks approximately aligned, one over the other. Tap the stud face near the lower end to make the studs plumb and check this with a level held against the stud face. If everything checks out, drive some concrete nails through the bottom plate into the concrete (remember to wear eye protection), then trim and toenail the remaining studs.

Mount the electrical box(es) for the outlets and make sure that the vent tube, hoses and any gas connections will clear all studs when the appliances are brought up to the wall. Staple up the insulation (foil side facing inward), and nail on the drywall. Finish up the wall by installing the panels with the appropriate color panel nails, cutting out for boxes and tubes as you go. Close up the electricals after inspection.

Suspended Ceiling

We found it easiest to install the suspended ceiling framework at this time—no reaching behind cabinets or climbing over appliances. In addition to the 2'×4' panels, a suspended ceiling requires wall angle, main runners, cross pieces and suspension wires. Try to leave about a 4" space between the joists and the ceiling framework so you'll be able to insert the panels easily.

Begin the ceiling by mounting the wall angle, using box nails or drywall nails. A stretched string and line level will help you to get a straight, horizontal installation. Continue this procedure around the perimeter of the room. Wall angle (runners and crosspieces as well) can easily be trimmed to length with a metal snips.

In order to center the panels in the room, measure the length of the room in inches. Divide this number by the width of the panel you're using in that direction. You'll get a number and a remainder. The whole number represents full-size panels. Add the remainder to the width of the panel you're using in that direction and divide the sum by two. The result is the width of the border panels. Do the same type of calculation for the adjacent wall. Example: The panel width is 48" and the wall dimension is 136". Divide 136" by 48" and get two full panels, plus 40". Add 40" to 48" to get 88". Divide by two and get 44" for the width of border panels.

Next, trim the ends of the main runners and locate them the appropriate distances from the walls parallel to them. Now, suspend the main runners with wires every 4' of their length and fill in the structure with 4' crosspieces, making a grid of 2'×4' openings, except as calculated at the borders. Then, adjust the structure with the wires to eliminate any sags or bulges, making sure that the openings are square. Drop in the panels, and you're done with this major job.

Cabinet Construction

The appliances in our laundry have a combined width of 55"; if your washer and dryer have the same combined width, use the dimensions given on the drawing for the right side cabinet. If the combined width of your appliances is other than 55", add the combined width of your washer and dryer to ¾" spacing requirement. Add this sum to 20¼" (left side cabinet minus the thickness of the outer side). Subtract this from 96" (width of upper cabinet) and then add ¾" (thickness of right side outer piece) to the result. Example: Combined width of washer and dryer is 56". Add ¾" and get 56¾". Add 20¼" and get 77". Subtract 77" from 96" and get 19". Add ¾" to 19" and get 19¾" for the actual width of the right side cabinet.

Next, modify the widths of the top, bottom, back, divider, front and shelf to accommodate the change.

The cabinet construction uses plywood surfaces and pine trim, assembled with white glue and nails. Cut out all cabinets and assemble them, except for the face frames. Fill and sand all exposed edges, or—even better—edge them with pine. Paint the cabinets, then hook up the appliances. Install the lower cabinets next to the appliances, allowing ¼" spacing between the appliances and between the appliances and the cabinets. Place the upper

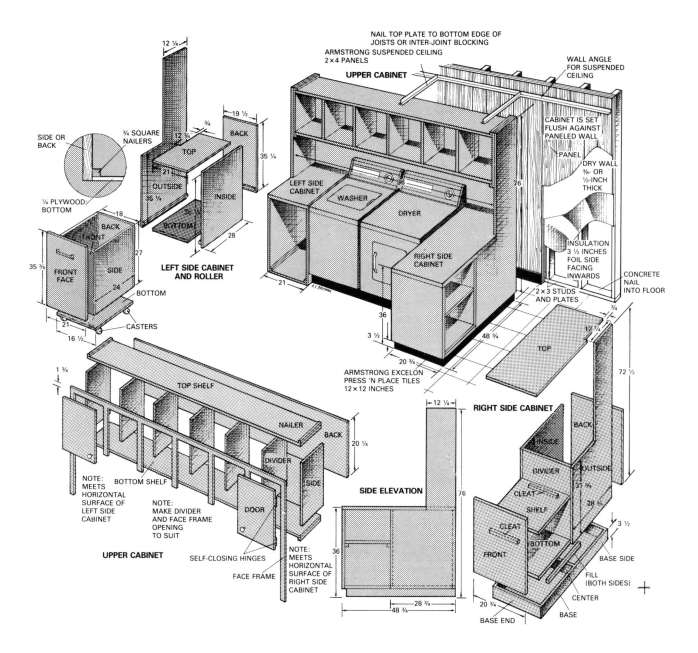

Flooring

cabinet in position and clamp it to the outer sides of both left- and right-hand cabinets with the front edges flush (to receive the face frame). Screw or nail all cabinets to the wall. Screw or nail the upper cabinet to the outer side extensions and for additional support, install a pre-painted cleat under it. Trim the face frame pieces to fit and install them with glue and nails. Set all nails, fill all holes and sand them smooth before touching up the paint.

Hang the prepainted doors, covering the end compartments of the upper cabinets with self-closing hinges designed for overlay doors and add the door pulls. Install a pull grip to the front face of the roller cabinet and check the cabinet's alignment with the left side, lower cabinet. Minor discrepancies can be corrected by shimming between the roller cabinet bottom and the castor mounting pads.

Center the floor tiles using the same method as with the ceiling. Before laying them, make sure the surface is smooth and free of dust. Minor bulges can be hammered down and hollows may be filled with cement patch (no aggregate).

Snap a chalk line on the floor at a convenient location according to your centering calculation, then simply peel off the protective papers and press the tiles in place. Butt them tightly to avoid any gapping. A scissors or shears will handle any trimming to an edge or around obstacles. Apply some compatible colored molding where applicable.

Part VIII

Techniques

37

Masonry

In projects such as garages or additions and, of course, entire houses, it is necessary to provide concrete footings and hollow concrete block foundations to support the wood structure above them in a stable and permanent manner so there will be no sagging or heaving. To ensure success, a concrete footing must have adequate depth to avoid cracking, adequate width to distribute the load, adequate compressive strength to prevent cracking and must rest on a firm base 1' below the frost line. Footings and foundations can be in the form of points, lines or complete perimeters.

Several factors influence the design of footings: the size, mass and type of structure, soil conditions and whether the concrete is linear, as a house footing, or isolated, as a pier support. The depth of pier footings is influenced by exposure or lack of exposure to freezing conditions plus concentrated loads.

To determine the depth necessary for pier footings and the amount of concentrated loads that can be carried, you must know what type of soil you have. (For example, soft clay will support only 1 ton per square foot, whereas gravel will support 6 tons per square foot.) The soil test (paid for by you) is performed and validated by a licensed engineer or architect, and the results give a core sample, which indicates the various strata from grade to approximately a 10' depth. This test is part of the site engineering for building a house, so if you already have these data with your survey, you might be able to use them.

For a deck supported by piers resting on concrete pads, the required loading is relatively light so the pads, although they should extend past the frost line, can be cast within a 12"-diameter strippable cardboard tube.

On the other hand, pier pads to support structural columns and girders inside a basement are typically 2' or more square and 1' deep, while the perimeter concrete footings supporting those basement concrete block wall foundations and house walls might be 8" deep and 20"

Cylindrical or point footings, such as those used to support decks or other relatively lightweight structures, can be cast in special paperboard tubes from concrete mixed by hand.

Pads to support lally columns in the basement of a home are typically 2' square and 1' deep. They are the same level as the perimeter footing for the walls.

wide. The perimeter wall footing will support perhaps seven rows of 12″ block plus six rows of 8″ block and will be considerably below the frost line. All pier pads support concentrated loads while linear and perimeter wall footings have a fairly equally distributed load.

A structure such as a garage with a concrete slab floor and no basement doesn't need such a heavy foundation and footing. The footing and foundation can be 8″ thick and the slab 4″ thick. The footing and foundation are sometimes an integrated concrete casting (monolithic pour), while at other times, a separate 8″×16″ concrete footing is poured and a mortar-joined, hollow, 8″ concrete block wall is built over it. In either case the footing should be 12″ below the frost line.

Another common situation occurs when an addition to the house requires the foundation to be enlarged. If the footing and foundation will enclose only a crawl space, the typical requirement would be an 8″-thick perimeter or line foundation on an 8″×16″ concrete footing, 12″ below the frost line. This foundation should be tied into the existing foundation with rebars (reinforcing rods) set into the new footing and locked into holes drilled in the existing footing.

If the addition has a full basement, the footing should be tied in to the existing footing, but, in this case, much deeper than 12″ into the ground. This situation requires an 8″×20″ concrete footing, perhaps seven courses of 12″ hollow, concrete block with the remaining 8″ block. The basement floor would be 4″-thick poured concrete.

All footings should rest on undisturbed soil of an ap-

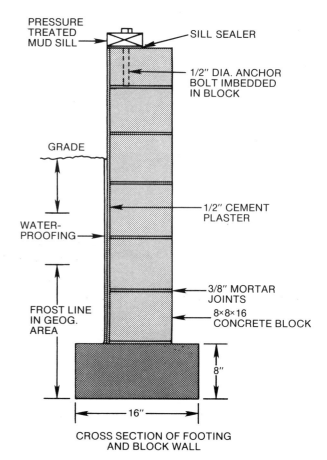

CROSS SECTION OF FOOTING
AND BLOCK WALL

Cross section of footing and block wall.

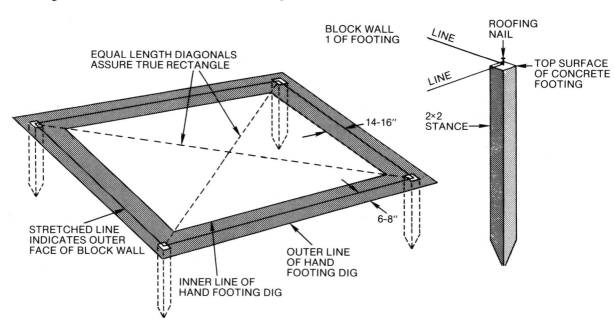

1—EXCAVATE ROUGH.
2—SET UP AND LEVEL STAKES TO TOP CONCRETE FOOTING.
3—STRETCH LINE BETWEEN STAKES INDICATING OUTER FACE OF BLOCK WALL.
4—MARK SHOVEL HAND INDICATING FOOTING DEPTH *BELOW* STAKE TOP.
5—HAND DIG FOOTINGS TO HANDLE MARK DEPTH AND ABOVE 6-8″ OUTSIDE INNER LINE TO ALLOW ROOM FOR FORMS AND SUPPORT STAKES.

Excavation, footing layout, controlling depth, keeping it square, location of block wall perimeter relative to footing perimeter.

proved load-carrying capacity and should be poured with concrete whose compression rating equals or exceeds 2500 psi (3000 is preferable). Rebars are generally not required in footings except to deal with specific problems such as being in an earthquake area or being poured on sloppy or wet soil. All foundations should be at least 8″ higher than grade to get away from ground moisture.

If the footing cannot be put on undisturbed soil, then an approved fill, such as compacted gravel, should be used. Many times this problem can be totally avoided by not overdigging. All block wall foundations should be given a complete exterior, plaster coat (mortar is basically cement with some lime and no coarse aggregate), then waterproofed.

Most small excavations around the home, whether they are isolated piers, lines or perimeters, can be done by hand—if not by you, then by people who are hired to do the work. So before you go for a backhoe, small bulldozer or end loader, estimate the cost of doing the job both ways. In most cases, the hand dig is cheaper and more practical because, first, the chances of overdigging are minimal and second, getting a piece of construction equipment to a site next to a house over a lawn and past

shrubbery can cause a lot of damage. However, before a shovel hits the ground, you must check with your local building authorities to make sure what you do is acceptable. When you apply for a permit, you will learn the rules of the game and might even be given required changes and modifications in your plan.

Prepare for the excavation, especially if it's a perimeter type, with an intersecting layout done with mason's cord strung between stakes or batter boards. Square the layout using either the 3-4-5 engineering triangle or equal diagonals between opposite corners of a rectangle. From the intersections of the lines, drop a plumb bob or small weight to indicate corners.

Point excavation locations are straightforward: the point (a stake, for example) represents the center of a posthole and a small rectangular dig represents a pad. Lines and perimeter excavations are usually for concrete footings that will have masonry hollow concrete block wall on top. Therefore, the stakes should represent the outer face of the block wall where it contacts the footing. This means that the depth of the stake is important, too. When the rough excavation is about the level of the top surface of the footings, drive in enough 2′-long 2″×2″

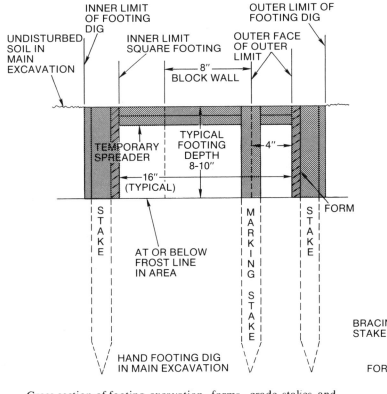

Cross section of footing excavation, forms, grade stakes and spreader prior to pouring concrete.

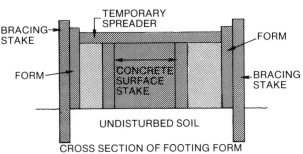

Cross section of footing excavation, forms, grade stakes after pour.

stakes spaced between 4′ and 8′ apart to outline the wall's outer face.

To ensure a level footing top surface, place a marked stick on top of each stake in turn and take a reading with a dumpy (surveyors's) level. (These levels can be rented for a reasonable price.) If you have no optical level, place a straight 2×4 on edge between the stake tops, lay a carpenter's level on this and read the bubble for horizontal. Check with a marked stick, comparing the reading with grade to get the general depth correct. Note that the top surface of the footing should be 4″ to 6″ below the frost line. When the stake tops are driven down firmly and leveled, drive roofing nails into the stake tops to hold the stretched mason's cord outline of the wall face. Make a final check of the outline to see that the cords are lined up the way you want them to be.

Then, dig out the footing both downward and to the sides. Let's assume that you're putting in an 8″ block wall over an 8″×16″ footing. This means that you must dig down a consistent 8″ to the outside of the cords (4″ outside the outer block wall face) and 12″ to the inside of the cords (4″ inside the inner block wall face). Keeping the depth constant while you're digging is easy: just place a mark or tape ring 8″ from the handle of your shovel and periodically invert the shovel to compare the mark with the cords or stake tops.

If you plan on placing wooden forms on either side of the footing, dig outward a few inches further to provide room for the extra stakes and plywood or board forms. If you can use the soil walls to control the footing sides, make the total width 16″. In either case, after the pour has cured, you can backfill to the footing.

If you're using side forms, you can brace them with stakes on their outer sides and make them level with the marking stakes. However, this is very time-consuming. Instead of trying to have all the top edges of the forms level with the marking stakes, an easier way is to make sure that the tops of the forms are at least as high as the stakes. They can be somewhat higher; it doesn't matter. Then, drive some auxiliary stakes in between the existing marking stakes and check with a level. These stakes can be placed where the middle of the footing would be, if you like. Just make sure they're at the same level as the marking stakes. At this point, you're ready to pour.

Concrete Estimation and Sources

Estimating the amount of concrete you need is simple. For a 1′-diameter cylinder that is 3′ high (such as a pier footing for a deck), the formula is pi/4 times the diameter squared times the height.

In this case, 3.14/4.00×(1×1)×3=2.36 cubic feet. There are 27 cubic feet in a cubic yard, so this column requires 2.36/27=0.087, or about 1/12 of a cubic yard. Therefore, 1 cubic yard could do almost 12 of these columns.

Concrete can be mixed and delivered in a variety of ways. It is measured in quantities of 27 cubic feet, or what

The level is rotated to view readings on a marked rod, which is placed atop each footing grade stake in turn to assure that they are all on the same horizontal plane.

Forms are positioned and locked in place with stakes and backfill. They are held apart by scrap spreaders and their inner surfaces oiled for easier removal following the pour. These spreaders are removed as the pour fills the forms.

Parts by Volume for Footing Concrete		
Portland Cement	Sand	Gravel
1	2¾ to 3	4

Concrete mixing table.

is known as a cubic yard or simply *yard*. This is why we convert from cubic feet into cubic yards. Suppose you were making a pad 2′ on a side and 1′ deep, which is typical of a structural column footing in a basement. Multiply the length times the width times the height to get the cubic feet; then divide that number by 27 to get the cubic yards. L×W×H/27= number of cubic yards, so 2×2×1/27=0.148, or about 1/7 of a cubic yard.

The same formula is used for a slab 12′×16′×4″ thick. Since 4″ is 1/3 foot, we use 1/3 to keep all dimensions in feet.

Therefore, L×W×T/27 here is 12×16×1/3/27=2.37 cubic yards, or about 2⅜ cubic yards.

The final example is a perimeter footing that is 8″ deep, 16″ wide and 24′ long. So, L×W×T/27 is 24×4/3× 2/3/27=0.79 cubic yards, or almost 4/5 cubic yard.

If you need only a small amount of concrete, half a yard or less, it's feasible to do a hand mix in a mortar box (a metal mixing pane). You might consider dry mix, which comes in 80-pound bags. When mixed with water, one bag of dry mix will produce 0.6 cubic feet of concrete. You could also start with the makings, which are cement, sand and gravel, but for this small amount, it's a bit messy and quite expensive for such a small delivery.

For handling quantities of concrete that are a bit too much for a mortar box, portable gas-powered mixers can produce batches of up to 6 cubic feet from the basic ingredients.

If you need at least several yards of concrete, you could rent a mixer and buy the makings. Also, there are rental places that mix concrete and provide a wheeled hopper and a hitch so you can tow it by car. Or, you can contact a concrete delivery service that will mix and meter out as much as you ask for. You'll pay a little more per yard, but you'll get exactly what you need. Keep access to the site in mind. If the truck can't drive up to the site directly or get within range of the chute, the concrete will have to be moved by wheelbarrow or Georgia buggy (both rentable items). You'll be charged a waiting fee while this is going on, so have some able bodies and 'barrows on hand.

If you need more than 5 yards of concrete, it might pay you to order a straight concrete delivery truck. However, if you don't have direct access to the site, you'll still need some helpers with wheelbarrows.

Tips and Safety

If you can get the truck chute within 8′ to 12′ of the pouring site, you might want to build a chute with a plywood base and 2×6 or 2×4 sides. This should be built before the truck arrives. It can be attached to the chute with a chain and bolt that you provide. When the concrete is ready to pour, hose down the chute to reduce friction.

Concrete is caustic and can cause severe burns. Consequently, when working with concrete, certain safety precautions should be observed. Use eye protection, heavy work gloves and high rubber boots or galoshes.

Aside from trucks, mixers or pans and level, you'll also need a shovel (not a flat garden spade), a masonry hoe, for both mixing and pulling concrete, or a special concrete placer tool, called a come-along, which is excellent for pulling concrete. You'll also need a heavy hammer or small sledgehammer to drive the stakes, plus a hammer to nail the forms in place.

Pouring Concrete Footings

Remove the cords and the roofing nails from the stakes. Coat the inside of the forms with used automobile engine oil so the form can be easily removed. When pouring, try to distribute the concrete as evenly as possible with either chute, auxiliary chute, buggy, wheelbarrow or shovel.

For large jobs, such as this house wall footing, a concrete truck is the ticket for quantities of about 10 cubic yards. The metal chute can be raised, lowered and rotated.

If the metal chute won't quite reach the forms, a quick and dirty auxiliary chute of plywood and 2×4s can be chained onto the truck chute to extend its reach.

The idea is to distribute the concrete continuously but slowly enough so that the people pulling the concrete can achieve an approximate level with the marking stakes. With enough helpers, this operation is not as difficult as you might think. First, gravity is with you, as well as the natural tendency of concrete to flatten out—to seek the lowest common level. The tops of the marking stakes and the auxiliary stakes serve as height gauges, so the best tool for the leveling job is the bottom surface of the shovel. Just smooth down the concrete far enough so you can see the stake tops. Let the concrete set and cure for three days or more before removing the forms.

With the forms removed, you can drive the roofing nails into their original holes in the marking stakes and reconnect the mason's cords indicating the outer face of the blocks. These cords will serve as a guide for the first course of blocks.

The flat side of a shovel is an excellent tool for trowelling the final grade of the footing surface. It's done by moving from one grade stake to another in turn.

The chute must be guided and the flow regulated (usually by the driver) to keep pace with the people pulling the concrete along in the form and establishing a rough level with the footing stakes.

A final touchup eliminates any lumps or hollows. This method is accurate to within a 1/4″ of requirements, well within the correction range of the block wall mortar bed...the next step.

Standard Mortar Mixes (ASTM C270)							
		Parts by Volume					
Specification	Mortar Type	Portland Cement or Portland Blast-Furnace Slag Cement	Masonry Cement*	Hydrated Lime or Lime Putty	Aggregate		
For plain masonry, ASTM C270	M	1 1	1 –	– ¼	Not less than 2¼ and not more than 3 times the sum of the volumes of cement and lime used.	↑ Highest Strength	Highest Plasticity ↓
	S	½ 1	1 –	— Over ¼ to ½			
	N	– 1	1 –	– Over ½ to 1¼			
	O	– 1	1 –	– Over 1¼ to 2½			
	K	1	–	Over 2½ to 4			

*N is most commonly used because of the blend of strength and plasticity (workability). On the average: 1 shovel of portland cement, 1 shovel of lime, and 4 to 6 shovels of masonry sand.

Mortar mixing table.

Preparing Mortar

The choice of mixing mortar, as of concrete, depends on how much you need and how fast you need it. For a relatively small amount, you can use the dry bagged mortar mix in a mortar box. You could also hand mix a larger quantity from the makings, which are portland cement, masonry cement, mason's sand, hydrated lime and water, all mixed in prescribed proportions to suit the existing conditions. This could be done either in a mortar box or a power mixer. Regardless of the method or the prescription, mix all dry ingredients before adding the water.

The most efficient hand tool for mixing is the mason's hoe, which has passage holes in the blade. Mix enough to work with. Don't mix too much or the mortar will start drying and setting up before you're ready to use it. This is a matter of trial and error, highly dependent upon how efficiently you can lay the blocks and use up the mortar. Probably the hand mix method is best for the homeowner or do-it-yourselfer, because a reasonably able mason's helper can supply two or more masons with mortar if using a power mixer.

Laying Blocks

Most of the block work is done using two or three core stretchers. These blocks are actually 7⅝"×7⅝"×15⅝", although they are known as 8"×8"×16" because the normal mortar joint, which should be ⅜" thick on top, bottom or end, brings the total dimension of the block plus the mortar to the nominal size.

If you're laying just a small number of concrete blocks, mix by hand in a mortar box or use the dry mix. If not, these gasoline-driven types will handle as much as 7 cubic feet (2 bags).

The outer faces of the block wall are marked by a line stretched between the nail holes in the tops of the footing grade stakes. Lay the blocks along these lines in a dry run to determine the necessary block cuts.

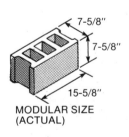

MODULAR SIZE (ACTUAL)

7-5/8"
7-5/8"
15-5/8"

REGULAR STRETCHER

TWO-CORE 8"×8"×16" UNITS

7-5/8"
7-5/8"
15-5/8"

ONE PLAIN END (SINGLE CORNER)

7-5/8"
7-5/8"
15-5/8"

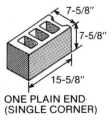

BOTH ENDS PLAIN (DOUBLE CORNER OR PIER)

SLOT FOR BREAKING
7-5/8"
7-5/8"
7-5/8"
7-5/8"
15-5/8"
15-5/8"

NOMINAL SIZE (USUALLY FICTITIOUS)

8"
8"
16"

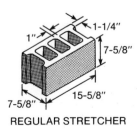

REGULAR STRETCHER

1"
1-1/4"
7-5/8"
7-5/8"
15-5/8"

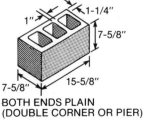

ONE PLAIN END (SINGLE CORNER)

7-5/8"
7-5/8"
15-5/8"

BOTH ENDS PLAIN (DOUBLE CORNER OR PIER)

1"
1-1/4"
7-5/8"
7-5/8"
15-5/8"

Typical concrete block shapes.

Before mixing the mortar, lay the first course of block in place dry to check the fit. If one block must be chopped down to complete the course evenly—and this is usually the case—the dry-lay will show how much. To cut a block, use the sharp edge of a mason's hammer to score an outline completely around the block at the place you want to cut it. Then give the block a sharp blow or two along the score line.

The basic approach to laying blocks is to deposit a bed of mortar on the footing and set the blocks on this bed. The end of each block must be buttered with mortar to fill the joint between the block and the one before it. Any row of blocks must form a plane across the face, while the tops of the blocks must be level across both length and width. Once the first course is in place and level, the corners, both internal and external, are built up a few courses. Then they are checked for level, and the block wall is checked for plumb in the vertical plane. After this they

can serve as guides for the courses that must be completed in between the corners.

To set this up, hold a mason's cord at opposite corners stretched across the outer face of the wall at the top of the course to be laid next. Then, as the blocks are set in place with mortar, they are dressed to this cord or line. As the work progresses, the cord is raised a course at a time and continues to serve as an accurate guide.

The prime tools for this operation, excluding an optical level, are a trowel, level and mason's cord with blocks. Other necessary equipment includes a mortar pan and mason's hoe, a wheelbarrow and shovel and a mortar-board.

The blocks are never wet. Any adjustments made to compensate for temperature or humidity are made in the mortar mix. The heaviest deposit of mortar is made on the footing to start and level the first course. This is relatively easy because you're throwing mortar on a solid surface,

The blocks can be cut easily by scoring an outline with the sharp end of the brick hammer and tapping along the scoreline.

The beginning blocks at the first corners are critical, so use care when setting them onto the mortar bed. After a couple have been laid, check the line and make minor corrections.

Remove blocks from footing surface and lay in a generous, full-width bed of mortar. Use the trowel point to furrow down the middle to ensure full contact with bottom edges of blocks.

Applying mortar to the ends of a block is called *buttering*. These buttered ends provide the joint mortar between the blocks.

Bring the buttered block into position. Then, press it down into the bed and against the next block.

Check cocking of the first course: place the level in a vertical position against the outer block face and make minor corrections by tapping on the appropriate edge with the trowel handle.

Use the level as a straightedge by placing it against several blocks already laid. For true alignment make minor corrections.

On all courses after the first, bed mortar is applied on the inner and outer top edges only (face shell mortar bedding).

Place the level along the row of blocks on the top and make any minor grade corrections by tapping down with trowel handle.

The procedure is to build up the corners 4 to 6 courses high, then work the blocks between them.

the footing. From the second course on, you have only the hollow concrete block shell edges on which to throw mortar (as well as the end, as mentioned).

Experience enables the professional mason to keep his joints constant, so he doesn't have to check every row with a level. In a basement foundation wall 13 courses high, he may check only two or three times with the dumpy level. But amateurs don't have as much experience and must rely more on instruments. This means you should check every row with a level as you proceed. If you find you've really got a feel for this work, then you might want to skip a few rows between levels.

As you butter the end of a block and set it in place on the bed mortar on the top edges of the blocks beneath, you'll need to adjust it. Gauge this with the level, but make the actual adjustment by tapping down on the edges in

strategic locations with the butt end of the trowel handle to get the required orientation.

As you lay the blocks and adjust them, a certain amount of mortar will be extruded or squeezed out at the joints. This excess should be cut off with a stroke of the trowel. However, in certain cases where the mix is too loose for the prevailing conditions, it might be necessary to wait a bit for the excess mortar to partially set up and cut it off then. Otherwise, this excess might get smeared over the surface. This won't matter on below-grade work because the block surface must be plastered and water-proofed, but if you're working above grade and using struck or tooled joint, smeared mortar is unsightly.

Notice that where walls intersect, such as at corners, the blocks interlock for additional strength. Also, the wall itself is done in a running bond. This means that the end of

They should be checked across the face again for alignment and vertically on the face for plumb. In addition, the level can serve again as a straightedge for a true plane.

The echelon or stepped arrangement of the block, where each block overlaps the block below by a half block, can be checked by positioning the level diagonally against the corners.

You can easily make a story pole to check that each block plus its 3/8″ thick mortar joint totals 8″.

Stretch mason's line between adjacent corners with plastic or wooden line blocks. Address intermediate blocks to line.

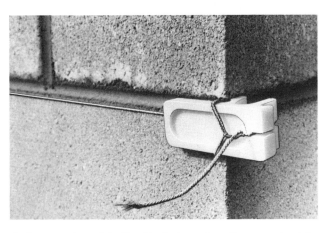

A close-up view of the line block shows how it gets a grip at the corner block edge and keeps the line taut.

One way to reuse this excess mortar is to "throw" it on the top edges or face shell, preparing a bed for the next block.

The line can also be stretched and held in place by using a pair of adjustable line stretchers, which fit over the block top.

When fitting the last or closure block into a course, butter the edges of the blocks forming the opening.

The weight of the block forces excess mortar out of the joint. Cut off this mortar with a flick of the trowel and reuse it.

Also butter the closure block, be it full or cut down, in the normal manner before setting it in place.

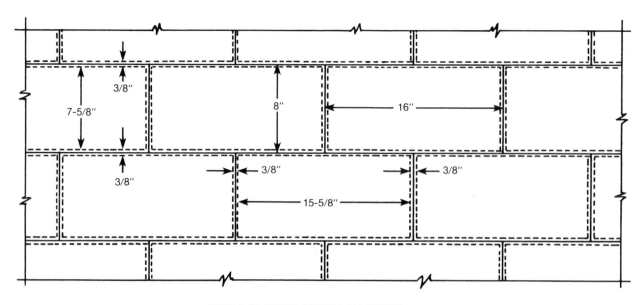

MODULAR UNITS IN WALL MASONRY

Elevation drawing showing dimensions of typical running bond concrete block wall.

a block in the higher course is positioned in the middle of the block in the course just below. In short, the blocks are overlapped.

Foundations for basements will have windows. In many homes and additions, no masonry lintel (header) is found; only the mud sill or sill plate is over the window. This will cause problems if the basement is to be finished. So, if you're involved with this type of project, order a concrete lintel. This will rest on blocks adjacent to the window as well as create a concrete header space over it.

Foundations that will support a wood structure must have mechanical connections to the structure. Therefore,

at least two anchor bolts must be set in the foundation of every wall at a maximum distance of 8' apart. The bolts are 1/2" diameter and must protrude up high enough from the top block to penetrate either a single- or double-sill plate, allowing enough threads for washers and nuts.

To imbed these anchor bolts in the block wall, lay pieces of metal lath on the top surface of the course, just below the top course. Then, lay up the top course in the normal manner, checking for level, because there will be no other opportunity to do so. Throw some mortar into the hollows where the bolts are to be placed. Put the bolts in their respective places, protruding out enough so they'll

Finish off the closure block by compressing the joint with the trowel tip and replacing any mortar that fell out.

To determine when you can tool or compress most mortar joints, press joint and a thumbprint should hardly be seen.

Concave horizontal tooling is done first with a jointer, or sled runner, so named for the kickup at the front end.

Remaining residue should be whisked off with a stiff brush.

A shorter, modified "S"-shaped jointer is used for the concave tooling of the vertical joints.

The top course of block will support the mud sills or sill plates of the house structure, and 1/2″-diameter anchor bolts are imbedded in the block and bolted to the sills.

Tooling causes flash or burrs at the joint edges. This should be cut off flush with a flick of the trowel.

A cement plaster or parge is applied to the complete outer face of the block wall. Sometimes this is done with a roughened scratch coat and a second finish coat.

be able to penetrate the sill plate(s). Fill the remainder of the hollow with mortar, and smooth it out at the top. The lath will support this, allowing the mortar to set.

The entire outer surface of the block wall, both below and above grade, is plastered or parged with approximately a ½"-thick coat of mortar. This is troweled out as smoothly as possible and, when thoroughly dry, is given a coat of waterproofer up to grade.

For those areas or special circumstances that require reinforcements, such as rebar for tying in new footings to existing ones, footings in earthquake areas, footings with sharp changes in elevations or undesirable soil conditions, consult your local building authority to check the requirement. This holds true for frost-line depth, compressive concrete strength, footing width and depth, as well as below-grade use of 12" (or at least wider than 8") block in full basement foundations and drainage considerations. Also find out what stages of the work require inspection.

38

House Carpentry

Almost all of the carpentry that the home do-it-yourselfer faces is concerned with projects in or around the house. This holds true whether the project is the replacement of a door or window, the building of storage space or shelving or the creation of an addition, complete with plumbing and electricals.

The principles and techniques used in the construction of the house are applicable to the building of sheds, fences, decks, outdoor furniture and similar structures. A further advantage is knowing what's behind a wall or inside a ceiling *before* you open it up. Therefore, a rapid refresher course in general house construction is an excellent starting point.

Woodwork Starting at the Plates

House carpentry starts directly on top of the foundation. The main considerations for the interface between the first piece of wood structure, called the mud sill or sill plate, and the masonry foundation are level, solid attachment of the sill and termite protection.

The attachment problem is solved quickly by the use of anchor bolts, concreted into the foundation. These bolts pierce the sills through predrilled holes and lock them down with large washers and nuts.

The insect problem may be prevented in several ways: (1) by inserting sill sealer (a sandwich of insulation between a pair of plastic membranes) between the foundation top and the mud sill; (2) by using sills of pressure-treated lumber (lumber containing copper chromium arsenate, which tends to repel insects and withstand water damage) or (3) by installing a copper-clad anti-termite shield between the sill and the foundation. This method is preferred in the south where termite damage can be devastating.

Many builders install a double layer of mud sills, overlapping all joints in the bottom layer. In this case, pressure-treated lumber should be used in both layers.

The framing of a house starts at the top of the foundation. In this case doubled, lapped mud sills (sill plates) of pressure-treated lumber are separated from the concrete block by a compressible laminate sill sealer.

Floor joists span between the sill plates on the exterior walls and a central girder, typically spaced 16″ on center.

225

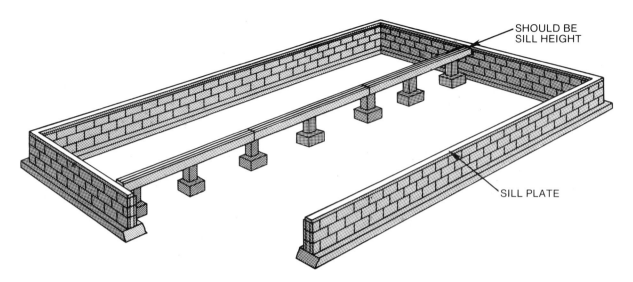

The foundation with girder supported, ready for the framing.

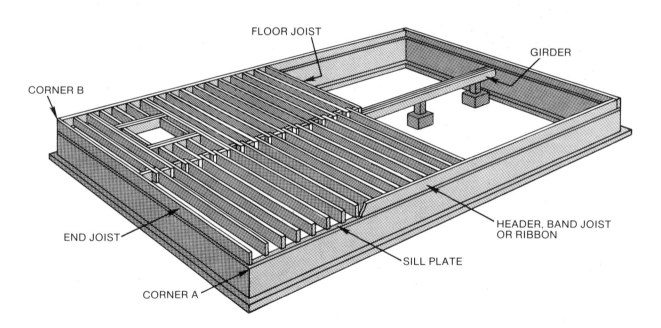

Sill plates, joists and joist headers in place; opening to basement shown.

The Column, Girder and Joist Array

The first floor of a house is supported by a structural network consisting of parallel members called joists. These are erected on edge and most commonly spaced 16″ on center (O.C.). They typically span the width of the building, supported at their outer ends by the sills, while a girder supports their inner ends where they meet at or near the centerline of the building foundation.

Although it is quite common for the joists to overlap at the girder, they may also be butted and spliced, thus eliminating the 1½″ offset. In either case, there should be solid blocking between the joists over the girder to prevent possible twisting and warping.

The typical lumber girder is a stagger-jointed sandwich of three 2×8s, 2×10s or 2×12s spiked together, supported by a row of columns, running parallel to the ridge, if the house has a simple gable roof. Sometimes, these girders are built in sections, with the butt-jointed ends meeting over the column plates. These lally columns are cast iron cylinders filled with concrete and most often spaced at 8′ intervals. These columns, in turn, rest on concrete pads that are at least 1′ thick and 2′ on a side.

Certain areas in the joist network are reinforced, either by doubling, tripling or extra close spacing. In homes with large joist spans, the 16″ centers are sometimes reduced to 12″ centers to beef up the area above without

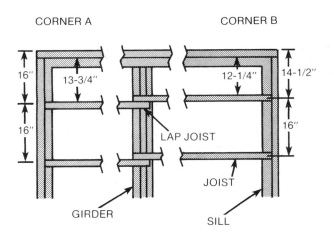

Detail shows the effect of the joist overlap at the girder.

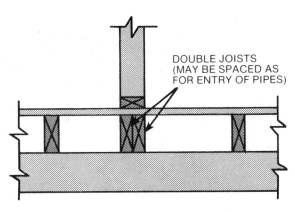

Detail shows double joist lending extra support for an interior wall.

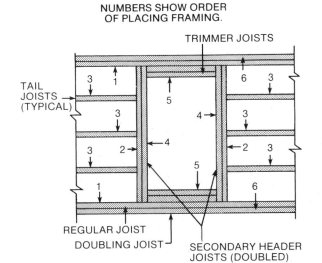

Detail shows joist opening with headers and trimmers and their assembly order.

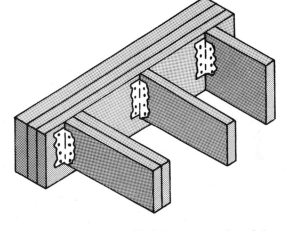

Detail shows single and double joists connected to girder with metal joist hangers.

doubling the joists. However, certain areas will require still more support. These include locations that will support heavy plumbing fixtures such as cast iron tubs or spas, or locations where an interior, load-bearing wall runs parallel to the joists.

Floor openings in the joist network are always required. These include stairway openings in first or second floor joists and openings in ceiling joists for attic access, such as trapdoors, stairways and disappearing stairways.

These openings are bordered on the long sides by doubled joists called trimmers, and by doubled headers on the short sides. The headers support the ends of the rafters interrupted by the openings. They may be fastened in place with nails or metal hangers, and in some cases are partially supported by ledger strips which mate with notches in these members.

Bridging and Blocking

To prevent joists from twisting and warping, rows of bridging or blocking, spaced a maximum of 8' apart, are nailed into the joist bays. This may be in the form of solid, joist-depth, staggered blocking, or bevel-ended 1¼"×3" wood struts or steel struts applied in crisscrossed pairs like "X's."

Finally, where the joists end 1½" from the outer mud sill edge and the joist bays on opposite sides of the building would be exposed, they must be headed off by joist-sized lumber whose outer faces are flush with the outer sill edge.

Subfloor Construction

Generally, the subfloor consists of a number of span-rated ½"-, ⅝"-, or ¾"-thick plywood panels, integrated into a deck by directly nailing the subflooring with 6d to 8d cement-coated nails to the joist network that supports it. It may also be attached to the joists with screws, or with adhesive for a non-squeak deck.

All plywood subfloors are installed with the ends centered over the joists, and the facegrains (or long edges) perpendicular to the joist runs. Alternate rows are staggered by a nominal 4' for strength, with both end and edge gaps provided between adjacent panels to allow for the normal expansion and contraction of the entire structure.

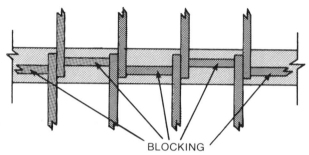

BLOCKING

Because the joists, which can be single or double depending upon their load, are relatively deep, 5/4×3 wood bridging (shown) or blocking is used to constrain any tendency to twist.

Blocking is one of the alternate methods to prevent joist winding and distortion.

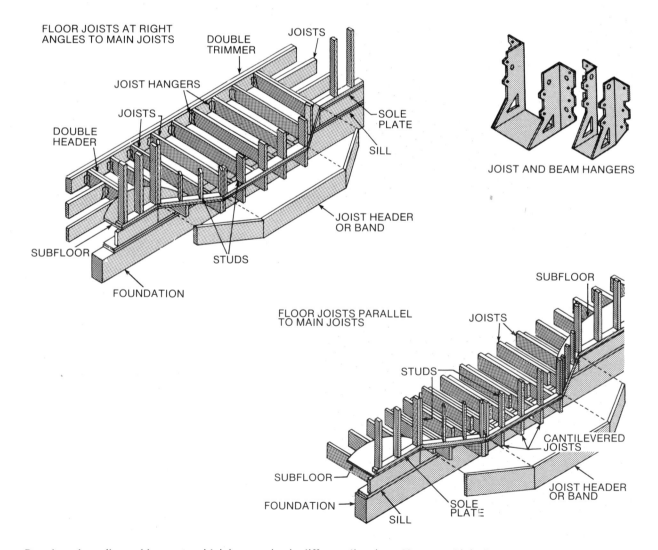

JOIST AND BEAM HANGERS

Bay-shaped cantilevered bumpout with joists running in different directions. Note metal joist hangers.

The typical deck can vary in thickness between ½″ and ¾″ or even more in some cases. The panel ends are staggered for maximum strength, and a prescribed nailing pattern for both perimeter and field is used.

The plates, one bottom or sole plus two top plates, are laid out according to the house plan. The sole plates are nailed directly to the deck and joists, whereas the top plates are spiked together as a pair and tacked on top of the sole plate for accurate stud location marking, including door and window openings.

The wall, with temporary bracing nailed on at strategic locations, is then propped up on the sole plate, and the bottom ends of the studs are toenailed to the sole plate. Then the braces are nailed to the deck, joists and/or joist headers in a plumb (vertical) attitude.

Framing Exterior and Interior Walls

Most houses are framed with 2×4 (actually 1½″×3½″) studding, which will allow 3½″-thick insulation to be installed in the stud bays (providing an R value of 11 or 13, depending upon whether roll or batt insulation is used). However, the so-called electric home uses 2×6 studding, allowing 5½″-thick insulation (for an R value of 19).

The construction principles are the same for both 2×4 and 2×6 dimensioned lumber, though sometimes the 2×6 framing systems are built on 24″ centers instead of 16″. But, regardless of thickness of the framing lumber, basic exterior wall framing consists of precut studs, cripple studs, single sole and doubled top plates, plus headers, doubled rough sills and trimmers.

Studs, usually spaced parallel and 16″ O.C., are positioned between the plates, separating the plates by a consistent 92⅝″ (thus ensuring that the plates are parallel, and that the ceiling is parallel with the floor). Precut studs of this exact length may be purchased from your local lumberyard. It's the smart way to go, whether retrofitting a patio door or building a complete addition.

The rough openings (R.O.) for exterior doors and windows are bounded on the top by a header, on the bottom by a doubled rough sill and on the sides by trimmers, which also support the header. The trimmers are doubled by nailing them to precut studs on both sides of the openings. Cripple studs, also 16″ O.C., are positioned between the sole plate and the rough sill. These cripple studs will continue the 16″ O.C. pattern across the R.O. to the other side, to accommodate the modular sheathing and drywall, although the precut studs and trimmers may crowd the pattern somewhat.

The header provides vertical support for the top plate (and eventually the load of the roof members) where the normal stud pattern is interrupted. The deeper the header, the wider the opening it can span. But most carpenters make them all the same maximum depth for convenience of production. Note that the headers 5′ or longer will have two trimmers supporting each side instead of one.

The majority of these headers are built up from two pieces of 2×10 capped off at the bottom by a 2×4. The capping makes the thickness at the bottom of the header equal to the thickness at the top plates. In some instances, where the spans are large, a pair of 2×12s will be spiked together. This leaves no room for a cap, so the bottom of the head must be furred out with lath or similar wood.

Some topics of special interest are the treatment of exterior corners, and the junctions of interior and exterior walls. Both exterior corners and interior/exterior wall junctions must provide strength at the end of walls, connect adjacent walls, and provide an interior vertical nailing area for the ends or edges of the drywall panels.

Therefore, it is preferable to lap-join the top plates where exterior walls meet at the corners, at the perpendicular junctions where the interior and exterior walls

After all first floor walls, both exterior and interior, have been nailed in place, another set of joists is erected over the top plates. If the house is colonial or multistoried, this set of joists becomes the second floor joists. It will be bridged or blocked out and decked over. Joist areas under toilets are headed off, boxed out and the opening planked over with ledger support to provide room for toilet closet bends.

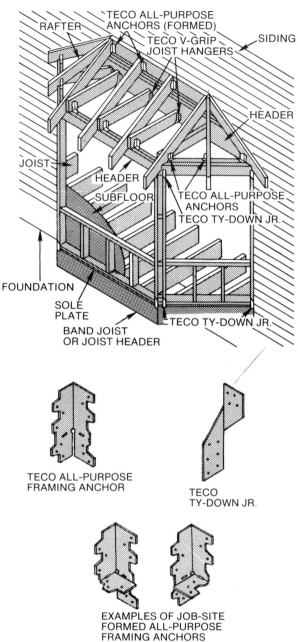

Wall structure at the bumpout.

meet, and where the interior walls meet. If the exterior wall top plates are not lapped at the corners, then metal straps should be added.

Corner posts are usually built up in one of three ways: (1) a pair of 2×4s is sandwiched over several short pieces of 2×4; (2) three 2×4s are spiked together and then a fourth is face-nailed to the edges of the sandwich, flush with one of the faces; or (3) face-nail one 2×4 to the edge of another, and then nail a third one into the internal corner thus formed. Note that all three methods are strong and provide nailing surfaces for the drywall. One advantage of the first method is that the voids may be filled with insulation.

Where interior walls meet exterior or other interior walls, the top plates are lapped. In addition, studs are arranged below this point so that there is a 3½″ space between them. This void is filled with another stud, the edges of which are nailed to the faces of the surrounding studs. This provides a good grip along the full stud length for the adjoining wall.

Where a wall meets another wall, and studs are spaced closer than 3½″, the studs of the adjoining wall may be toenailed to the two studs.

An alternate method of strengthening the meeting of walls is to block between two normally spaced (16″ O.C.) studs at several heights, and then nail the studs of the meeting wall to the blocking.

Interior Walls

Interior walls are usually the same as exterior walls, with certain exceptions. There are plates, studs, headers (if desired) and trimmers in interior walls, but rarely any sills and cripples, because of the absence of windows. The

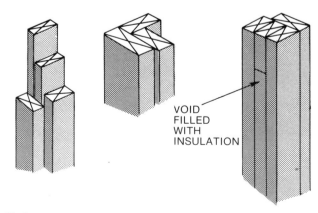

Various ways to assemble wall corner posts.

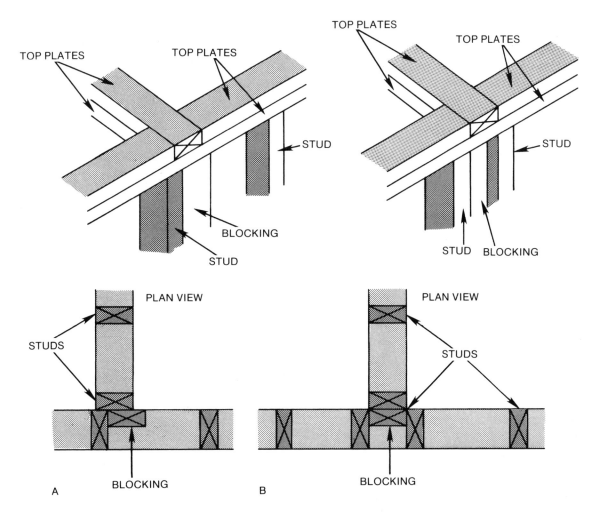

Two methods of connecting walls: isometric view at the top and plan view at the bottom.

upper top plate on an interior wall should overhang the lower top plate on either end by a length equal to the plate width of the walls to which it will be joined. For example, if it will meet a 2×4 wall, the overhang should be 3½″; and if a 2×6 wall, 5½″. These interior walls should be of 2×4 construction, unless they are used to conceal large plumbing or to house acoustic insulation or pocket doors.

Ceiling or Second Floor Joists

If the house has no second floor, the joists installed over and supported by the exterior walls and interior load bearing walls are ceiling joists. If the house has a second floor, these joists are floor joists. Floor joists are deeper in order to carry both the dead load (the weight of the construction materials) and the live load (the weight of people and furniture) of the second floor, which includes a second deck and another group of interior walls.

Assuming that the joists are floor joists, they are installed in a manner similar to that used with the first floor joists: They would be spaced on 16″ centers and their inner ends either lapped or butted and spliced as well as

If the building is single-storied or ranch style, the joists are ceiling joists and not as deep as second-story joists inasmuch as they won't have to carry a live load. They need not be decked over, but they do require strong backs (topside, two-piece, "L"-shaped bracing) and blocking. Note the use of metal joist hangers.

blocked over the load-bearing interior wall. They require bridging for rigidity and headers installed at right angles (to the joist run) to close off the exposed joist bays.

The decking over these floor joists is installed in the same manner as the decking over the first floor joists: with staggered end joints. Exterior and interior walls are all constructed just as the first floor walls except that there are no exterior door openings (except when needed to provide access to a second floor deck or similar structure).

Ceiling Joists

Ceiling joists require no headers. But they do require both bridging and strongbacks to keep them from twisting and warping, because there is no deck over them (unless the attic area has been converted into living space). If there is an attic deck, they will have been reinforced to carry the additional live load. Joists which run perpendicular to interior walls are toenailed to them, but sometimes joists and interior walls are parallel to each other. In these cases, mechanical connections such as blocking and drywall nailers are needed. The nailers can be fastened directly to the upper top plate, allowing equal overhang on each side. Then, blocking is nailed between and perpendicular to the adjacent joists, flush with the top of the nailers and fastened to them.

There is another requirement for ceiling or second floor joists: to provide a nailing surface for ceiling drywall at the bearing wall. This is typically handled by short 2×6 inserts along the top plate of the bearing wall between the joists or joist splices.

It should be noted that a different stud and joist layout scheme is used for houses with a hip roof. All hip roofs have a straight ridge section where rafters of the same length (common rafters) span between the wall top plate and the ridge, or spine of the roof. This entire section of the roof is centered between (equidistant from) the ridge ends and the ends of the building. This distance can be spanned by inserting common rafters, of the same length as those connected to the ridgeboard, at 90° angles between the ridgeboard ends and the building end walls.

To bring this about, the structure of the building from the girders and first joists and up is geared to provide maximum support and symmetry of roof members. For example, the joists are counted out in both directions on 16″ centers from the building centerline. Also, rafters must be nailed to joists on all four sides of the building, and this accounts for the necessity of lookout rafters (short rafters) on the tro side of the building.

Roof Structure

Simple gable roof framing consists of a number of rafter pairs, a ridgeboard, collar beams and end wall studs. The rafters span the distance from the ridgeboard to the exterior walls, and many times their tails extend

Ceiling joists have been headed off to create an opening beneath the skylight. Here, the walls of a light shaft are being installed. This area will have to be insulated and drywalled later.

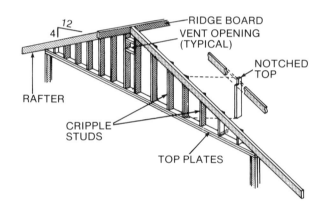

View of gable end wall with cripple studs, ridge, rafters.

somewhat beyond. The ridgeboard, which is the highest point of the roof, extends the full length of the roof, sometimes beyond the gable ends. Collar beams are horizontal members in tension that keep the rafters tight against the ridgeboard. Gable end wall studs are vertical members on the gable end that rest on the end wall top plates and seat the rafters directly above them in their top notches. The weight of the roof is sustained by the exterior walls for the most part, but there is another laterally outward force due to the roof's weight and geometry. This outward force is balanced by the ceiling joists, which are in tension, "holding the walls together," so to speak.

As a roof becomes more complex in shape, clearly more members are needed. For example, if the roof overhangs the gable ends, additional members, generally called fly rafters, are connected to the inboard rafters. The combination of the inboard rafter, lookouts and fly rafter takes on the look of a ladder going up the roof plane. This ladder is always integrated into the roof—in the case of relatively narrow fly rafters, by the roof sheathing attachment to the inboard rafter and the fascia at the lower

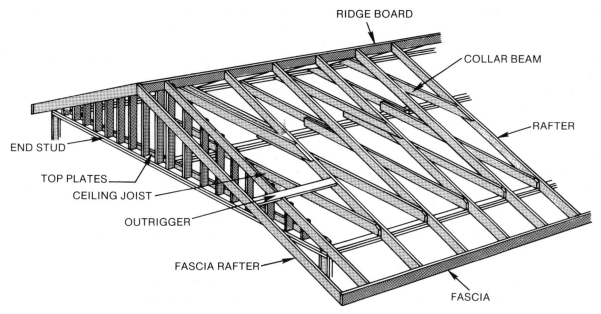

View of gable roof end with fly (fascia) rafters and outriggers (lookouts) supporting them. Gable end wall with cripples ridge, collars and fascia at the rafter tails can also be seen.

But here's the real thing...at least the bare bones. Again, we can see plates, studs, headers with cripple studs this time, header joists, braces, rough sill and cripples at the window rough openings, gable end wall studs, lookouts supporting the fly rafters, ridge and many common rafters.

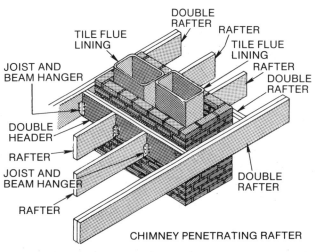

Doubled rafter (trimmer) with doubled headers and rafters tailing into the headers supported by metal joist hangers. This structure surrounds the chimney, which penetrates it.

end; wider fly rafters require more support, and the lookout rafters for them must span across several common rafters.

Roofs may have either shed or gable dormers. Both of these require modifications to the planes of the gable roof, such as doubled trimmer rafters (forming side borders). Both kinds of dormers require studs and top plates. The gable dormer has a ridgeboard, dormer rafters, valley rafters and doubled headers bordering the top and bottom of the roof opening. The shed dormer may rest either on the exterior wall top plates or on a doubled header and

sill combination further up the plane of the roof; while there is no ridge, there are shed rafters that span between the shed dormer top plate and the main roof ridge.

Another typical roof form occurs when there is a perpendicular intersection of two gable roofs. The intersection lines are called valleys, and the rafters which run from the intersecting gable wall plates to the ridge are common rafters, while those that run from the valley rafters to the ridge are called valley jack rafters.

When the gable ends of a gable roof are tilted inward at the top, a hip roof is formed. The rafters marking the intersections of the roof planes and extending out to or past the exterior walls are called hip rafters. Rafters spanning between the wall plates and the ridge are common rafters, but the rafters spanning from the exterior wall top plates to the hip rafters are called hip jack rafters. In cases where a gable roof intersects a hip roof, rafters running between the hip and valley rafters are called hip valley cripple jacks.

In gambrel roofs, there are some common rafters running between the exterior wall top plates and the purlin (which in some cases are the top plates of a wall), while other common rafters run between the purlin and the ridge. Collar beams hold the upper rafters tight against the ridge, and in some cases serve as ceiling joists.

End wall studs at the gables are installed 16″ O.C. and are notched at the top to seat the rafter. Vents are installed in these gable end walls, so that the openings for these vents must be framed out with headers and cripple studs.

Wall Sheathing

The sheathing most commonly used is ½″ thick with a 32/16 span rating, manufactured with exterior glue. The span rating numbers mean that if used as roof sheathing, the maximum span between rafter centers is 32″, and if used as subflooring, the maximum span is 16″ between joist centers. This sheathing, when combined with the stud and plate structure, forms what is called in engineering terms a shear wall, just as the joist network and deck forms a diaphragm.

Wall sheathing covers the entire vertical surface of the house, with the exception of the window and door openings. The end joints are usually staggered if the sheathing is applied with the long ends horizontally, but it may also be applied with the long edges vertical. When locked to the framing with 6d to 8d cement-coated nails, it provides stability against racking (where a rectangle becomes a rhombus). Sheathing also serves as a base for siding or as the ties for a masonry veneer wall.

Roof Sheathing

The roof sheathing should be ½″-thick exterior plywood with a 24/0 or a 24/16 span rating when the rafters are spaced 24″ O.C. or less. The sheathing panel end joints are staggered just like the decking and wall sheathing end joints. The roof sheathing serves as the base for the roofing material, and can be pierced to accommodate plumbing vent stacks, skylights and chimneys.

When the house has overhanging eaves and closed soffits, the rafters must have tails to accommodate these structures. The rafter tail ends will be covered with a fascia board, and the lower soffit surface will be sheathed with plywood. It is at this stage that the average home will receive roofing and window installation.

What's Inside the Walls

Where heavy plumbing fixtures are located, there are ribbon- or blocking-type let-ins for support. Plumbing

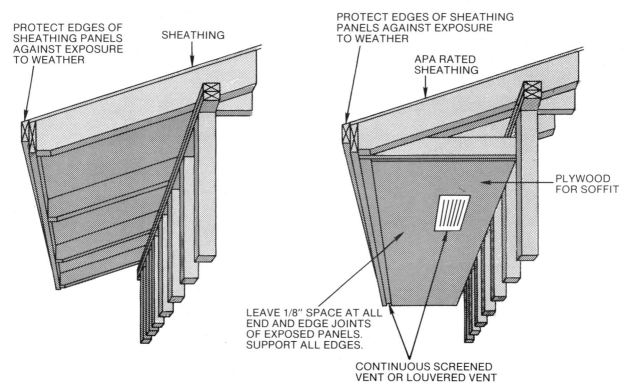

Detail of open and closed soffits with rafters, plates, studs, fascia and trim. Note vent in closed soffit for circulation.

Here, sheathing is being installed on furring strips nailed to the rafters of a low-pitch gable roof. The furring strips allow air coming from vents to circulate in the rafter area. This is necessary because it's a cathedral ceiling inside and will be closed in on the lower surface with drywall following insulation.

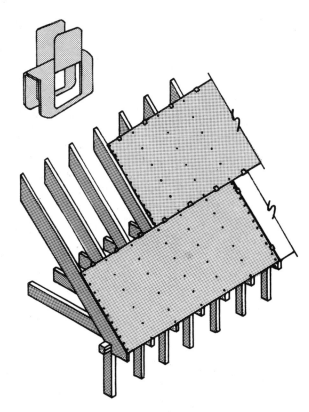

When roof sheathing joints appear too flexible in the rafter bays, metal "H" clips can be inserted during the assembly to add rigidity.

pipes are also found in the walls. Copper tubing of about ½" to ¾" diameter, for both hot and cold water supplies, normally runs through holes drilled in studs, joists and plates. There are also stacks and other pipes running vertically through the walls, to vent interior air to fans and passive ventilators in the roof, and to pick up waste drainage from the sinks, toilets, showers and baths.

Electrical cable also runs through the walls, connecting the electrical panel and its breakers with switches, receptacles and other electrical fixtures and devices. In addition, there is the telephone wiring and thermostat wiring, and there may be vacuum tubing, security wiring and television cable.

These are not the only materials stuffed inside the walls: The exterior walls also have insulation and, in many cases, forced air ducting or forced hot water piping.

According to many building codes, house wiring and plumbing should have steel protective plates mounted on the living space edge of the adjacent studs and plates to guard against drywall nail damage or damage from other home improvement work. Unfortunately, this is not always the case, so cautious work is your best defense against costly damage, when doing projects in the house.

39

Installation and Repair of Gypsum Board

Almost 5/6ths of the living space in your average home is surfaced with gypsum board. You'll need to install it in additions and remodeling projects; and in some cases you will need to repair existing gypsum board (also called gypsum drywall), due to accidental damage, improper installation, framing shrinkage, foundation settling damage or intentional destruction caused by other repairs or modifications. Finally, there are the more modest drywall operations, including the application of wall covering, panelling and tiling, each of which will be covered separately.

According to the Gypsum Association, gypsum board is the generic name for a family of panel products consisting of a noncombustible core composed primarily of gypsum, and a paper surface covering on the face, back and long edges.

Some Hard Facts about Gypsum Board

There are a number of advantages to be gained by the use of gypsum board or drywall, due to its physical properties. Among these are fire resistance due to the noncombustible core, sound control due to the density and ease of installation due both to its chemical makeup and its large, smooth, modular physical character.

Gypsum board is manufactured in a variety of types, face skins, cores, edge shapes, thicknesses, sizes and configurations. Three types most commonly used for the surfacing of residential walls and ceilings are: regular gypsum board, Type X board (which is used in fire-rated assemblies) and water-resistant gypsum board (used in wet locations, such as bathrooms and laundry areas, where it may be painted, wallpapered or used as a base for the installation of ceramic tile).

The ends of standard gypsum boards are square sawn, leaving the core exposed (but temporarily covered with shipping paper, which keeps pairs of boards locked together during transportation and delivery).

There are five paperbound edge shapes from which to choose: (1) tapered, (2) rounded, (3) beveled, (4) square and (5) tongue and groove. Of these, the tapered edge is by far the most practical, certainly for residential work.

The standard manufactured width is 4', which is compatible with the 4' modular sizes used in construction. Standard lengths are 8' to 16' (in 2' increments). Regular gypsum board and Type X board are both manufactured in 1/4", 5/16", 3/8", 1/2", 5/8" and 1" thicknesses. The thicker dimensions are used primarily in commercial applications, while the 1/2" thickness is used in residential work. The thinner boards are useful when treating curved walls.

General Installation Facts

Although gypsum board can be installed over furring, masonry, concrete, metal and wood framing, or even other gypsum board products, the most typical residential application is over wood studding and ceiling joists to provide interior wall and ceiling surfaces.

Gypsum board may be installed in a single layer (1 ply) or a double layer (2 ply). With the extra ply, fire resistance and sound control improve, as would be expected.

A number of fastening methods are available, including nails, screws, staples (in certain applications) and adhesives. Nail types and lengths vary according to the thickness of the assembly, whereas screw types and lengths vary both with the thickness and with the type of substrate (wood, metal or gypsum) to which the board is being applied. These methods will be handled in greater detail shortly.

Regardless of the fastening method used, all flat joints and internal corner joints are treated with paper tape and joint compound. All external corners are treated with corner bead and compound.

Once the taped and jointed areas have been sanded to blend in with the immediately adjacent drywall, the entire wall becomes integrated into a smooth, continuous surface, which may be painted, textured, tiled or decorated with paper, plastic or cloth wall covering. If the choice of wall covering is panel, the taping and jointing may be omitted.

Openings at electrical boxes are covered with switch or receptacle cover plates, while forced air boot openings are covered with registers. At the windows and doors, case moldings bridge the insulated gaps between the jambs and the drywall, while the bottom of the drywall and the adjacent flooring edges are trimmed off even with the base molding or base and shoe molding.

Tools Needed to Work with Gypsum Board

The aspect of drywall application and repair that has been most fascinating for me is the relatively small number of tools required to do a workman-like job. On the average, you'll need a straightedge (or better, a 48″ drywall T square), a drywall saw and utility knife for cutting, a flexible tape for measurements not taken on the T square, a hammer to drive nails, a Surform to smooth edges, a hawk or pan or board to hold the compound, a few taping knives for applying and feathering the compound and a sanding block (with or without handle) to finish the dry, jointed surfaces. If alternate fastening methods are used, a screwgun or adhesive cartridge gun will be needed.

Final Framing Preparations before Drywall Installation

Make sure that all joists are crowned alike, with the convex curves all facing up, and that these crowns are of a minor nature to being with—less than, say, 1/2″ per 14′ or 15′. Check that the stud spacing is 16″ O.C. (or 24″, in some cases) and that the joist spacing is 24″ O.C.

Replace any twisted or bowed studs, and bring any misaligned studs or plates into proper position. Replace any framing that is split out to an edge. Make sure all internal areas have nailers and that the framing members are dry. If necessary, correct this problem with a space heater. You don't want to have framing with a life of its own under a gypsum board installation.

Particularly in bathroom or laundry room areas, where fixtures may be wall-mounted, check that there are ribbon let-ins where required, and that these are flush with the surrounding studs.

To ensure minimal drywall movement, give the headers and their trimmers a final check for gaps, which might result in slight sagging over a window, archway or exterior door, causing stress cracks in the drywall later on.

Let's assume that everything that's going into the stud or joist bays is in place. This includes rough electric, rough plumbing, telephone cable, TV cable, central vac tubing, heat ducting and insulation (with facing vapor barrier or with a separate vapor barrier). Steel protection plates should be installed over critical areas on stud or joist edges which might be penetrated by drywall nails or screws, causing damage to electrical or plumbing parts within. Forced air register boots as well as electrical boxes should be firmly mounted on the framing, to fit into the drywall, but not so far out past the studs or joists that they penetrate it. Penetrations can allow excessive and annoying sound vibrations to be transmitted through the wall.

T.L.C. for Gypsum Board before, during and after Installation

Excessively high and low temperature and humidity can cause not only unsatisfactory results with tape and joint compound, but unnecessary delays in installation work as well. Work should not be done in temperatures of less than 50° F or more than 80° F.

When gypsum drywall is installed during periods of rain or high humidity, the use of fans for ventilation is recommended to speed up the drying time of the compound. Allow additional drying time between applications of compound during damp periods to avoid putting fresh compound on a wet base (which can cause shrinkage and cracking). The problem of high humidity can also be overcome by the use of space heaters.

A different problem occurs when weather conditions are hot and dry. Here the low vapor pressure and high temperature of the ambient air encourage excessively rapid drying. Excessive ventilation or breezes acting upon wet compound surfaces must be avoided, since the moving air can speed up the drying process even more.

Installation Basics—Single Layer

The basic procedure is to cut each piece of gypsum board so that it fits in place neatly without having to be forced. After measuring and marking, straight cuts on gypsum board are made by scoring a line on the front face skin with a utility knife guided by a straightedge or T square. The waste end or edge is folded back to crack the core (accomplished most easily over a table end), and then the second skin is cut through, separating the pieces.

When an electrical box or mechanical device such as a heating register boot falls within the area of a gypsum board installation, take accurate measurements and mark the face skin with a pencil and square. The rectangular waste may then be removed with a hand-operated drywall saw or a jigsaw. This procedure is used for all irregular cutouts as well as the "crosscuts" of rectangular cutouts and notches. All rough edges can be trimmed smooth in seconds with a "block plane"-size Surform.

The order of installation is important. In all cases, the ceiling gypsum board panels should be installed before the walls. This provides additional end and edge support of ceiling panels—by the wall panels installed just beneath them.

There are a number of ways to mark and cut gypsum board. This piece was marked with a folding rule, and a level served as a guide for the utility knife score on the face side.

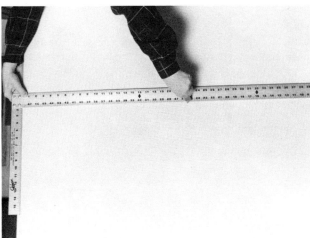

This 4' square is used by drywall pros when rectangular marks or cuts are required. It will guide either pencil or knife fully across the panel width and yet clear the floor.

The piece is flipped over with the back side up, then folded to crack it along the scoreline on the front side. Then a final utility knife cut through the fold line completes the cut.

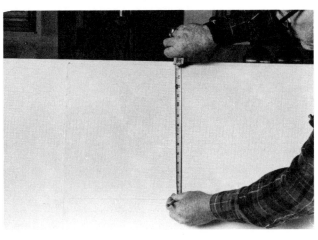

Take a technique from the pro's bag of tricks for marking or scoring a full-length (rip) cut. One hand rides the long edge holding the flexible tape body, while the other holds both the moving tape end with either a knife or pencil.

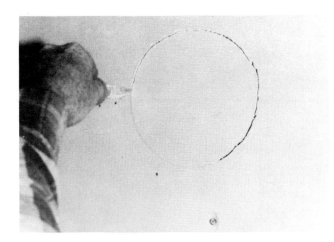

Round holes are necessary for most built-in ceiling light fixtures (top hats). The saw will cut to a circular outline with no problem if your location measurement is accurate.

Always put the ceiling panels up first in a full room, and unless the room dimension is more than 16', span it with full-length panels to avoid troublesome taping problems.

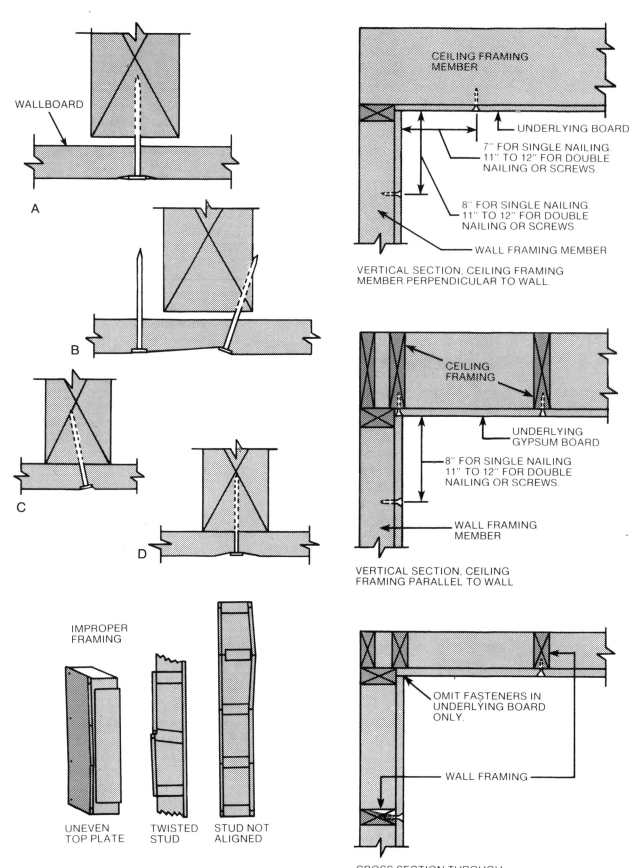

WALLBOARD

A

B

C

D

IMPROPER FRAMING

UNEVEN TOP PLATE

TWISTED STUD

STUD NOT ALIGNED

CEILING FRAMING MEMBER

UNDERLYING BOARD

7" FOR SINGLE NAILING. 11" TO 12" FOR DOUBLE NAILING OR SCREWS.

8" FOR SINGLE NAILING. 11" TO 12" FOR DOUBLE NAILING OR SCREWS

WALL FRAMING MEMBER

VERTICAL SECTION, CEILING FRAMING MEMBER PERPENDICULAR TO WALL.

CEILING FRAMING

UNDERLYING GYPSUM BOARD

8" FOR SINGLE NAILING. 11" TO 12" FOR DOUBLE NAILING OR SCREWS.

WALL FRAMING MEMBER

VERTICAL SECTION, CEILING FRAMING PARALLEL TO WALL

OMIT FASTENERS IN UNDERLYING BOARD ONLY.

WALL FRAMING

CROSS SECTION THROUGH INTERIOR VERTICAL ANGLE

Avoid framing and installation errors: (A) Gypsum board not flush with framing; (B) Cocked nail splitting board and not pulling board flush with framing; (C) Cocked nail, breaking skin; (D) This is how framing, gypsum board and nail should be.

Various views showing wall, ceiling junction and framing.

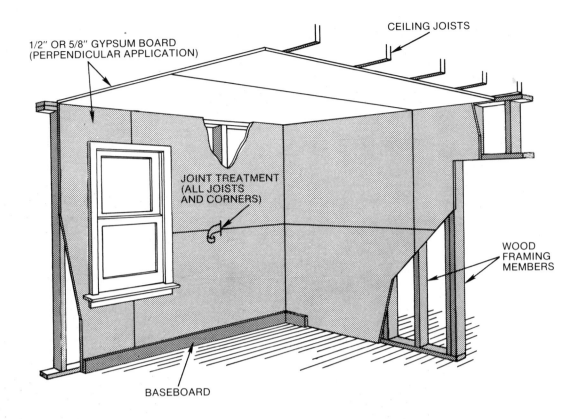

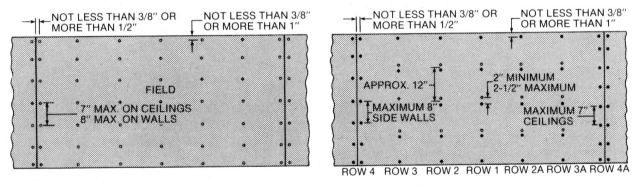

Typical ceiling and wall gypsum board positions when installed in the respective framing (top); wall gypsum board nailing pattern (left); ceiling gypsum board nailing pattern (right).

As to orientation, gypsum board may be placed either parallel or perpendicular to both joist and stud runs, but when placed in position for nailing, the ends and edges should match the equivalent ends and edges of all adjacent pieces, except where a surface such as a ceiling meets a wall.

If at all possible, try to go completely across the span of a wall or ceiling with a single piece to minimize the number of ends to be taped and jointed. This reduces the number of end joints. You can tape and joint the tapered and paperbound edges rather quickly, but the ends are sawn with the cores exposed, making the blending job somewhat more difficult. It's a good idea to stagger these end joints and to locate them in less conspicuous areas where the eye will not pick them up as easily.

Nails and Nailing

The panels may be single- or double-nailed, both on ceiling and wall installations, with double-nailing the preferred method on ceilings. In both single- and double-nailing, the perimeter nails are more closely spaced than the field nails. Also, in both methods, the end and edge minimum and maximum distances are specified.

You can use either smooth shank- or annular ring-type nails in drywall installation. Both have thin heads with diameters ranging between 1/4″ and 5/16″. The length chosen depends on the type of nail used as well as the thickness of the panel. This is because the accepted standard for penetration into the framing is 7/8″ for smooth shank and 3/4″ for the annular ring-type.

The idea when nailing is to drive the nail straight in through the panel, firmly into the supporting framing behind it, bringing the panel up tight against the framing, and at the same time creating a shallow (1/32″ deep) dimple with the nailhead in the center. This should be done without breaking the face skin.

One of the keys to success is to start nailing in the center of the panel and work gradually outward to the perimeter; another key is to apply hand pressure on the panel in the immediate nailing area, holding the panel tight against the framing. The correct choice of hammer can help, too. It should weigh no more than 16 ounces, and should have a crowned head, which forms a dimple more easily. This dimple surrounding the countersunk nail provides a place where several applications of joint compound will hide the nail and produce a smooth, continuous surface. If the face skin is accidentally broken, another nail should be driven in through the intact face skin a couple of inches away.

In the critical area of the wall/ceiling joint, there's a little trick used to reduce the chance of cracks and nail or screw pops caused by structural stress due to the natural movement of the house framing. It's called the floating interior angle and here's how to do it: Where joists are perpendicular to an approaching wall, do not nail the ceiling panel all the way to the wall. Instead, stop the nail pattern 7″ from the wall or 12″ in the case of double-nailing. In cases where the joists run parallel to the wall, nail right up to the end. In both cases the taping and jointing will be done in the normal manner.

When the ceilings and wall panels have been installed, the room geometry often leaves external corners where panels from adjacent walls meet. These corners must be touched up with the Surform to make them smooth; then, lengths of "L"-shaped corner bead are placed over the joint, and nails are driven through both of its flanges. Joint compound is applied at the appropriate time.

Taping and Jointing

The tape used in drywall is typically 2″ wide and pre-creased (with an embossed fold line running down the center of the roll). The tape is used in conjunction with joint compound to seal internal corners and flat, matched tapered joints, and in some cases to effect a repair.

The first thing is to learn to use the right equipment to apply compound and tape efficiently. You don't want your hands encumbered, so bend a belt loop for the tape roll from a wire hanger or compound bucket handle, and keep the tape roll centered on your belt. After opening a compound bucket, as you use the compound, continually scrape the unused compound remaining on the sides of the bucket down into the main mass. This will prevent the thin residue on the sides from drying prematurely, and the resulting dry grit from contaminating the rest of the mix and causing gouges in the compound when it is applied to the wall or ceiling.

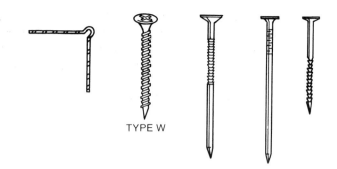

Drywall hardware from top to bottom: Three typical drywall nails; drywall screw; metal corner bead sectional view.

Nailing Schedule for Single-Ply Gypsum Board	
Gypsym Board Thickness in Inches	Minimum Nail Length in Inches
¼	(2)
⅜	1¼
½	1⅜
⅝	1½

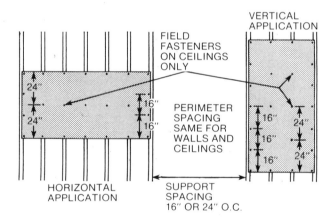

When panels are applied with stud adhesive, supplemental nails or screws are required. They should be installed according to the patterns shown.

Now, you have a choice: Hold a small mass of compound either in a so-called California pan or on a hawk. These tools can be held in one hand and will give you a wide radius of mobility away from the bucket.

All nail dimples must be spotted with compound alone, but flat joints on walls and ceilings require both flat tape and compound. External corner joints require only compound over the corner bead, while the internal corners need both folded tape and compound. The internal corners are the hardest to handle, due to the right angle apex. Therefore, after the initial tape imbedment dries, you must alternate from one flange to another when applying subsequent compound layers. Also, there are the

A lightweight drywall saw similar to a carpenter's handsaw can be used to make the cuts between the window jamb and rough opening in new construction or addition walls. The head area of the panel has already been scored before installation. The waste can then be folded in to crack it along the scoreline, and the internal cut made in the fold to separate it from the panel.

The last mechanical operation before taping and jointing is to apply metal corner bead to all external corners including vertical wall intersections, horizontal wall intersections at drop ceilings and drywalled openings. Care must be exercised not to dent the bead at the outer edge.

internal corners where three surfaces intersect—for example, where two walls meet the ceiling. In these places, three alternations are needed.

There is a normal amount of shrinkage when compound dries, so that even the dimples will have to be spotted more than once. Spotting is done by first transferring compound from the hawk or pan to a 4″ to 6″ taping knife, and then executing a broad, sweeping, continuous arc, covering as many dimples as possible. During this motion keep the knife at a shallow angle relative to the

wall or ceiling. Only a few minutes of experience are needed to get the "feel" of the correct angle. Check that the compound has not been dragged out of the dimples and, at the same time, that the maximum fill has been made.

To fill the long, flat joints, lay a continuous bed of compound in the depression formed by the matched tapers. Then, center the flat tape over this bed. Next, hold one end of the tape and, with the taping knife, squeeze the tape smoothly and continuously into the compound. The idea here is to use enough pressure to effect a bond, but not so much as to squeeze out the bed of compound completely. This would cause a bonding failure. Avoid wrinkles while bonding the tape and, make sure that both ends are bonded down. If you don't like the results, do it again—no one's looking. Once the bond is satisfactory, reload your taping knife with compound and apply a leveling coat over the bedded tape. Although you level the compound with the main wall, completely filling the tapered area, there will be some unavoidable shrinkage during the drying process. Two or three more finish coats of compound, applied to the area with increasingly wider taping knives, will finish it off.

Now for those end joints, where you don't have the taper to make life easier. Fill any joint cracks and apply a thin bed of compound to bond the tape over the joint, as flat as possible without losing the bond. Follow this up with a thin coat over the tape and allow the joint to dry. Then, add enough thin, feathered-out coats to blend the "high" joint with the adjacent panels. This may require a band of compound more than a foot wide. All this extra work is one reason you should try to limit the number of end joints.

At this point, the exterior corners will be no problem at all. Just load up your taping knife with compound and lay a wide bed of it along both sides of the corner bead. Then, with the blade guided by both one wall and the bead radius, pull the knife down at the usual shallow angle, blending the radius in with the rest of the wall. This must be done on both sides of the bead when dry, additional coats will be required.

When handling an internal corner formed by the intersection of two walls, prefold the necessary length of tape by pulling it with one hand through the shape formed by thumbnail and curled index finger of the other hand. Be careful here, since it is very easy to get a nasty paper cut. Then, apply a bed of compound several inches wide to both sides of the corner. Next, tuck the prefolded tape into the apex and bond it in place with the taping knife, one side at a time, again avoiding wrinkles. After this dries, fresh compound must be applied to one side at a time only, and allowed to dry. Otherwise, smoothing the compound on one side damages the other side. The treatment of internal corners where three walls meet is the same except that instead of alternating between two sides, you must alternate between two sides of each of three intersecting pieces of tape.

At the wall/ceiling intersections apply a coat of compound first to one surface for the full length of the room. On the reverse pass, apply compound to the adjacent surface also for the full length of the room. Flat joints on ceilings are handled in the same manner.

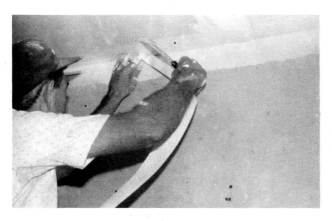

On the third pass, start the tape at one corner, fold it as you move along and center it in the internal corner all the way across the room. Pros walk on stilts to do this ceiling work. Do-it-yourselfers can set up planks on low benches or boxes in a safe manner to get just about the same advantage.

On the fourth pass, press the blade on one surface of the bedded tape, again at a shallow and go the full length of the room. The fifth pass takes care of the adjacent surface. The vertical wall intersections are handled in the same manner.

The horizontal tapered joints of the walls can be taped in three to four passes, depending upon the craftsman's skill. Begin by applying compound to the joint area with a 4″ knife.

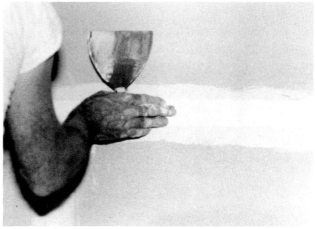

Next, center the tape on the bedded area for the full length of the room. This can be done with the hand alone or the knife in combination with the hand.

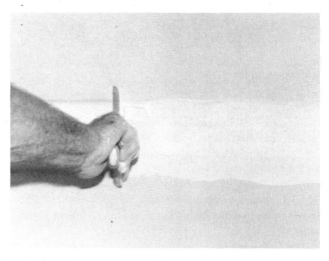

On the third pass, place the knife on the bedded tape at a shallow angle and drag the knife across the full length of the room. Press hard enough to bond the tape, but not so hard as to squeeze out the compound completely, because this would cause tape separation.

Once all the finish layers of compound have been applied and allowed to dry, it's time for a final sanding to blend in all the tape and compound applications with the adjacent wall and ceiling surfaces. But exercise care so as not to sand into the tape, causing eruptions that will have to be repaired. The correct time for sanding is at the end of all compound applications, *not* after each coat, although it's very tempting. There are abrasive sheets available that fit the spring-loaded locks of both handle and pole-handled swiveled sanders.

Using Screw Fasteners

As already mentioned, the gypsum board may be fastened with nails, screws or adhesive. The approach with screw fasteners is basically the same as the nailing method, but the pattern spacing is looser and the required depth of penetration into wood framing is less than that for nails.

Gypsum board screw fasteners come in three types. The Type W screw, used to fasten gypsum board to wood, must penetrate 5/8″ into the framing for single-layer gypsum board. The spacing is 12″ O.C. for ceilings, 16″ O.C. for 16″ O.C. studding and 12″ for 24″ O.C. studding. Obviously, considerably fewer fasteners are required to install a gypsum board by the screw-fastening method than in a nail installation.

In all cases, screws are power-driven with a drill-like tool that has an adjustable depth control to limit the countersinking of the screw into the gypsum board. The Type W screw has a diamond point for "drilling" into the wood, and a high lead thread for rapid driving. All drive screws for gypsum board have Phillips head slots for use with the driver.

Using Adhesive as a Gypsum Board Fastener

There are several advantages to using adhesive as the main fastener of gypsum board panels to wood framed structures: The screws or nails used are supplemental and reduced in number by 50%; and also, as a result of the bonding power of continuous beads of adhesive, not only are small discrepancies in the framing eliminated, but a more integrated, considerably stronger wall is formed.

With an adhesive as the main fastener, supplementary nails or screws are required on the perimeter at all times, but when the gypsum board panels are applied to the ceiling, nails or screws are required on the intermediate joists as well. Specifically, this means that the screws or nails must be 16″ O.C. on all edges and ends parallel to the long edge. They must also be at all crossing points of the edges or ends and perpendicular framing. On ceilings only, field fasteners must be used on the intermediate framing members—along the studs and joists at 24″ O.C. spacing. If this is done with metal studs, both perimeter and field screws are required, but spacing and screw

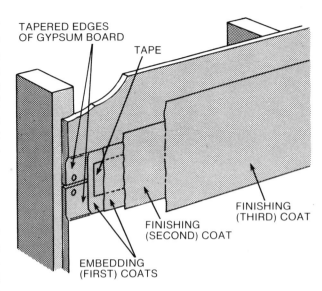

A typical horizontal joint where tapered edges meet and the taping and jointing processes required prior to sanding.

length should be done as specified in the Gypsum Association Fire Resistance Manual.

To eliminate the double line of fasteners where two ends or edges join over a stud, preset a curve in gypsum board so that a convex belly or arc is formed on the back faces. Then, in addition to the adhesive applied to the studs, fasteners are needed on the top and sole plates.

The adhesive is applied as a 3/8″ bead with a hand-operated cartridge gun (available in consumer and commercial sizes, as is the adhesive). The normal tendency is to run a wavy bead of adhesive on the studs or joists, and this is fine, except at studs where adjacent panels abut. Here you want two straight lines of adhesive, separated by 1/2″ to 3/4″, to avoid squeeze-out on the face skin. It is not necessary to apply adhesive to top and sole plates, bridging, cats, bracing, let-ins, blocking or internal corners.

Wet Locations

In baths, showers, kitchens and laundry rooms, the preferred material is the water-resistant gypsum board (and backer board, if the design requires). There typically are higher-than-average moisture levels in these areas, and quite often tile is attached to these walls with organic adhesive. At tubs and showers, special precautions must be taken to prevent moisture from gaining access to the bottom edges of the gypsum board by wicking (basically a capillary action process), or to the upper areas by spray action and soaking. These precautions include the allowance of a minimum distance between the top of the shower receptor or tub lip and the bottom of the gypsum board, and observing the minimum tile heights for showers and tubs.

Drywall Repair

Drywall repairs fall into a number of categories, with various levels of difficulty. Some of the simpler problems include nail popping, shadowing, and minor stress cracks—whereas water damage, intentional holes (made necessary by repairs to plumbing or electrical items), and ridging are among the more troublesome items to put right.

Let's work up from the easier problems: Nail popping is probably the most common one. It is caused by improper nailing (by insufficient penetration into framing, by obliquely driven nails or by having the drywall not locked tight against the framing), or by the normal shrinkage of green framing members. After a heating season or two, green lumber will have dried out sufficiently for repair. Start by finding and removing any loose nails and dimple compound. Then drive additional nails into these spots, and refinish them with fresh compound.

Begin by cutting out a piece of drywall about an inch larger than the hole on all sides. Then make scorelines on the back side that are the size of the hole. Crack off the drywall along these scorelines and pull the perimeter away from the front skin without tearing it.

The last job is the easiest. Stroke the knife with compound over each dimple (nail depression caused by the hammer shape). Note that when dry all taping must be compounded again, and when that has dried, again.

Butter up the edges of the patch and stuff some compound into the hole's edges as well.

These two small holes in the drywall are best handled by combining them into one using the drywall saw and closing it with a "balloon patch."

Place the patch in the hole, flatten the skin perimeter by hand and then bond and smooth it with a taping knife. A coat or two more compound with drying time in between will do it.

Small cracks that may be the result of foundation or framing settlement are repaired with compound alone, if they are very narrow, or else with tape and compound, with a fairly large surrounding area allowed for feathering and blending. Shadowing, which is caused by low-angle viewing of raised finish areas, can be reduced or eliminated by simply broadening the feathered finishing area.

Small holes that don't cross studs or joists are best repaired with the so-called balloon patch. Start by sawing the hole into a rectangular shape with the drywall saw.

But be careful not to damage any wiring or plumbing behind the hole. Then, cut out a piece of gypsum board about 1 1/2" larger than the hole on all sides. Next, on the back skin of the patch, outline the hole dimensions, and score this outline with a utility knife, all the way to the edges. Crack these edges and remove both back skin and core on all four sides, leaving only a face skin border around the body of the patch. Then work compound around the inner edge of the hole and around the outside of its perimeter, so that it is spread widely enough to bond

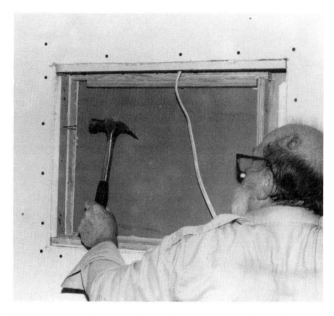

This is a larger hole that basically extends the width of the stud bay. The hole has 2 × 4 blocking at the top and bottom, and nailers have been installed on the studs.

This is an extensive rip out, caused by a plumbing leak. It extends across several stud bays and so far down that the base molding had to be removed. The hole should be outlined and cut out to a clean, rectangular shape. Then, the drywall and nails should be removed from half the width of the bordering studs, and new nails installed around the perimeter to the remaining drywall.

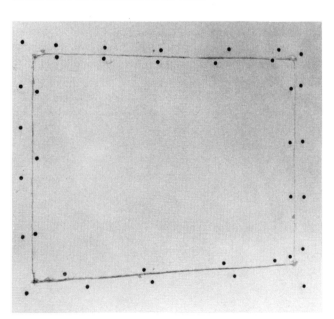

All drywall and drywall nails have been cleared from the studs and a full width piece has been nailed in place. A bed of compound is spread around the joint area. This will be followed by taping and finishing coats after drying.

The large drywall patch should be nailed in place around the perimeter and to the intermediate studs and blocking. Saw out the duct register boot waste. Then tape and joint the edges in the normal manner. Sand smooth when the finish coats have dried.

the patch skin. Position the patch and apply pressure around the perimeter skin with a drywall knife. When dry, apply additional finish coats.

To repair large holes or damage that crosses framing, enlarge the damaged area to the centerlines of the two nearest parallel framing members. This requires the removal of perimeter fasteners, and sometimes also field fasteners, and the smoothing of any disrupted adjacent edges. Then, cut a patch to size, nail it in and apply the tape and joint compound.

Large waterlogged pieces should be replaced with new panels to avoid the accumulation of end joints. If you're dealing with a ceiling, be sure to tuck the edges in on top of the wall pieces.

Ridging or bulging of gypsum board along one side of a joint is usually caused by framing movement, and should not be repaired during the heating season. The recommended repair method is to apply tape and joint compound in thin layers on the low side until it's even with the high side. Compound and feather as required.

40

Trim Carpentry

In this section, the term *trim carpentry* includes hinged interior doors and jambs, modular panelling, plank panelling, standard molding and some custom molding applications. We'll cover the hanging of prehung doors as well as separate doors and jambs.

General Door Information

Hinged interior doors may be purchased in a variety of surfaces, materials and styles. Among the many kinds available are the flush surfaced doors and the raised panel doors.

The flush doors are available either with a full solid wood core or with a cardboard honeycomb core and a solid wood perimeter (including the lock frame). The latter type is more common due to its lower cost plus the fact that the average interior door receives relatively little abuse and usually doesn't need the strength of solid wood.

Surfaces for these doors come in several wood species, such as birch, mahogany and oak. Surface skins for the hollow core doors may be purchased separately, in case a repair is required.

The typical raised panel door is constructed of solid wood, with its panels locked in by an array of rails and stiles. Its raised and fielded panels, sized according to classic proportions and combined with shaped edges, make it quite an attractive package. But it's quite a bit more expensive than a flush door of comparable size. Both flush surfaced and raised panel doors may be finished with stain, shellac and varnish, or painted to match the room decor.

Both flush surfaced and raised panel doors may be purchased separately from the jamb assembly that supports them; or they can be purchased as prehung units, already hinged to the side jamb of an assembled jamb set (with the door itself already prebored for the lockset.). If you buy separate jambs and doors, you'll find that jamb sets consist of two side jambs connected to a head jamb (almost always with rabbeted or dadoed joints). In many cases, jamb sets are packaged to include stop and case molding as well.

Jambs are conventionally 4 9/16″ wide, to accommodate the standard interior wall. This standard interior wall is framed with 2×4 studs and a single layer of ½″ gypsum board on either side for a total thickness of 4½″.

Most interior hinged doors are 1⅜″ thick, but they can be as thick as 1¾″. They range in width from 1′0″ to 3′0″, and come 6′8″, 6′10″, or 7′0″ in height. The standard interior door is 2′6″×6′8″ to allow normal household traffic and furniture clearance. Bathroom doors and some linen closet doors are typically smaller in width.

If you're planning an addition, and you have large furniture, it's a smart move to install a 2′8″ door, which costs only a fraction more than the 2′6″ size and won't take up much more room, but will make it a good deal easier to jockey furniture around.

Prehung Door Installation.

For ease of installation, the prehung door is the way to go because you are saved the trouble of chiseling hinge mortises in the door and jamb, as well as the job of boring the lockset and latch holes.

Before starting to hang the door, make a quick check of the hinge fits. Be sure that they are tight on the surfaces, and that they are squarely mounted, so that the hinge knuckles are tight on the pins. If you find any slop at the top hinge pin, remove the hinge as a unit from the door and jamb. Protect it from damage with a piece of scrap rubber or carpet and give the knuckle a squeeze between the vise jaws. If this problem exists and is not corrected, you'll never be able to set up a proper gap between the side jamb and the door edge, especially near the upper hinge. Clearly, a loose hinge pin at the top causes a gap, while

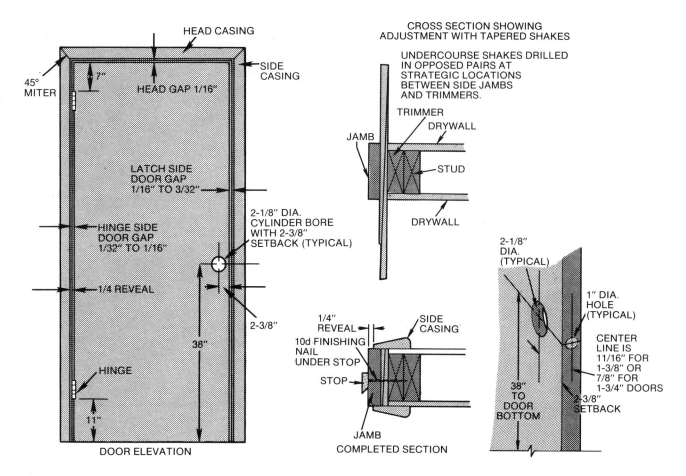

Door details show hinge and lock locations, gaps, reveals, rough opening, jamb, shimming and molding.

one at the bottom tends to reduce the gap. At this time the door itself should be inspected for any warpage that may have occurred during storage and exchanged for another door, if necessary.

To actually hang a prehung door, the door and its jamb must be fitted into the rough opening of the wall with the hinges and lockset holes correctly aligned. This involves choosing a left-hand or a right-hand fit, and an inward or outward opening direction. Bedroom, bathroom and dining room doors normally open inward; broom, utility and linen closet doors open outward, and so on.

Next, check to see if the floor is level in the threshold area. If the floor is sloped, the side jambs, both the same length, will cause the head jamb to be sloped. The correction for floor slope discrepancy is to trim off the bottom of the jamb that would fit over the high side of the threshold, and then trim the bottom of the door to match.

The major tool for checking the plumb attitude of the side jambs and the level attitude of the head jam is the carpenter's level. Use it generously for a professional-looking job.

You will notice spaces between the jambs and the rough opening trimmers. These spaces are for jamb adjustments, which are used to plumb the jambs as well as to control the small gaps that appear between the door and the jambs. These two adjustments are carried out by inserting tapered undercourse shakes in pairs, with their tapers opposed, into the spaces at strategic locations, and then adjusting and locking the shakes in place.

The opposed tapers ensure that the jamb will be parallel to the trimmer and allow you to make continuous, minute adjustments. To move the jamb away from the trimmer (to increase the space), drive the shakes from the butt ends toward each other. Pull them apart to decrease the space.

Start the actual installation by removing all three door-stop moldings, and then position the door in the rough opening so that the jamb edges are flush with drywall. Drive 10d finishing nails through the jambs into the rough opening trimmers in the stop areas. Note that the rough opening will grip the nails better than the pine jambs, so that the jambs can be pried away from the trimmer to create the necessary adjustment spaces. For the best results in the shortest time, the pairs of tapered shake spacers should be installed behind the hinges, behind the strike, at the top and bottom, and in as many other places as required to keep the side jambs straight. Try to make the gaps between the door and the jambs 1/32" to 1/16" wide on the hinge side and 1/16" to 3/32" wide on the lock side.

Place the jamb and door(s) inside the rough opening and nail through the side jambs into the 2×4 trimmer studs behind. This is a closet door because it opens outward.

These professional trimmers drive the 10d nails through the stop and jamb. It's neater to remove the stop, drive the nails and replace the stop later.

Do this first near the top hinge and then the lower hinge. Tapered shims provide continuous adjustment range.

The trimmer is checking the door gap, controlled by shim adjustment. With single doors check door-to-jamb gap.

After adjustment and nailing, trim the shakes flush with the jamb with a utility knife so they are ready for the case molding.

Apply the case molding to both sides of the door jambs, nailing both at the jamb and at the drywall-covered rough opening. Generally, 4d finishing nails are used at the jamb and 6d finishing nails at the drywall. If you can do this with 6d and 8d nails, respectively, without any splitting, so much the better. Note that jamb corners are 45° miters

and that there is a reveal or backset of about ¼″ between the inner face of the jambs and the inner edge of the case molding.

Now, install the lockset, following the manufacturer's instructions. Then, mount the strike on the side jamb at the mortise provided and check the latchbolt engagement. This should be smooth, but positive. Next, reinstall the three stop trims. If they were stapled in place by the manufacturer, remove the staples and use 4d to 6d finishing nails instead. Do this with the door latched. Again, snug but not tight is the fit you want. Set the nails in the casing and the stop. Plug these holes, and paint or stain.

How to Hang a Door and Separate Jamb

There may be occasions when a prehung door just won't give you the results your design demands. In this case, purchase the door and the jamb set separately. You could easily make the jamb set, but with the prohibitive cost of white pine it really doesn't pay, except for special jambs (such as those used in combinations for front exterior doors with sidelights, or jambs that must be made wider than the standard of 4 9/16″—such as 4 13/16″ wide jambs required to accommodate ¼″ interior panelling). Note also that jambs may be purchased fingerlap-jointed or in clear full-length pine. The latter costs more but may be necessary if you're planning to stain rather than paint.

The job here consists of assembling and setting the jamb, mortising the door for hinges and mounting them, drilling for the lockset and backset latch, mortising the jambs for the hinges and strike and finally mounting the door.

To begin, assemble the jamb head and sides with 10d finishing nails. If the head jamb must be trimmed first, saw it so as to allow a distance of the actual door width plus ⅛″ between the inner jamb faces. Again, check the level of the floor and shorten one of the side jambs, if necessary. Position the jamb in the rough opening so that its edges are flush with the drywall surrounding the opening. Again, drive 10d finishing nails through the side jambs into the rough opening trimmers. Do this in the area where the stops will hide them, about 2″ in from the edge of the jamb where the face of the door will be.

Go through the shimming procedure using tapered shakes as before, but constantly monitor the distance between the jamb faces from top to bottom. Don't cut the

shakes off at this time. Instead, wait until the door is hung, in case any minor adjustments are required.

Now, set up the door on a long edge. There are commercial holders for this purpose, or you can make a homemade one in a jiffy. If the door has one beveled long edge, set up the hinges on the opposite long edge. Note that the low part of such bevel faces the stop to provide closing clearance when the jamb/door gaps are small.

For a two-hinge interior door, the top of the upper hinge should be 7″ from the top edge of the door, and the bottom of the lower hinge 11″ from the bottom edge. Strike a butt marker with a hammer at the appropriate locations to outline the hinge and mark the stop cuts. Note that butt markers match the standard hinge sizes, 3″, 3½″, and 4″ (with 3½″ being the most common).

Remove the waste within the butt marker outlines with a butt chisel and hammer to create the mortises and fit the hinges. Then, mount the hinges by positioning them in their mortises and punchmarking the screw holes. Drive the screws home.

Now take the template from the lockset package and fold it for the correct backset. The most common backset dimension is 2⅜″. Place the fold of the template on the door edge with the lockset centered at a point 38″ from the door bottom. Then punchmark both the lockset bore hole center on the door face, and the cross bore for the backset bolt latch on the door edge.

There are several ways to locate the hinges on the side jamb: (1) Place the butt marker on the jamb 7 1/16″ down from the head jamb, then measure from the top of the top hinge to the top of the bottom hinge and transfer this dimension to the jamb; (2) prop the door in place next to the jamb so that its top edge is 1/16″ down from the head jamb with the free hinge leaves folded out onto the side jamb, and then mark their positions; (3) make up a story pole or story stick with the appropriate dimensions taken from the door, and then transfer these dimensions to the jamb.

Nail the butt hinge template to the door edge. Hinges should be 7″ down from the top and 11″ up from the bottom.

Place the hinge leaves on the template and the router base on the leaves. Adjust the router plug so the bit just touches the door edge. Remove the hinges and rout out the hinges mortises.

Check the fit of butt hinge leaf in mortise. Transfer hinge position measurements to the jamb, allowing a 1/16″ gap at head. Machine the hinge mortises in jamb with the same technique.

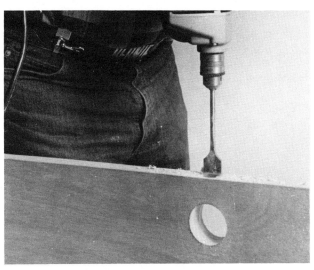

With a 1″-diameter (check lock instructions) spade bit or holesaw, drill the crossbore for the latch.

Tape cardboard template in place on door edge, centered 38″ from bottom. Use correct backset from lock instructions and door edge center according to thickness. Punchmark centers.

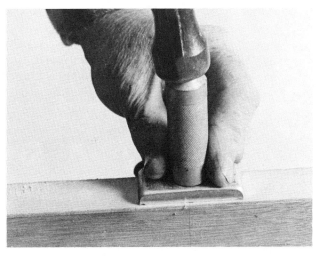

Punch the outline for the rectangular latch plate with a latch mortiser (available at lumberyards).

Set up the drill in guide with a typical 2⅛″-diameter holesaw (check lock instructions) and bore cylinder hole.

Test the latch fit. Install hinges on the door, then on the jamb. Now you're back to a prehung door.

Use the butt marker and butt chisel to make the hinge mortises in the jamb. An alternate method of making all these hinge mortises is to use a router with a surfacing bit, a guide and a template that is nailed in place on either the door or jamb edge. This method leaves a small radius in each corner that must be squared out with a chisel.

Mount the door by screwing the hinges into the hinge mortises on the jamb. Next, check the jamb/door gaps and adjust them, if necessary. Install the lockset and partially close the door to mark the strike position on the side jamb. Mark the strike mortise (to seat the bolt) location using the strike as a template; then chisel or drill it out and mount the strike.

Add the stops, then the molding. Set the nails, plug the holes and apply the finish. See Chapter 38 for a more definitive treatment of fitting and cutting.

Modular Panelling

Panelling for interior walls is available as individual planks with tongue and groove interlocking edges as well as large modular panels. Although 4′×8′ is the typical modular panel size, panels up to 10′ long are readily available. Panelling may be all wood with a prefinished veneer of the chosen species over a plywood substrate; it may also be composed entirely of man-made materials, such as hardboard; or it may be a combination of a composition substrate with a prefinished wood or plastic veneer surface.

On the average, panels range in thickness between ⅛″ and ¼″. A few panelling types are slightly thicker, but the majority fall between the two major thicknesses.

Most rooms are finished with the large 4′-wide modular panels, as opposed to the relatively narrow solid wood planking. This is due mainly to the higher initial material cost of planking and the more time-consuming installation, which further increases the cost unless handled by a Do-It-Yourselfer. But panelling of both kinds can be trimmed out with various readily available moldings.

Preparing the Walls for Modular Panels

Although many carpenters will apply panels directly to the wall studs, especially if the panels are ¼″ thick, this doesn't make for the best results. The best method for achieving a beautifully panelled wall is to install the panels over drywall. You automatically get rid of any drumming effects, as well as possible cusps and troughs due to a thin panel being installed on narrow edges separated by relatively wide, empty spans.

If you need to erect a wall before panelling, please refer to Chapter 2 if you're panelling in an attic. If you're plan-

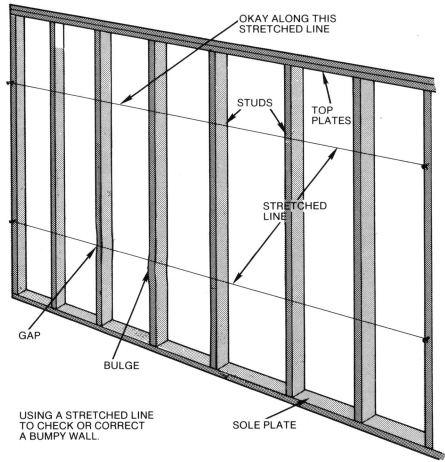

Method of furring out, shimming and checking a wall in preparation for modular paneling.

ning to install panelling in a basement, erecting a free-standing stud wall away from the foundation is really the way to go. In this situation, you should remove all causes of dampness before starting the wall. This means filling any foundation wall cracks, applying sealer as necessary, providing reasonable ventilation, and checking that the sump pump (if one is needed) is in tip-top shape.

Should you be starting in an existing structure with bare studs, check that the walls are plane and plumb before proceeding. If the room already has panelling, cut off all electrical power to the area by throwing the appropriate breaker or removing the right fuse before beginning work on the wall. Then, remove the existing panels as well as all moldings from the wall. If there is drywall under the panelling, and if the surface is flat, you're ready to begin the new panelling installation immediately. But with a stud wall, it will be necessary to install the drywall before you can being panelling.

What if the wall studs are crooked or bent, and the wall is not really flat? The best way to prepare a wall with bumps and hollows for the installation of modular panelling is to fur out the wall studs and plates into a true plane surface, using a network of furring strips and shims. First, you'll need to find and mark some reference points; then, the final positions of the furring faces can be established.

Begin at the wall end studs. Check their edges for plumbness with a level. If they are definitely plumb, they should require no modification at all, or, if anything, only a regular furring strip (or plywood or lattice furring strip)

added to the edges, from top to bottom. But if they're not plumb, the wall end studs must be modified with furring strips, and shims of varying thickness must be placed along the length of the studs between the stud edges and the furring strips. This shimming should be equally thick on both end studs.

When you know that the wall end studs are truly plumb, then tack in some nails at various heights, about 1½′ apart, along the length of the plumbed end studs; stretch cords between the nails from one end of the room to the other. If the cords stay flat, fur these intermediate studs out to the cord levels. Should there prove to be insufficient space to insert furring between the cords and the intermediate studs without bending the cords, simply fur out the wall end studs a bit, then nail and stretch the cords again until there is sufficient space. But if the cords are actually bent outward by the intermediate studs, the wall end studs must be furred out much farther to compensate. When all the vertical stud furring has been made plumb and flat, fur the plates out flush with the vertical furring.

Now, make sure that the power to the room has been turned off, then remount any thermostats, electrical receptacles or similar wall units so that they will end up flush with the surface of the new panelling.

Install the drywall using the methods described in Chapter 39 (except for the taping and jointing procedures, which may be skipped). Then, build out the jambs of all the windows and doors within the wall area to the

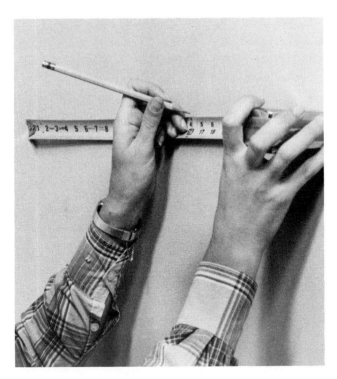

Sound out the wall by thumping lightly with fist, hammer or stud finder. Mark the stud pattern.

Use a plumb bob (shown) or level to get a true plumb line.

level of the drywall plus the thickness of the new panelling to be installed. It's the smart move to build out these jambs with the same (color) material as the molding will be; for example, pine jamb extensions with pine casing.

Estimating the Number of Panels

To figure the number of panels needed for a wall or an entire room, measure the length of the wall or the perimeter of the room to be panelled, then divide this length or perimeter by 4' (the width of a standard modular panel). Add to this number enough extra panels to handle any special enclosures, piers, columns, girder boxes and closets. Measure the height of the room if you don't already know it. If the height is 8' or less, the standard panel will do the job. If the room is between 8' and 10' high, generally 9' or 10' panels are available, although at a considerably higher cost. You might wish to butt a standard panel on top of a short cut panel and hide the joint with some form of molding. This is also the procedure for rooms taller than 10'.

Starting the Panelling

Check the position of the electrical boxes, forced air heating register boots, or forced hot water convectors. Make sure that all power to the room has been turned off at the fuse or breaker box. Then remount any switches, receptacles or similar wall units and devices and pull the wiring up to the level of the new panelling. The new panels must be measured and openings must be cut to accommodate all electrical and mechanical wall units and devices.

The two methods of installing modular panels are nailing and adhesive fastening. Nails are available in various colors, compatible with the panels. These ringed nails, designed to install panels directly to studs or over drywall, are 1" and 1⅝" long, respectively. Suggested nailing patterns include every 8" for fastening the wall edge studs, and every 12" for intermediate studs. The minimum nailing distance from the edge of any stud or substrate is ¼". As mentioned previously, studs on the average wall are spaced 16" on center (in some homes you may find them on 24" centers, but this is relatively rare). In either case, the stud locations should coincide with the panel grooves (found on the vast majority of modular panels) in which nails can be placed most unobtrusively or nearly hidden.

Those who prefer not to use nails may install panels with adhesive. The adhesive is used to bond the main portion of the panel to the wall, but some supplemental nailing is necessary along the top and bottom edges.

The bottom panel edge will also be held in by a base molding and its nails. At the top edge you will use a crown, cove or similar type molding to hide the nails.

The adhesive comes in cartridges, which will fit the standard caulking cartridge gun. In general, adhesive should be applied to the drywall along vertical lines on approximately 16" centers in a wavy or serpentine pattern. Keep back from the panel edge locations just a bit to avoid excess adhesive from being squeezed out between panels.

When a prefitted panel is positioned against a section of drywall that has already received an application of adhesive, the entire back panel surface should be pressed against the wall over the adhesive, pulled away momentarily, and then replaced finally. This flattens out the adhesive and covers more of the back surface, provides more "tooth" and speeds the adhesive setup time.

Contact between the panel and the drywall is enhanced by applying both percussive and long-term pressure against the panel. The percussive pressure is applied by moving a fairly broad piece of wood scrap (surfaced with cloth or carpet) over the panel surface vertically along the 16" centers while striking the scrap piece with a hammer. In cases where the panel may have been warped or bent due to improper storage, temporary blocks are pressed against the panel surface with braces secured to the floor.

As discussed in other sections, when dealing with wood-constructed houses and wood products, it makes sense to take into account their "live" nature—that they breathe, expand and contract. There are several procedures that will minimize or prevent problems caused by the natural process of expansion and contraction.

A simple method is to equalize the ambient conditions of both the panels and the room. This is done by bringing the panels into the room and stacking them flat with wood spacers between each panel for at least two days before starting the installation.

Another method is to select a stain that matches the color of the panels. When you have determined where the panel edges will meet all around the room (every 4'), stain

Saw the first panel to match the stud pattern, slightly oversized to fit to the corner.

You can also do this cutting with a portable circular saw on the reverse side.

If attaching the panels with adhesive, apply it near the perimeter, but back from the edge to prevent squeezeout. Then use a serpentine line of adhesive on the intermediate areas. Nails are required at the top and bottom.

Position the first panel nearest wall so that the edge away from the corner is plumb and centered on a stud. Then, scribe the panel to the corner with a compass. Block the plane scribe to fit the corner.

Panel openings at switches, outlets or vents should be marked and the corners drilled for starter holes. This can be done with power tools as well.

Spray the wall where the panel joints will occur with approximately the same color or tone as the panels. This will hide minor discrepancies.

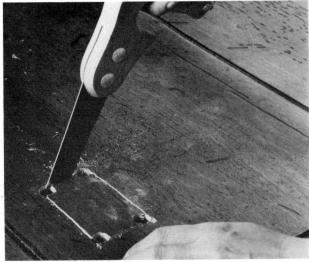

Cut between holes with keyhole or jigsaw. If using a jigsaw, cut hole on reverse side.

the drywall from top to bottom at these points. Then, if the panels shrink at all, there will be no telltale white lines. A slight gap due to normal shrinkage won't even be noticed.

So much for shrinking, but what about expansion due to high humidity? Easy—just leave a very slight joint space between each panel, about a couple of matchbook cover thicknesses (about 1/32"). Use matching stain on the drywall to hide these very slight expansion joints.

Before starting the actual panel installation, figure out the placement of your panels. Generally, it's best to start in a corner. Trim the length of the panel at the bottom, if trimming is necessary. Then, set the panel's outer edge plumb with a level, with the inner edge touching the corner. If the fit is good, install the panel. If not, scribe the adjacent wall profile on the mating panel corner edge.

You can do this with either a set of compasses or with a small pencil or nail holder. In either case, move the marking tool down the adjacent wall at the corner, using its surface as a fence or guide, while the business end of the tool scores or marks the mating edge of the first panel.

Then block plane, file or sand the scribed edge until a match is obtained with the wall. Mount the panel in one of the two ways described above. If you're thinking that the edge you just scribed will be hidden anyway, you're right. But it's better to have the results of your practice run hidden—just in case. The next scribing you do will be the real thing, but you have a little experience under your belt, and the scribing should be a snap.

The tool used for cutting the panel determines whether to saw on the face or the reverse side. If using a table saw with the teeth facing downward (toward the reverse face), saw with the face side up. If using a portable circular saw or most jigsaws with the teeth facing up, cut with the face side down. The exception to this is when you're using a superfine blade. Be sure to test it to be certain it won't cause the face to splinter on a piece of scrap. You might also want to cover the base plate of your jigsaw with some slick-backed tape such as vinyl electrical. This will prevent the plate from accidentally marring the panel face.

As you proceed to install subsequent panels, you will come across switch boxes, receptacle boxes, registers and other wall-mounted mechanical and electrical devices. The power in the room should be turned off at the electrical panel just as before when you moved these boxes out.

The panels will have to be fitted to or around these parts as well as window and doorjambs. You can measure with either a flexible tape or folding rule and mark accurate outlines with the aid of a square.

When sawing out rectangular cutouts, it's good technique to first drill holes at or near the corners. These holes should be large enough to allow the jigsaw blade to fit. Then the corners can be cut cleanly.

It might be necessary to frame around girders, posts, columns, stairways, windows or other special areas. But once a framework is up, the procedures are similar to those mentioned previously.

You'll need molding in these special areas as well as in the main part of the room, but be sure to install the molding in the correct sequence. The door casing should be applied first. Then the base or base and shoe, unless you plan on hiding the flooring under the base molding. If that's the case, install the flooring first, followed by the case molding around the doors, then the base or base and shoe. If a cove or crown is used at the wall/ceiling joint, add this next.

Finally, add the vertical inside and outside corners, the window case, chair rail, cap and all other moldings. Saw or cut the molding as shown in the molding detail section. Touch up of any goofs, scars, gouges and scratches may be handled using colored wax crayons, felt-tip markers, touch-up paint or small cans of spray paint. The crayons are available in all lumberyards, and the other repair media can be obtained either from a cabinet shop or their suppliers.

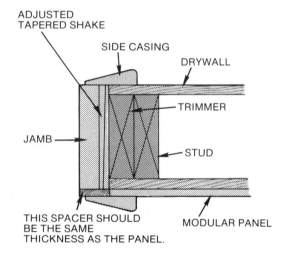

Modular panel steps: Cross section of door (or window without the shims) showing jamb, spacer molding and panel.

The completed job makes the room look like new.

Panelling with Planks

In the sauna chapter, you saw the horizontally applied redwood tongue and groove V-joint planking. Individual planks can also be installed vertically or diagonally. The vertical studs may be used as nailers for a diagonal application, but for a vertical planking application a network of horizontal furring nailers must be installed.

Tongue and groove planking is also available with V-groove or square groove in a variety of hardwood species including ash, red oak, white oak, cherry, cottonwood, pecan, walnut and pecky cypress. Planking comes in two thicknesses, ½″ and ¾″, with random widths and lengths. No piece of planking is smaller than 1′, and it is packed in modules 8′ long with no more than four pieces per 8′ length. Both edges and ends are tongued and grooved. Except for certain purposely roughsawn types, all planks are sanded and prefinished.

Estimating Plank Panelling

To figure the amount of material required, find the wall area by multiplying the room perimeter by the room height. Multiply this figure by 1.18 to account for tongue and groove loss and waste. Bundles are available in 30 and 60 board feet. (A board foot is 12″×1′×1″).

Wall Preparation for Plank Panelling

There are two area situations you might encounter in preparing a wall for plank panelling: (1) installations on exterior walls that require a polyethylene vapor barrier between the back of the plank and the wall; and (2) installations on interior walls that do not require the vapor barrier.

If you're going to install this planking on new construction such as on an addition stud wall, the manufacturer suggests that you prepare the nailers for a vertical installation by interposing 2×4 fire blocking between the studs. This blocking, spaced between 18″ to 24″ apart, will provide the necessary horizontal nailing surface for the planks. An alternate method of providing nailers is to install furring strips over the new stud wall as in the existing wall shown below. Of course the spacing is the same, and provisions for padding the openings around doors and windows must be treated accordingly.

On existing walls, nail a horizontal array of furring strips to the studs, again with 18″ to 24″ spacing. Whether you're installing planking on new construction or on existing walls, in both cases you're probably going to have windows and/or doors in the room. To build the entire wall out to one level, first pad around the perimeters of the openings, keeping the pads flush with the inner faces of their jambs. Using wood of the same thickness as the furring will put all of the wall on one level.

Now you must account for the thickness of the planking to be added. So, add spacers of the same thickness as the planks around the window and door openings, flush with the jambs. If you want to case the doors and windows with the same material as the planking, you have two options. One is to rip and joint smooth some planking stock and use this for casing. The other is to buy some wood of the same species, rip that, joint it smooth, install it as casing and finish it.

This method allows you to butt planking against the spacer without accurate fitting and scribing because the casing will conceal the joint. For you more experienced woodworkers who wish to keep the door jamb thickness to a minimum, add the casing right over the pads, skipping the spacer, and fit to the casing edge. Make sure to use casing that is thicker than the planking. In this way, the casing will protrude past the face of the planking and can be routed or shaped to suit your taste.

The completed plank paneling shows both the beauty of natural wood as well as the depth provided by the deep joints.

Another shot of the sauna, emphasizing the esthetic impact of the wood, a welcome addition to its practical features.

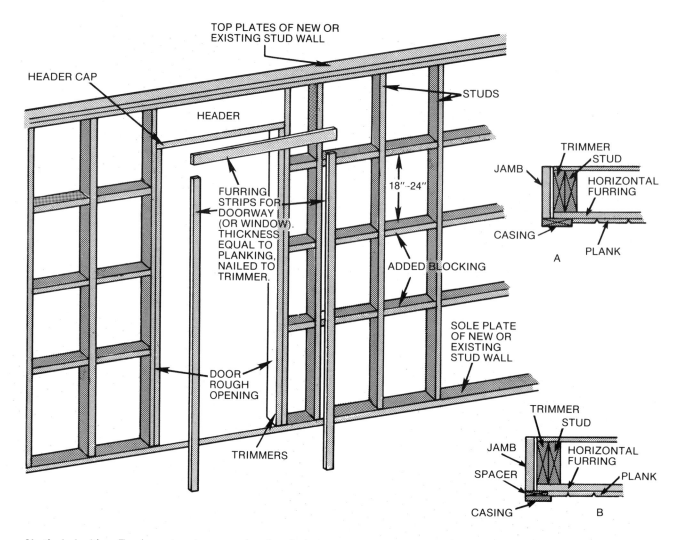

Vertical planking: Furring out and open stud wall and window or door treatments.

Where fire blocking is used as the nailing surface, the easy way to account for the thickness is to pad the opening with plank thickness stock, install the planking and add the casing, which will hide the joints. The alternate way is to case the openings first with stock that is thicker than the planking and fit to its edges.

Starting the Plank Panelling

Planks can be nailed or glued, but if you glue, face nails, which can be hidden by molding, are required at both the top and bottom. Blind nailing is used in the planking field here as it was on the hardwood strip floor and the sauna redwood wall. Fourpenny nails are driven into the internal corners of the tongues at a 45° angle, set and hidden by the grooves of the adjacent planks. However, it is not a bad move to keep a drill handy and predrill the nail holes to eliminate any possibility of splitting.

To control expansion, several approaches are recommended. First, use the vapor barrier on exterior walls. Second, the house should be totally enclosed, with all drywall, plaster and masonry completely dry. Third, do not open the bundles of planking until ready for use and, especially, do not expose them to wet weather. Fourth, use the inside corner joints shown. Fifth, allow about ⅛″ total gap (a slightly loose fit) for every 9 lineal feet of applied planks. Sixth, work with a dehumidifier turned on where a lot of masonry has been used in the house.

As to actual installation, on 8′ ceiling rooms, use one carton of planks at a time; with higher ceilings, use the planks from three cartons. The planks are of random width. Use them in this manner for the most pleasing effect. Don't put two planks of the same width side by side, and don't allow the end joints on adjacent planks to line up. Randomize these joints as well. It doesn't matter if the end joints are not supported by a nailer. The tongues and grooves of the adjacent planks lock them in firmly.

As stated, inside corners are expansion joints. Outside corners can be mitered and molded or fitted with a corner strip, which is flush with the surfaces of both adjacent walls as shown. You'll have to cut the power at the electrical panel because the electrical boxes should be moved up to the new wall level. This goes for forced air registers and thermostats, too.

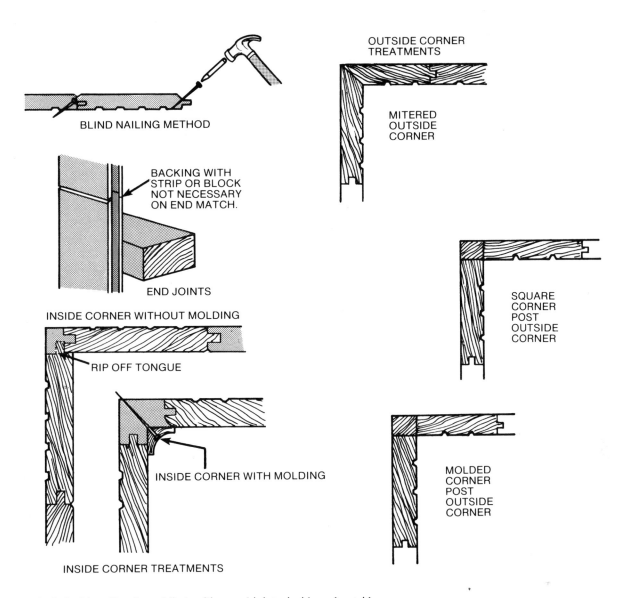

BLIND NAILING METHOD

BACKING WITH STRIP OR BLOCK NOT NECESSARY ON END MATCH.

END JOINTS

INSIDE CORNER WITHOUT MOLDING

RIP OFF TONGUE

INSIDE CORNER WITH MOLDING

INSIDE CORNER TREATMENTS

OUTSIDE CORNER TREATMENTS

MITERED OUTSIDE CORNER

SQUARE CORNER POST OUTSIDE CORNER

MOLDED CORNER POST OUTSIDE CORNER

Vertical planking: Details on blind nailing, end joints, inside and outside corner.

Moldings

Moldings, which come in a variety of shapes and several sizes in many of these shapes, are used to carry out the following interior trim functions: (1) To close gaps and hide joints that normally occur in construction, such as casing does between the jambs of windows or door and the rough openings surrounding them; (2) to hide joints that occur at wall/floor intersections, such as base molding; (3) to perform a mechanical job, such as door and window stop or window parting strip; (4) to act as a standard decorative strip, as cove or crown; (5) to achieve an architectural effect as part of a customized molding or group of moldings.

All lumberyards stock standard pine molding milled to a listed number of standard shapes, which represents most of the molding sold. Hardwood moldings are available at a higher cost as are architectural hardwood moldings for even more. In addition, many window manufac-

turers supply their own molding to go with casement, bow and bay windows. Plastic moldings are also manufactured but do not come in the variety of shapes and sizes of wood products.

Window and door casing and base are the most common molding shapes found in the home. These are readily available in two standard profiles, clam and colonial. There are window and door stops, window stool, cap, cove, crown, bed, astragals, mullions, balusters, bar rails, bar, band, back band, chair rail, outside corners, inside corners, shoe, rounds, half rounds, parting strip, quarter rounds, skewback, lattice, shelf edge, screen molding, picture molding (chamfer strip), picture frame, pilasters, hand rail, glass beads, base caps, panel molding, wainscot, battens, squares and S4S stock. This long list still is incomplete. It doesn't list the style variations or sizes within each category. However, you see that choice should not be a problem.

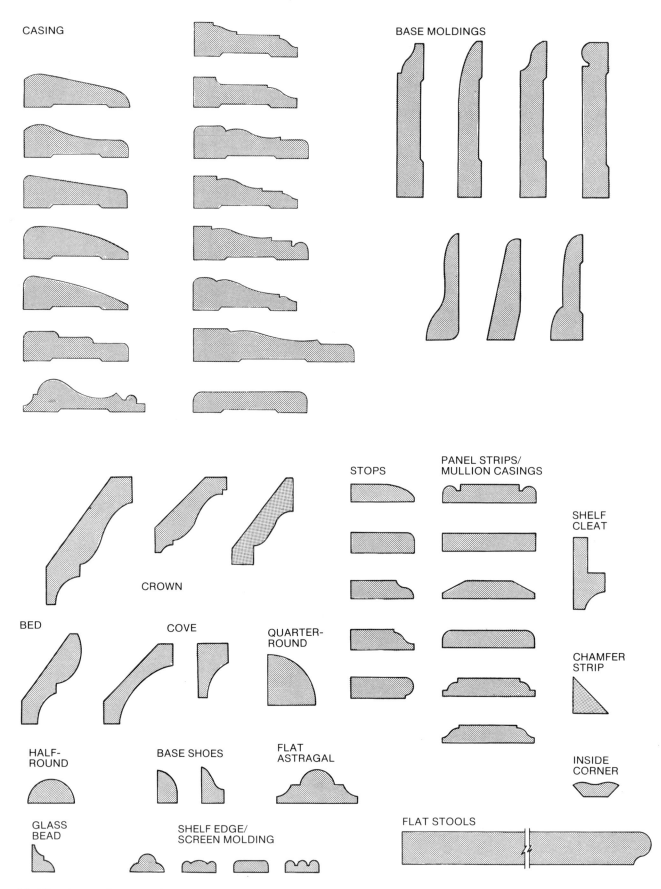

CASING

BASE MOLDINGS

STOPS

PANEL STRIPS/
MULLION CASINGS

SHELF
CLEAT

CROWN

BED

COVE

QUARTER-
ROUND

CHAMFER
STRIP

HALF-
ROUND

BASE SHOES

FLAT
ASTRAGAL

INSIDE
CORNER

GLASS
BEAD

SHELF EDGE/
SCREEN MOLDING

FLAT STOOLS

Molding shapes. (Courtesy of Wood Moulding and Millwork Producers. For further information, please contact Wood Moulding and Millwork Producers, 1730 S.W. Skyline, P.O. Box 25278, Portland, Ore. 97225.)

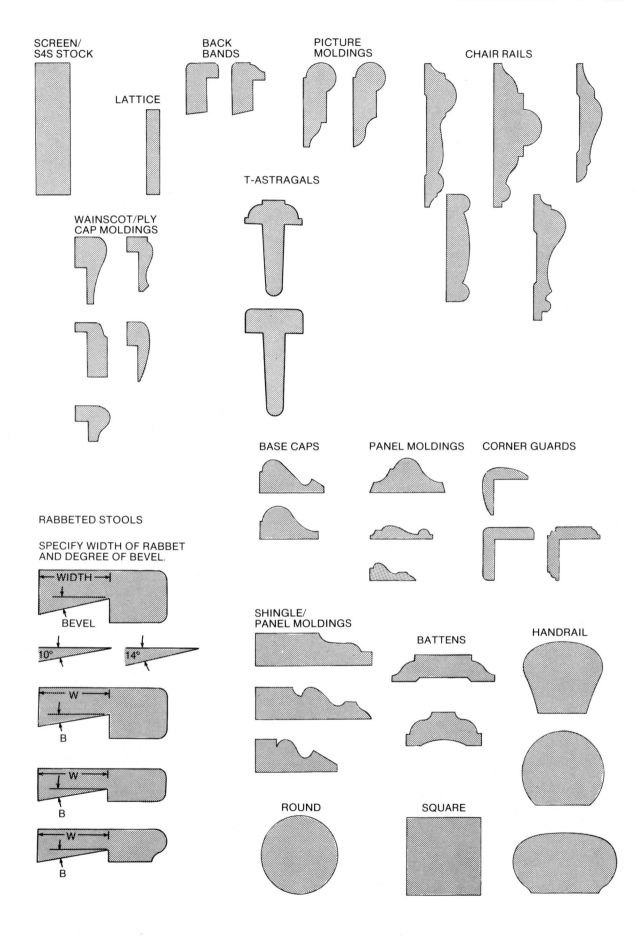

SCREEN/
S4S STOCK

LATTICE

BACK
BANDS

PICTURE
MOLDINGS

CHAIR RAILS

WAINSCOT/PLY
CAP MOLDINGS

T-ASTRAGALS

BASE CAPS

PANEL MOLDINGS

CORNER GUARDS

RABBETED STOOLS

SPECIFY WIDTH OF RABBET
AND DEGREE OF BEVEL.

WIDTH

BEVEL

10°

14°

W

B

W

B

W

B

SHINGLE/
PANEL MOLDINGS

BATTENS

HANDRAIL

ROUND

SQUARE

Using Moldings

To use standard moldings, you'll have to be able to miter, bevel, cope, stain, seal and varnish or paint, nail, set nails and plug and, most important of all, measure correctly. Outside of painting and staining, the basic tools required for working with moldings are a hand or power miter box, coping saw, hammer, nailset and flexible and/or folding rule.

The order of installation is important because many moldings down the line, so to speak, are fitted to those already in place. For example, the base is fitted to the side door casing. Also, if painting or wall covering is your next project, have the casing, base, cove and any other moldings completely finished and dry before beginning to treat the walls.

Door and Window Casings

All hinged interior passage doors are cased on both sides of the jamb with one head and two side casings on each side. They are joined at the corners with 45° miters and nailed both to the jamb and to the wall over the rough opening. Typically, a 3/16″ to 1/4″ reveal or setback from the jamb face is used. Therefore, if you are using a 1/4″ reveal,

A window with a stool molding should be notched to fit and installed before the casing. Side casings can be cut at 90°, abutted to stool surface and marked for mitering at top corners.

Next, the head casing is measured, mitered and installed.

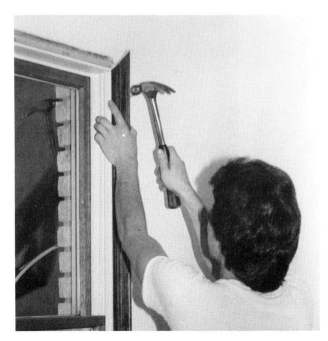

The mitered side casings are then nailed into the rough opening on its outer border and to the jamb on its inner border.

Finally, the apron, the piece of casing trimmed at the ends, is nailed in place under the stool's molding.

measure the distance between the jamb faces, add ½″ to this and you'll have the length of head case on the short side of the miters. Once the head case is nailed up, measure the distance to the floor for the side casings. The head case requires a 45° miter on either end, while the side casings (one left and one right) have a 90° cut on one end and a 45° miter on the other.

Windows can be treated in many ways; a common way is to case a window on all four edges. To do this, measure horizontally between the side jambs, add ½″ and you'll have the head casing short side miter measurement. If the window is made accurately, you should also have the lower casing dimension, but check it to be sure. Install these two casings while holding an accurate reveal. Then, measure vertically to get the side case dimensions. When working windows and doors, check the (assumed) 90° corners with a square, just to be sure.

Another common window treatment is to use a stool at the bottom, over the sill, with two sides and one head casing. In this case, the stool must be notched on the inner edges of its ends to fit within the side jambs of the window, then nailed in place. The bottom 90° cuts of the side cases butt against the top face of the stool, and the meeting at the top with the head casing is standard.

The miters and butt cuts are all done in a straightforward manner on the miter box. After nailing in the molding pieces with 4d to 6d nails or, if you can do it without splitting, 6d to 8d finishing nails, set these nails and plug the holes. Do this with putty alone, if you're going to paint, or with putty, tinted with stain, if you're going to stain. An even better way of handling this situation is to prepaint or prestain, shellac and varnish (sanding between the shellac and the varnish) before installation. In this way, you need only set the nails, plug and touch up to complete the job.

Base Molding

With the door casings in place, you can go on to the standard base. For the best appearance and easiest instal-

When you can't make the full length of the room with one piece of molding, make a scarf joint for the neatest appearance.

lation, fit all walls less than 16′ with one continuous piece of base. If the long walls exceed 16′, use a scarf (bevelled) joint where the pieces meet and try to get the joint in the least obvious place. Never use butt joints to join two pieces of base (crown, cove, cap). Note that scarf joints, bevels, miters and butt cuts can be done on the miter box.

Using the Miter Box

All adjustable angle miter boxes have a base, rear fence and movable protractor table, which can be easily rotated to cut the desired angle. Most have detents at 90° as well as 45° on either side. They all can be locked at these detents or at any angle in between.

Manually operated miter boxes have a pair of standards with bearings and uplocks to allow the long backsaw to slide through easily and to lock it in the UP position while adjusting the workpiece. They also have a set of downstops to limit the vertical position of the saw at the completion of a cut. Most are equipped with some form of locking clamp which holds down the workpiece.

Power miter boxes, also known as chop saws, have the motor and blade mounted in a single pivot arm that allows the blade to come down in an arc to and through the workpiece. Most saws of this type have various safety features such as guards, mechanical brakes and trigger interlocks.

To cut a miter on either power- or hand-operated miter boxes, place the molding flat on the table, resting against the fence at the rear. Adjust the table to the angle you want and lock it. Then hold the molding with one hand in a safe position on the table away from the blade path and cut the molding. You may hold the molding with the clamp on saws so equipped.

To cut a bevel, rest the bottom or edge of the molding on the table with the back of the molding against the fence at the rear. Hold it or lock it as before in a safe manner and saw through the piece. Note that a scarf joint is merely two mating bevels (a left hand and a right hand).

When using a motorized miter box, keep the thumb of the hand that is operating the arm and trigger on the trigger interlock on saws so equipped. Do this until the cut is complete, then remove the thumb from this interlock to press the brake with that thumb. On saws without an interlock, release the trigger at the completion of the cut and press the brake button to stop the saw. A somewhat different technique is used on crowns and coves; we'll look at that shortly.

To fit the base, you should be able to complete two of the four walls with one piece of base butt-fitted to the adjacent walls. Then, to do an inside corner, the adjacent base will be coped to match the profiles of the molding already installed. It's easiest to fit the coped end of the molding first and fit the butt cut last; as, for example, when the butt cut meets a piece of side jamb casing. In certain situations, you'll have to cope both ends to meet the base on the adjacent walls.

The power miter box or "chop saw" is designed for trim work. Here, a piece of molding is set up to cut a bevel or a scarf joint. Note the protractor table angle.

In this manner, the saw will make a straight 90° or butt cut, such as when fitting a complete piece of molding between walls.

With the molding flat on the table and the protractor set at 45°, you can make a mitered cut. With the protractor table at 90°, you'd get a butt cut.

Coping

Coping is a two-step operation that requires a miter box and coping saw. First, the molding to be coped must be bevelled at a 45° angle on the miter box to expose the profile. This is done so that the long edge of the bevel, in the back, is toward the adjacent base molding to which you are fitting. If it's hard to see the profile edge, darken it with a pencil. Then, the profile is cut with the coping saw, with the teeth facing toward the back of the molding to eliminate splintering. When coping complex moldings, don't saw at exactly 90° to the molding. Instead, angle the saw slightly to provide just a bit of undercut to get a neater fit. Although the teeth must always face the back of the molding, there are two ways to orient the coping saw. The purist holds the handle down and pulls the blade along, eliminating most of the chatter and ending up with the cleanest cut. Most amateurs and many pros push the blade by holding the saw handle above the work because it seems easier to position themselves. Try it both ways and gauge the results on a piece of scrap.

Outside Corners and Finishing

The outside corner is a much simpler and quicker operation. The two pieces of base molding are bevelled at 45° on the miter box, with the longest parts of the bevels at the face of the moldings. It's a good idea to glue these pieces at the joint and touch up with stain or paint as needed.

Working with Crowns and Coves

The trickiest moldings to fit are crowns at the intersections of ceiling and walls. They are up out of the way and difficult to reach, measure and install; plus they are sawn upside down on the miter box, so you have to think a little bit differently when cutting it.

To cope a piece of flat molding (for example, base at an inside corner) with another piece of the same profile, put a 45° bevel on the piece to expose the profile. Then, cut it or, better, undercut it slightly with a coping saw along the line formed by the face of the molding and the bevel.

With small crowns, less than 4″, the average power miter box will do the job. But if you're dealing with large crowns, you'll have to saw these on a hand miter box.

Modification of the Miter Box for Coves and Crowns

To handle these crowns and coves with the hand or power miter boxes, a small addition must be made to the older type units, which the newer models have already built in. This is a pair of auxiliary fences, fitted to the table, one on either side of the blade. They keep the moldings from "falling down." Note that a crown or similar molding is sitting on both the table and the fence at a 45° angle and it must remain that way for sawing. Hence, the edge sitting on the table, which eventually will rest on the ceiling, rests against these auxiliary fences. (Remember that this molding is sawn upside down.) These auxiliary fences may be either screwed or clamped in place in a position that will ensure the molding is at an actual 45° angle. If you're going to work with only one size molding, the fences may have a permanent mount, such as a pair of screws each, tapped into the table, but if you plan on using several sizes, you might be better off simply marking the table and clamping the fences into position for each use.

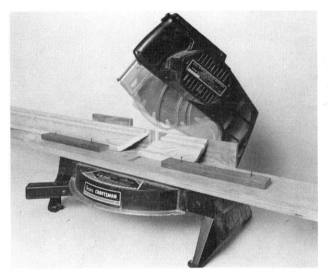

The power miter box setup for crown molding requires a pair of additional fences on the table on either side of the blade to keep the molding piece stable. This is because the crown molding rests partly on the fence and partly on the table. Also, remember that the part on the table is actually the top, when installed.

With the molding to the left of the blade, and blade path in left miter position, you are preparing a left-end miter; with the molding to the right of the blade and blade path in right miter position (shown), you are preparing a right-end miter.

Once the measurement from wall to wall is obtained, a crown molding should be installed flush (with butt cuts) at wall/ceiling junctions on opposite ends of the room. Here, a trim carpenter is performing a butt cut on the crown.

The trim carpenter is checking the fit of the mitered and coped end of a crown molding with the butt-cut piece already installed on the adjacent wall/ceiling joint.

Measuring for Crowns and Coves

Measuring from wall to wall at the ceiling can be awkward because there are limits to how far you can "stand out" a flexible rule. Therefore, do it the easy way: Measure the distance using two thinner, lighter moldings, each a bit longer than half the wall dimension. Get up on your ladder near the middle of the wall carrying the two "sticks," one of which has already been measured on the floor. Slide both sticks to meet the adjacent walls and mark the second stick where the inside end of the measured stick stops. Get down off the ladder and add up the measurements of the sticks. If you have a wall whose dimension is greater than 16', the crowns will have to be scarfed or mitered with mating cuts. Get the first crown up on the wall/ceiling intersection and measure from there to the adjacent wall. Try to cover the spans of two walls with one piece of crown butt-fitted to the adjacent walls. Then, cope both ends of the last two crowns to meet those already in place.

These same methods of measurement, mitering, bevelling, scarfing, butt cutting, installation and the use of the miter box and coping saw can be used in handling most standard moldings.

Custom and Combination Moldings

You can do much more with molding than just the standard applications. In fact, you can create and develop architectural and cabinet level effects. For example, instead of a standard or Norman chair rail, you can use a combination of moldings to build one up, assuming it will fit in with the remaining size, shape and decor. One way to do this is to use two solid crowns separated by a spacer and capped off with an astragal. This combination can continue up a stairway as a false rail on the outer wall in a colonial style home.

Another attractive molding application that can decorate either an interior wall, a cabinet door or an entryway is an array of panels formed with rectangular surface frames. These can be made from shapes such as panel molding, base cap, picture moldings or lattice. This technique can be used on drywall and plywood as well as other surfaces.

If you take a quick glance at the dining room makeover chapter, you'll see that the sliding doors have "raised panels" bordered by "shaped" rails and stiles. The raised part of the panel is actually a slab of ¼" plywood, and the shaped edges are quarter-round molding tacked to S4S (surfaced four sides) rails and stiles that have been dadoed to nest the main ½" plywood panel.

This idea can be expanded to a complete wall or all walls of a room to give the effect of the Wren Chapel at the College of William and Mary in Williamsburg, Virginia. The basic wall is vertical stud-mounted modular 4'×8' pine or hardwood-faced plywood ½" to ¾" thick. A gridwork of rails and stiles, arranged to cover all vertical

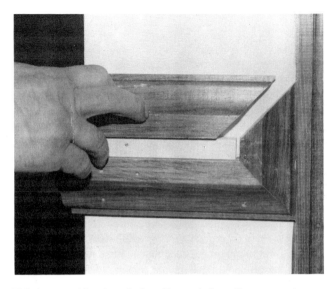

This is a combination chair rail, consisting of an upper, lower and end solid crown, with an S4S spacer between.

The molding finally surrounds the newel post base.

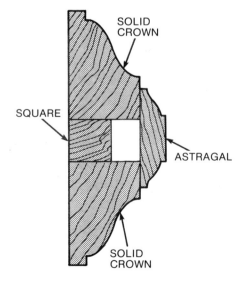

SOLID CROWN

SQUARE

ASTRAGAL

SOLID CROWN

Cross section of combination chair rail.

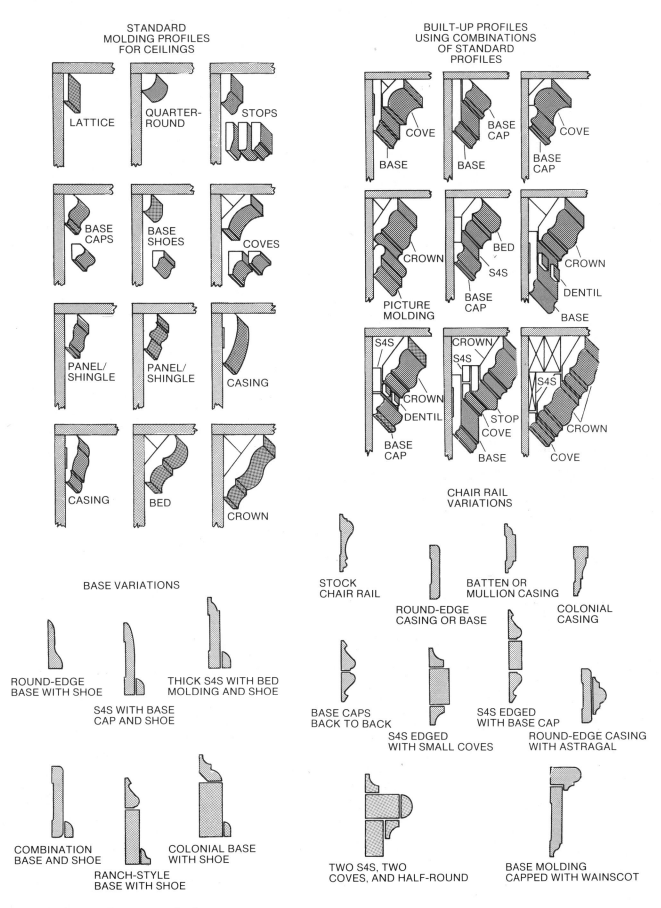

STANDARD
MOLDING PROFILES
FOR CEILINGS

LATTICE

QUARTER-ROUND

STOPS

BASE CAPS

BASE SHOES

COVES

PANEL/SHINGLE

PANEL/SHINGLE

CASING

CASING

BED

CROWN

BUILT-UP PROFILES
USING COMBINATIONS
OF STANDARD
PROFILES

COVE
BASE

BASE CAP
BASE

COVE
BASE CAP

CROWN
PICTURE MOLDING

BED
S4S
BASE CAP

CROWN
DENTIL
BASE

S4S
CROWN
DENTIL
BASE CAP

CROWN
S4S
STOP
COVE
BASE

S4S
CROWN
COVE

CHAIR RAIL VARIATIONS

STOCK CHAIR RAIL

BATTEN OR MULLION CASING

ROUND-EDGE CASING OR BASE

COLONIAL CASING

BASE CAPS BACK TO BACK

S4S EDGED WITH SMALL COVES

S4S EDGED WITH BASE CAP

ROUND-EDGE CASING WITH ASTRAGAL

BASE VARIATIONS

ROUND-EDGE BASE WITH SHOE

S4S WITH BASE CAP AND SHOE

THICK S4S WITH BED MOLDING AND SHOE

COMBINATION BASE AND SHOE

RANCH-STYLE BASE WITH SHOE

COLONIAL BASE WITH SHOE

TWO S4S, TWO COVES, AND HALF-ROUND

BASE MOLDING CAPPED WITH WAINSCOT

Combination moldings and applications.

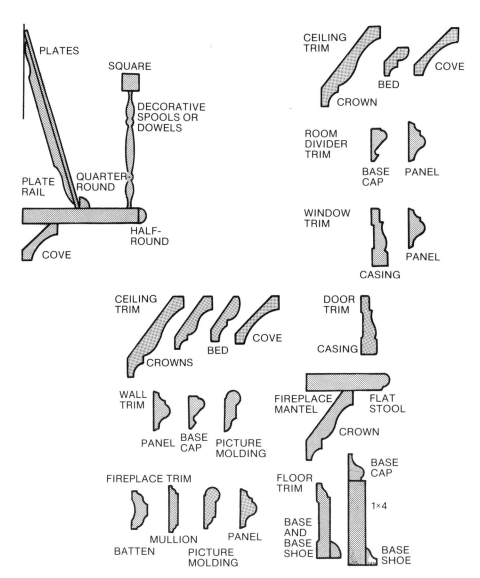

Combination moldings and applications.

joints, is nailed to the wall. Then, quarter-round, glass bead, base cap, panel molding or similar small molding is mitered at the corners and fit to the edges of the rails and stiles to give the shaped effect. This may be painted or stained after setting nails and plugging nail holes.

On a more modest level, you don't have to settle for plain clam or more decorative colonial base. Base can be built up by combining S4S board with base caps and shoes or quarter-rounds. Complex and attractive ceiling

moldings can be greatly varied by different recombinations of coves and crowns, beds, bases, S4S and base cap. This is an area where you are limited only by your imagination. It's a sure way to get some pizazz into your home decor at a reasonable cost. The place to start is with a set of standard molding profile drawings. Make reproductions of these shapes and do a bit of cutting and pasting on the drawing board until you get a combination that you find appealing.

41

Flooring

There are many methods of installing house floors. For example, parquet floor is mentioned in the dining room makeover chapter, adhesive-bond strip is shown in the plank floor chapter and ceramic tile is shown in the front hall tile floor chapter plus in both the sauna and whirlpool bath chapters.

This chapter will cover other floor treatments including hardwood strip, vinyl squares, vinyl sheet and wall-to-wall carpet.

Hardwood Strip Floors

By far the most mysterious floor installation to the do-it-yourselfer is the hardwood strip floor, even though it is probably the most ubiquitous of all flooring (with the possible exception of carpeting). Although installing hardwood strip floor is physically arduous, it's not technically difficult.

You'll need a portable saw, flat bar, utility knife, a special, heavy rubber-nosed mallet and two flooring guns—a top nailer, which drives in fasteners straight through the face of the strips, and a blind nailer, which drives in fasteners at a 45° angle. You need a top nailer when you're close to the walls parallel to the strips, and you need the second gun to handle the blind nailing in the field of the floor.

The blind nailer gets the lion's share of the work. It's used to drive the fasteners through the internal corner of the tongue of the strip floor piece. Both the nailing and the tongue itself are hidden by the groove of the subsequent piece.

All edges and ends of every manufactured piece of standard strip flooring have either a tongue or groove. Hence, all edges and ends mate with an adjacent strip. The only exception to this is at the end wall where pieces are sawn off to fit in the remaining space. Strip floor is typically ¾″ thick, 2¼″ wide (not including the tongue [dressed from 1×3]), and comes in strapped bundles that contain 3 board feet per lineal foot of bundle. The bundles are made up of assorted lengths of wood strips. Various species are used for strip flooring, such as beech, birch, walnut and, the most popular, oak.

If a plywood subfloor at least ½″ thick is solidly in place over the joists, the first step is to staple down No. 15 saturated felt with the lengths slightly overlapping and running perpendicular to the joist runs. In a room where the drywall is already up, such as when remodeling, first remove all base, case and shoe molding. The doorjamb must also be removed temporarily, or undercut, if possible, to slip the wood strip beneath it. Joist locations should be marked on with chalk (on new construction use the exposed edge of a drywall scrap) so that the nailing will be into the joists as much as possible. (Joist locations can easily be spotted from the plywood joints and nail runs.)

Next, the strips are loose-laid on the paper or felt, starting ⅜″ from the wall, with the edge tongues facing away from the wall, running perpendicular to the joist run. Since the pieces come in various lengths, it's easy to stagger the end joints in an echelon, or stepped, pattern. Naturally, there will be a remainder at the end of each row that will require fitting. To do this, take the piece to be fitted and invert it end-for-end and hold it ⅜″ from the wall where it will stop. See where the opposite end is relative to the end of the adjacent piece and mark the piece for sawing. Trim off the waste with a portable saw, invert the piece end-for-end again and it's ready for nailing.

Lay out about 6 to 8 rows before starting to nail. Then, load the top nailer and fasten the first strips against the wall. The strips should be parallel to the wall, with the end tongues and grooves tightly matched and a gap of ⅜″ at each end of the row. Nail into the joists through the strip face and plywood deck.

After a couple of rows are fastened, use the blind nailer to continue nailing. Because of its weight and the friction of its rubber nose, the hammer can be used to maneuver the pieces into their exact nailing positions by drawing them together for tight end and edge tongue-and-groove matches.

When the opposite wall is close, you'll have to switch back to the top nailer. Also, because of the close quarters, you won't be able to tighten up the edge tongues and grooves with the hammer, so it will require a pry bar between the sole plate and the last pieces.

After the floor has been installed completely, it can be sanded or stained, if desired, shellacked and varnished. Then the jambs and moldings can be replaced. In new construction such as an addition, the completion of the plumbing and the electrical and exterior wall insulation would be followed by applying drywall, hanging the doors, painting, sanding the floor, shellacking, varnishing and adding the molding.

Once past the beginning strips, the blind nailer can be used. The rubber poll of the hammer is used to herd the pieces to their approximate locations and to pretighten both edge and end joints. The gun will tighten the edge joints as it strikes, but it can't bring the end joints together.

Rows of 15-pound saturated felt are rolled out on the wood (or plywood) subfloor, overlapped, marked with chalk for joist location and stapled. This limits moisture, dust and squeaks in dry weather. Over this the strips should be loosely arrayed in a stepped pattern to random the end joints.

As you move out from the starting wall, you must also add on the ends of the strips already fastened down in the first stepped array or echelon. If a particular strip requires more than one additional piece to reach the end wall, no cutting will be required on the second piece.

The strip grooves face the starting wall so the tongue will be on the leading edge for the nailing gun. Because of tight quarters the beginning strips at the starting wall must be face nailed, using a flat-platen gun, which drives in the fasteners perpendicular to the floor surface.

Now, use a pry bar to wedge between the last strip and the sole or bottom plate of the wall. This will compress the edge joints of the non-nailed strips. Place the gun in position, hold the pressure on the bar with your foot or leg and start the face nailing. Work across the room from one side to another.

You can rent the power nailers as well as the mallet from a local tool rental.

Self-Adhering Vinyl Tiles

This is the simplest of all vinyl floor installations. The 12″×12″ tiles are packed 45 to a box and have contact adhesive already in place on the backs, protected by removable paper. There are 9″×9″ vinyl tiles available, but to install them you have to spread adhesive on the subfloor or underlayment. (Subfloor means the structural floor; underlayment can be plywood on top of the subfloor or a mastic underlayment, which is a leveling technique to flatten cracks and discrepancies.)

Self-adhering tile flooring can be applied directly on top of plywood, concrete, particleboard, linoleum or existing resilient tile floors as long as they're clean of wax, dirt, oil or other materials that would impair adhesion. No matter what type of surface you have, it should be free of protruding nailheads or moving subfloor joints.

To install the tiles, vacuum the floor, then snap chalk lines at right angles, preferably laid out so that the floor will be balanced at the main edges. This means that the width of the tiles along opposite edges should be equal for a symmetrical appearance.

From here, it's simply a matter of removing the protective papers from the tiles, one at a time, positioning the tile and pressing down to lock the adhesive. Always start at the intersection of the lines and make sure that each tile butts cleanly against its neighbors.

When you have completed the field, use either a shears or utility knife to cut the tiles at the perimeter to fit. Make sure that you fit the tiles close enough to the edge so that the molding will hide them after it's installed.

Applying Vinyl Tiles with Adhesive

Be sure that your subfloor is compatible with the tile you have chosen. Remove all base or shoe molding from the room you are going to tile. Then measure the length and width of the room and snap a pair of perpendicular chalk lines on the floor, intersecting at the midpoint of both the length and width. Check the instructions on the adhesive can because most of these products require a short set-up time. Apply the adhesive using a notched trowel designed for the job. This is usually a trowel with notches that are 1/16″ wide and 1/32″ deep with a 5/64″ space separating them. (Some adhesive can be brushed on the subfloor.) Spread the adhesive up to the chalk lines and set the tiles along them, gradually building out a stepped triangle pattern. Complete the entire field in the four quarters divided by the chalk lines, then work the edges. The edges will probably require cutting, and most tiles respond better when the reverse surface is heated slightly. Then they can be cut with a linoleum or utility knife. Finish up by replacing the molding. If any adhesive gets on the tile surface, check the can for the proper solvent to remove it.

Vinyl Sheet Goods

Two features make it easy for the do-it-yourselfer to work with vinyl floor covering: it's quite flexible, even foldable in many cases; and it comes in widths up to 12′ as well as 6′ and 9′. The first feature makes it easily transportable, and once you reach your destination, fitting into corners and around various objects such as kitchen cabinets or heat pipes is a snap. The second feature provides for minimum or no seams in the average room. If you've ever wrestled with linoleum or some of the early vinyls in

Required tools include a scissors, pencil, long straightedge or chalk line and flexible tape. Begin the installation on a clean surface by positioning the tiles right at the intersections of the lines and pressing them down to bond them. Then, work outward to establish a snugly jointed field.

When you reach the perimeter of the room, measure the distance to either the toe space beneath cabinets or the wall with baseboard or the shoe molding removed. Transfer these measurements to the tiles using a square, if one is handy, and cut the tiles with a common household scissors or shears.

the good old days, you'll really appreciate the advantage of using this "state of the art," modern vinyl. It doesn't crack, it cuts easily and can be seamed, if necessary.

Among the methods for installing vinyl sheet goods are the loose-lay method, the perimeter bond and the full-spread adhesive. The method of installation as well as the type of vinyl and where it can be used depends on the type of subfloor or underlayment, whether the floor is above or below grade and the backing on the vinyl.

Vinyl Floor Requirements

Certain conditions prohibit a vinyl floor installation, such as concrete subfloors that are subject to hydrostatic pressure and/or alkaline (various hydroxides) solutions rising to the surface. Another condition to avoid is a subfloor over a crawl space with poor ventilation beneath it, which allows moisture to collect. Also not recommended is laying the vinyl floor over an existing resilient floor that is highly embossed, rough, sponge-backed, loosely bonded to its subfloor or underlayment or shows signs of wax, moisture, alkaline salts or hydrostatic pressure. And, certain subfloors, known as *monolithic,* such

as concrete, will occasionally require patching or leveling with crack filler and/or a latex leveling agent.

On the plus side, however, most surfaces will accept a vinyl floor, including wood, plywood, particleboard, wood strip, concrete, metal and certain resilient floors. It is important to remember that you must match the method and the material to the existing subfloor conditions.

Vinyl Floor Fitting

With the loose-lay method, no adhesive is spread over the subfloor or underlayment, and no bonding or stapling is used to lock down the perimeter, although molding can be used to hide the edge. For a readily accessible room with a simple rectangular floor area no more than 12' wide, the job is a breeze.

First, remove the base molding. (After the floor has been installed, either replace the molding over the edge of the vinyl floor or leave the existing base molding in place and add a shoe molding to the base to hide the vinyl edge.) Then, with the room stripped of furniture, align the roll with the exposed edge facing the starting wall so that the

First, get the vinyl into position in the room so it can be trimmed to fit. Notice the relief cut to allow the main area of the material to pass the cabinets at the right.

Relief cuts at the opening for the dishwasher permit the material to be tucked into the cabinet toe space at the right and into the opening at the left.

At a right-hand return on the cabinet ell section, a vertical relief cut has been made to allow the material to fold up separately at the return and the toe space to be trimmed.

A relief cut allows the material to tuck under the toe space of a tall cabinet to trim into the doorway and around molding.

body of the vinyl can be rolled out onto the remaining floor. Just make sure that the roll is laid out flat and parallel to one of the long walls.

If you're working with folded vinyl, plan the unfolding so that the same criteria used for the roll vinyl are met. By doing this you'll avoid a lot of grunting and the possibility of a misaligned floor pattern. In either case, make the final adjustments so that the pattern is square with the room and all edges are covered, and that there is some flash or excess material rolled up on the three remaining walls. This will allow trimming to these walls.

Then, with a utility or linoleum knife, make what the trade calls safety cuts at all inside and outside corners. This holds true not only for handling wall intersections but for working around appliances or cabinets as well. So, at all inside or internal corners, make a diagonal cut across the corner at or near the bottom of the corner. At all outside or external corners, make a vertical cut to the bottom of the corner. This will allow you to trim the flash along each wall as separate planes without the troublesome corner fold.

Next, to get as close as possible to the baseboard or wall floor junction, use a rafter or carpenter's square to force the material into the horizontal internal corner and make a continuous cut down the length of the room with a utility or linoleum knife, guided on the outer edge of the square. To avoid damaging the baseboard area with the knife, hold the handle so that the blade is almost vertical.

You might have to trim around pipes as well as fit around casing and doorjambs. Let's consider the pipes first.

With the vinyl fitted to the two end walls, for example, and the pipes on one of the long walls, draw perpendiculars out from the wall, indicating the pipe locations along the long wall. Then, mark the inner- and outermost extent of each pipe. Using these marks, draw a circle representing each pipe in its proper position on the vinyl. Next, with a square, draw lines perpendicular to the long wall so they split the pipe circles and cut the circles themselves. The vinyl can then be moved into the long wall and the split circles set around the pipes.

A couple of approaches can be used to fit the vinyl to doorjambs and casings. One is to use the safety cuts and the square to force the vinyl close to the jamb and cut it. The casing can be treated somewhat like a pipe by drawing perpendicular lines out from the walls where the molding begins, ends and changes shape sharply. With these lines in place, scribe the shape (transfer it from the molding to the vinyl) onto the vinyl using a compass or similar marking device.

You might want to handle the moldings the way ceramic tile setters do. Lay a scrap piece of vinyl next to the casing and jamb. Then, lay a crosscut or similar saw down on the scrap to serve as a thickness gauge, and undercut both the casing and jamb. After appropriate fitting the actual vinyl floor can be slid beneath the jamb and casing.

A completely different method of fitting is to start with the room stripped of furniture and base molding and make a paper pattern of the entire room. Once this pattern has been completed, it is removed and laid over the vinyl in another room and the vinyl is cut to match the pattern. The vinyl is then moved into the actual room and installed. The pattern should be made close enough to the walls so that the base molding will cover the edges. You might want to use the undercut jamb and case or scribe them with the major portion of the floor prefit.

Vinyl Floor Installation

To complete a loose-lay floor once it's fitted, simply replace the base molding or add a shoe molding to hide the edges. If you're doing a perimeter bond, you can staple down the edge and hide it with molding. This is fine for

When fitting and trimming are complete, roll or fold the material halfway back, but don't change its position. Then, apply the adhesive to the exposed half subfloor with a notched trowel.

Reposition the half that had been folded back onto the adhesive and smooth it out by hand, if necessary. Then repeat the procedure for the second half to complete the adhesive work.

Bond down the entire flooring material with numerous passes in random directions using a 100-pound roller.

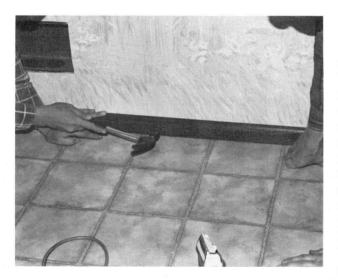

With the floor locked down, replace the base moldings.

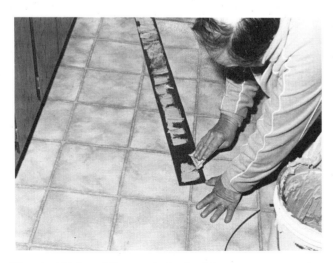

The vinyl kick moldings at the back of the toe spaces must be fitted up and adhered to complete the job.

wood floors if you're on top of concrete or another type of surface that cannot be penetrated by staples. Or, if you prefer another method, you can bond the perimeter with an adhesive band.

If you go for the traditional full-spread adhesive method, the fitting is still done the same way. But, when you're done fitting, roll the vinyl back halfway, trowel adhesive on the exposed subfloor or underlayment and roll the vinyl back over it. Then, simply repeat the operation from the other end. When both halves have been rolled back into position, go over the vinyl in a random pattern with a 100-pound roller to lock and flatten everything.

Seaming

If your room is more than 12' wide, you'll have to make a seam because vinyl's maximum width is 12'. The general seaming procedure is to cut a matching pattern seam where the first and second pieces of vinyl meet and lock down the seam. As a rule, this involves accurate cutting of the edges and notched-trowel application of seam adhesive below and seam sealer above.

The only critical part of seaming, however, is the edge matching and actual cutting. This may be done in a number of ways, but probably the easiest way for the do-it-yourselfer to cut is this: Align both pieces with one piece overlapping the other so the pattern matches all across the room. Then, use a metal straightedge as a guide and double cut the edges holding the knife blade so it's perpendicular to the floor. Remove the waste and check the matchup. Finish off the joint with the adhesive and sealer as described above. Most seams require rolling in a manner similar to that used on wall covering butt joints plus rolling with a 100-pound roller to lock the adhesive. Note also that there are various kinds of adhesive used, both on perimeters and seams, including latex- and solvent-base types. Be sure to check first which type goes with your vinyl and subfloor or underlayment.

Repairs

Most repairs, especially in vinyl sheet goods called *rotovinyls,* can be completed by placing double-faced tape over the damaged area and a fresh piece of vinyl over this, with the patterns aligned. Then, both the patch and the damaged area can be double cut. Remove the repair piece, tape and the damaged piece. Check the fit between the area surrounding the damage and the repair piece. If the match is good, treat it like a seam with adhesive, seam sealer and the rollers.

Wall-to-Wall Carpeting

Strip the room of furniture and with a small, flat pry bar, remove shoe molding if it is next to the base. Also remove any forced-air registers that are floor-mounted as well as any doors that are in the way.

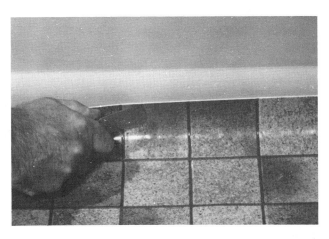

This is freehand cutting based on photos from the Armstrong Installation Manual. Base molding is in place, but shoe molding is not. When confronted with an irregular wall, make vertical safety cuts at critical locations in flash (folded-up vinyl) to allow material to conform more closely to wall contours.

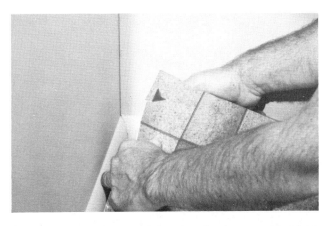

At inside corners, the material can't make the compound fold, so a series of diagonal safety cuts should be made to allow the material to conform and fold separately on the adjacent walls.

When relieved sufficiently, this is the result. You can now fold in each side close enough to the wall to trim as required.

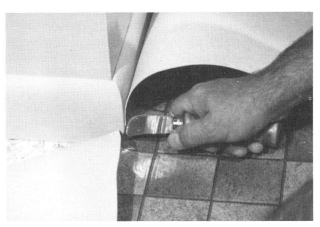

The outside corner also must be separated by a safety cut. This is a vertical cut which follows the corner down to the floor.

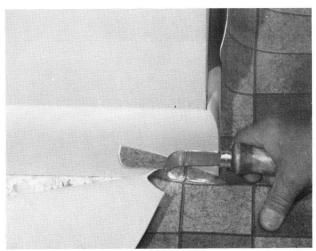

There is still stress concentrated at the bottom end of the safety cut. To avoid a possible tear this must be removed by trimming the material on both sides of the safety cut flat with the floor.

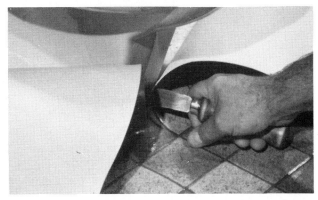

It is necessary at times to cut around fixed obstacles such as a toilet. Push the material to the floor at the front and make a vertical safety cut, just short of the floor. Then, relieve the stress at that point with a small, horizontal cut.

Continue with the safety cuts on both sides of the first cut.

Make additional vertical cuts to the floor at the other stress points, such as the other edge of the stop, jamb edges and casing.

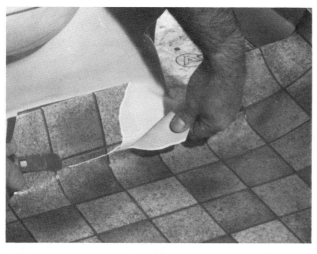

Push the material flat to the floor and continue the safety and relief cuts. Then, with the material pushed to the floor, make horizontal cuts between the safety cuts.

Finish the area by trimming between the vertical cuts at the floor level; in effect, trimming around the jamb and its molding.

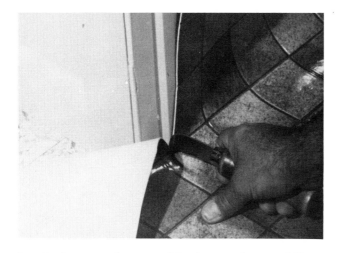

Doorjamb, case and stop combinations can be treated like a complex outside corner. Start by making a vertical safety cut down to the floor at one edge of the stop.

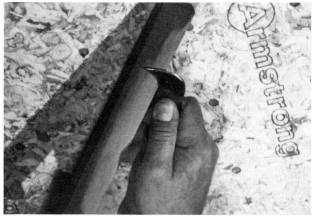

The pros in this sequence use a hook knife, which must remain sharp throughout the course of the work. When sharpening, do the entire radius of the knife so it retains its shape. Keep the bevels of edge equal on both sides of the blade.

Tackless strip must be nailed to the floor all around the room's perimeter. These strips can be found at flooring outlets or flooring supply houses. Their function is to retain the trimmed carpet edge close to the wall. The strips are fastened to the floor by several nails that protrude out of the bottom surface of each 4'-long strip. Protruding out of the top surface of these strips are pins that face outward toward the walls, when installed. These pins hold the tension on the rug. Strips are graded A, B, C and D for the compatibility of their pin length with various thicknesses of carpeting, but the two most common grades used are B and C. It's a good idea to have the dealer match the strip with the carpet.

Start nailing down the strips with the tacks facing toward the wall. Use a small handsaw, jigsaw, chisel, special strip cutter or heavy-duty shears to trim them to length. Patch in small pieces around any obstacles, but do not nails the strip in doorways.

Next, lay out the underpadding in rows and trim it with a utility knife so it just fits within the tackless perimeter. Then staple it in place with a stapler or hammer tacker. The next operation is fitting and trimming the carpet.

If the carpet is rolled on a core or tube, unroll the carpet, discard the tube and reroll the carpet face side in before bringing it into the room. You might find getting the carpet into the room easier yet by folding the carpet and then unfolding it. Then, unroll the remainder. Place the exposed carpet end so it faces one of the shorter end walls. This allows you to roll the remainder into the room. Finally, maneuver the carpet so that it's square with the floor area with the excess rolling up the various walls.

Start trimming and fitting by making relief cuts at doorways and obstacles such as radiators and pipes. Make a vertical relief cut in one corner, then kick the carpet toward the wall near the corner on one side of the cut and then the other. The overhanging carpet at the walls will be treated later. Repeat this cutting and kicking procedure at each corner. The idea behind this procedure is to kick the rug tight by tensioning it across a span with the tackless strip pins or points on opposite sides of the room retaining the carpet. Then, gradually kick the carpet edges that are between the corners.

Make a starter cut somewhere in the middle of each wall, insert the edge trimmer and push it toward the corners while holding pressure along the walls. As the carpet edge is trimmed, tuck it in and down with the back side of a hook knife or utility knife blade.

The carpet in the threshold areas can be either doubled under and locked in place with staples or seamed to an existing carpet. Seaming can be done with a hot plate seaming tool available at rental stores.

For carpet work you'll need a kicker, hammer, a tool to cut the tackless strip, a utility knife, hook knife or angled carpet knife (available at carpet supply shops), pry bar, hammer tacker or stapler, edge trimmer. Edge trimmers, hook knives, hammer tackers and kickers are available at tool rental stores.

For installing wall-to-wall carpeting you'll need some standard tools such as a hammer, pry bar, hook knife, utility knife and hammer tacker, but you'll also need a few special tools, including a kicker, edge trimmer and tackless strip cutter (available at tool rental stores).

Remove only the shoe molding, if it exists, and the furniture; also, it might be a good idea to remove the doors from the room.

Lay out the tackless strip along the perimeter of the room except in the doorways. Use the cutter to trim them to length. Orient them so that the carpet pins face outward and nail them down.

Staple down this underpadding with the hammer tacker.

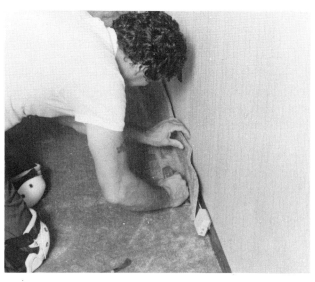

Make a relief cut and start the edger moving to trim the excess.

Move the carpet into the room and position it.

Tuck in the edge behind the tackless pins and clear any loose threads or pilling (fuzzing).

Starting at the corners and working opposite ends of the room, use the kicker to stretch the carpet and retain it with one of the tackless pins.

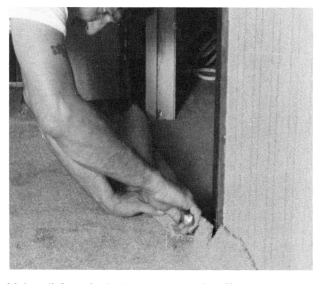

Make relief cuts in the doorways and trim off carpet squarely.

Wood Parquet Floors

Attractive patterned hardwood floors are well within the skill and tool range of the average do-it-yourselfer. These floors can be installed within a day, so if the idea suits your taste and the cost of materials fits your budget, why not try it? As with any project, there are rules of the game, but if you follow them, you can't go wrong.

Parquet flooring is typically square-foot units of factory-assembled, prefinished hardwood modules. Modules vary in thickness—⅜″ is common—and most have tongues or grooves on all four edges. The modules are locked to the floor below with troweled-on adhesive and can be trimmed with various moldings such as base, shoe, nosing, quarter-round, reducers and feature strip. The manufacturer can supply these trims in most cases. For the purposes of validating your warranty, use the adhesive recommended and marketed by the manufacturer and install these floors only on acceptable subfloors.

In this regard, many of these floors are not recommended for below-grade, wet area installations (such as baths) or over cushioned floor covering. However, they can be installed over concrete slabs, maximum 1×4 width tongue-and-groove wood, plywood, particleboard, linoleum or tile. Obviously, any of these floor coverings or subfloors must be firmly secured to the structure below. In the case of the wood product subfloors, extra nails or screws might be required to eliminate movement or noise, and these must not be sealed because the adhesive won't grab hard enough. As with vinyl sheet goods, concrete with moisture problems, hydrostatic pressure or alkaline salts (from the addition of calcium chloride to prevent freezing at the time of the pour) is not suitable for this flooring.

To avoid dirt and damage, flooring should be done after all ceiling and wall work, with the possible exception of moldings. Stair nosings and similar pieces should be

The floor layout was started by snapping perpendicular lines on the plywood subfloor to assure a square start and determine the width of the border tiles. Install stair nosings now. Use a 3/32″ square-notched trowel to spread the adhesive in broad, sweeping strokes in the first area. Don't obliterate the layout lines.

Apply more adhesive and set more tiles. Once tiles have been set, don't stand or kneel on them. Also, after a number of tiles are down, their friction eliminates any tendency for them to move when you engage the tongues and grooves of the next tiles.

Start the installation by placing the first few tiles in position against the layout lines, one of which, in this case, coincides with the inner nosing edge. Lock the tongues and grooves during the placement. Check that you are square with the lines.

The completed floor needs only the base molding and cap extended around the entire perimeter.

installed first, whereas base molding, doorstop and case should be installed last to hide the edges. If this is not possible and the case molding is already in place, it should be removed or undercut with a crosscut or backsaw (just in a ceramic tile job), using a parquet tile over the subfloor to gauge the crosscut height. Subfloors must be free of all substances such as wax, fat, oil, grease, dirt or any other foreign substance that might prevent the adhesive from grabbing. To this end, sweeping and vacuuming are imperative. Also, check the plane of the subfloor with a level or long straightedge for discrepancies no greater than $\frac{1}{4}''$ in 10'. Depressions can be brought up to level with latex patching compound and high spots sanded or abraded to conform to this criterion.

Before starting, measure the room in both directions. You might want to balance the floor by arranging to have equal-width edge tiles on opposite sides of the room. But, if this requires a lot of extra trimming, it might be better to arrange to start laying the tiles so that full tiles form the border on two adjacent walls. Personally, I like to balance these floors—it doesn't amount to that much extra work.

If you're going for two full-border tile walls, snap two intersecting chalk lines on the floor perpendicular to each other and each $24\frac{1}{2}''$ out from the wall (with the base molding removed or not yet installed). If you're balancing, figure the partial tile widths on both the long and short walls, add $12\frac{1}{2}''$ to these numbers (one full tile plus an expansion gap) and snap the perpendicular lines in the appropriate locations.

If you're using nosing, install it now. All other moldings, except feature strip, which is interposed between tiles as the work progresses, can be added after the floor tile. Otherwise, the work consists of trowelling on adhesive and setting and trimming tiles.

For the best possible grip, adhesive should be trowelled on at a rate of 1 gallon per 100 square feet for relatively smooth surfaces, such as plywood, or 1 gallon per 50 square feet for rougher surfaces, such as tile or wood-floated concrete. To get these results, the manufacturer suggests his adhesive and a square-notched trowel with $3/32''$ teeth for smooth surfaces, $\frac{1}{8}''$ for tough surfaces.

In either case the adhesive should be swept over the surface in continuous strokes with the trowel angled at 45°. You should not lean on tiles already set, so apply adhesive to an area no wider than you can reach. In this case, this means the area between one of the chalk lines and the wall. Do not cover the lines because you need them as a guide. With this adhesive, there is no waiting time, so start setting the tiles right away.

If you are using full tiles, there's no problem; but if you're fitting to an edge, prepare the partial-width tiles in advance by measuring and cutting them to fit, alowing for the $\frac{1}{2}''$ expansion gap at the edge. For this, you might use a small bandsaw, jigsaw or portable saw. The portable saw, however, is last choice here because you'd be working with rather small pieces in a somewhat dangerous situation. The person shown cutting with the portable saw is a pro.

In any event, start setting the tiles according to the graphic scheme shown and take particular care that the starting tiles are absolutely square with the lines. You can check this with a rafter or carpenter's square so that the remainder of the tile field will be square with the room. As you set the tiles, carefully interlock matching tongues and grooves together. This start is the most critical part of the entire job. You must be careful not to cause any of the tiles in the first group to move from their set positions. This problem will not exist in the second group due to increased resistance to shear of the greater number of tiles and setting up of the adhesive.

Continue to work the groups trowelling, setting and trimming where necessary. At times you may accidentally get a bit of adhesive on the tile surface. This can be removed easily with the solvent provided by the tile manufacturer. (This solvent can also be used for tool cleanup.) When the floor has been completely set, allow at least 24 hours before people walk on it or before setting furniture on it. At this time, moldings can be installed, including those to hide the expansion gaps at the edges.

42

Wall Covering

In the average home, about 80% of the rooms are painted, and the rest are surfaced with wall covering. *Wall covering* (not wallpaper) is the correct term for the broad group of flexible wall decorations available in roll form. Only a small amount of actual wallpaper is sold today.

The more popular coverings sold currently are vinyl-coated paper, paper-backed vinyl and the more expensive fabric-backed vinyl. However, fabric-backed vinyl is not as big a seller because of the cost difference.

These coverings are typically, but not always, constructed in a three-part laminate. The outer or decorative layer is usually a print on vinyl with a protective layer or coating over the print. It may or may not be embossed and varies from 0.0001″ to 0.0003″ in thickness. The intermediate layer, if present, contains the background color. This layer may be between zero and 0.0100″. The third layer, or substrate (backing), may be either woven or nonwoven fabric or paper, and its thickness varies from 0.004″ to 0.012″.

In addition to the basic wall coverings, there are specialty types, which, as you would suspect, are more expensive than the basics. But they can give you a lot more pizazz, if the room decor warrants it. These types include grass cloths, foils, textiles, suedes, string flocks, corks and expanded prints. In general, the specialty coverings are more difficult to install for both the professional and the do-it-yourselfer.

All coverings have certain characteristics such as being strippable and peelable that affect their performance during and following hanging. *Strippable* means that without steaming or wetting the covering can be pulled completely off the wall after it has dried or at some later date. *Peelable* means that the outer layers (surface and intermediate) can be removed, leaving the substrate in place. This provides a smooth wall surface for an alternate covering.

Coverings are also scrubbable and washable. *Scrubbable* means they can withstand a prescribed amount of scrubbing with a brush and a given detergent without damage. *Washable* means the coverings can withstand a prescribed amount of detergent sponging without damage.

Stain and abrasion resistance refer to the covering's ability to clean up after exposure to certain materials and to withstand mechanical abuse such as scuffing, rubbing and scraping. Stain resistance pertains to kitchen and dining areas where the covering is exposed to foods,

TYPICAL WALLCOVERING CROSS SECTION
DECORATIVE SURFACE (0.0001″–0.0003″)

| INTERMEDIATE LAYER (0–0.010″) |
| SUBSTRATE (0.004″–0.012″) |

VINYL-COATED PAPER
DECORATIVE SURFACE (0.0001″)

| GROUNDS COATING (0.0003″) |
| PAPER SUBSTRATE (0.005″) |

PAPER-BACKED VINYL
DECORATIVE SURFACE (0.0001″)

| SOLID VINYL (0.002″–0.005″) |
| PAPER SUBSTRATE (0.006″) |

FABRIC-BACKED VINYL
DECORATIVE SURFACE (0.0001″)

| SOLID VINYL (0.002″–0.010″) |
| WOVEN FABRIC BACKING (0.012″) OR NON-WOVEN SUBSTRATE (0.006″) |

Wall covering construction. (Courtesy of the Wallcovering Information Bureau.)

beverages, fruit stains, butter, margarine, fat and oil. Abrasion resistance is important in high traffic or rough traffic areas such as halls, foyers and places where children play frequently or dogs run.

Colorfast is the ability of the covering's print to resist the bleaching effects of sun; tear strength is the covering's resistance to the spreading or expanding of a nick or cut; and break strength is the covering's ability to remain intact under tension. These characteristics are covered under ASTM (American Society for Testing Materials) F793.

Planning Your Wall Covering

Before purchasing wall covering, you'll want to consider a few factors that will narrow your choices and, at the same time, give you the most pleasing and long-lasting results. First, estimate the number of square feet of covering required. If you're doing only the walls, to get the area, add up the total wall perimeter and multiply this number by the wall height. For example, if the length is 16, the width is 12 and the height is 8, the computation would be 16+16+12+12=60 and 60×8=480 square feet. If you're also doing the ceiling, multiply the width times the length to get the additional area, or 12×16=192 square feet. Don't worry about the windows and doors. The extra covering might be needed or, if not used, it usually can be returned if it is still in double-roll quantities.

With a sufficient material estimate in hand, you can zero in on a covering that suits both your taste and your budget. Look at the walls and ceiling. Are they lumpy and bumpy? If they are, skip stripe patterns, foils and Mylars. Try for a "busy" pattern or an embossed covering that will hide the wall's discrepancies. If the room is short, don't go for vertical stripes; they will make the room look shorter. In general, patterns with brilliant colors or dazzling designs are best for special-purpose rooms, not family or living rooms where you'll be spending a lot of time. It is important to take into account the rugs, drapes and furniture for the room. For example, if your room is colonial, try to pick a pattern to match this decor, such as a small print.

In addition to choosing from the various materials, colors and patterns available, you will also have the problem of matching adjacent pieces of wall covering. There are three basic categories: (1) straight-across match; (2) drop match and (3) random match. The random match, typically found in ribbed or vertical stripe patterns, is the easiest to hang, and there's no waste at all. The other two matches may repeat at either large or small intervals. If they repeat at small intervals, the waste will be minor, and the physical matching will be easy; but if they repeat at a large interval, such as 18″ to 24″, there may be considerable waste and extra care required.

Before you make your purchases, here are some final thoughts. Never buy wall covering that is not pretrimmed.

Each piece requires the full length of the edges to be razor cut along an 8′ steel edge. It is best to leave this to the professionals. Match the wall covering paste and the method of installation to the wall covering (if you're not using prepasted wall covering). You can get this information from the dealer or from the instructions packaged with the covering. Make sure that all covering is from the same dye lot or run. Before the purchase, understand what your responsibility is and what the dealer's is in case anything goes wrong, such as a bad run, a bad edge or a misindexed pattern.

If it's your first time, stick to easy patterns and material such as a prepasted, pretrimmed, random match pattern. Don't be afraid to seek advice. The dealer is there to help you. He wants you to be successful so you'll come back again. In the beginning, avoid specialties such as metallics, foils, grass cloths and heavy embossings. Choose a covering that's prepasted instead of unpasted, if possible.

Tools and Equipment

To mark a plumb line on the wall at the starting point, you'll need either a level or a plumb bob and straightedge. To apply the paste, either a roller and cover or a paste brush can be used. If the wall covering is prepasted, no brush or roller is required, but a special, inexpensive water tray will wet the covering. For applying the covering to the wall or ceiling, either a smoothing brush or a smooth plastic edge will do.

The covering must be trimmed off at the base molding and at the ceiling or its molding, so use either a razor knife or a utility knife with spare blades, plus a 6″ putty or drywall taping knife for a guide.

It's best to have a scissors handy to cut off lengths of wall covering and trim in the electrical switch and outlet areas and sometimes corners. There's also a small roller that is used to lock down the vertical seams where adjacent pieces of wall covering butt. Finally, a couple of spare buckets and a sponge will cover the cleanup at the base molding, ceiling, seams and on the field area of the wall covering.

Preparing the Room and the Walls

Regardless of the wall covering chosen, most of the rules of procedure are the same. For instance, the room should be totally ready for you to work in; there should be nothing for you to worry about but hanging the wall covering. This means that the room should be cleared of all furniture and rugs, if possible, and all curtains, drapes, hinged or sliding doors should be removed.

The ceilings should be painted if they are not going to be covered, and the door and window moldings, including casing, base stool and apron plus all other moldings such as crown, cap or chair rail, should be finished and dry before beginning any wall covering.

A worktable or tabletop at least 8' long to put the paper on should be in the center of the room. You should have a reliable ladder, about 3' high, to put you eye-to-eye with the wall top or ceiling. All breakers controlling the room switches and outlets should be turned off. All surfaces to be covered, both walls and ceiling, should be given a coat of sealer. Depending on the surface, this sealer can be latex or oil-based and can be rolled on. Generally, porous surfaces such as fresh- or latex-painted drywall can be treated with a latex sealer; oil-painted, ceramic, glass or other hard, nonporous surfaces require an oil-based sealer. No matter which sealer you use, make sure it is dry before you apply the wall covering.

A Few Tips Before Starting

The rolls of wall covering should be examined to be sure there is no damage, loss of index (pattern positioned differently on the roll, such as different edge distances) or differing run numbers. The match should be rolled out and checked for its repeat, if such exists, as well as a clean and accurate edge match. If any of these criteria have not been met, do not start. Instead, return the wall covering to the dealer and clear up any problems.

Getting Started

When you're ready to start hanging wall covering, choose a place that is not too obvious, such as a corner or a short area between the top of a window or door. This way you can control any single minor mismatch that might occur where the first and last pieces meet. Also, decide which part of the pattern looks best at the ceiling. Allow a couple of extra inches above this spot before cutting across the covering. Then, measure the wall height and transfer this to the covering on the table. Allow a bit extra at the bottom and cut the first piece. All full-length wall pieces will be cut the same way.

Most of the time the paste will be applied to the covering on the table with either a brush or roller, and then the covering will be booked; that is, folded up on each end, paste-to-paste. However, this is not always the case. When dealing with Mylars or coverings that are prone to crease and remain that way from handling, apply the paste only to the wall and gently position the covering over it before carefully smoothing.

On the other hand, when dealing with coverings that are heavily embossed or have a powerful "memory" (they like to stay in the rolled position), it might be necessary to double paste (apply two coats of paste to the covering) or

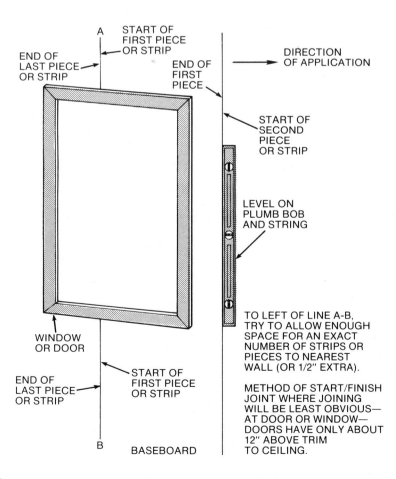

Hanging the first strip.

apply paste to both wall and covering. Part of the problem with embossed coverings is their reduced gripping area, while the powerful memory coverings require "relaxing" as well as paste-to-paste contact to assure grip and full-contact flat adhesion to the wall.

All rooms will have inside corners; some will have outside corners as well. As a general rule, never continue a large amount of wall covering across an inside corner onto the adjacent wall because there's no assurance that the walls meet squarely. If they don't, you might have to continue the adjacent wall with a starting edge that is not vertical, or out of plumb. That's bad news. To avoid this, run the covering from the previous wall into the inside corner and about ½" to ¾" onto the adjacent wall. If more covering than this is on the adjacent wall, trim it with your knife and straightedge. Then, start the adjacent wall in the corner, but make sure that its opposite edge is plumb by checking it with your level. If the corner is out of plumb, you might have to slightly trim the corner edge of the piece of wall covering. By doing this you'll have an excellent start for the adjacent wall.

If there's an outside corner, such as for a jog or closet, use a large strip to wrap around it, but be sure to cut a small relief slit at both the top and bottom of the piece to allow a clean and snug wraparound. It's important to avoid seams at or very near the corner itself. Check the edges for plumb and make any minor corrections right away. This can be done by plumbing the far edge of the next piece with the near edge just slightly overlapping the wraparound edge, and then double cutting through both edges simultaneously. After that, just remove the waste and match up the seams.

All butt seams should be rolled following fitting, smoothing and trimming at the ceiling and base molding. Areas that won't be covered, such as the ceiling, as well as the seam and field areas that get unwanted paste on them should be cleaned off as soon as possible with a sponge and clean water. To make this job easier, keep wringing out the sponge and changing the water in the bucket.

Many places in a room, such as window openings without moldings, forced-air registers, light switches, electrical outlets and intercoms, require special considerations. The photo sequence shows the various steps involved, including double cutting, cutting into electrical boxes and wall devices, treating both cased and noncased windows (trimming to a casing is the same as trimming to a base or crown molding) as well as covering electrical plates and registers.

Finally, the best advice for your first attempt is to try to do a neat job with the simplest type of wall covering. Then, when you've got the mechanics down, you can go on to more sophisticated patterns and materials.

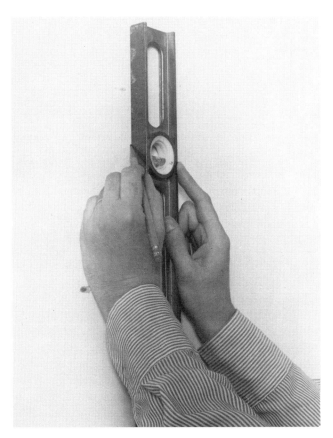

Wherever you plan to start hanging wall covering, use a level or plumb bob to establish a true vertical as a reference line for the edge of the first strip.

Once the room height is measured, and you've chosen the area of the pattern to be at the top, measure out the length. Allow a few extra inches and cut the first strip. Then, use this first strip to set up cutting a number of strips in advance.

Most pastes can be applied to the covering using either a brush or roller. In certain cases, the paste should be applied to the wall.

The pasted strip should be unfolded at the top and aligned with the preceding strip, both edge-to-edge and vertically, with the pattern or repeat. When the top is set, unfold the bottom and continue downward.

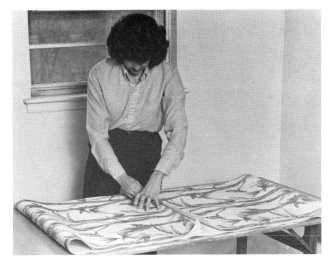

If applied to the strip as shown, the covering should be folded up at both ends (booked) to keep the paste moist and allow better control of the strip.

The strip is then smoothed, eliminating any bubbles, wrinkles or misalignments, working from the center of the strip to the edges. This squeegee action can be done using either a smoothing brush or smooth piece of plastic.

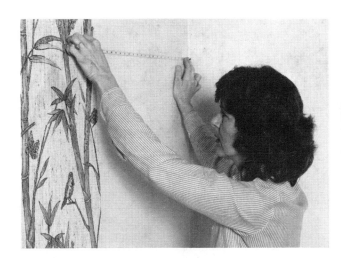

When less than a strip width from an inside corner, measure the distance to that corner and add ½″ to ¾″. This will provide a slight start onto the adjacent wall to be covered by the next strip.

Where strip edges butt together (without overlap), use a wooden roller to secure them. Then sponge off the joint to eliminate any possibility of paste on the surface.

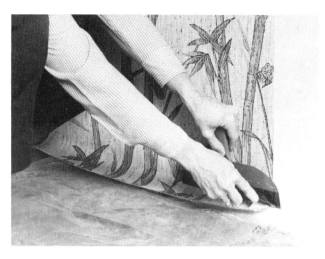

Strip must be trimmed cleanly at the ceiling (or molding) and at the base molding (plus under the window apron molding, etc.). Press covering home with a drywall taping knife and cut off excess with a utility knife, guided by the taping knife.

Now, cut a partial strip to cover from the corner to the line, using the measurement taken just before.

To handle an uncased window just ahead, a full strip must be started a few inches out from the corner just completed. Working backward from the window edge, make a mark and measure the width of the partial strip that's needed.

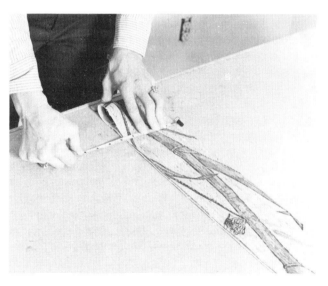

Check the width of the partial strip cut, either with several measurements along its length or dry against the wall.

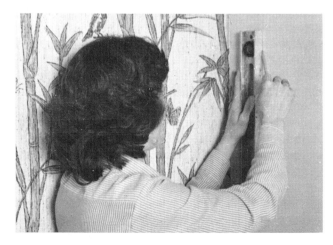

This partial must have its manufactured right edge perfectly straight and plumb, so use the level again to strike a plumb line.

Paste the partial strip and position it on the wall with its left, hand-cut edge to the corner and the manufactured edge to the line. Make the fit against the line perfect.

The full strip, to the left of the window, has been positioned and smoothed. Note that the extra covering on the right edge is wide enough to be folded into the left side jamb area. The fold-in cut is about to be made at the top.

Hold a short piece cut off the top of a full-length, partial-width strip with a manufactured right edge and get a pattern match just to the left of the window opening.

The fold-in cut at the bottom of the window opening is being made at the stool molding. This extra work is necessary because one piece cannot simultaneously cover the head and side jamb areas of the window opening.

Temporarily paste or tape the short piece in place over the existing full strip, indexing the pattern. Then, using a wide-blade taping knife or other straightedge as a guide, double-cut through both the short piece and the full piece.

Fold-in piece at left side jamb is trimmed in the usual way.

Remove scrap from the full piece and short piece. Align cut left side of the short piece with cut right side of full piece.

Smooth short piece and trim its top at the ceiling as usual.

Fit and smooth this piece in place over the window.

Tuck its bottom into the head area of the window opening, cutting as required to fold it in. Smooth it and trim it. Double-cut in a longer piece the same width as the short piece under the window to keep the strips even.

Trim off this piece at the ceiling. Fold it into the head area and trim it off there.

Cut the top off a full piece long enough to fit over the window to the ceiling and fold in at the head.

Fit the next full-sized strip on the right side of the window. Then, work backward and fit the partial strip underneath the window. Trim it off at the apron, just below the stool.

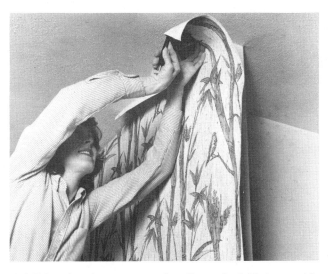

A full-length strip next to a stub wall must be folded around it. In order to do this relief cuts are required at both the ceiling and at the baseboard ends.

With the power to the room cut off at the electrical panel as suggested in the text, it's no problem to cut in at switches and duplex receptacles using the utility knife.

Thus relieved, the strip can easily be positioned, smoothed and trimmed at the ceiling and the baseboard.

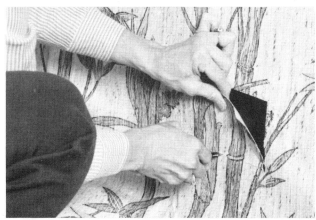

Register boot openings are cleared with four quick cuts of the utility knife, and the register can be reinstalled.

This intercom station and similar wall-mounted devices don't necessarily have to be unwired. All that's required is to dismount them temporarily from their rough-ins and provide relief cuts in the covering strips.

To handle patches on damaged wallcovering, begin by matching a scrap repair piece to the pattern of the damaged area. Then either tape it or paste it in place.

Using a guide, cut through both covering layers (double-cut) in an irregular pattern, if possible. We used a rectangle for clarity.

Inner area of repair piece is removed, exposing damaged area, cut to the same size and shape. Remove it, too.

The outer border of the repair piece is removed.

The patch can now be positioned, smoothed and its edges rolled before cleaning with the sponge.

43

Ceramic Tile

In the hall tile floor shown in Part II, the tile is Italian; the tile in the hearth, domestic. Both were adhered to a plywood substrate with three-part epoxy mortar (resin, hardener and portland cement). The whirlpool bath chapter shows several ways to adhere a domestic tile: with organic adhesive for tile-over-tile; with organic adhesive for tile over drywall and with thinset mortar over cement board. So, having already covered some floor and wall methods, here's a bit more on floors and kitchen and bath countertops.

Large-Area Tile Floors

Throughout the book there are many references to the natural expansion and contraction of wood products and structures, including joist-supported plywood floors. However an alternative, straightforward method to overcome this problem of setting a tile floor over large, plywood subfloors has evolved.

An underlayment, which is somewhat independent of the plywood, is provided over the plywood. When the plywood expands or contracts, the underlayment does not; or does so only minimally. Black diamond metal lath is stapled to the plywood throughout the field and the perimeter, then gray, thinset mortar is mixed with latex additive and spread in a thin layer with a steel trowel so that it barely covers the lath.

Once the thinset has dried, the tile is set in a standard manner. To assure straight, square tile rows, perpendicular intersecting chalk lines are snapped on the underlayment. Remove all base molding and undercut all jambs, case and stop molding with a crosscut or backsaw that rests flat on the tile as a gauge.

Next, dry-lay all the tiles in the field. Score and crack all border tiles that require straight cuts with a tile cutter and fit all irregular shapes with a carbide-tip tile nipper. An alternative method is to mark some of the tougher cuts and take them to a tile store to be cut.

However, there are times when a power-driven, water-cooled tile saw is the best answer. In this case, mark the tiles and pay a tile service outfit by the piece to make your cuts.

Once the entire floor is fitted, stack the tiles in back of the work area in sequence, keeping the work area clear, making it easy for a helper to hand you the tiles as you need them. Then, mix up some thinset mortar with latex additive in an expendable vessel, such as an old drywall compound bucket. Use a drill and mixing paddle if you want, but keep the speed low to avoid forming of air bubbles that tend to weaken the mortar.

Spread some mortar on the underlayment in a sweeping motion with the trowel angled at about 45°. The trowel should be square-notched to create troughs and ridges, and the notch size should be matched to the type of tile being set. This is typically 3/16″ to 1/4″; the tile distributor can supply exact information. The mixture should be stiff enough so that the ridges hold their form without any sagging.

Do not trowel over the intersecting lines and obliterate them. Instead, use the lines as a guide to keep the joints straight. When you have set a number of tiles, you can beat them in to flatten and level the general surface as well as to lock them down. With certain types and sizes of tile, especially large squares, this beating won't be necessary. However, check with your distributor to be sure.

After waiting a minimum of 24 hours, mix and apply the grout, forcing it into the joints with a rubber-soled grout float. After allowing the grout to set up a bit, damp-sponge the entire surface several times, continually cleaning the sponge in a bucket of fresh water. Allow at least 24 hours before walking on the tile floor.

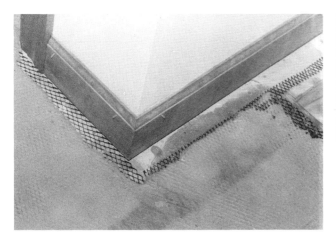

This hall is being prepared for the installation of a tile floor. The base molding has been fitted, but only tacked. To control expansion and contraction, a layer of expanded diamond pattern metal has been stapled to the plywood subfloor, and a skim coat of gray thinset mortar applied to it with a steel trowel.

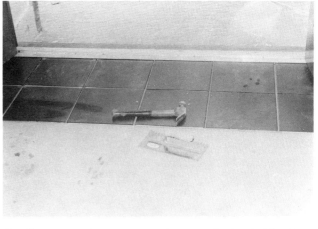

The first couple of rows are set up between the threshold and one of the snapped lines. Note its perpendicular, barely visible, coming out from the area of the hammer handle. In this particular case, this line is dividing the room exactly in half.

The thinset mortar for setting the actual tile is mixed with a paddle wheel, driven by a heavy-duty drill. Preparing the dry ingredients and the latex additive (for dampproofing) takes only a minute or so this way.

To handle closets, bathrooms, borders or obstacles, certain tiles must be trimmed straight. To make accurate markings requires that you use a square.

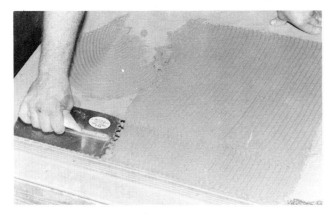

A square-notched trowel is used to spread the mortar on the prepared surface. Note that the far end of the mortar ends along a straight line. This line, not visible here, is one of the two perpendicular intersecting lines used to lay out the job squarely, parallel with the room, and to position the tile field so as to minimize possible difficult cuts.

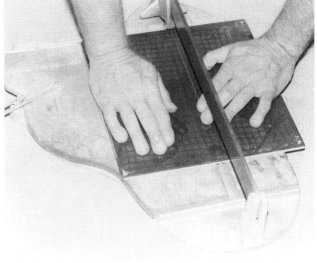

Straight cuts can be made on the tile cutter.

Irregular cuts are made with a carbide-tipped tile nipper.

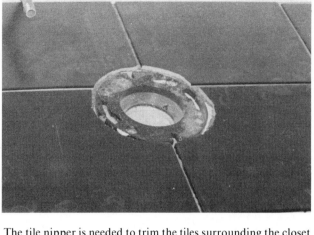

The tile nipper is needed to trim the tiles surrounding the closet bend in this bathroom.

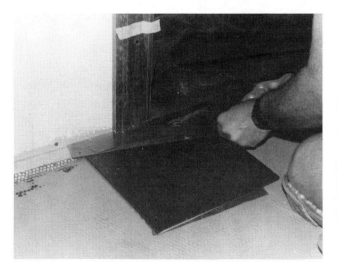

To undercut the jamb, stop and casing, lay the saw on its side on top of a tile to be used on the floor. This will make a perfect fit.

The completed hall tile floor, before it was cleaned and the base molding installed.

Kitchen and Bath Tile Countertops

Kitchen and bath tile countertops are durable and easily installed. Most kitchen countertops, which are laminated with some type of high-pressure laminate (such as Formica, Nevamar or Wilsonart), can be tiled right on the spot. All that has to be done to convert the slick, plastic surface to a suitable substrate for tile installation is abrade it with rough sandpaper to give it "tooth." Reverse drip moldings at the joint where the top meets the backsplash, or edge moldings must be removed. The sink must also be removed along with any built-ins such as mixers, chopping boards or rimmed ceramic units. At this point your top is the same as a newly constructed plywood substrate.

If you're using the second method and have constructed a plywood substrate to fit over either kitchen or bath cabinets, fasten the substrate to those cabinets from below by driving screws up through the cabinet nailers into the countertop or sink top doublers, but make sure that the top and the cabinet are firmly secure to the wall.

A third substrate is also quite feasible because it can be applied over plywood quite quickly. This is done with cement board. It has the advantage of adding absolute rigidity to the substrate (due to the weight of the extra, locked-down lamination), and it virtually eliminates any expansion from moisture. If moisture gets at it, the concrete core only hardens. Cement board can be sawn with special-purpose blades in a portable saw, or scored and cracked something like gypsum board. It is fastened to the plywood with roofing nails, and its many joints are sealed with fiberglass tape and thinset mortar, much like taping and jointing gypsum board.

To figure the amount of tile required, add the total length of the entire outer edges of the countertop. Edge trim runners are 6″ long, so it is easy to calculate how many are needed. Count up all inside and outside corners on the edge. Inside corners take edge trim square-in mitered runners (two pieces each), and outside corners take edge trim runner-out angles (one piece each). Then, compute the field areas of both the countertop and backsplash

Some trims and their installation use.

for the number of flat tiles. These 4¼″-square tiles come 12½ square feet per box.

Now, if you're using a short backsplash, which leaves a large space between the bottom of the wall cabinets and tile, the top row must all be bullnose runners. But, if you're using an 18″ backsplash right up to the bottom

edges of the wall cabinets, then the top row can be flat tiles, but the tile borders that do not contact cabinets must be bullnose runners. You may also require outside corner or inside corner bullnose. These are called, respectively, bullnose round-out angles and bullnose square-up angles. Add 5% or 10% to your estimate to account for breakage

Cut out the opening in the countertop for the sink, using a jigsaw. There are no drilled holes at the corners because the radii are large enough and this saw will cut its own starter hole.

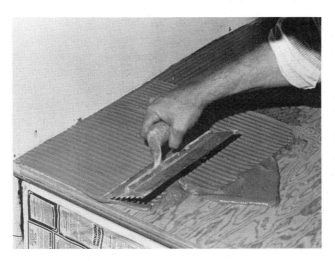

Thinset mortar made with latex additive, again for dampproofing in a wet area, is applied directly to the plywood substrate with a ¼″×¼″-notched trowel.

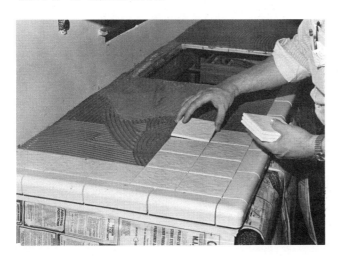

Paper is taped around cabinets to prevent damage. The edge runners and round-out corners are set first, followed by the field of flat tile.

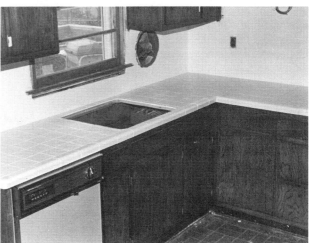

This is the countertop's appearance after the tile has been set, the surface cleaned and a day allowed for mortar curing.

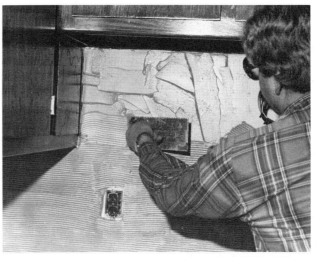

Apply organic adhesive with a triangular-notched trowel to the backsplash area.

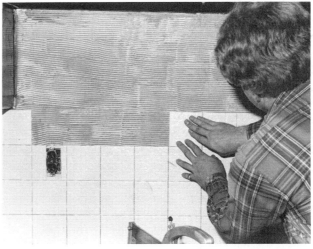

Tiles should be installed with a pushing, twisting motion. If switch or receptacle cuts cause problems, use a carbide-tipped masonry drill bit to remove waste.

When all tile has set for at least 24 hours, mix grout with latex grout additive into a creamy consistency and work into the joints with a rubber-soled grouting float. This is done on both the backsplash and countertop.

Polish the surface with slightly damp rags or sponges to remove cementicious residue. Clean rags or sponges frequently.

and/or spares. In addition, you'll need either epoxy mortar mix or thinset mortar and latex additive, organic adhesive, grout and latex grout additive and plumber's putty to set the sink and fixtures.

Tool requirements include a tile cutter, which can be rented, a tile nipper as described above, a notched trowel for the mortar, a serrated trowel for the organic adhesive, a grout float, a bucket, sponges, a small block of wood and a mallet or small hammer.

The most practical approach to this project is to purchase a drop-in china sink and mark the outline on the counterop in the correct location. Use either the sink as a pattern or a pattern that is supplied. If you use the sink, you'll have to draw a second outline within the first outline to allow for the width of the rim. Jigsaw out the waste, working from drilled starter holes at the corners or the small radii at the corners. Test the sink fit and if it's all right, put the sink aside.

Next, lay out the countertop tiles, flats, edge trim runners and angles, and fit where necessary, especially in the sink area. Remove the tiles when the fitting is completed, but keep them in exact order so that they may be set quickly on the mortar. Mix up the mortar and trowel in onto the substrate with long, sweeping strokes. Use a square-notched trowel for this, but remember that the notch size depends on the type of tile used.

Set the tiles and beat them as before. Make a final check to see that the joints are straight and that no mortar is on the surface or flush with the surface at the joints. Allow a day or so for the thinset mortar to harden before proceeding.

Then, fit up the backsplash area tiles. When this dry fit is satisfactory, spread organic adhesvie on the drywall behind the countertop and below the cabinets with a serrated trowel. The tiles may be installed with light pressure and a slight twisting motion to get the best possible grip. Allow an additional day for setting up. Finish by applying the grout as before and damp-sponging the surface many times.

The A-C plywood countertop has been beefed up along front edge to increase overhang. Backsplash is also A-C plywood.

Both the top and the backsplash will be covered with noncombustible cement board. It can be cut to shape with a portable saw and special-purpose blade, or scored and cracked like gypsum board, using a special knife available at tile suppliers.

Place a 4-mil polyethylene film or 15-pound saturated felt barrier over the entire top. Then nail the cement board to it using 1½″ galvanized roofing nails spaced 1′ apart along the perimeter and the intermediate area. Interboard gaps will be filled with mortar later.

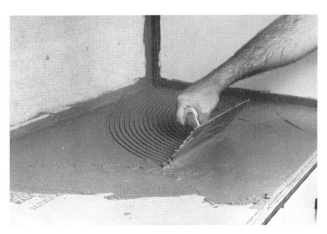

Spread thinset mortar over cement board surface with a ¼″×¼″ square-notched trowel held at an angle.

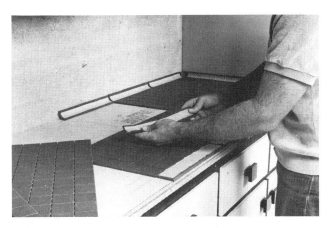

Dry-lay 2″×2″ mosaic tile, using thinset bullnose in front row and cove in back row. Both trim tiles are face-mounted in strips. The 2″×2″ tiles are back-mounted and joined in 1′×2′ sheets.

With the smooth trowel edge, spread a ⅛″ layer of mortar on the beefed-up front edge. Press the front edge trim into this mortar. Press the front edge bullnose trim onto the top surface mortar. Adjust both strips so that the front edge of the bullnose is flush with the edge tile trim surface.

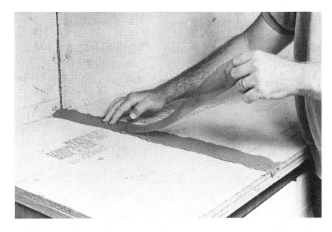

At each joint, apply a band of thinset mortar. Embed fiberglass tape in this mortar and smooth it out with the smooth edge of the trowel.

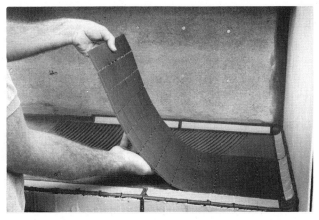

Lay 1′×2′ sheets of tile on top surface, between front and back trim. For cuts, use a tile cutter or nipper.

Fit tiles around the sink opening and press each tile firmly to bond it and resist vibration from the garbage disposal unit, to be installed later.

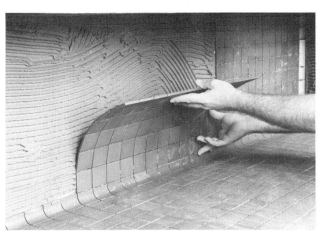

Set tile 1'×2' sheets on the backsplash. Press them in and align their joint line with those on the countertop. Dampen and peel the paper from cove trim. Clean surfaces with a damp sponge.

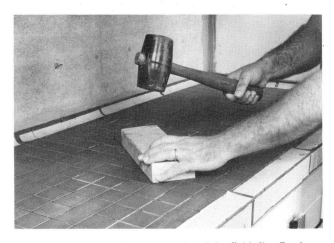

Use beater block and hammer to bond the field tiles firmly to mortar. Dampen paper on trim strips and peel it off. Clean surface with wet sponge and check joints for alignment.

Set tile 1'×2' sheets and bullnose trim on side wall of the backsplash. Dampen and peel paper from the trim. Clean surfaces with a damp sponge. Beat in all of the field tile.

Apply thinset to the backsplash in the same manner as before. Press in the cove tile at the vertical joint.

Apply grout to the joints with a rubber-soled grout float. After forcing grout into all joints, remove excess grout with a squeegee or an angled float moved diagonally.

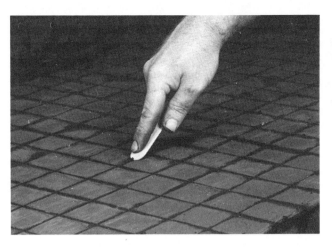

To assure maximum joint compaction, run a wooden spatula along each joint line, pressing grout further into joints. This makes stain resistance greater and reduces cleaning.

Now sprinkle dry sawdust over the damp grout surface film. Rub with a dry burlap rag and brush off sawdust. Any remaining spots of grout haze can be damp-sponged.

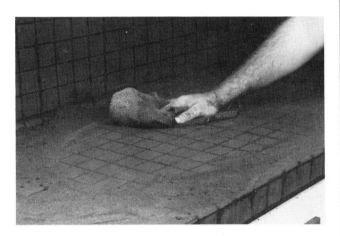

Sprinkle dry grout powder over surface and dry or polish with burlap rag. This makes joints denser, makes them dry evenly and loosens film to make final cleaning easier.

Caulk around sink opening and drop in the sink.

44

Tools, Techniques and Safety

A lot of tools for both general and specialized use have been shown so far in this book. Some are manually operated; others are powered. They run the gamut from tools for measurement, alignment and marking, such as flexible rules, levels and squares, to tools for cutting, drilling and fastening, such as various kinds of saws, drills and bits, staplers and hammers.

Because so many of these tools are for general use, it pays to buy them as your budget allows if you plan on completing a lot of DIY projects over a period of years. However, because some of them are for specialized use, it pays to rent them unless they are either inexpensive or expendable.

When buying tools for a lifetime of use, remember to buy quality tools, not low-quality tools at so-called bargain prices, and buy a tool that is good enough to last long enough to need *and* warrant a repair. Only the very rich can buy low-quality tools because they can afford to buy the same tool over and over. So, before spending your money, take a few moments and check out the library— you'll find books and periodicals that review and rate tools.

Only you know which tools you need, since you decide on the type of projects, maintenance or hobbies you intend to pursue. Many surveys show that the most commonly owned power tools are the electric drill and jigsaw, and topping the list of hand tools are the hammer, screwdriver and pliers. If these are sufficient for your needs, stop there. It's senseless to buy tools and just let them sit idly in a closet. If you need the tool for a one-shot job, try to rent it. If you need the tool for consistent, long-term use, buy it. Whatever tool, aid, device or machine you buy, you should look for safety, accuracy and, if possible, efficiency.

Safety is the primary goal. You can always replace wood, concrete, brick, laminate or hardware. But there are only two eyes and two hands per customer. You, as a home craftsman, are not in the same boat as many pros whose living depends upon very quick completion of a job. Look at DIY work as something you want to do, or must do, in the safest manner to achieve the most pleasing results and not as a "race for the lifeboat."

Safety Tips

As the posters say, "Safety is no accident." You should always wear eye protection (goggles or full face mask) when using power tools or striking tools, and wear a dust mask when sanding or a special filtration respirator when spraying. Wear high galoshes or rubber boots, eye protection and gloves when working with concrete because it's very caustic and can burn you badly.

For exterior work, if you have to work in a high awkward or dangerous position where a ladder won't do the job, take the time to build a safe scaffold. Incidentally, scaffolds and similar devices can be rented. This includes pump jacks, kickers and mason's X-braced steel scaffolding. You no doubt have seen masons working from scaffolding and siders using pump jacks and kickers (flat, narrow platforms that rest on the pump jack arms). The pump jacks are typically used in pairs, each mounted on a double pair of 2×4s spiked together.

When using machines such as table saws, jointers, bandsaws and drill presses, always wear eye protection. In addition, use hold-downs, fences, push sticks and guides with the saws, and remember to remove the chuck key from the drill press before starting it (the same goes for drills). Also with drill presses as well as electric drills, you should understand the effect of torque when drilling small objects. The bit can catch in the workpiece, causing it to spin suddenly and violently in a clockwise rotation and injure you. Prevent this by using vises, hold-downs and stopblocks as each case dictates.

Most safety information is given in the instructions or owner's manual packaged with the tool, and it is very important that you read it and become familiar with the tool before using it. The information will include the electrical safety precautions and advice about voltage drops over large power cord distances.

Machine tools or stationary tools usually have provisions for controlling, guiding and holding down the workpiece, or the manufacturer will sell optional accessories for these purposes. In many cases, however, with some experience and common sense, you can make your own in the shop for very little cost and in almost no time.

The portable power tool, on the other hand, is a bit different. Many operations can be controlled by eye and hand coordination, as during the day of the handcraftsman in Colonial America. But, as fascinating as that might appear, it is much safer and certainly more accurate to operate the portable power tool with minimum dependence upon the hand and eye. The ideal in many cases is for the hand merely to supply the feeding power to bring the tools to the work. (This is the opposite of working with stationary tools, where the work is brought to the machine.)

For example, if you've seen house sheathers at work, you know they measure out a shape on a piece of plywood, snap a chalk line and follow the line with the portable saw. The smarter move for the DIY craftsman is to use a guide such as the straight edge of a long, narrow piece of plywood, which acts as a fence against the saw base edge. The fence can be nailed or clamped in place. An alternative is to buy one of the inexpensive, commercially available sawing guides, some of which come with their own clamps.

Another common example is using trammels or edge guides, which constrain routers or jigsaw, to execute circles or cuts parallel to the edge of the workpiece, respectively. The drill guide is fairly new and was developed for use with the portable drill. It allows you to drill into a workpiece at any chosen angle, including the perpendicular, and provides drill depth-stopping as well.

Portable Saw Safety

Most of DIY work is with wood or wood products, and an ever-present part of woodworking involves sawing. Therefore, safe, accurate and efficient use of saws, especially the portable circular saw, has to be a high-priority item.

If you're working in a cabinet shop atmosphere, the use of the portable saw is either limited or nonexistent, but in all probability, this won't be the case for the average home craftsman. Safety is a big factor when working with a portable saw, as it is with any tools. By using common sense, intelligence and proper technique, injury can be avoided. No one writing in a book or teaching in a school or showing by example in a workplace can cover every

situation one encounters when using a portable saw. But, by showing the principles involved, one can try to keep others from injury and help improve their craft skills.

First of all, portable circular saws are manufactured in a variety of sizes, rated by blade diameter. They are also made in a fairly wide power range in two styles: direct and worm drive. All standard saws have a base or platen that can be adjusted to control the depth of cut by exposing more or less blade as well as the angle of the base for bevel cutting. All have a fixed upper blade guard and a spring-loaded, automatic-closing lower guard. Some have one handle with an enclosed trigger, but more and more are equipped with two handles, with the trigger enclosed in the rear one. All woodworking blades for these saws, regardless of tooth style or material, rotate so as to emerge out of the workpiece near the leading edge of the saw at the base level.

Standard accessories for these saws are edge guides (which I've rarely used in my experience) and a choice of blades ranging from high-speed steel with chisel teeth to 40-tooth carbide-tip types with alternate tooth bevel design. There are other special-purpose blades that are used for masonry, but these are not applicable to the things covered in this book.

The choice of saw and blade can be made on the basis of the work being done. For instance, there are small (5½″ blade diameter), lightweight saws, designed for use on modular, interior wall panels or other ¼″-thick wood products. This saw can be equipped with a standard general-purpose blade, a fine-tooth veneer blade or a carbide-tip blade.

Then, on the other end of the spectrum, there's the standard middle-level (7¼″ blade diameter) worm drive, a two-handled brute that won't take no for an answer. It's an industrial-level saw, designed for full-time use on construction grade materials. Due to the weight, most carpenters or framers use it on ground level.

Somewhere in the middle is the standard workhorse portable circular saw. It's a relatively lightweight, general-purpose saw with a 6½″-diameter blade, which professional carpenters or framers use above ground level.

In addition to the electrical caveats in the instructions or owner's manual, there are a number of mechanical items that must be checked before using the saw. For example, the blade must be inspected to be sure that it is sharp, has no teeth missing and is not warped. The blade should be tight on the shaft and correctly oriented so that the teeth face up at the forward end of the saw at the base level.

Whatever depth of cut or bevel angle has been chosen, the adjustment locks must be tight. The lower guard must be free to snap closed. If it's not, disconnect the power and correct the problem.

When the saw is in use, the blade cuts a path for itself in the workpiece. This is called a kerf. Should this path be cramped or closed, the motor will continue to try and turn the blade, but the blade can't move at the point of contact

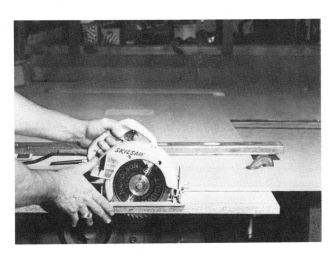

Here a portable saw is cutting off a piece of particleboard, guided by a plywood straightedge clamped to the workpiece. Eye protection is a must.

A light workpiece such as this should be controlled while sawing.

A very powerful worm-drive portable saw makes the second cut in a rafter bird's-mouth. The first angle cut required the lower guard (black handle) raised to start.

If you clamp a portable circular saw in this, you can safely cut through 1×12 boards as shown or up to 2×12s. With this setup you can make miter, bevel or combination cuts. It will do miters, bevels or combinations. It can be used with a router as well.

A supported plywood panel is ripped, using an aluminum guide. It's good up to 8′, has its own clamps in extruded tracks and can be used with routers or jigsaws, too.

You can also clamp your portable circular saw into a saw guide and rip long panels with cuts up to 24″ wide accurately. Its fence rides the outer panel edge.

with the workpiece. This is called kickback—it's the saw's reaction to motor torque and a locked blade in a tight or closed kerf. This is a very dangerous condition and can cause serious injury.

Try to crosscut construction lumber, boards or planks so that the waste or desired-length piece will fall off the end past the support, horse or table. Never support a piece of lumber or similar material at two points that are so far out from the blade on either side that when you cut in the middle, the weight of the saw and the workpiece causes the middle to drop and close the kerf. If you ever watch professional carpenters, careful observation will show that they lift the workpiece slightly with their free hand to raise the area of the cut and keep the kerf open.

Note that when making a 90° crosscut, the lower guard will contact the workpiece and automatically rotate out of the way to clear it. However, when cutting miters and certain bevels, the lower guard must be manually rotated by lifting its handle, allowing it to get a purchase on the workpiece. At that time, the lower guard handle can be released. This situation also might occur when the workpiece has been cut just a bit oversize, which requires only a sliver to be removed from the end. The procedure is the same as for a miter.

Other ways to crosscut lumber include using a radial saw or a sawing aid. One sawing aid has an adjustable, lockable protractor table that supports a portable saw carriage. For crosscutting long workpieces, the device should be set up with a table on either side, something like a radial saw setup. The lumber or board is then set under the carriage, and the depth of cut and bevel angle, if required, is adjusted on the saw. Any desired miter angle can be set on the protractor. This saw aid can also hold a router.

If you're rough-cutting plywood, take a tip from the sheather's book and stack all your rough plywood on supports. Then set the depth of cut for just a tiny bit more than the thickness of the plywood and make the freehand or guided cut. If you don't have a stack of plywood, set up support for the plywood with horses and 2×4s. Crosscutting 4'×8' plywood pieces can be safely done by using parallel supports under both sides of the cut and under the outboard ends as well. This method can be used either freehand or guided.

Ripping long cuts on plywood, such as a 1×8 piece, can be done with parallel supports. The cut can be made freehand or guided as the work requires.

A guide can be a simple, straight-edged plywood fence clamped to the workpiece or a commercially available, lightweight straightedge with its own clamps, as mentioned above. There's another way. Your saw can be clamped quickly into another type of sawing aid that can rip a piece from the workpiece varying in width from almost nothing to 24". This lightweight, relatively inexpensive device has a fence that rides the edge of the workpiece and an adjustable width carriage for the saw.

Just set the depth of cut and bevel angle, if desired, and perform the cut. This is an extremely safe way of getting the job done.

Sawhorse and Bench Supports

Supporting the work is a basic requirement, whether assembling or performing operations such as sawing, drilling, routing, sanding, gluing or fastening. If your working space is limited or you must move between different areas, you'll want a support that is strong, yet light and portable. The simplest type of support is the sawhorse.

Sawhorses can support work directly, or the space between them can be spanned with lumber. If a table is needed, a cull door can be laid directly over the horses, or if more strength is required, the door can be used on top of lumber already laid flat over the horses. Even more strength can be built into the door by nailing lumber to the door edges with lumber on edge instead of flat.

A horse can be a length of 2×4 that fits into clampable metal legs. It can be assembled from four 2×4 legs, a 2×4

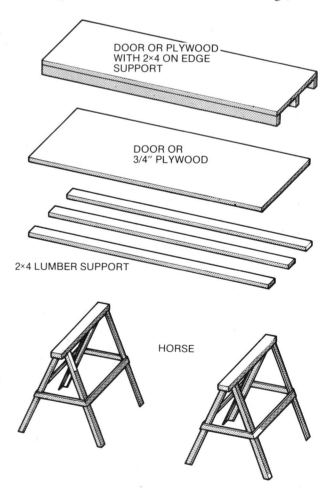

DOOR OR PLYWOOD WITH 2×4 ON EDGE SUPPORT

DOOR OR 3/4" PLYWOOD

2×4 LUMBER SUPPORT

HORSE

This is a simple work surface resting on horses. (1) The basic table support is 2×4s. (2) A door can rest on these. (3) For heavier loads, use the setup where the 2×4s are placed on edge and nailed to the door to limit sagging or deflection in the center.

A, B, C, D AT RIGHT ANGLES
TO SUB-SUPPORTS, BENCHES,
OR HOSES (E, F)

WORKPIECE

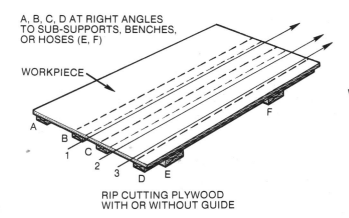

RIP CUTTING PLYWOOD
WITH OR WITHOUT GUIDE

RIPPING CUT BLADE 1 PATH BETWEEN SUPPORTS B, C MADE
WITH SUPPORTS A, B, C, D.

RIPPING CUT BLADE 2 PATH CAN BE MADE WITH SUPPORTS
A, B, C BUT WITHOUT D.

RIPPING CUT BLADE 3 PATH CAN BE MADE WITHOUT
SUPPORT D, BUT WITH SUPPORTS A, B, C MOVED OVER JUST
TO THE LEFT OF PATH.

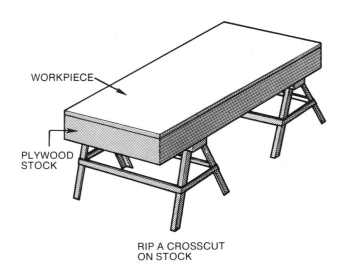

WORKPIECE

PLYWOOD
STOCK

RIP A CROSSCUT
ON STOCK

BOTH RIP AND CROSSCUTS CAN BE MADE ON WORKPIECE IN
THIS CONFIGURATION.

SAW

BLADE SET TO
CUT WORKPIECE
THICKNESS

A setup for supporting large panels for ripping (top). The horses
(E,F) support four longitudinal 2×4s (A-D). The stack method
(bottom) for ripping or crosscutting, where the stack is supported on horses.

A, B, C, D WORKPIECE SUPPORTS
E, F SUB-SUPPORT ON HORSES.

WORKPIECE

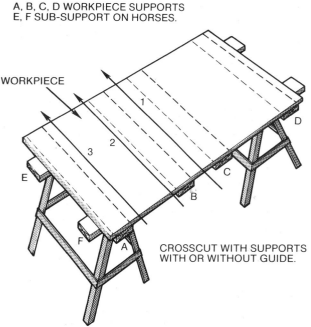

CROSSCUT WITH SUPPORTS
WITH OR WITHOUT GUIDE.

CROSSCUT BLADE 1 PATH BETWEEN B, C WITH SUPPORTS
A, B, C, D.

CROSSCUT BLADE 2 PATH CAN BE MADE WITH B, C, D AND
WITHOUT A.

CROSSCUT BLADE 3 PATH CAN BE MADE WITH SUPPORTS
C, D AND B MOVED JUST TO RIGHT OF BLADE PATH.

A setup for crosscutting large panels. Here the longitudinal 2×4
supports (E,F) span the distance between the horses, and the
transverse 2×4 supports (A–D) rest on rop of those.

stretcher and a pair of connecting units. Lightweight
horses that require you to assemble a 2×4 stretcher to
metal legs and braces are available commercially. These
can fold flat for transportation or storage and are strong
enough for your average job.

Horses can be built from 2×4 legs and a stretcher with
plywood gussets and board bracing to add rigidity. When
you want more from a support, such as a built-in trough
to hold small tools or hardware, build a small bench. You
see many "quick and dirty" benches built on the spot at
any construction site, but most of these are used to support work for sawing or as a stool. Very few have storage.
Of course there's a trade-off. With the bench type, you
gain a tool holder but you lose portability.

Another alternative work support is a group of commercially available devices, all of which can be closed or
folded for easy storage and transportation. They all have
an articulated, dual-handle vice that can hold workpieces
upright or flat and handle both rectangular and irregular
shapes using either the vice's jaws or a dog-and-hole
system. These units have a flat top surface and some have
tool storage space below. Some are free-standing while
others are bench-mounted.

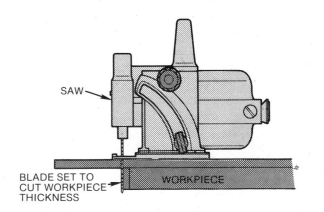

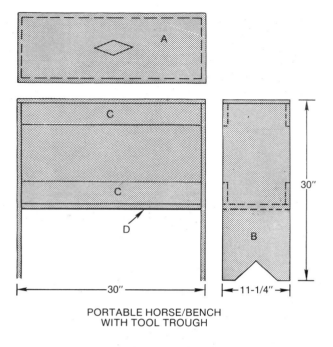

PORTABLE HORSE/BENCH
WITH TOOL TROUGH

Point	Quantity	Dimension
A	1	1×12*×30
B	2	1×12*×29-1/4
C	4	1×4**×28-1/2
D	1	1×12*×28-1/2

*1×12 Nom = 3/4×11-1/4″
**1×4 Nom = 3/4×3-1/2″

Materials

(1) 1′×12′×10′
(1) 1′×4′×10′

A bench/horse with tool tray.

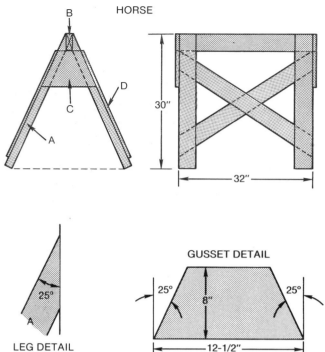

A simple horse.

Point	Quantity	Dimension	Material
A	4	2″×4*×32-1/2″	Fir
B	1	2″×4*×32″	Fir
C	2	1/2″×8″×12-1/2	Plywood CDX
D	2	1″×4**×40″	Spruce

*2×4 Nom = 1-1/2×3-1/2″
**1×4 Nom = 3/4×3-1/2″

Materials

(1) 2′×4′×14′ D/Fir
(1) 1′×4′×7′ Spruce
(1) 1/2″×8″×26″ Plywood CDX

Benchtop Power Tools

Many benchtop, down-sized or three-quarter size power tools are on the market today. One of the main reasons they are available is many manufacturers believe residential storage space is at a premium; that is, many homes are built without basements or garages; consequently, the size of the home shop is reduced—to the size of a closet in some cases.

The most common benchtop power tools are probably the bandsaw and drill press. They can't handle all of the jobs that a full-size press or bandsaw can, but they can make your life easier when used in the right situation. And besides, what's so bad about a power tool that can be stuck under the bench, out of harm's way, when not in use?

My first pleasant experience with a benchtop bandsaw was during the installation of a hardwood parquet tile floor. I had worked out the dimensions and layout of the tiles to balance them on both the long and short walls. This meant that a whole bunch of tiles had to be sawn to fit the perimeter, so I hauled out my little bandsaw. This was easy because of its minimal weight. Then, its real advantage showed up. It whizzed through those tiles almost faster than I could mark them.

This saw is also quite useful for hobbies, home maintenance and modest-size wood projects. Its features include a 10″ capacity, power safety interlock, tilting table, miter gauge, adjustable tension, variable speed and the ability to cut wood, metal and plastic.

In addition to variable speed control, the drill press also has an electric interlock for safety, a 2″ vertical quill movement, a 7½"×10½" slotted table, large knob head lock, double-knurled quill depth lock and a 15 drill index from 1/16" to ½" by 1/32" increments. The three-armed quill crank can be removed for storage. The interlock safety feature requires that the chuck key be removed from the chuck and inserted into the head to provide power.

This ½", variable speed, benchtop drill press has a safety chuck key interlock, drill index, speed vs. material guide, three-arm quill crank and a slotted table. It can be stored in approximately a square foot area.

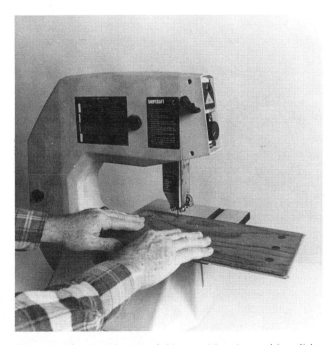

There also is a benchtop variable speed bandsaw with a tilting table, miter gauge, adjustable tension for the blade and adjustable guides. It's a good alternative to the jig or portable circular saw for cutting strip or parquet flooring quickly and safely.

Lay out the disc or wheel with compasses and make a pronounced center mark.

Cut the circle shape on the bandsaw leaving a slight overage from the line.

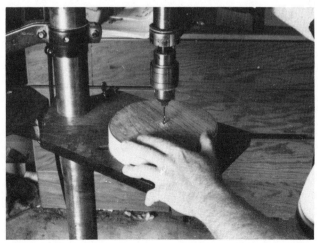

On the drill press, or with a portable drill with guide, drill a 3/32"–⅛" diameter center hole completely through the workpiece.

Tap a nail through the center hole into a plywood scrap. Clamp one end of the plywood to a disc or belt sander (shown). Gradually move the other end of the plywood toward the sander as you rotate the wheel.

Plug cutter chucked in a drill press or in a portable drill with guide will make a short "dowel" or a plug. Hold-down prevents sudden spinning.

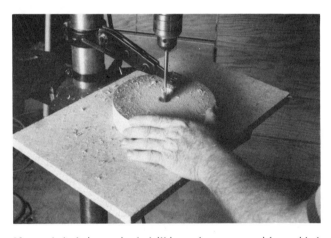

If an axle hole is required, drill it on the press or with a guided portable drill.

Forstner or bradpoint drill with plug diameter makes a blind hole in the main workpiece. Then the point hole can center a combination bit for the screw.

To machine radii on the edges, set up the router with a ball bearing-guided rounding-over bit in a router table. Slowly rotate the wheel against the bearing. These safety glasses are not as good as goggles or a face mask.

The plug can be glued into the hole after the screw is driven. When dry, the plug can be sawn close to flush and sanded.

Portable Power Tools

As noted before, the jigsaw and drill are the tools owned by most DIYers. However, there are a number of other portable power tools available for the home craftsman's use. This section will look at some of the most common and widely used portable power tools.

Bandsaws and Jigsaws

Both bandsaws and jigsaws have narrow blades for cutting curves, irregular shapes and fairly tight radii. Actually, the principle is that the more narrow the blade, the tighter the radius that can be handled. A comparison between a bandsaw and jigsaw shows the following:

- The jigsaw requires an up-and-down (reciprocating) motion to complete each cutting stroke, whereas the bandsaw is on a continuous loop with what might be called a 100% duty cycle.
- The bandsaw cuts through the work with its teeth facing downward, while the jigsaw cuts through the work on the upstroke.
- The jigsaw can pierce the work to create its own start or can be started in a drilled hole to complete a pocket cut (that is, to cut the waste out of the inside of a rectangle or curved shape without cutting through the perimeter). The bandsaw cannot generally do this, although some very expensive ones are equipped to cut the blade and later spot-weld and grind it after it has been started in a drilled hole in the workpiece.
- The work is brought to and fed into the blade of a bandsaw, while the jigsaw is brought to the work.
- The jigsaw can be set up with a trammel to perform an accurate circular cut from a center. To do this on a bandsaw, you must clamp a scrap board to the table and establish a pilot, such as a nail, through the center of the workpiece and fixed in the scrap.

Rotate the platen, set the edge guide and make a 45° bevel rip on this plywood piece. The saw has orbital blade control for speed or extra-smooth cuts. It can start its own hole or make circles with guide (trammel) and center point.

- Depth of cut is limited on the bandsaw to the horizontal distance between the vertical post and blade path, whereas there is no limit on a jigsaw.
- The base of the jigsaw can be adjusted and locked to perform bevel cuts. This is done on the bandsaw by tilting the table.
- Many bandsaws can be set up as narrow belt sanders by installing an accessory platen and belt. There is no equivalent to this on the jigsaw.
- The jigsaw has an edge guide accessory to cut parallel to a workpiece edge. A bandsaw can do this with fences and/or miter gauges.
- Both saws can cut through a variety of materials by the selective use of special blades.
- Some benchtop bandsaws have continuous speed ranges, while larger ones have discreet speeds, based on belt and pulley arrangements. Some jigsaws are single-speed, while others have discreet speeds or continuous speed ranges.

Portable Drills and Drill Presses

Most modern portable drills are ⅜″ chuck size instead of the traditional ¼″ size that was preferred so much by home craftsmen in the past. This is due not only to price considerations, but also to the varied accessories for drills, some of which put a heavy electrical load on the tools. These would include hole saws, angle drives and carbide-tip masonry bits. Another effect of working with more powerful, higher torque drills is the introduction of stabilizing handles to control the torque reactions should the bit jam in the hole. In many cases, it is just not possible to keep a firm grip on the drill with one hand on the pistol or "D" handle and the other hand on the body of the drill. The larger the drill, the more of a consideration this becomes. If possible, especially when using ½″ chuck drills, try and brace the stabilizing handle or extension pipe against a fixed object so the drill can't spin suddenly and injure you.

The development of the drill guide has also given a boost to portable drill applications. This accessory attaches to a drill and allows the user to control both the angle and depth of the hole being made. It can be used with twist drill bits, spade bits, brad-point bits, forstner bits, plug cutters and hole saws up to 2⅛″ diameter. For example, this allows the guided drilling of lock cylinders and crossbore holes for setback latch bolts. With a plug cutter and a matching size piloted bit, you can counterbore a perfect hole in a wood surface over a screw clearance hole, drive the assembly screw home and hide the screw with a wood plug of the same or contrasting wood species.

Among the numerous tasks a drill can perform with accessories are angle drilling to get the drill bit into a confined space with a right angle attachement. A rubber disc can be chucked into the drill and will support a buffer or a sanding disc. This is particularly useful for cleaning the perimeter of a hardwood floor that can't be reached with the large sander. There are paint-stirring attachments as well as mixing paddles for drywall compound, tile mortar and wallcovering adhesive. Then, for various edge sandings, there are circular rasps and sanders to speed the work and wire brushes for metal cleaning.

A comparison of a portable drill with a drill press reveals the following:

- Both will drill holes with numerous bits, but the press will handle a wider variety of bits as well as larger sizes.
- The speed controls are discreet on the full-size presses and continuous on benchtop presses and portable drills.
- To drill at an angle, you must hold the portable drill at the desired angle with or without a drill guide (you get much more accuracy with a drill guide); with a press you tilt the table and check the angle with a protractor, if other than standard detent angles are chosen.
- The work can be held in several vise types that can be bolted to the table of a drill press. This is much tougher to do using a drill unless you make special jigs or fixtures.
- You can add a mortising accessory (yoke, hollow chisel and drill) to most full-size drill presses and hold the workpiece in a special clamp or vise on the table. This is not possible with a drill.
- You can use a drill press chuck to hold work for sanding or filing, while a sanding disc must be chucked into the portable drill and then addressed to the work.
- Special bits such as fly cutters can be used safely on the full-size drill press to cut out large holes. This is not an acceptable operation with a portable drill.
- It is pretty simple to jig up a baluster, cylinder or spindle on the full-size drill press with the table offset to the side of the quill travel. Then the spindle end can be either drilled out with a bit or round-tenoned with a plug cutter. This could be done with a portable drill, but a vise would be needed to hold the work and, without a special jig, true axial alignment would not be possible.
- You bring the work to the drill press, but you bring the portable drill to the work.

This is only a partial list of the major differences and similarities in the drills.

Reciprocating Saws

The reciprocating saw is a portable saw designed for two-handed operation on either wood or metal under typically rough or field conditions. It usually has two speeds (one for wood; one for metal) and accepts blades either 6″ or 12″ long that can pierce wood given an angled start. All reciprocating saws, such as jigsaws, require two oppositely directed motions of the blade for one cycle, with the cutting done on the backstroke.

The jigsaw's base sits flat on the workpiece, whereas the reciprocating saw has no base, only an articulating slipper at the front end where the blade enters the body. This is used to brace against the work. The reciprocating saw blade is in line with the body of the tool so that it can be "stuck" into awkward construction spots and saw out waste from areas almost no other tool could reach. For example, the saw is used to cut clearance holes for pipes, cables and ducts and is highly favored by plumbing, heating and electrical professionals. If you plan on building additions to your home, you might want to rent or buy this lifesaver.

Power Planers and Jointer/Planers

The portable version of the reciprocating saw is the power planer, while the stationary tool is the jointer/planer. They do some of the same jobs, but not all. The portable power planer will surface a face up to 3½″ wide and therefore is good for 1×4 boards or 2×4 lumber. Jointer/planers come in 4″, 6″, 8″ and greater widths with the combined length of the front and rear tables increasing with the width of the blade. Both the portable and stationary machines are operated by a number of razor-sharp blades mounted on a cylinder rotating at high speed, passing over a wood edge or surface. The jointer/planer has a movable, tiltable fence, whereas the power planer has a rabbet shoe, edge guide and bevel edge guide. The jointer/planer increases the depth of cut by lowering the rear table, but the power planer does this by raising the front shoe.

There are commercial users among the pros. For example, you'll find these power planers owned and operated by trimmers and carpenters who hang exterior doors and by carpenters or installers who put in overhead garage doors. The planer is especially useful in fitting exterior door edges to jambs and applying the 5° bevel to the door edge. In hanging double doors it's virtually a necessity. The power planer can most easily fit the bottom edge of the bottom garage door section to the concrete floor and make the top edge of the bottom section set level.

Probably the greatest number of jointer/planers would be found in cabinet shops where they are an integral part of the work. This is because the typical cabinetmaker must start with S2S (surfaced two sides) hardwood and make straight pieces out of some pretty weird-looking stuff. Mostly, he runs the wood on one edge through a large jointer to provide a clean and straight surface to ride against the table saw fence. Upon completing a sawing operation, which is made slightly oversize, he joints the second side and now has an S4S piece of the required size.

A comparison of the power planer and jointer/planer shows the following:

- The power planer is brought up to and over the work, while the work is brought up to and over the surface of the jointer/planer.
- You can bevel and edge with either machine.
- You can plane the surface of a workpiece as wide as

the jointer/planer, but with some skill you can plane a larger surface with the power planer.

• You can joint (true and clean up an edge either for gluing to another jointed edge or dress it as a rail or stile after sawing) an edge with either machine.
• You can do shallow rabbets with a power planer. You cannot do this with most modern jointer/planers because the guard must be removed and the manufacturers consider this unsafe (rightly so).
• You can chamfer (flatten or smooth off a corner) with both machines.
• You can bevel edges with both machines.
• You can perform accurate tapers on a jointer/planer, using stop blocks clamped to the rear table. You

The power planer can take down a door edge or trim the bottom section of an overhead garage door virtually in less time than it takes you to read about it here. Power planes with 3½″ or wider blades can be used to reduce the thickness of boards or lumber up to 4″.

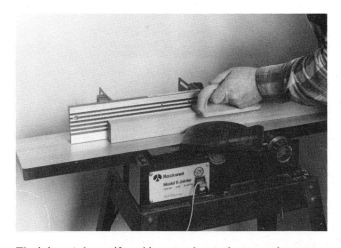

The jointer/planer, if used incorrectly, can be a very dangerous tool, so follow the manufacturer's warnings about never removing guards, never working short pieces, always using pushers (shown here for jointing) or similar devices with thin or narrow stock...and a lot more. But, for cabinet or furniture work it's an indispensable tool that can smooth out or joint rough edges, plane surfaces and taper.

might do tapers with the power planer, but they would have to be done by eye.

• Octagons and hexagons can be cut on the jointer/planer with the fence tilted at 30° or 45°. This could only be approximated with the power planer, unless you made an indexing jig to rotate the workpiece in 45° and 60° increments.

Routers

The router is one of the most versatile tools you can buy. With it you can bead edges, emboss surfaces, cove, rabbet, dado, decorate, make signs with the aid of a pantograph, trim laminates, shape moldings, make dovetail drawers with a bushing and dovetail pattern, mortise for hinges in jambs and door edges with guide bushing and template, do small shaping jobs with the router inverted in a table, follow male and female patterns to shape a workpiece, make concentric circles with a trammel, make sunken surface trays or tables with trammels, make picture frames,...the list is almost endless.

All this comes about by mounting what might be called an ultra high-speed chisel in a base, which allows depth control for the tool bit, accepts accessory items such as straightedge guides, irregular edge guides, trammels and special base plates.

Tool bits are quite varied, too. They come in high-speed steel or carbide tip, with or without pilots, some with roller-bearing pilots. Standard tool bit shapes include straight, ogee, core box, rounding over, surfacing, veining and a number of decorative shapes. There are special bits to trim laminates as well as bits and arbors that make slots for plastic trim or glass retainers.

The business end of the router is a locknut and shaft collet used to hold the bits in place when locked with a wrench against the shaft detent. Routers are rated by shaft size and power; a ¼″ shaft router with a 6″-diameter base is the most popular. Routers with a ½″ shaft, several large bases and horsepower are found in industry, where the tool is expected to run all day.

When the router is spinning a pilotless bit, position of the machining depends entirely on guides or bushings attached to the base, but when using a roller-bearing pilot on the bit, this bearing can serve as a guide against an edge. In the dovetail template, a bushing attached to the base follows the fingerlike contour of the template or pattern and executes the pins and tails on the workpieces.

To trim plastic laminate, I have found the best bit to be solid carbide. This is a compound bit, with both straight and bevel profiles. Which one is in play at the moment depends on the depth of the bit relative to the work edge. As with all other router applications, the depth is controlled by the lands on the motor section threading up or down in the grooves of the base section. This depth control is indexed and lockable so you have total control.

The final quality of work being routed is highly dependent upon feed and speed. The speed is the rotation

The basic router shown with its collet nut lock wrench and an assortment of bits, arbors and bearings including from the left: (1) bevel laminate trimmer; (2) dovetail; (3) straight; (4) rounding-over; (5) cove; (6) surfacing; (7) ogee; (8) hinge mortising; (9) combination panel cutter; (10) combination v-groove and chamfering cutter.

If you substitute longer ¼″ diameter rods, the circles can become quite large as shown here cutting an arc in a substrate for a modern table leg/support.

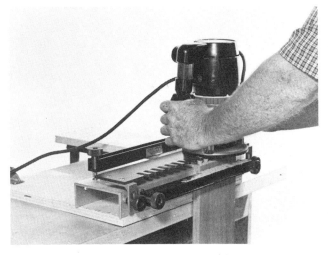

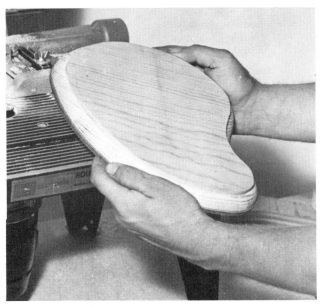

Dovetailing for drawers is done with a dovetail bit, guide bushing and dovetail template. Two mating pieces are done at one cutting, using this device.

The rounded-over shaped edge results can be seen by inverting the workpiece.

The results are not only striking but form really strong joints.

per minute made by the tool bit (usually 18,000 to 20,000 revolutions per minute). The feed is how rapidly the tool bit is moved (fed) into the work. This is a matter of feel, which must be developed with some practice runs. You can burn or ruin the work or dull the tool by moving either too slowly or too fast. Never allow the tool to sit in one position spinning wildly. The direction of feed must be such that the work is always on the left of the tool as the tool is moving to the right, as viewed from above. Failure to observe this direction can cause the tool bit to splinter or chunk out an edge.

Always use tool bits that are razor sharp. If you don't, you'll get heat problems, dull the tool bit further (and possibly ruin it) and scorch or foul the work. To avoid this keep a small combination shape bevel and straight stone handy to dress the tool bit before starting.

Sanders

Whether you're working on cabinet face frames, panel doors, plain hardwood surfaces or shelving, you can't avoid sanding if you want to do a first-class job. The power sander is the answer for the job. If you don't think so, try knocking out a project by hand-sanding.

Sanders can be either portable or stationary. A few portables can be mounted on a bench like a stationary tool. Most of the stationary sanders are large belt or disc types. Various sizes of drum sanding attachments that fit a portable drill can also be chucked in a drill press for smoothing and cleaning up the edges of curved pieces that have just been jigsawed, coped or bandsawed.

There are special multiple-strip sanding attachments that come mounted on a thick disc and integral mandrel with springlike backing and adjustment for winding out more abrasive strip. These devices may be used on radial saws, drill presses or some larger drills. Some grinders have optional sanding disc ends, and there are a few narrow belt tools such as the sander/grinder or bandsaw that can be converted for the task. These last two are more properly thought of as benchtop tools.

On the portable side, for limited applications there's the disc attachment for the portable drill, as mentioned. But the major tools in this area are the belt and pad sanders. For roughing down a surface that has been glue-assembled from a number of small pieces, such as a butcher's block, you could use fore and jointer planes. But that's truly time-consuming and can be done more efficiently with belt sanders whose width and length suit the size of the work surface. Note that belt sanders are rated by belt size as well as power—for example, 3″×21″ or 4″×24″.

Obviously, for large surfaces you want the widest belt. But what about the length? The way to look at this is like a ship of a given length in a sea with waves. The ideal case for a smooth sail would be the longest possible length at the waterline, relative to the peak-to-peak wave length. The same is true for sanding large surfaces without creating troughs and waves. But what is the longest flat part of a sander? This is not necessarily a function of the belt length, but of the flat platen area behind the belt. Therefore, when buying a belt sander, look at the bottom of it without a belt in place to see how long the flat platen is. It's possible to level a large area with a short platen sander, but you must be an expert because it's a tricky task.

The belt grit is also important. For rough work, use 50- to 80-grit belts. Leveling a large surface is best done by making broad, sweeping arcs with the sander in the beginning, constantly checking with a metal straightedge. Never allow the sander to stay in one place. Always keep it moving. The straightedge should be positioned again in a number of random directions to get an overall view of the high and low spots. Then, when the gross corrections have been made, make another straightedge check and continue sanding, but from this point on, sand with the grain.

Make sure any cross-grain sanding marks are gone and continue down to 100- to 120-grit belts.

Once a level surface has been established, the worst is over. From here, it's a matter of working the level surface smooth. This is done with one or more pad sanders, which are designed to execute rapid orbital motion with either a half- or quarter-size sheet. The pad or orbital sander should be moved over the surface with a circular motion, with finer and finer abrasive sheets until the desired finish is reached. Precut aluminum oxide open coat (nonloading) sheets can be purchased for these sanders in grits ranging from 40 to 150 for half-sheet sanders or 60 to 220 for quarter-sheet models. You may, at your option, cut your own to size from full sheets.

Some sanding jobs can be efficiently done with either hand or power sanding, including breaking corners (sanding a tiny radius on a sharp corner for easier handling and better finishing), sanding the profiles left by machine processes, such as routing or shaping, and sanding the corners of veneered pieces.

Other jobs such as cabinet face frame surface and edge work, cleaning the combined edges of a substrate with laminate in preparation for the laminate application on the adjacent edge and cabinet or casework shelving are best left to power sanders.

Table Saws

To my way of thinking, which is colored by having done a fair amount of cabinet and casework, the table saw is the mainstay of the home shop. It's true that a lot of radial saws are sold, and they surely have their place. They are really efficient when cutoffs, repeat shelf dadoes or planing bevel edges for a raised panel are required, but radial saws are not meant for accurate ripping operations. A table saw is. Cutting cabinet rails, stiles or door blanks, ripping out sides, backs or shelves all come naturally to this saw. So do vertical dadoes for sinking pilasters or joining pieces, as well as rabbeting.

The table saw's basic controls are blade height and bevel angle, along with the rip fence, which can be moved toward or away from the blade and locked at any position along its supporting rails. Its safety feature is a combination plastic blade guardsplitter (which keeps the kerf open) on the output side of the blade, and the antikickback pawls on the infeed side of the blade. Kickback is most likely to occur when a workpiece gets pinched between the blade and the fence; the speed and direction of the blade portion above the table insert can propel the workpiece backward toward the operator.

The essential accessory for performing miters and other crosscuts is the miter gauge, which is supplied with the table saw. The miter gauge can be equipped with extensions and hold-downs to extend its capabilities. Tapers can be sawn on short pieces by means of a taper jig, whose taper is marked in inches, feet and degrees. Special-purpose miters are available for 45° work. These miters have clamps and stops to handle repetitive work safely.

Any number of special-purpose jigs can be shopmade quite easily to get full control over specific operations. Among these are a miter or V-jig with a base equipped with runners to ride in the miter gauge grooves, making it independent of the rip fence. There are a number of rip fence-riding jigs to help you make tenons or shape discs and multiple hold-downs that attach to the rip fence via an auxiliary fence. There are also auxiliary fences, which bolt to the rip fence and allow rabbeting or molding. For molding thin stock, there are simple rabbeted hold-downs that trap the workpiece between their rabbets and an auxiliary fence bolted to the rip fence. You can make a jig in minutes that will index stock for box or fingerlap joints.

In fact, there's virtually no end to the sawing jigs you can design and put together with a few pennies' worth of wood and hardware. Wood-sprung hold-downs are another example of what can be designed. The whole idea is to take the control of the workpiece from the hand/eye coordination area and trap or constrain the piece to move along a single path to be machined. This procedure limits the operator's role to providing straight ahead feed, with push sticks or whatever is applicable, as well as a virtually risk-free environment.

Much of the versatility of a table saw depends upon what's spinning around on the shaft. Table saws can be equipped with steel discs, which can accept sanding discs with a form of mastic or they can take a plethora of high-speed steel blades, ranging from general rip to general crosscut, or a veneer blade, a general-purpose

Here's how this dado looks, installed in the saw with the dado insert removed. Adjustment takes only seconds. Note that this extreme height is only for adjustment.

Hold-downs should control the workpiece totally when using molding cutters. The high auxiliary wood fence keeps the workpiece upright, while high-riding featherboards keep the workpiece against the auxiliary fence. The operator's only job is to advance the workpiece. You can see the edge shape on the output end.

A test performed on plywood held in the miter gauge hold-down proved the dado to be a clean cutter.

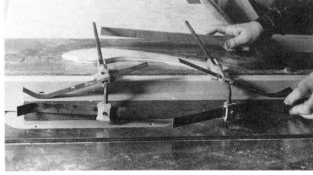

When grooving or molding (on the wood auxiliary fence edge) low and fairly narrow workpieces, use commercially available spring-type hold-downs. These hold-downs attach to the wood auxiliary fence and the rip fence, too. They can be adjusted vertically, laterally and along the infeed line.

combination or a special thin kerf blade. Their carbide-tipped cousins also run the gamut from straight rip to straight crosscut, with a combination general-purpose blade in between.

For getting a contoured edge on the work, there's a molding head that accepts a variety of cutters in groups of three. You can do amazing things with these cutters by changing the height or bevel angle of the blade or by varying permutations in the lateral position of the workpiece. This involves some planning on paper, because to try to figure combinations of shapes on the spot can boggle the mind.

Rabbets can be made in a variety of ways on the table saw. One way is to make two perpendicular single-blade cuts; another way is to make successive, adjacent single-blade cuts combined with appropriate rip fence adjust-ments to free the waste. A third way is to use square top molding cutters, while a fourth way is to use a dado blade. If the rabbet is made on the edge of the workpiece away from the rip fence, no auxiliary wood fence is required; but if the rabbet is made on the rip fence side, an auxiliary wood fence is required to allow the blade to be raised safely.

Dado blades are designed to plough out troughs of selected widths and depths. To do this, dado blades were originally (and still are) in packs with the outer blades outlining the cut width limits and the inner, chipper blades hogging out the main waste.

The wobble blade was developed after the dado blade. This blade allows the operator to change the width of the cut by temporarily loosening the shaft locknut and rotating the hub; this pitches the single blade at a different

Note the use of the high, wood auxiliary fence and the high-riding double featherboards to control the raised panel. The blade is angled to the desired bevel and depth of cut. Then the operator need only advance the workpiece (mahogany shown).

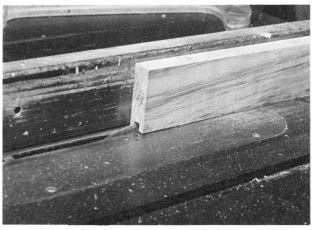

To make the stiles, joint the wood edges, rip the pieces slightly oversize and joint those edges smooth. Then, machine dadoes (grooves) on the inner edges. No hold-downs are shown here.

Here is the previous setup viewed from the side and above. Note that beveling and raising are occurring on the opposite side of the workpiece.

Rails are the stiles with tenons. Make tenon shoulder stop cuts on both ends using miter gauge, fence and a single blade. Remove waste without the miter gauge. Fence to outer blade face distance is tenon length. Rapidly oscillate the workpiece across the blade while moving slowly in the outfeed direction. Keep hands away from the blade.

angle. The older type adjustment was made by adding or removing chippers and/or shims. The newest type dado uses twin blades and an eccentric hub with very rapid adjustment with the locknut temporarily loosened. The blades in this new type look like real carbide-tipped cutters rather than revised chippers and afford a relatively splinter-free cut.

To cut a dado or groove, several adjacent single-blade passes with appropriate fence adjustments can do the job, but the dado blade is more accurate and faster. Note that many table saws have table inserts specifically designed for either a single-blade, dado or molding cutter. Damage or injury can occur if this is not observed. Note also that the guard must be removed for certain operations such as dadoing, rabbeting or molding cutters, but the guard should be in place for any single-blade operation that pierces the top of the workpiece. In other operations where the guard is removed, appropriate hold-downs should be used and safety measures should be observed.

The mortise and tenon joint is extremely strong and universally used. Although the mortise (rectangular hole) is made on the drill press with an adapter or by hand with drills and chisels, the tenon can be made on the table saw. For two-shouldered tenons, the workpiece can be clamped vertically in a universal or shopmade jig. The blade height is set for the tenon depth and the cheek stock cut off according to the adjustment of the universal jig base or the rip fence setting, if using a shopmade jig. It's good practice to make the stop cuts first, using the miter gauge and the fence or auxiliary fence as a stop.

For four-shouldered tenons, make all four stop cuts first as above. Then, remove the miter gauge and carefully oscillate the workpiece tenon end crosswise over the blade, set at the correct height for the depth of the shoulder being cut. The piece should be slowly advanced toward the output part of the blade so the full depth of cut can occur. This is the exception to the rule. Here, you must use hand/eye coordination. But, before there were power saws, people made tenons by hand in a vise, using a fret or backsaw, and cut both stops and cheeks with no problem.

45

Replacing Windows

Homes with older, double-hung windows can be modernized quickly and easily by first removing the inner stops, parting strips and sashes, and then installing replacement windows right into the existing window jambs. You can do this without disturbing the window jambs, head and sill in their location in the rough opening.

If your home has a full set of the old-style, five-section aluminum combination windows (inner and outer upper sash, inner and outer lower sash and a half screen), you might be interested in what is involved in retrofitting windows with thermal breaks, insulated glass, removable sash and balances and a flip-down sash for cleaning the outside glass from the inside. This will improve your energy status, from both the insulation and infiltration angles, provide easy light replacement and cleaning convenience and perk up the appearance of your home.

This approach to modernization requires complete window replacement and alteration of the rough opening. You'll have to work from a ladder part of the time, but the work is not at all complicated.

To keep within the building codes regarding fire safety, check with your local authorities to find out what the minimum window area and dimensions must be if located in upstairs bedrooms (if your house is other than ranch style). Building Officials and Code Administration (BOCA) requirements call for a net clear minimum opening area of 5.7 square feet, with a minimum width of 20″ and minimum height of 24″. Also, the sill height should be no more than 44″ off the floor because you'll be downsizing the rough openings to the rough openings required for the new windows.

Removing the Old Windows

The worst part of the job is getting rid of the old materials. First, remove all of the glass that can be taken out easily. Be careful when freeing the spiral spring-loaded balances that control the movement of the windows and prevent them from falling down in their tracks. They work something like the old counterbalancing sash weights, but in a much more confined area. When releasing the balances, it's best to wear goggles or a face mask and hold the spiral parts with a heavy pliers because they could snap suddenly and cause injury if not constrained. The storm window section, or the outer upper and lower sashes, is in a separate frame that's screwed to the main frame with Phillips-head screw fasteners. These can be removed easily using a drill equipped with a No. 2 Phillips bit. Also remove the half screen.

Because the typical window frame is nailed to the sheathing around its perimeter flange underneath the siding, the siding must be stripped back somewhat to make the flange removal easier. Before dislodging the window frame you might want to hacksaw through the aluminum sill and pop it up with a flat bar to break the strength of the aluminum jamb.

If your home has more than one floor and you have to use a ladder, make sure that the ladder top is set firmly against the house wall and that the ladder feet are set firmly on the ground. Use scrap plywood as support pads if the ground is uncertain. Keep the ladder feet 1′ away from the house wall for each 4′ or 5′ of height from the ground to the top of the ladder. If you're using an aluminum ladder and think it's unsteady, bolt a stabilizer close to the top of the ladder. Ladder stabilizers are available at discount stores at reasonable prices. However, a wooden or fiberglass ladder is the better choice.

KEEP CLEAR OF ALL ELECTRICAL LINES. Do not do this ladder work when it's windy. It's possible for the piece you're working with to act as a sail and blow you off the ladder. For the same reason, try to keep all work hanging below you unless you're working against the wall. If you must remove shutters, carry a spray bomb in your tool pouch because wasps and other little nasties

319

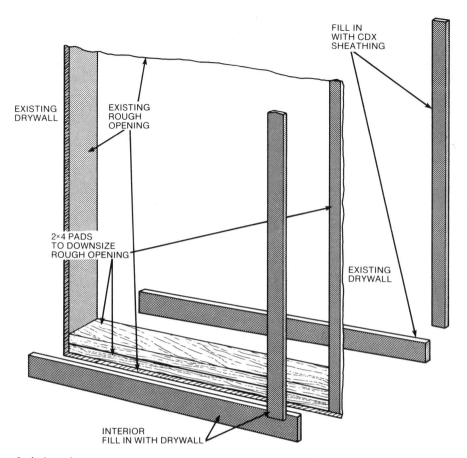

EXISTING
DRYWALL

EXISTING
ROUGH
OPENING

FILL IN
WITH CDX
SHEATHING

2×4 PADS
TO DOWNSIZE
ROUGH OPENING

EXISTING
DRYWALL

INTERIOR
FILL IN WITH DRYWALL

Isometric view of window changes.

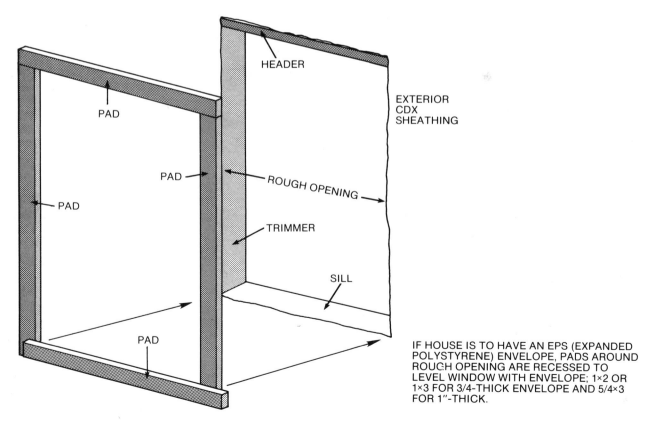

HEADER

PAD

PAD

PAD

PAD

EXTERIOR
CDX
SHEATHING

ROUGH OPENING

TRIMMER

SILL

IF HOUSE IS TO HAVE AN EPS (EXPANDED
POLYSTYRENE) ENVELOPE, PADS AROUND
ROUGH OPENING ARE RECESSED TO
LEVEL WINDOW WITH ENVELOPE; 1×2 OR
1×3 FOR 3/4-THICK ENVELOPE AND 5/4×3
FOR 1"-THICK.

Optional window pads if adding EPS insulation envelope.

First remove the sash, leaving the metal frame in place. There is no casing, so begin by removing the stool and apron molding below, if present.

Weaken the bottom of the aluminum frame with a hacksaw cut and pop it up with a flat pry bar to break it.

Remove the frame from the outside and clear the window perimeter of shakes or alternate existing siding.

Rip out the metal corner bead from the inner perimeter of window opening to expose the drywall in the jamb area.

Rip out all drywall from within the window opening exposing the header, rough sill and trimmers of rough opening.

often build nests around or behind shutters and don't take kindly to eviction. Therefore you should be prepared for aerial combat.

To recap, remove the sashes, strip the siding around the frame perimeter and remove the frame. Then, from the inside, strip away the wood stool (sometimes erroneously called the sill) as well as all the drywall from the head and sides within the rough opening. Since this is all that must be taken out, from here on you'll be building back the rough opening to its new, smaller size.

Downsizing the Rough Openings

The new downsized windows listed in the manufacturer's catalogue will have their own rough opening requirements, so the width and height differences between the old and new rough openings can be filled in using standard-dimension lumber and/or boards. It's physically easier to make up most or all of the height difference by adding to the rough sill at the bottom of the existing rough opening (unless by doing so, you'll raise the sill level above 44″), as opposed to adding to the head or cap at the top. When filling in for the width difference, add to the trimmer (the rough opening side member), which will either tend to center a single window or keep the spacing symmetrical if dealing with more than one window on a room wall.

In most cases 2×4 lumber and 1×4 boards—face dimensions are actually 3½″—will do fine unless your home has 6″ walls. If so, you'll have to move up to 2×6 and 1×6 (5½″). Whatever the case, be sure that the completed rough opening exceeds the measured physical dimensions of the new window by about ½″ in both directions to allow for squaring up the window.

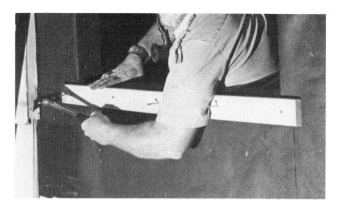

Renew the building paper or saturated felt around the window, and the opening is ready for an average new window installation. However, in this particular case, a re-siding with a 1″-thick EPS envelope was planned, hence the 5/4 × 3 pads to bring the window out the additional inch.

Check the replacement window or catalogue for the correct rough opening dimensions and downsize the old rough opening to meet these criteria, using dimensioned lumber, if possible.

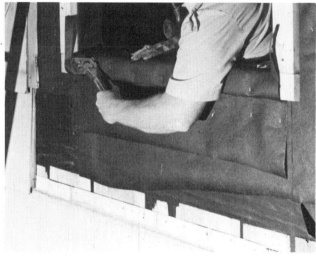

As added insurance, the pads too were given a layer of saturated felt (or building paper).

Apply sheathing patches to the exterior faces of the dimensioned lumber just installed.

Whether using pads or not, always work the felt or building paper up from the bottom, with each piece overlapping the one below by 2″ or 3″.

Once you've padded in the rough opening to the new dimensions, you must sheathe the exterior wall and patch the drywall on the interior wall. The drywall can be done either before or after the window installation, but the sheathing must be finished before. The sheathing can be either ½″ CDX or whatever thickness matches the existing sheathing. Fasten the sheathing with 6d to 8d cement-coated nails flush with the head, rough sill and trimmers of the rough opening.

Now staple the 15# felt or building paper over the sheathing. Make sure that each piece overlaps the piece below it by several inches and fold all pieces in and onto the head, trimmer and sill of the rough opening. This is the standard job, but our house was not quite standard. We planned to reside almost immediately so we applied a 1″ layer of Condec. This is expanded polystyrene with protective skins on both surfaces, which gives an additional R5 insulation. The material comes in 4′×8′ sheets. All door and window opening perimeters had to be padded out about 1″ to make a level siding surface, so this accounted for the 5/4″×3″ (actually 1 1/16″×2½″) pads that were applied over the sheathing around the window perimeters. In our case we stapled the felt both over and under the pads.

Installing the New Windows

The windows can be installed now. With these particular windows (Caradco double-hung aluminum clad), the sash can be removed so the frames can be installed in the prepared rough openings more easily and safely at a reduced weight due to the absence of glass.

The perimeter flanges around the window must be nailed to the sheathing bordering the window rough opening. But there's another requirement: The window must be square within the opening. Be sure to have a level and carpenter's square when you put in the windows. You'll also need a hammer and some 1½″ roofing nails.

Position the window in the opening and tack a nail through one of the flanges at the corner so that the window has play for level and plumb adjustment. Place the level on the opposite side, bring the window into plumb (one side dead vertical) and tack in that position. Now check the top or bottom for level (dead horizontal). Adjust as required, then drive in all nails. In our case, we nailed the window flanges to the 5/4″×3″ pads on the rough opening perimeter.

Inasmuch as no additional drip cap is required over the window head, all you have to do is bring the siding back to meet the window frame. If you've got shake siding, check out the garage add-on chapter, but the only tools you'll need are a square, block plane, utility knife and hammer. Use galvanized shake nails, at least on the finish course, if you're double coursing. When the siding is complete, caulk the edges of the window frame where the siding butts against it.

Carefully lift the window in place in the opening, resting it on the rough sill. Note that these particular windows, among others, have a removable sash, so you can install the empty frame and reinstall the sash later, if you wish.

Center and square the window within the opening and check this with a level. Tack-nail a corner, recheck and nail it at the opposite corner.

After a final check that the frame is square, either with a carpenter's square or the level, nail the flanges completely, using roofing nails.

Back on the inside, stuff, but do not compress, insulation in the cracks between the window frame and the new rough opening to cut down any possibility of infiltration.

Apply the drywall to the inner faces of the dimensioned lumber (the inner equivalent to the exterior sheathing).

Finishing Up

Back on the inside, you're all weatherproof, so if you haven't as yet patched the drywall, do it now. The drywall should be on the same plane as the edges of the window jambs, head and sill. Replace the sash at your convenience and paint or stain and varnish both the exposed parts of the frame and the sash rails and stiles. Note that those of you who have 6″ walls must have requested deeper extension jambs and should have been provided with appropriately deeper window frame heads, sills and jambs from the dealer.

When the drywall taping and jointing have been completed, gently tuck fiberglass insulation into the cracks around the frame of the window, between it and the rough opening. Do this using a small putty knife or the reverse side of the utility knife blade (in the handle, of course). Do not compress the insulation or you'll ruin its efficiency.

Use a miter box to cut the corners of the window casing and nail it to the wall and the window frame head, jambs and sill. After setting the nails, plug the holes with putty (putty mixed with stain if you're not painting). Then, paint or stain and varnish the casing. Install the grilles after applying finish.

Note that these windows are designed for use in both new construction and renovation. Also, from the flipped-

Tape, joint and sand the drywall patching. All you need to do on the inside is add molding. On the outside, refit the siding and caulk where it touches the window frame.

down cleaning position, the sashes can be rotated slightly and removed from the frame. Further, by removing four Phillips-head screws from the sash corners, the rails and stiles can be disassembled for replacement of the insulated glass. Finally, with the sash removed from the frame, the balances can be squeezed and removed from the frame.

Index